SAINT SHENOUDA COPTIC ORTHODOX MONASTERY

SYDNEY   AUSTRALIA

THE KIAHK PSALMODY

Ϯⲯⲁⲗⲙⲟⲇⲓⲁ ⲛ̀ⲧⲉ ⲭⲟⲓⲁⲕ

ألتسبحة الكيهكية

In English, Coptic and Arabic

The Kiahk Psalmody

ϮψΑλΜΟΔΙΑ ΝΤΕ ΧΟΙΑΚ

ألتسبحة الكيهكية

In English, Coptic and Arabic

§

ST SHENOUDA COPTIC ORTHODOX MONASTERY AUSTRALIA 2010

8419 Putty Rd, Putty, NSW, 2330

http://www.stshenoudamonastery.org.au/

Our Lord Jesus Christ and

The Virgin Saint Mary

**His Holiness Pope Shenouda III - 117th Pope
and Patriarch of the Apostolic See of St Mark**

His Grace Bishop Daniel.

Bishop and Abbot of St Shenouda Monastery.

Contents

Sunday Vespers for the Month of Kiahk – تسبحة عشية الاحاد   1

Niethnos Tiro - Ⲛⲓⲉⲑⲛⲟⲥ ⲧⲏⲣⲟⲩ - لحن نى اثنوس تيرو   1

Fourth Hoos – Ⲡⲓϩⲱⲥ ⲙ̄ⲙⲁϩ-ⲇ̄ - الهوس الرابع   3

PSALI WATOS FOR THE VESPERS OF SUNDAY'S OF KIAHK – ابصالية واطس   14

ANOTHER PSALI WATOS (By ABU EL-SAAD) – مديح واطس للعذراء   22

Introduction to Watos Theotokeias - - مقدمة الثيؤطوكيات الواطس   28

First Part of the Saturday Theotokia - ثيؤطوكية السبت القطعه الاولى   29

   FIRST EXPLANATION BY ABU EL-SAAD - القطعة الاولى من نظم المعلم ابو السعد   30

   FIRST EXPLANATION BY GABRIEL EL-KAI - القطعة الاولى من نظم المعلم غبريال   31

   THE FIRST EXPLANATION BY AMBA MORCOS - القطعة الاولى من نظم البطريرك انبا مرقس   34

Second Part of the Saturday Theotokia - ثيؤطوكية السبت القطعه الثانية   35

   SECOND EXPLANATION BY ABU EL-SAAD - القطعة الثانية من نظم المعلم ابو السعد   37

   SECOND EXPLANATION BY GABRIEL EL-KAI - القطعة الثانية من نظم المعلم غبريال   38

   THE SECOND EXPLANATION BY AMBA MORCOS القطعة الثانية من نظم البطريرك انبا مرقس   41

Third Part of the Saturday Theotokia - ثيؤطوكية السبت القطعه الثالثة   43

   THE THIRD EXPLANATION BY ABU EL-SAAD - القطعة الثالثة من نظم المعلم ابو السعد   44

   THE THIRD EXPLANATION BY GABRIEL EL-KAI - القطعة الثالثة من نظم المعلم غبريال   46

   THE THIRD EXPLANATION BY AMBA MORCOS - القطعة الثالثة من نظم البطريرك انبا مرقس   48

Fourth Part of the Saturday Theotokia - ثيؤطوكية السبت القطعه الرابعة   50

   FOURTH EXPLANATION BY ABU EL-SAAD - القطعة الرابعة من نظم المعلم ابو السعد   51

   FOURTH EXPLANATION BY GABRIEL EL-KAI - القطعة الرابعة من نظم المعلم غبريال   53

   THE FOURTH EXPLANATION BY AMBA MORCOS - القطعة الرابعة من نظم البطريرك انبا مرقس   55

Fifth Part of the Saturday Theotokia - ثيؤطوكية السبت القطعه الخامسة   57

FIFTH EXPLANATION BY ABU EL-SAAD- القطعة الخامسة من نظم المعلم ابو السعد   58

FIFTH EXPLANATION BY GABRIEL EL-KAI- القطعة الخامسة من نظم المعلم غبريال   60

THE FIFTH EXPLANATION BY AMBA MORCOS- القطعة الخامسة من نظم البطريرك انبا مرقس   63

Sixth Part of the Saturday Theotokia - ثيؤطوكية السبت القطعه السادسة   65

SIXTH EXPLANATION BY ABU EL-SAAD- القطعة السادس من نظم المعلم ابو السعد   67

SIXTH EXPLANATION BY GABRIEL EL-KAI- القطعة السادسة من نظم المعلم غبريال   68

THE SIXTH EXPLANATION BY AMBA MORCOS- القطعة السادسة من نظم البطريرك انبا مرقس   71

Seventh Part of the Saturday Theotokia - ثيؤطوكية السبت القطعه السابعة   72

SEVENTH EXPLANATION BY ABU EL-SAAD- القطعة السابعة من نظم المعلم ابو السعد   74

SEVENTH EXPLANATION BY GABRIEL EL-KAI- القطعة السابعة من نظم المعلم غبريال   75

THE SEVENTH EXPLANATION BY AMBA MORCOS- القطعة السابعة من نظم البطريرك انبا مرقس   78

Eighth Part of the Saturday Theotokia - ثيؤطوكية السبت القطعه الثامنة   80

EIGHTH EXPLANATION BY ABU EL-SAAD- القطعة الثامن من نظم المعلم ابو السعد   82

EIGHTH EXPLANATION BY GABRIEL EL-KAI- القطعة الثامنة من نظم المعلم غبريال   83

THE EIGHTH EXPLANATION BY AMBA MORCOS- القطعة الثامنة من نظم البطريرك انبا مرقس   86

9th Part of the Saturday Theotokia - ثيؤطوكية السبت القطعه التاسعة   88

NINTH EXPLANATION BY ABU EL-SAAD- القطعة التاسعة من نظم المعلم ابو السعد   89

NINTH EXPLANATION BY GABRIEL EL-KAI- القطعة التاسعة من نظم المعلم غبريال   90

THE NINTH EXPLANATION BY AMBA MORCOS- القطعة التاسعة من نظم البطريرك انبا مرقس   94

The Sherat - Saturday Lobsh - Ϧⲉⲣⲉ ⲑⲏⲉⲑⲙⲉϩ ⲛ̀ϩⲙⲟⲧ - الشيرات   96

Exposition of the First Week - طرح للإسبوع الأول   104

Exposition of the Second Week - طرح للإسبوع الثاني   107

Exposition of the Third Week - طرح للإسبوع الثالث   110

Exposition of the Fourth Week - طرح للإسبوع الرابع   112

The Conclusion of Watos Theotokeias - ⲱ ⲡⲉⲛⲟⲥ Ⲓⲏⲥ Ⲡ̅ⲭ̅ⲥ̅ - ختام الثؤطوكيات الواطس   116

THE KIAHK PSALMODY FOR SUNDAY   121

Arise, O Children - Ⲧⲉⲛⲑⲏⲛⲟⲩ –قوموا يا بني 122

The Kiahk's Ode - ⲎⲱⲥⲉⲠϭ̅ⲟⲓⲥ - الهوس الكيهكي 129

Agios O Theos اجيوس اوثيئوس 141

First Hoos – Ⲡⲓ̅ϩⲱⲥ ⲛ̅ϩⲟⲩⲓⲧ – الهوس الأول 150

Hymn After the 1st Hoos مديح يقال بعد لبش الهوس الأول 161

Praise Before Monday Theotokia مديح على ثيؤطوكية يوم الأثنين 171

Praise Before Tuesday Theotokia مديح على ثيؤطوكية يوم الثلاثاء 178

Psali Adam on the 2nd Hoos - ابصالية آدم على الهوس الثاني 182

Second Hoos – Ⲡⲓϩⲱⲥ ⲙ̅ⲙⲁⲩ Ⲃ الهوس الثاني 189

Hymn after the 2nd Hoos مديح بعد الهوس الثاني 200

Hymn Before Wednesday Theotokia - مديح واطس على ثيؤطوكية يوم الأربعاء 206

Hmyn Before Thursday Theotokia مديح على ثيؤطوكية الخميس العليقة 213

Psali Adam on the Third Hoos ابصالية آدم على الهوس الثالث 226

Third Hoos – Ⲡⲓϩⲱⲥ ⲙ̅ⲙⲁϩ Ⲅ̅الهوس الثالث 231

Praise of the Three Young Men ابصالية الثلاثة فتية 242

Hmyn after Praise of the Three Young Men مديح بعد ابصالية الثلاثة فتية 251

Hymn Of Tenen - Ⲧⲉⲛⲉⲛ - لحن تينين 260

Psali Batos for the Three Young Men أبصالية واطس للثلاثة القديسين 262

The Commemoration-المجمع 264

Praises For the Saints مدايح للقديسين: 284

    Praise for St Shenoudaمديحة للأنبا شنوده 284

    Praise for St. Bishoy-مديحة للأنبا بيشوي 291

    Praise for St. Anthony the Great-مديحة للأنبا أنطونيوس 297

    Praise for Saints Maximos and Domadios مديحة للقديسين مكسيموس و دوماديوس 301

The Doxologiesالذوكصولوجيات 305

    The Doxology for Kiahk - ذكصولوجية كيهك 305

    St Virgin Mary's Kiahk Doxologyذكصولوجية العذراء 309

iii

Doxology For Archangel Gabriel for Kiahk ذكصولوجية الملاك غبريال	311
Conclusion of the Doxologies ختام الذوكصولوجيات	313
Hymn Before Friday Theotokia - مديح واطس على ثيؤطوكية يوم الجمعة	315
Fourth Hoos – Ⲡⲓϩⲱⲥ ⲙ̀ⲙⲁϩ ⲇ̅ - الهوس الرابع	322
The Sunday Psali – Ⲁⲓⲕⲱϯ – ابصالية الأحد	335
I Open my Mouth with Praise - افتح فاىبالتسبيح	343
Adam Conclusion ختام الآدام	353
The Sunday Theotokia ثيؤطوكية يوم الأحد	356
The First Explanation التفسير الأول	360
The Second Explanation التفسير الثانى	369
The Third Explanation التفسير الثالث	377
The Fourth Explanation -التفسير الرابع	385
The Fifth Explanationالتفسير الخامس	394
The Sixth Explanationالتفسير السادس	402
The Seventh Explanationالتفسير السابع	410
Shere ne Maria - Ⲭⲉⲣⲉ ⲛⲉ Ⲙⲁⲣⲓⲁ̀ – السلام لك يا مريم	414
O Mary - Ya Mem Reh Yeh Mem- يا م ر ى م	427
I Praise the Virgin - أمدح فى البتول	439
You are More Worthy - Ⲧⲉⲟⲓ ⲛ̀ϩⲓⲕⲁⲛⲟⲥ - أنت مستحقة	449
Your Mercies O my God - مراحمك يا إلهى	469
The Conclusion - الختام	473

Sunday Vespers for the Month of Kiahk

تسبحة عشية الاحاد ـ

Niethnos Tiro - Ⲛⲓⲉⲑⲛⲟⲥ ⲧⲏⲣⲟⲩ - لحن نى اثنوس تيرو

Glory be to God. O praise the Lord all you nations. Praise Him, all you people. For His merciful kindness is great toward us and the truth of the Lord endures forever, Alleluia.	Ⲇⲟⲝⲁ ⲥⲓ ⲟ̀ Ⲑⲉⲟⲥ ⲩ̀ⲱⲛ: Ⲛⲓⲉⲑⲛⲟⲥ ⲧⲏⲣⲟⲩ ⲥ̀ⲙⲟⲩ ⲉ̀Ⲡⲟⲥ: ⲙⲁⲣⲟⲩ̀ⲥⲙⲟⲩ ⲉ̀ⲣⲟϥ ⲛ̀ⲭⲉ ⲛⲓⲗⲁⲟⲥ ⲧⲏⲣⲟⲩ: ⲝⲉ ⲁ ⲡⲉϥⲛⲁⲓ ⲧⲁϫⲁⲣⲟ ⲉ̀ϩ̀ⲣⲏⲓ ⲉ̀ϫⲱⲛ: ⲟⲩⲟϩ ϯⲙⲉⲑⲙⲏⲓ ⲛ̀ⲧⲉ Ⲡⲟⲥ ϣⲟⲡ ϣⲁ ⲉ̀ⲛⲉϩ: ⲁ̅ⲗ̅.	المجد الهنا.ياجميع الامم سبحوا الرب ولتباركه كافة الشعوب لأن رحمته قد قويت علينا وحق الرب يدوم إلى الأبد الليلويا
Glory be to the Father and the Son and the Holy Spirit. Now and forever and unto the ages of ages, Amen, Alle-	Ⲇⲟⲝⲁ Ⲡⲁⲧⲣⲓ ⲕⲉ Ⲩⲓⲱ ⲕⲉ ⲁ̀ⲅⲓⲱ Ⲡⲛⲉⲩⲙⲁⲧⲓ: Ⲕⲉ ⲛⲩⲛ ⲕⲉ ⲁ̀ⲓ ⲕⲉ ⲓⲥ ⲧⲟⲩⲥ ⲉ̀ⲱⲛⲁⲥ ⲧⲱⲛ ⲉ̀ⲱⲛⲱⲛ ⲁ̀ⲙⲏⲛ: ⲁ̅ⲗ̅	المجد للآب والأبن والروح القدس الآن وكل اوان: والى دهر الدهور

luia, Alleluia.

Glory be to God.

$\overline{\alpha\lambda}$: Ⲇⲟⲝⲁ ⲥⲓ ⲟ̀ Ⲑⲉⲟⲥ
ⲓ̀ⲙⲱⲛ.

آمين الليلويا.

المجد لالهنا.

Fourth Hoos – Ⲡⲓϩⲱⲥ ⲙ̅ⲙⲁϩ ⲇ̄ -

الهوس الرابع

*Praise the Lord from the heavens Alleluia. Praise Him in the heights.	*Ⲥⲙⲟⲩ ⲉ̀Ⲡⲟ̅ⲥ̅ ⲉ̀ⲃⲟⲗ ϧⲉⲛ ⲛⲓⲫⲏⲟⲩⲓ̀ Ⲁ̅ⲗ̅ : ⲥ̀ⲙⲟⲩ ⲉ̀ⲣⲟϥ ϧⲉⲛ ⲛⲏⲉⲧϭⲟⲥⲓ.	*سبحوا الرب من السموات الليلويا. سبحوه فى الأعالى.
Praise Him all His angels Alleluia. Praise Him all His hosts.	Ⲥⲙⲟⲩ ⲉ̀ⲣⲟϥ ⲛⲉϥⲁⲅⲅⲉ-ⲗⲟⲥ ⲧⲏⲣⲟⲩ Ⲁ̅ⲗ̅: ⲥ̀ⲙⲟⲩ ⲉ̀ⲣⲟϥ ⲛⲉϥⲇⲩⲛⲁⲙⲓⲥ ⲧⲏⲣⲟⲩ.	سبحوه ياجميع ملائكته الليلويا. سبحوه يا جميع جنوده.
*Praise Him sun and moon Alleluia. Praise Him all you stars of light.	*Ⲥⲙⲟⲩ ⲉ̀ⲣⲟϥ ⲡⲓⲣⲏ ⲛⲉⲙ ⲡⲓⲟϩ Ⲁ̅ⲗ̅ : ⲥ̀ⲙⲟⲩ ⲉⲣⲟϥ ⲛⲓⲥⲓⲟⲩ ⲧⲏⲣⲟⲩ ⲛ̀ⲧⲉ ⲡⲓⲟⲩⲱⲓⲛⲓ.	*سبحيه ايتها الشمس والقمر الليــلويا. سبحيه ياجميع كواكب النور.
Praise Him you heavens of heavens Alleluia. And you waters above the heavens.	Ⲥⲙⲟⲩ ⲉ̀ⲣⲟϥ ⲛⲓⲫⲏ-ⲟⲩⲓ̀ ⲛ̀ⲧⲉ ⲛⲓⲫⲏⲟⲩⲓ̀ Ⲁ̅ⲗ̅ :ⲛⲉⲙ ⲛⲓⲕⲉⲙⲱⲟⲩ ⲉⲧⲥⲁ ⲡ̀-ϣⲱⲓ ⲛ̀ⲛⲓⲫⲏⲟⲩⲓ̀.	سبحيه يا سماء السموات الليلويا. وياايتها المياه التى فوق السموات.

*Let them praise the Name of the Lord Alleluia. For He commanded and they were created.

He has ordered and they were created Alleluia. He has established them forever and ever.

*He has made a decree and it will be enforced Alleluia. Praise the Lord from the earth.

All you dragons and all depths Alleluia. Fire and hail, snow and vapor and stormy wind fulfilling His word.

*Ⲙⲁⲣⲟⲩⲥⲙⲟⲩ ⲧⲏⲣⲟⲩ ⲉ̀ⲫⲣⲁⲛ ⲙ̀Ⲡϭⲟⲓⲥ ⲁ̅ⲗ̅ ⲭⲉ ⲛ̀ⲑⲟϥ ⲁϥϫⲟⲥ ⲟⲩⲟⲅ ⲁⲩϣⲱⲡⲓ.

Ⲛ̀ⲑⲟϥ ⲁϥⲅⲟⲛⲅⲉⲛ ⲟⲩⲟⲅ ⲁⲩⲥⲱⲛⲧ ⲁ̅ⲗ̅: ⲁϥⲧⲁⲅⲱⲟⲩ ⲉ̀ⲣⲁⲧⲟⲩ ϣⲁ ⲉ̀ⲛⲉⲅ ⲛⲉⲙ ϣⲁ ⲉ̀ⲛⲉⲅ ⲛ̀ⲧⲉ ⲡⲓⲉ̀ⲛⲉⲅ.

*Ⲁϥⲭⲱ ⲛ̀ⲟⲩⲅⲱⲛ ⲟⲩ-ⲟⲅ ⲛ̀ⲛⲉϥⲥⲓⲛⲓ ⲁ̅ⲗ̅: ⲥ̀ⲙⲟⲩ ⲉ̀Ⲡϭⲟⲓⲥ ⲉ̀ⲃⲟⲗϧⲉⲛ ⲡ̀-ⲭⲁⲅⲓ.

Ⲛⲓⲇⲣⲁⲕⲱⲛ ⲛⲉⲙ ⲛⲓⲛ-ⲟⲩⲛ ⲧⲏⲣⲟⲩ ⲁ̅ⲗ̅: ⲟⲩⲭⲣⲱⲙ ⲟⲩⲁⲗ ⲟⲩⲭ-ⲓⲱⲛ ⲟⲩⲭⲣⲩⲥⲧⲁⲗⲗⲟⲥ ⲟⲩⲡⲛⲉⲩⲙⲁ ⲛ̀ⲥⲁⲣⲁⲑⲏ-ⲟⲩ ⲛⲏⲉⲧⲓⲣⲓ ⲙ̀ⲡⲉϥⲥⲁϫⲓ.

*لتسبح جميعها لاسم الرب الليلويا. لانه قـال فكانت.

وأمر فخلقت الليلويا. اقامها إلى الأبد والى ابـد الابد.

*وضع لها امرا فلن تتجاوزه الليلويا. سبحى الرب من الارض.

ايتها التنانين وجميع الاعماق الليلويا. النار والبرد والثلج والجليد والريح العاصفة الصانعة كلمته.

*Mountains and all hills Alleluia. Fruitful trees and all cedars.	*Ⲛⲓⲧⲱⲟⲩ ⲉⲧϭⲟⲥⲓ ⲛⲉⲙ ⲛⲓⲕⲁⲗⲁⲙⲫⲱⲟⲩ ⲧⲏ-ⲣⲟⲩ Ⲁ̅ⲗ̅: ⲛⲓϣ̇ϣⲏ ⲙ̇-ⲫⲁⲓⲟⲩⲧⲁϩ ⲛⲉⲙ ⲛⲓϣ̇-ⲉⲛⲥⲓϥⲓ ⲧⲏⲣⲟⲩ.	*الجبال العالية وجميع الآكام الليلويا. الاشجار المثمرة وكل الأرز.
Beasts and all cattle Alleluia. Creeping things and flying birds.	Ⲛⲓⲑⲏⲣⲓⲟⲛ ⲛⲉⲙ ⲛⲓⲧⲉ-ⲃⲛⲱⲟⲩⲓ̀ ⲧⲏⲣⲟⲩ Ⲁ̅ⲗ̅: ⲛⲓϭⲁⲧϥⲓ ⲛⲉⲙ ⲛⲓϩⲁⲗⲁϯ ⲉⲧⲟⲓ ⲛ̇ⲧⲉⲛϩ.	الوحوش وكل البهائم الليلويا. الهوام وكل الطيور ذات الاجنحة.
*Kings of the earth and all people Alleluia. Princes and all judges of the earth.	*Ⲛⲓⲟⲩⲣⲱⲟⲩ ⲛ̇ⲧⲉ ⲡ̇ⲕⲁ ϩⲓ ⲛⲉⲙ ⲛⲓⲗⲁⲟⲥ ⲧⲏⲣⲟⲩ Ⲁ̅ⲗ̅ : ⲛⲓⲁⲣⲭⲱⲛ ⲛⲉⲙ ⲛⲓⲣⲉϥϯϩⲁⲡ ⲧⲏⲣⲟⲩ ⲛ̇-ⲧⲉ ⲡ̇ⲕⲁϩⲓ.	*ملوك الارض وكل الشعوب الليلويا. الرؤساء وكل حكام الارض.
Both young men and maidens Alleluia. Old men and children.	Ϩⲁⲛϧⲉⲗϣⲓⲣⲓ ⲛⲉⲙ ϩⲁⲛ-ⲡⲁⲣⲑⲉⲛⲟⲥ Ⲁ̅ⲗ̅: ϩⲁⲛϧ-ⲉⲗⲗⲟⲓ ⲛⲉⲙ ϩⲁⲛⲁ̀ⲗⲱⲟⲩⲓ.	الشبان والعذارى الليلويا. الشيوخ والصبيان.
*Let them praise the Name of the Lord Alleluia. For His Name alone is	*Ⲙⲁⲣⲟⲩⲥⲙⲟⲩ ⲧⲏⲣ-ⲟⲩ ⲉ̀ⲫⲣⲁⲛ ⲙ̇Ⲡ̅ⲟ̅ⲥ̅ Ⲁ̅ⲗ̅ : ϫⲉ ⲁϥϭⲓⲥⲓ ⲛ̇ϫⲉ	*فليسبحوا جميعاً اسم الرب الليلويا. لانه قد تعالى اسمه

exalted.	ⲡⲉϥⲣⲁⲛ ⲙ̇ⲙⲁⲩⲁⲧϥ.	.وحده
His glory is above the earth and heaven Alleluia. He also exalts the horn of His people.	Ⲡⲉϥⲟⲩⲱⲛϩ ⲉ̇ⲃⲟⲗ ϣⲟⲡ ϩⲓⲭⲉⲛ ⲡ̇ⲕⲁϩⲓ ⲛⲉⲙ ⲛ̇ⲉ̇ⲣⲏⲓ ϧⲉⲛ ⲧ̇ⲫⲉ ⲁⲗ ⲋ ϥⲛⲁϭ̇ⲓⲥⲓ ⲙ̇ⲡ̇ⲧⲁⲡ ⲛ̇ⲧⲉ ⲡⲉϥⲗⲁⲟⲥ.	شكره كائن على الارض وفى السماء الليلويا. ويرفع قرن شعبه.
*The praise of all His saints Alleluia. The children of Israel a people near unto Him.	*Ⲟⲩⲥⲙⲟⲩ ⲛ̇ⲧⲉ ⲛⲏⲉⲑⲟⲩⲁⲃ ⲧⲏⲣⲟⲩ ⲛ̇ⲧⲁϥ ⲁⲗ ⲋ ⲛⲉⲛϣⲏⲣⲓ ⲙ̇ⲡ̇ⲓⲥⲣⲁⲏⲗ ⲡⲓⲗⲁⲟⲥ ⲉⲧϧⲉⲛⲧ̇ ⲉ̇ⲣⲟϥ.	*سبحاً لجميع قديسيه الليلويا. بنى اسرائيل الشعب القريب اليه.
Alleluia, Alleluia, Alleluia.	ⲁⲗ ⲁⲗ ⲁⲗ	الليلويا الليلويا الليلويا.
Sing unto the Lord a new song Alleluia. And His praise in the congregation of the saints.	Ⲭⲱ ⲙ̇Ⲡⲟⲥ ϧⲉⲛ ⲟⲩⲭⲱ ⲙ̇ⲃⲉⲣⲓ ⲁⲗ ⲋ ϫⲉ ⲁ̇ⲣⲉ ⲡⲉϥⲥⲙⲟⲩ ϧⲉⲛ ⲧⲉⲕⲕⲗ̇ⲏⲥⲓⲁ̇ ⲛ̇ⲧⲉ ⲛⲏⲉⲑⲟⲩⲁⲃ.	انشدوا للرب نشيداً جديداً الليلويا. لان تسبحته فى بيعة القديسين.
*Let Israel rejoice in Him that made Him	*Ⲙⲁⲣⲉϥⲟⲩⲛⲟϥ ⲛ̇ϫⲉ Ⲡⲓⲥⲣⲁⲏⲗ ⲉ̇ϫⲉⲛ ⲫⲏⲉⲧ-	*فليفرح اسرائيل بخالقه الليلويا.

Alleluia. Let the children of Zion be joyful in their King.	ⲁϥⲑⲁⲙⲓⲟϥ Ⲁⲗ: ⲛⲉⲛϣⲏⲣⲓ ⲛ̀Ⲥⲓⲱⲛ ⲙⲁⲣⲟⲧⲟⲉⲗⲏⲗ ⲉ̀ϫⲉⲛ ⲡⲟⲩⲟⲩⲣⲟ.	وبنوا صهيون فليتهللوا بملكهم.
Let them praise His Name in the chorus Alleluia. Let them sing praises unto Him with timbrel and harp.	Ⲙⲁⲣⲟⲩ̀ⲥⲙⲟⲩ ⲉ̀ⲡⲉϥⲣⲁⲛ ⲉⲑⲟⲩⲁⲃ ϧⲉⲛ ⲟⲩⲭⲟⲣⲟⲥ Ⲁⲗ: ϧⲉⲛ ⲟⲩⲕⲉⲙⲕⲉⲙ ⲛⲉⲙ ⲟⲩⲯⲁⲗⲧⲏⲣⲓⲟⲛ ⲙⲁⲣⲟⲩⲉⲣⲯⲁⲗⲓⲛⲉ̀ⲣⲟϥ.	فليسبحوا اسمه القدوس بصف الليلويا. بدف ومزمار فليرتلوا له.
*For the Lord takes pleasure in His people Alleluia. He will raise the meek with salvation.	*Ϫⲉ Ⲡϭⲟⲓⲥ ⲛⲁϯⲙⲁϯ ⲉ̀ϫⲉⲛ ⲡⲉϥⲗⲁⲟⲥ Ⲁⲗ : ϥⲛⲁϭⲓⲥⲓ ⲛ̀ⲛⲓⲣⲉⲙⲣⲁⲩϣ ϧⲉⲛ ⲟⲩⲟⲩϫⲁⲓ.	*لان الرب يُسر بشعبه الليلويا. يعلى الودعاء بالخلاص.
Let the saints be joyful in glory Alleluia. Let them sing aloud upon their beds.	Ⲉ̀ⲣⲉϣⲟⲩϣⲟⲩ ⲙ̀ⲙⲱⲟⲩ ⲛ̀ϫⲉ ⲛⲏⲉⲑⲟⲩⲁⲃ ϧⲉⲛ ⲟⲩⲱⲟⲩ Ⲁⲗ: ⲉⲩⲉ̀ⲑⲉⲗⲏⲗ ⲙ̀ⲙⲱⲟⲩ ϩⲓϫⲉⲛ ⲛⲟⲩⲙⲁ̀ⲛⲉⲛⲕⲟⲧ.	يفتخر القديسون بمجد الليلويا. ويتهللون على مضاجعهم.

*Let the high praises of God be in their mouth Alleluia. And a two edged sword in their hand.	*Ⲛⲓϭⲓⲥⲓ ⲛ̀ⲧⲉ Ⲫ̀ϯ ⲉⲧⲭⲏ ϧⲉⲛ ⲧⲟⲩϣⲃⲱⲃⲓ Ⲁⲗ: ϩⲁⲛⲥⲏϥⲓ ⲛ̀ⲣⲟ ⲥⲛⲁⲩ ⲉ-ⲧⲭⲏ ϧⲉⲛ ⲛⲟⲩϫⲓϫ.	*تعليات الله فى حناجرهم الليلويا. وسيوف ذات حدين فى أيديهم.
To execute venge-ance upon the heathen Alleluia. And punishment upon the people.	Ⲉ̀ⲡϫⲓⲛⲓ̀ⲣⲓ ⲛ̀ⲟⲩϭⲓⲙ̀ⲡϣ-ⲓϣ ϧⲉⲛ ⲛⲓⲉⲑⲛⲟⲥ Ⲁⲗ: ⲛⲉⲙ ϩⲁⲛⲥⲟϩⲓ ϧⲉⲛ ⲛⲓⲗⲁⲟⲥ.	ليصنعوا نقمة فى الامم الليلويا. وتوبيخات فى الشعوب.
*To bind their kings with chains Alleluia. And their nobles with fetters of iron.	*Ⲉ̀ⲡϫⲓⲛⲥⲱⲛϩ ⲛ̀ϩⲁⲛ-ⲟⲩⲣⲱⲟⲩ ϧⲉⲛ ϩⲁⲛⲡ-ⲉⲗⲏⲥ Ⲁⲗ: ⲛⲉⲙ ⲛⲏⲉⲧⲧⲁⲓⲏⲟⲩⲧ ⲛ̀ⲧⲱ-ⲟⲩ ϧⲉⲛ ϩⲁⲛⲡⲉⲗⲏⲥ ⲛ̀ϫ-ⲓϫ ⲙ̀ⲃⲉⲛⲓⲡⲓ.	*ليوثقوا ملوكهم بقيود الليلويا. واشرافهم باغلال للايدى من حديد.
To execute on them the written judge-ment Alleluia. This honor have all His saints.	Ⲉ̀ⲡϫⲓⲛⲓ̀ⲣⲓ ⲛ̀ϧⲏⲧⲟⲩ ⲛ̀-ⲟⲩϩⲁⲡ ⲉϥⲥ̀ϧⲏⲟⲩⲧ ⲁ̅ⲗ̅ : ⲡⲁⲓⲱⲟⲩ ⲫⲁⲓ ⲁϥϣⲱⲡ ϧⲉⲛ ⲛⲏⲉⲑⲟⲩⲁⲃ ⲧⲏⲣ-ⲟⲩ ⲛ̀ⲧⲁϥ.	ليصنعوا بهم حكما مكتوباً الليلويا. هذا المجد كائن فى جميع قديسيه.

*Alleluia, Alleluia, Alleluia.	*Ⲁⲗ ⲁⲗ ⲁⲗ.	*الليلويا الليلويا الليلويا
*Praise God in all his saints Alleluia.	*Ⲥⲙⲟⲩ ⲉⲪⲛⲟⲩϯ ϧⲉⲛ ⲛⲏⲉⲑⲟⲩⲁⲃ ⲧⲏⲣⲟⲩ ⲛ̀ⲧⲁϥ. Ⲁⲗ.	*سبحوا الله في جميع قديسيه الليلويا.
*Unto our God is due glory and praise. Praise the Lord our God with a joyful psalm.	*Ⲉϥⲉⲣⲁⲛⲁϥ ⲙ̀ⲡⲉⲛⲛⲟⲩϯ ⲛ̀ϫⲉ ⲡⲓⲱⲟⲩ ⲛⲉⲙ ⲡⲓⲥⲙⲟⲩ. Ⲥⲙⲟⲩ ⲉ̀Ⲡϭⲟⲓⲥ ⲡⲉⲛⲛⲟⲩϯ ϫⲉ ⲛⲁⲛⲉ ⲟⲩⲯⲁⲗⲙⲟⲥ.	*يليق لإلهنا المجد والتسبيح. سبحوا الرب الهنا بحسن المزمار.
Praise Him in the firmament of His power Alleluia.	Ⲥⲙⲟⲩ ⲉ̀ⲣⲟϥ ϧⲉⲛ ⲡⲓⲧⲁϫⲣⲟ ⲛ̀ⲧⲉ ⲧⲉϥϫⲟⲙ. Ⲁⲗ.	سبحوه في جلد قوته الليلويا.
Unto our God is due glory and praise. Praise the Lord our God with a joyful psalm.	Ⲉϥⲉⲣⲁⲛⲁϥ ⲙ̀ⲡⲉⲛⲛⲟⲩϯ ⲛ̀ϫⲉ ⲡⲓⲱⲟⲩ ⲛⲉⲙ ⲡⲓⲥⲙⲟⲩ. Ⲥⲙⲟⲩ ⲉ̀Ⲡϭⲟⲓⲥ ⲡⲉⲛⲛⲟⲩϯ ϫⲉ ⲛⲁⲛⲉ ⲟⲩⲯⲁⲗⲙⲟⲥ.	يليق لإلهنا المجد والتسبيح. سبحوا الرب الهنا بحسن المزمار.
*Praise Him for His mighty acts Alleluia.	*Ⲥⲙⲟⲩ ⲉ̀ⲣⲟϥ ⲉ̀ϩⲣⲏⲓ ϩⲓϫⲉⲛ ⲧⲉϥⲙⲉⲧϫⲱⲣⲓ.	*سبحوه على مقدرته الليلويا.

	Ⲁ̅ⲗ.	
*Unto our God is due glory and praise. Praise the Lord our God with a joyful psalm.	*Ⲉϥⲉⲣⲁⲛⲁϥ ⲙ̇ⲡⲉⲛⲛⲟ-ⲩϯ ⲛ̇ⲭⲉ ⲡⲓⲱⲟⲩ ⲛⲉⲙ ⲡⲓⲥ̇ⲙⲟⲩ. Ⲥⲙⲟⲩ ⲉ̇Ⲡ̇ϭⲟⲓⲥ ⲡⲉⲛⲛⲟⲩϯ ⲝⲉ ⲛⲁⲛⲉ ⲟⲩⲯⲁⲗⲙⲟⲥ.	*يليق لإلهنا المجد والتسبيح. سبحوا الرب الهنا بحسن المزمار.
Praise Him according to His excellent greatness Alleluia.	Ⲥⲙⲟⲩ ⲉ̇ⲣⲟϥ ⲕⲁⲧⲁ ⲡ̇ⲁ-ϣⲁⲓ ⲛ̇ⲧⲉ ⲧⲉϥⲙⲉ-ⲧⲛⲓϣϯ. Ⲁ̅ⲗ.	سبحوه ككثرة عظمته الليلويا.
Unto our God is due glory and praise. Praise the Lord our God with a joyful psalm.	Ⲉϥⲉⲣⲁⲛⲁϥ ⲙ̇ⲡⲉⲛⲛⲟⲩϯ ⲛ̇ⲭⲉ ⲡⲓⲱⲟⲩ ⲛⲉⲙ ⲡⲓⲥ̇ⲙⲟⲩ. Ⲥⲙⲟⲩ ⲉ̇Ⲡ̇ϭⲟⲓⲥ ⲡⲉⲛⲛⲟⲩϯ ⲝⲉ ⲛⲁⲛⲉ ⲟⲩⲯⲁⲗⲙⲟⲥ.	يليق لإلهنا المجد والتسبيح. سبحوا الرب الهنا بحسن المزمار.
*Praise Him with the sound of the trumpet Alleluia.	*Ⲥⲙⲟⲩ ⲉ̇ⲣⲟϥ ϧⲉⲛ ⲟⲩⲥⲙⲏ ⲛ̇ⲥⲁⲗⲡⲓⲅⲅⲟⲥ. Ⲁ̅ⲗ.	*سبحوه بصوت البوق الليلويا.
*Unto our God is due glory and praise. Praise the	*Ⲉϥⲉⲣⲁⲛⲁϥ ⲙ̇ⲡⲉⲛⲛⲟ-ⲩϯ ⲛ̇ⲭⲉ ⲡⲓⲱⲟⲩ ⲛⲉⲙ	*يليق لإلهنا المجد والتسبيح. سبحوا الرب

Lord our God with a joyful psalm.	ⲡⲓⲥⲙⲟⲩ. Ⲥⲙⲟⲩ ⲉⲠϭⲟⲓⲥ ⲡⲉⲛⲛⲟⲩϯ ϫⲉ ⲛⲁⲛⲉ ⲟⲩⲯⲁⲗⲙⲟⲥ.	الهنا بحسن المزمار.
Praise Him with the psaltery and harp Alleluia.	Ⲥⲙⲟⲩ ⲉⲣⲟϥ ϧⲉⲛ ⲟⲩⲯⲁⲗⲧⲏⲣⲓⲟⲛ ⲛⲉⲙ ⲟⲩⲕⲩⲑⲁⲣⲁ.Ⲁ̅ⲗ̅.	سبحوه بمزمار وقيثارة الليلويا.
Unto our God is due glory and praise. Praise the Lord our God with a joyful psalm.	Ⲉϥⲉⲣⲁⲛⲁϥ ⲙⲡⲉⲛⲛⲟⲩϯ ⲛ̀ϫⲉ ⲡⲓⲱⲟⲩ ⲛⲉⲙ ⲡⲓⲥⲙⲟⲩ. Ⲥⲙⲟⲩ ⲉ̀Ⲡϭⲟⲓⲥ ⲡⲉⲛⲛⲟⲩϯ ϫⲉ ⲛⲁⲛⲉ ⲟⲩⲯⲁⲗⲙⲟⲥ.	يليق لإلهنا المجد والتسبيح. سبحوا الرب الهنا بحسن المزمار.
*Praise Him with timbrel and chorus Alleluia.	*Ⲥⲙⲟⲩ ⲉ̀ⲣⲟϥ ϧⲉⲛ ϩⲁⲛⲕⲉⲙⲕⲉⲙ ⲛⲉⲙ ϩⲁⲛⲭⲟⲣⲟⲥ.Ⲁ̅ⲗ̅.	*سبحوه بدفوف وصفوف الليلويا.
*Unto our God is due glory and praise. Praise the Lord our God with a joyful psalm.	*Ⲉϥⲉⲣⲁⲛⲁϥ ⲙⲡⲉⲛⲛⲟⲩϯ ⲛ̀ϫⲉ ⲡⲓⲱⲟⲩ ⲛⲉⲙ ⲡⲓⲥⲙⲟⲩ. Ⲥⲙⲟⲩ ⲉ̀Ⲡϭⲟⲓⲥ ⲡⲉⲛⲛⲟⲩϯ ϫⲉ ⲛⲁⲛⲉ ⲟⲩⲯⲁⲗⲙⲟⲥ.	*يليق لإلهنا المجد والتسبيح. سبحوا الرب الهنا بحسن المزمار.
Praise Him with	Ⲥⲙⲟⲩ ⲉ̀ⲣⲟϥ ϧⲉⲛ	سبحوه بأوتار

stringed instruments and organs Alleluia.	ϩⲁⲛⲕⲁⲡ ⲛⲉⲙ ⲟⲩⲟⲣⲅⲁ-ⲛⲟⲛ. Ⲁ̅ⲗ̅.	وأرغن الليلويا.
Unto our God is due glory and praise. Praise the Lord our God with a joyful psalm.	Ⲉϥⲉⲣⲁⲛⲁϥ ⲙ̀ⲡⲉⲛⲛⲟⲩϯ ⲛ̀ⲭⲉ ⲡⲓⲱⲟⲩ ⲛⲉⲙ ⲡⲓⲥⲙⲟⲩ. Ⲥⲙⲟⲩ ⲉ̀Ⲡϭⲟⲓⲥ ⲡⲉⲛⲛⲟⲩϯ ⲭⲉ ⲛⲁⲛⲉ ⲟⲩⲯⲁⲗⲙⲟⲥ.	يليق لإلهنا المجد والتسبيح. سبحوا الرب الهنا بحسن المزمار.
*Praise Him with loud sounding cymbals Alleluia.	*Ⲥⲙⲟⲩ ⲉ̀ⲣⲟϥ ϧⲉⲛ ϩⲁⲛⲕⲩⲙⲃⲁⲗⲟⲛ ⲉⲛⲉⲥⲉ ⲧⲟⲩ̀ⲥⲙⲏ. Ⲁ̅ⲗ̅.	*سبحوه بصنوج حسنة الصوت الليلويا.
*Unto our God is due glory and praise. Praise the Lord our God with a joyful psalm.	*Ⲉϥⲉⲣⲁⲛⲁϥ ⲙ̀ⲡⲉⲛⲛⲟ-ⲩϯ ⲛ̀ⲭⲉ ⲡⲓⲱⲟⲩ ⲛⲉⲙ ⲡⲓⲥⲙⲟⲩ. Ⲥⲙⲟⲩ ⲉ̀Ⲡϭⲟⲓⲥ ⲡⲉⲛⲛⲟⲩϯ ⲭⲉ ⲛⲁⲛⲉ ⲟⲩⲯⲁⲗⲙⲟⲥ.	*يليق لإلهنا المجد والتسبيح. سبحوا الرب الهنا بحسن المزمار.
Praise Him with cymbals of joy Alleluia.	Ⲥⲙⲟⲩ ⲉ̀ⲣⲟϥ ϧⲉⲛ ϩⲁⲛⲕⲩⲙⲃⲁⲗⲟⲛ ⲛ̀ⲧⲉ ⲟⲩⲉ̀ϣ̀ⲗⲏⲗⲟⲩⲓ̀. Ⲁ̅ⲗ̅.	سبحوه بصنوج التهليل الليلويا.
Unto our God is due glory and praise.	Ⲉϥⲉⲣⲁⲛⲁϥ ⲙ̀ⲡⲉⲛⲛⲟⲩϯ	يليق لإلهنا المجد والتسبيح. سبحوا

Praise the Lord our God with a joyful psalm.	ⲛ̀ϫⲉ ⲡⲓⲱⲟⲩ ⲛⲉⲙ ⲡⲓⲥⲙⲟⲩ. Ⲥⲙⲟⲩ ⲉ̀Ⲡϭⲟⲓⲥ ⲡⲉⲛⲛⲟⲩϯ ϫⲉ ⲛⲁⲛⲉ ⲟⲩⲯⲁⲗⲙⲟⲥ.	الرب الهنا بحسن المزمار.
*Let everything that has breath praise the name of the Lord our God Alleluia.	*Ⲛⲓϥⲓ ⲛⲓⲃⲉⲛ ⲙⲁⲣⲟⲩ̀ⲥⲙⲟⲩ ⲧⲏⲣⲟⲩ ⲉ̀ϥ̀ⲣⲁⲛ ⲙ̀Ⲡϭⲟⲓⲥ Ⲡⲉⲛⲛⲟⲩϯ. Ⲁ̅ⲗ̅.	*كل نسمة فلتسبح اسم الرب الهنا الليلويا.
Glory be to the Father, the Son and the Holy Spirit Alleluia.	Ⲇⲟⲝⲁ Ⲡⲁⲧⲣⲓ ⲕⲉ Ⲩⲓⲱ ⲕⲉ Ⲁⲅⲓⲱ Ⲡⲛⲉⲩⲙⲁⲧⲓ. Ⲁ̅ⲗ̅.	المجد للآب والأبن والروح القدس الليلويا.
*Now and forever and unto the ages of ages Amen Alleluia.	*Ⲕⲉ ⲛⲩⲛ ⲕⲉ ⲁ̀ⲓ ⲕⲉ ⲓⲥⲧⲟⲩⲥ ⲉ̀ⲱⲛⲁⲥ ⲧⲱⲛ ⲉ̀ⲱⲛⲱⲛ ⲁ̀ⲙⲏⲛ. Ⲁ̅ⲗ̅.	*الآن وكل أوان وإلى دهر الداهرين آمين الليلويا.
Alleluia, Alleluia, Glory be to our God Alleluia.	Ⲁ̅ⲗ̅ Ⲁ̅ⲗ̅ Ⲇⲟⲝⲁ ⲥⲓ ⲟ̀ Ⲑⲉⲟⲥ ⲩ̀ⲙⲱⲛ Ⲁ̅ⲗ̅.	المجد لإلهنا الليلويا.
*Alleluia, Alleluia, Glory be to our God Alleluia.	*Ⲁ̅ⲗ̅ Ⲁ̅ⲗ̅ Ⲡⲓⲱⲟⲩ ⲫⲁ Ⲡⲉⲛⲛⲟⲩϯ ⲡⲉ Ⲁ̅ⲗ̅.	*المجد لإلهنا الليلويا.

PSALI WATOS FOR THE VESPERS OF SUNDAY'S OF KIAHK – ابصالية واطس

Come all in -happiness: Come all rejoicing: Come all in gladness: All of mankind.	Ⲁⲙⲱⲓⲛⲓ ⲧⲏⲣⲟⲩ ϧⲉⲛ ⲟⲩⲣⲁϣⲓ: ⲁⲙⲱⲓⲛⲓ ⲧⲏⲣⲟⲩ ϧⲉⲛ ⲟⲩⲑⲉⲗⲏⲗ: ⲁⲙⲱⲓⲛⲓ ⲧⲏⲣⲟⲩ ϧⲉⲛ ⲟⲩⲟⲩⲛⲟϥ: ⲛⲉⲛϣⲏⲣⲓ ⲧⲏⲣⲟⲩ ⲛ̀ⲧⲉ ⲛⲓⲣⲱⲙⲓ.	تعالوا جميعاً بفرح: تعالوا جميعاً بتهليل: تعالوا جميعاً بسرور: يا جميع بني البشر.
The wise and -understanding: The elders and the -young men: The men and the -women: All the children of -Adam.	Ⲃⲟⲛ ⲟⲩⲥⲁⲃⲉ ⲃⲟⲛ ⲟⲩⲕⲁⲧϩⲏⲧ: ⲃⲟⲛ ⲟⲩϧⲉⲗⲗⲟⲓ ⲃⲟⲛ ⲟⲩϧⲉⲗϣⲓⲣⲓ: ⲃⲟⲛ ⲟⲩⲣⲱⲙⲓ ⲃⲟⲛ ⲟⲩⲥϩⲓⲙⲓ: ⲛⲉⲛϣⲏⲣⲓ ⲧⲏⲣⲟⲩ ⲛ̀ⲧⲉ Ⲁⲇⲁⲙ.	الحكماء والفهماء: الشيوخ والشبان: الرجال النساء: جميع بني آدم.
*Come and hear -from me: For I will tell you: That the true God: Has come and	* Ϫⲉ ⲅⲁⲣ ⲁⲙⲱⲓⲛⲓ ⲥⲱⲧⲉⲙ ⲉ̀ⲣⲟⲓ: ϫⲉ ⲅⲁⲣ ⲁ̀ⲛⲟⲕ ϯⲛⲁⲧⲁⲙⲱⲧⲉⲛ: ϫⲉ ⲅⲁⲣ ⲁϥⲓ̀	*تعالوا اسمعوا مني: لأني أنا اخبركم: أن الله الحقيقي أتي: وتجسد من

-incarnated from the -Virgin.	ⲛ̀ⲭⲉ Ⲫϯ ⲙ̀ⲙⲏⲓ: ⲁϥϭⲓⲥⲁⲣⲝ ϧⲉⲛ ϯⲠⲁⲣⲑⲉⲛⲟⲥ.	العذراء.
*Truly she gave birth -to Him: Without any defilement: Truly she gave birth -to the Word: And her virginity is -sealed.	* Ⲇⲓⲕⲉⲱⲥ ⲁⲥⲙⲓⲥⲓ ⲙ̀ⲙⲟϥ: Ⲇⲓⲕⲉⲱⲥ ⲉⲥⲟⲓ ⲛ̀ⲁⲧⲁϭⲛⲓ: Ⲇⲓⲕⲉⲟⲥ ⲁⲥⲙⲓⲥⲓ ⲙ̀ⲡⲓⲖⲟⲅⲟⲥ: ϧⲉⲛ ⲧⲉⲥⲡⲁⲣⲑⲉⲛⲓⲁ ⲙ̀ⲙⲏⲓ.	*حقاً ولدته: وهي حقا بغير عيب: حقاً ولدت الكلمة: ببتوليتها الحقيقية.
Who is among the -wise: Who are living on the -earth: Thier mind will -become heavenly: To proclaim the -honour of the Virgin.	Ⲉ̀ⲣⲉ ⲛⲓⲙ ϧⲉⲛ ⲛⲓⲥⲟⲫⲟⲥ: ⲛⲓⲣⲉⲙⲛ̀ⲕⲁϯ ⲉⲧϩⲓϫⲉⲛ ⲡⲓⲕⲁϩⲓ: ⲛⲁ̀ϣⲉⲣ ⲡⲉϥⲛⲟⲩⲥ ⲛ̀ⲣⲉⲙⲙ̀ⲫⲉ: ⲉϥϫⲱ ⲙ̀ⲡⲧⲁⲓⲟ ⲛ̀ϯⲠⲁⲣⲑⲉⲛⲟⲥ.	من في الحكماء و الفهماء: الذين علي الأرض: يصير عقله سمائيا: ينطق بكرامة العذراء.
The seven angelic -ranks: And the seven great -heavenly soldiers: And the seven ranks -in Zion :	Ϣⲁϣϥ ⲛ̀ⲧⲁⲅⲙⲁ ⲛⲁ̀ⲅⲅⲉⲗⲟⲥ: ϣⲁϣϥ ⲛ̀ⲛⲓϣϯ ⲛ̀ⲥⲧⲣⲁⲧⲓⲁ̀: ϣⲁϣϥ ⲛ̀ⲧ-	سبع طغمات الملائكة: السبعة العساكر العظماء: السبع الطغمات في صهيون: يرتلون

15

Are chanting to the -Virgin.	ⲁⲩⲙⲁ ϧⲉⲛ Ⲥⲓⲱⲛ: ⲥⲉⲉⲣϩⲩⲙⲛⲟⲥ ⲛ̀ϯⲡⲁⲣ-ⲑⲉⲛⲟⲥ.	للعذراء.
*Behold the whole -creation: Magnify the Virgin: From the rising of the -sun: To its going down.	* Ⲏⲥ ϯⲕⲧⲏⲥⲓⲥ ⲧⲏⲣⲥ ⲉⲩⲥⲟⲡ: ⲏⲥ ϯⲱⲟⲩ ⲛ̀ϯⲡⲁⲣⲑⲉⲛⲟⲥ: ⲏⲥϫⲉⲛ ⲛⲓⲙⲁⲛϣⲁⲓ ⲛ̀ⲧⲉ ⲫⲣⲏ: ⲛⲉⲙ ⲉ̀ⲃⲟⲗ ϣⲁ ⲛⲉϥⲙⲁⲛ̀ϩⲱⲧⲡ.	*ها الخليقة كلها معاً: يمجدون العذراء: من مشارق الشمس: إلي مغاربها.
*God is the true God: God the Word of the -Father: God the Son of the -Virgin: The daughter of -Joakim and Anna.	* Ⲑⲉⲟⲥ ⲅⲁⲣ ⲡⲉ Ⲫϯ ⲙ̀ⲙⲏⲓ: Ⲑⲉⲟⲥ ⲡⲓⲖⲟⲅⲟⲥ ⲛ̀ⲧⲉ Ⲫⲓⲱⲧ: Ⲑⲉⲟⲥ Ⲡϣⲏⲣⲓ ⲛ̀ϯⲠⲁⲣⲑⲉⲛⲟⲥ: ϯϣⲉⲣⲓ ⲛⲒⲱⲁ̀ⲕⲓⲙ ⲛⲉⲙ Ⲁⲛⲛⲁ.	*لأن الله هو الإله الحقيقي: الله الكلمة الآب: الله إبن العذراء: إبنة يواقيم وحنة.
Jesus Christ the -Name of salvation: Jesus Christ the -sweet name: Jesus Christ the -Giver of life:	Ⲓⲏⲥ Ⲡⲭ̅ⲥ̅ ⲫⲁ ⲡⲓⲣⲁⲛ ⲛ̀ⲟⲩϫⲁⲓ: Ⲓⲏⲥ Ⲡⲭ̅ⲥ̅ ⲫⲁ ⲡⲓⲣⲁⲛ ⲉⲧϩⲟⲗϫ: Ⲓⲏⲥ Ⲡⲭ̅ⲥ̅ ⲫ̀ⲣⲉϥϯ ⲙ̀ⲡ̀ⲱⲛϧ: ⲉ̀ⲧⲁϥϭⲓ-	يسوع المسيح ذو الإسم المخلص: يسوع المسيح ذو الإسم الحلو: يسوع المسيح

Was incarnated from -the Virgin.	capϩ ϧεν ϯπαρθενος.	معطي الحياة: تجسد من العذراء.
According to what -was spoken: **By Isaiah the Prophet:** **That the Virgin will -conceive:** **And give birth to -Emmanuel.**	Κατα ὃρηϯ ὲταϥϫος: ̀ⲛϫε Ⲏсⲁнⲁс πὶπροφ- ⲏⲧⲏс: ϫε εⲥⲉ̀ερβοκι ̀ⲛϫε ϯπαρθενος: ⲟⲩⲟϩ εⲥⲉ̀- ⲙιⲥι ̀ⲛⲈⲙⲙⲁⲛⲟⲩⲏⲗ.	كما قال: أشعياء النبي: أن العذراء تحبل: وتلد عمانوئيل.
*All congregations -and tribes: **All Orthodox people:** **All harbours for -salvation:** **Sprang from the -Virgin St. Mary.**	* Ⲗⲁⲟⲥ ⲛιβεⲛ ⲛεⲙ ⲫⲩⲗⲏ ⲛιβεⲛ: Ⲗⲁⲟⲥ ⲛιβεⲛ ̀ⲛⲟⲣθⲟⲆⲟⲝⲟⲥ: ⲗⲁⲩⲙⲏⲛ ⲛιβεⲛ ̀ⲛⲧε πιⲟⲩϫⲁι: βεβι ⲛⲱⲟⲩ ὲβⲟⲗ ̀ⲛϩⲏⲧⲥ.	*كل الشعوب وكل القبائل: كل الشعوب الارثوذكسيين: كل ميناء للخلاص: أنبع لهم منها.
*Moses the Law -giver: **Melchizedek and -Aaron:** **Mark the Apostle:** **Glorify the Virgin.**	* Ⲙⲱⲥⲏⲥ ⲅⲁⲣ πιⲛⲟ- ⲙⲟθεⲧⲏⲥ: ⲘⲉⲗϫιⲥεⲆεⲕ ⲛεⲙ Ⲁ̀ⲁⲣⲱⲛ: Ⲙⲁⲣⲕⲟⲥ πιⲁ̀πⲟⲥⲧⲟⲗⲟⲥ: ⲥεⲩⲟⲩ- ⲩⲟⲩ ̀ⲙⲙⲱⲟⲩ ὲϫεⲛ	*موسي واضع الناموس: وملكيصادق وهرون: ومرقس الرسول: يفتخرون بالعذراء.

17

	†ⲡⲁⲣⲑⲉⲛⲟⲥ.	
The Cherubim with -six wings: The Seraphim full of -eyes: All the Heavenly -Ranks: Glorify the Virgin.	Ⲛⲓ̀Ⲭⲉⲣⲟⲩⲃⲓⲙ ⲛⲁ ⲡⲓ ⲋ̅ ⲛ̀ⲧⲉⲛϩ: ⲛⲓⲤⲉⲣⲁⲫⲓⲙ ⲉⲧⲟⲩⲟⲩ ⲙ̀ⲃⲟⲗ: ⲛⲓⲧⲁⲅⲙⲁ ⲧⲏⲣⲟⲩ ⲛ̀ⲁⲅⲅⲉⲗⲓⲕⲟⲛ: ⲥⲉϯⲱⲟⲩ ⲛ̀ϯⲡⲁⲣⲑⲉⲛⲟⲥ.	الشاروبيم ذو الستة الأجنحة: والسيرافيم كثيرون الأعيُن: وكل الطغمات الملائكية: يمجدون العذراء.
All the trees of life: All that decorate the -Paradise: The pride of all -virgins: Is St Mary the Virgin.	Ⲍⲩⲗⲟⲛ ⲛⲓⲃⲉⲛ ⲛ̀ⲧⲉ ⲡ̀ⲱⲛϧ: ϫⲟⲗⲥⲉⲗ ⲙ̀ⲡ- ⲓⲡⲁⲣⲁⲇⲓⲥⲟⲥ: ϫⲟⲗⲥⲉⲗ ⲛ̀ⲛⲓⲡⲁⲣⲑⲉⲛⲟⲥ ⲧⲏⲣⲟⲩ: ⲡⲉ Ⲙⲁⲣⲓⲁ ϯⲡⲁⲣⲑⲉⲛⲟⲥ.	كل أشجار الحياة: زينة الفردوس: زينة كل العذاري: هي مريم العذراء.
* Glory to God the -Father Amen: Glory to His beloved -Son: Glory to the Holy -Spirit: And we glorify the -Virgin.	* Ⲟⲩⲱⲟⲩ ⲙ̀Ⲫϯ Ⲫⲓⲱⲧ ⲁ̀ⲙⲏⲛ: ⲟⲩⲱⲟⲩ ⲙ̀ⲡⲉϥϣⲏⲣⲓ ⲙ̀ⲙⲉⲛⲣⲓⲧ: ⲟⲩⲱⲟⲩ ⲙ̀ⲡⲓ ⲡ̅ⲛ̅ⲁ̅ ⲉ̅ⲑ̅ⲩ̅: ⲛ̀ⲧⲉⲛⲧⲁⲓⲟ ⲛ̀ϯⲠⲁⲣⲑⲉⲛⲟⲥ.	*المجد لله الآب أمين: المجد لإبنه الحبيب: المجد للروح القدس: ونكرم العذراء.

* The Throne of the -Most High: The chariot of the -Cherubim: The illuminated Ark: Is the Virgin St. Mary.	* Ⲡⲓⲑⲣⲟⲛⲟⲥ ⲛ̀ⲧⲉ ⲫⲏⲉⲧϭⲟⲥⲓ: ⲡ̀ϩⲁⲣⲙⲁ ⲛ̀ⲛⲓⲭⲉⲣⲟⲩⲃⲓⲙ̀ⲕⲟⲛ: ⲡⲓⲥⲧⲉⲣⲉ̀ⲱⲙⲁ ⲉ̀ⲧⲉⲣⲟⲩⲱⲓⲛⲓ: ⲡⲉ Ⲙⲁⲣⲓⲁ ϯⲡⲁⲣⲑⲉⲛⲟⲥ.	*الكرسي الذي للعلي: المركبة الشاروبيمية: الفلك المنير: هو مريم العذراء.
Rejoice O my Lady -mother of my Master: Rejoice O Queen -mother of the King: Rejoice O the true -bride: Who gave birth to the -Bridegroom.	Ⲣⲁϣⲓ ⲧⲁⲟⲥ̄ ⲑⲙⲁⲩ ⲙ̀Ⲡⲁⲟⲥ̄: ⲣⲁϣⲓ ϯⲟⲩⲣⲱ ⲑⲙⲁⲩ ⲙ̀ⲡⲓⲟⲩⲣⲟ: ⲣⲁϣⲓ ⲱ̀ ϯϣⲉⲗⲏⲧ ⲙ̀ⲙⲏⲓ: ⲉ̀ⲧⲁⲥⲙⲓⲥⲓ ⲙ̀ⲡⲓⲡⲁⲧϣⲉⲗⲉⲧ.	أفرحي يا سيدتي أم سيدي: إفرحي أيتها الملكة أم الملك: إفرحي أيتها العروسة الحقيقية: التي ولدت الختن.
Solomon son of -David: Samuel the prophet: Severus the patriarch: Magnify the virgin.	Ⲥⲟⲗⲟⲙⲱⲛ ⲡ̀ϣⲏⲣⲓ ⲛ̀Ⲇⲁⲩⲓⲇ: Ⲥⲁⲙⲟⲩⲏⲗ ⲡⲓⲡ̀ⲣⲟⲫⲏⲧⲏⲥ: Ⲥⲉⲩⲏⲣⲟⲥ ⲡⲓⲡⲁⲧⲣⲓⲁⲣⲭⲏⲥ: ⲥⲉϯⲱ̀ⲟⲩ ⲛ̀ϯⲡⲁⲣⲑⲉⲛⲟⲥ.	سليمان إبن داود: وصموئيل النبي: وساويرس البطريرك: يمجدون العذراء.
*Your greatness O -Mary:	* Ⲧⲉⲙⲉⲧⲛⲓϣϯ ⲱ̀ Ⲙⲁⲣⲓⲁ̀:	*عظمتك يا مريم: متعالية

Is exalted above -heaven: You will give birth to -a Son: His name will be -called Emmanuel.	ⲧⲉ-ⲥⲁⲡϣⲱⲓ ⲉ̀ϩⲟⲧⲉ ⲧ̀ⲫⲉ: ⲧⲉⲣⲁⲙⲓⲥⲓ ⲛ̀ⲟⲩϣⲏⲣⲓ: ⲉⲣⲉⲙⲟⲩϯ ⲉ̀ⲡⲉϥⲣⲁⲛ ⲭⲉ Ⲉⲙⲙⲁⲛⲟⲩⲏⲗ.	أكثر من السماء: تلدين إبناً: يدعي إسمه عمانوئيل.
*There is none like -you: Neither in heaven or -on earth: I find myself unable: To proclaim your -honour.	* Ⲩⲙⲟⲛ ⲫⲏⲉ̀ⲧⲉⲛⲑⲱⲛⲧ ⲉ̀ⲣⲟ: ⲩⲙⲟⲛ ϧⲉⲛ ⲧ̀ⲫⲉ ⲛⲉⲙ ϩⲓϫⲉⲛ ⲡⲓⲕⲁϩⲓ: ⲩⲙⲟⲛ ϣ̀ϫⲟⲙ ⲙ̀ⲙⲟⲓ ⲁⲛⲟⲕ: ⲉⲑⲣⲓⲥⲁϫⲓ ⲉ̀ⲡⲉⲧⲁⲓⲟ̀.	*ليس من يشبهك: ليس في السماء وعلي الأرض: ليس لي أنا استطاعة: أن أنطق بكرامتك.
He who created -heaven and earth: Who came to us from -the Father: Came and dwelt in -your womb: Nine complete months.	Ⲫⲏⲉ̀ⲧⲁϥⲑⲁⲙⲓⲟ̀ ⲛ̀ⲧ̀ⲫⲉ ⲛⲉⲙ ⲡ̀ⲕⲁϩⲓ: ⲫⲏⲉⲑⲛⲏⲟⲩ ⲉ̀ⲃⲟⲗ ϧⲉⲛ Ⲫ̀ⲓⲱⲧ: ⲁϥⲓ̀ ⲁϥϣⲱⲡⲓ ϧⲉⲛ ⲧⲉⲛⲉϫⲓ: ⲙ̀ⲯⲓⲧ ⲛ̀ⲁ̀ⲃⲟⲧ ⲛ̀ⲏⲡⲓ.	الذي خلق السماء والأرض: المولود من الآب: أتي وحل في بطنك: تسعة شهور عدداً.
Hail to the spring of -the Water of Life: Hail to the golden -vessel:	Ⲭⲉⲣⲉ ϯⲙⲟⲩⲙⲓ ⲙ̀ⲙⲱⲟⲩ ⲛ̀ⲱⲛϧ: ⲭⲉⲣⲉ ⲡⲓⲥⲧⲁⲙⲛⲟⲥ	السلام لينبوع ماء الحياة: السلام للقسط الذهب: السلام

Hail to the undefiled -ark: In the Dome of -Testimony.	ⲛ̀ⲛⲟⲩⲃ: ⲭⲉⲣⲉ ϯⲕⲩⲃⲱⲧⲟⲥ ⲛ̀ⲁⲧⲁϭⲛⲓ: ϧⲉⲛ ϯ̀ⲥⲕⲩⲛⲏ ⲛ̀ⲧⲉ ϯⲙⲉⲧⲙⲉⲑⲣⲉ.	للتابوت الذي بلا عين: في قبة الشهادة.
*The adornment of -all virgins: And the souls of the -orthodox: And all souls honour -you: O Mary the Virgin.	* Ⲯⲟⲗⲥⲉⲗ ⲛ̀ⲛⲓⲡⲁⲣⲑⲉⲛⲟⲥ ⲧⲏⲣⲟⲩ: ⲯⲩⲭⲏ ⲛⲓⲃⲉⲛ ⲛ̀ⲟ- ⲣⲑⲟⲇⲟⲝⲟⲥ: ⲯⲩⲭⲏ ⲛⲓⲃⲉⲛ ⲥⲉⲥ̀ⲙⲟⲩ ⲉ̀ⲣⲟ: ⲱ̀ Ⲙⲁⲣⲓⲁ̀ ϯⲡⲁⲣⲑⲉⲛⲟⲥ.	*زينة جميع العذاري: وكل أنفس الأرثوذكسيين: وكل الأنفس تباركت: يا مريم العذراء.
*O the luminous -Dove: And the filled with -grace: O the rod of Aaron: Which budded and -flourished.	* Ⲱ̀ ϯϭⲣⲟⲙⲡⲓ ⲛ̀ⲟⲩⲱⲓⲛⲓ: ⲱ̀ ⲡⲓϩ̀ⲙⲟⲧ ⲉⲧϫⲏⲕ ⲉ̀ⲃⲟⲗ: ⲱ̀ ⲡⲓϣ̀ⲃⲱⲧ ⲛ̀ⲧⲉ Ⲇⲁ̀ⲣⲱⲛ: ⲉ̀ⲧⲁϥⲫⲓⲣⲓ ⲉ̀ⲃⲟⲗ ⲟⲩⲟϩ ⲁϥϯⲕⲁⲣⲡⲟⲥ.	*أيتها الحمامة النورانية: أيتها النعمة الكاملة: يا عصاة هرون: التي أزهرت وأعطت ثمرة.

ANOTHER PSALI WATOS (By ABU EL-SAAD) — مديح واطس للعذراء

I praise a celibate virgin:
And proclaim vespers and matins:
With a loud voice saying:
Blessed are you O Virgin.

أمدح فى عذراء وبتول:
واصيح عشية مع بكرا:
بأعلى صوتى وأقول.
طوباك ايتها العذراء

Truly we are granted:
This coming goodness:
If we proclaim loudly:
Blessed are you O Virgin

بحق إننا نُعطى وننال:
تلك الخيرات المنتظرة:
إذا صحنا بالصوت العال:
طوباك أيتها العذراء

Gabriel came to you:
Proclaimed to you the good tidings:
He greeted you and said:
Blessed are you O Virgin.

تقدم نحوكِ غبريال:
وأعلن صوته بالبشرى:
وأعطاك السلام وقال:
طوباك أيتها العذراء

Your womb carried your Creator:
As the Prophets said:
That God the Lord dwells in you:
Blessed are you O Virgin.

جوف أحشاكِ حمل باريكِ:
كما قال أهل الخبرة:
إن الرب الإله يسكن فيكِ:
طوباك أيتها العذراء.

Your name is sweet and great:
One greatly wonders about it:
Even the wise could not comprehend
-it:

حلو هو اسمكِ وعظيم:
وتتحير فيه الفكرة:
ولم يبلغ إليه حكيم:
طوباك أيتها العذراء

Blessed are you O Virgin.

Adam was driven out of Paradise:
And he became grieved with sorrow:
And the Holy God restored him back:
Blessed are you O Virgin.

خرج آدم خارج الفردوس:
وصار كئيباً فى حسرة:
وأعاده الرب القدوس:
طوباك أيتها العذراء

One becomes intoxicated:
When one drinks from this wine:
Praising the pride of generations:
Blessed are you O Virgin.

عمرى جميعه وأنا سكران:
شارب من تلك الخمرة:
ومادح فى أم الديان:
طوباك أيتها العذراء

The Fakhory praised you:
And your name is a sweet aroma:
As said by the Psalmist:
Blessed are you O Virgin.

رتل فيك الفاخورى:
وسَماكِ زهرة عطرة:
وأخبر عنك المزموري:
طوباك أيتها العذراء

Adam fell and became enslaved:
He returned once more:
To his rank with happiness and joy:
Blessed are you O Virgin.

ذلَّ آدم وبقى مأسور:
ورجع بابنكِ ثانى مرة:
إلى رتبته فرحاً مسرور:
طوباك أيتها العذراء

Ezekiel has prophesized:
Said the Mighty will come:
And appear from you at the fullness
-of time:
Blessed are you O Virgin.

سبق وتنبأ حزقيال:
وقال يأتى ذو القدرة:
ويظهر منك فى عقبِ الأجيال:
طوباك أيتها العذراء

Micah the prophet witnessed:

شَهَدَ ميخا قال الجبار:

God will come and get the victory :
And God will destroy the evildoers:
Blessed are you O Virgin.

يأتى وتكون النُصرة:
ويقوم الله على الأشرار:
طوباك أيتها العذراء

David cried with a soft voice:
Played his ten stringed harp:
Saying the Lord loved the gates of
- Zion:
Blessed are you O Virgin.

صرخ داود بصوت
حنون:
وحرك أوتاره العشرة:
أحب الرب أبواب
صهيون:
طوباك أيتها العذراء

The devil cheated Adam craftily:
Made him to eat from the tree :
And the Son of God came and
-redeemed him:
Blessed are you O Virgin.

ضَلَّ إبليس آدم وأغواه:
وأكل من تلك الشجرة:
وأتى ابن الله وفداه:
طوباك أيتها العذراء

The Lord shook the Heaven of
-Heavens:
And came to our earth:
And He took the shape of His
-creation:
Blessed are you O Virgin.

طأطأ الرب سماء
السموات:
وجاءَ إلى الأرض
القفرة:
وتشَّبه هو بالمخلوقات:
طوباك أيتها العذراء

He came from the house of David:
And healed us from all harm:
And revealed to us the Secret of
-secrets:
Blessed are you O Virgin.

ظهر من بيت داود البار:
وشفانا من كل مضرة:
وعرفنا سر الأسرار:
طوباك أيتها العذراء

I have been wearied trying to explain:

عَييتُ وأنا أطلب تفسير:

And yet I have achieved small gain:
Only a little glorification and praise:
Blessed are you O Virgin.

ولم أبلغ شيئاً بكثرة:
سوى تمجيد ومديح
يسير:
طوباك أيتها العذراء

The Unseen how can He be seen
Creator of the seen and unseen:
How did the people crucify Him:
Blessed are you O Virgin.

غير المرئى كيف رأوه:
خالق ما يرى وما لا
يرى:
كيف أهل العالم صلبوه:
طوباك أيتها العذراء

They sinned and arrested the
-Righteous:
The evil people crucified Him:
They became greatly ashamed:
Blessed are you O Virgin.

فعلوا الشر ومسكوا البار:
وصلبوه القوم الكفرة:
وصار لهم الخزى مع
العار:
طوباك أيتها العذراء

He said I am putting in Zion:
A stumbling stone:
They stumbled on it and fell:
Blessed are you O Virgin.

قال إنى واضع فى
صهيون: صخرة شك
وحجر عثرة:
عثروا فيه وقد سقطوا:
طوباك أيتها العذراء

We have been captured by the devil:
Under bitter bondage:
And your Son made us free:
Blessed are you O Virgin.

كنَّا فى رق المكار:
تحت عبودية مُرة:
وابنكِ صيرنا الأحرار:
طوباك أيتها العذراء

You have been dressed with lights:
Mary you became a great tree:
That is full of fruits:

لبستي حلة من الأنوار:
صرتِ يا مريم شجرة:
عظيمة حاملة الأثمار:

Blessed are you O Virgin.	طوباك أيتها العذراء

Moses saw on Mount Sinai:	موسى رآك فوق جبل
Something like a green bush:	الطور:
That was decorated with lights	شبه العليقة الخضرة:
Blessed are you O Virgin.	مشتملة بشعاع النور:
	طوباك أيتها العذراء

We have been exiled and lost all	نفينا وعدمنا كل
-goodness:	الخيرات:
And by your Son we have returned	ورجعنا بابنكِ ثانى مرة:
-once more:	إلى الفردوس أرض
And all the Christians rejoiced:	الميعاد:
Blessed are you O Virgin.	طوباك أيتها العذراء

Your Son conquered the devilish	هزم ابنك حيل الشيطان:
-tricks:	وصار له الغلبة و
To Him belong the victory and	النصرة:
-Lordship:	وقد فرح أهل الإيمان:
And all the Christians rejoiced:	طوباك أيتها العذراء
Blessed are you O Virgin.	

You have found grace and had:	وجدت نعمة وقد نلت:
Joy, delight and happiness:	فرحاً مع بهجة ومسرة:
To tell about you is beyond my reach:	ووصفك يعلو على
Blessed are you O Virgin.	مقدرتى:
	طوباك أيتها العذراء

You are like the rock:	لأنه ظهر منك ينبوع:
Out of whom came a sweet spring :	حلو أيتها الصخرة:
Ask your Son the Lord Jesus:	أسألى فينا أبنك الرب

Blessed are you O Virgin.

يسوع:
طوباك أيتها العذراء

O Mother of Light how many
-servants:
Came at the last hour and were
-rewarded:
And I am the poor coming being the
-last:
Blessed are you O Virgin.

يا أم النور كم أجير: جاء
فى الآخر وأخذ الأجرة:
وأنا المسكين أتيت
الأخير:
طوباك أيتها العذراء.

Hail to Mary full of grace:
Everyone attending and I:
Proclaim saying loudly:
Blessed are you O Virgin.

السلام لمريم والغبطات:
وأنا وجميع من فى هذه
البيعة:
نصيح ونقول بأعلا
الأصوات:
طوباك أيتها العذراء.

Introduction to Watos Theotokeias -
مقدمة الثيؤطوكيات الواطس -

And whenever we sing, let us say tenderly, "Our Lord Jesus Christ, have mercy upon our souls."

Ⲉϣⲱⲡ ⲁⲛϣⲁⲛⲉⲣⲯⲁⲗⲓⲛ: ⲙⲁⲣⲉⲛⲭⲟⲥ ϧⲉⲛ ⲟⲩϩⲗ-ⲟⲭ: ϫⲉ ⲡⲉⲛⲟⲥ Ⲓⲏⲥⲟⲩⲥ Ⲡⲓⲭⲣⲓⲥⲧⲟⲥ: ⲁ̀ⲣⲓ ⲟⲩⲛⲁⲓ ⲛⲉⲙ ⲛⲉⲛⲯⲩⲭⲏ.

إذا ما رتلنا. فلننقل بعذوبة. يا ربنا يسوع المسيح. اصنع رحمة مع نفوسنا.

* Glory be to the Father and the Son, and the Holy Spirit, now and forever and unto the ages of ages, Amen.

* Ⲇⲟⲝⲁ ⲡⲁⲧⲣⲓ ⲕⲉ Ⲩⲓⲱ: ⲕⲉ ⲁ̀ⲅⲓⲱ Ⲡⲛⲉⲩⲙⲁⲧⲓ: ⲕⲉ ⲛⲩⲛ ⲕⲉ ⲁ̀ⲓ ⲕⲉ ⲓⲥⲧⲟⲩⲥ: ⲉ̀ⲱⲛⲁⲥ ⲧⲱⲛ ⲉ̀ⲱⲛⲱⲛ ⲁ̀ⲙⲏⲛ.

*المجد للآب والابن. والروح القدوس. الآن وكل أوان. والى دهر الداهرين. آمين.

28

First Part of the Saturday Theotokia -
ثيؤطوكية السبت القطعه الاولى

The First Part:	Пιϣορπ:	:القطعة الاولي

The First Part:

O chaste and undefiled, holy in everything, who brought God for us, carried in her arms.

Пιϣορπ:

Ϯатоωλεβ ̀ncεμне: oυος ε̅θ̅ ϧεν ςωβ niβεn: θηεταcιni nan ̀мФ̇ϯ: εϥταληoυτ ̀εϧεn neϲχφoι.

:القطعة الاولي

أيتها الغير دنسة العفيفة. القديسة في كل شئ. التى قدمت لنا. الله محمولا علي ذراعيها.

* The whole creation rejoiced with you, proclaiming and saying, "Hail to you O full of grace, the Lord is with you."

* Cραϣι nεμε ̀nχε ϯκτηcιc τηρc: εcωϣ ̀εβoλ εcχω ̀ммoc: χε χερε θηεθμες ̀ǹςμoτ: oυoς Π̅o̅c̅ ϣoπ nεμε.

*تفرح معكِ كل الخليقة. صارخة قائلة. السلام لك يا ممتلئة نعمة. الرب معكِ.

Hail to you O full of grace, hail to you who has found grace, hail to you who has given birth to Christ, the Lord is with you.

Χερε θηεθμες ̀ǹςμ- oτ: χερε θηεταcχεμ ̀ςμoτ: χερε θηετ- αcμεc Π̅χ̅c̅: oυoς

السلام لك يا ممتلئة نعمة. السلام لك يا من وجدت نعمة. السلام لك يا من ولدت المسيح. الرب معك.

Ⲡⲟⲥ ϣⲟⲡ ⲛⲉⲙⲉ.

FIRST EXPLANATION BY ABU EL-SAAD -
القطعة الاولى من نظم المعلم ابو السعد

Who is she who is undefiled:	من هي تدعى الغيرالدنسة:
But only Mary for her purity:	إلا مريم بطهارتها:
And all my thoughts are trying:	وجميع افكاري ملتمسة:
But could not proclaim her honour.	ولم تنطق بكرامتها.
This Saint has given birth:	وضعت هذه القديسة:
And yet she remained a virgin:	وهي عذراء بطبيعتها:
And she became a mother and a leader	وصارت امأ ورئيسة:
And her rank is above the whole -world.	وفوق العالم رتبتها.
You have been greatly exalted O -Mary:	عليت يا مريم جداً:
And honoured above all ranks:	وتشرفك فوق المقدار:
And exalted more than the martyrs:	وفقتِ مقدار الشهداء:
And higher than all the righteous.	وتفضلتِ على الأبرار.
You have conquered the armies of the -enemies:	هزمتِ كراديس الأعداء:
Through your Son we have been saved -from hell:	وبابنك نجوْنا من النار:
We magnify you O Virgin:	نعظمك يا بكر مدى:
All our life and forever.	العمر إلى عقب الأدهار.

30

Every living body and soul:
Come and congratulate us:
With every language and tune:
Chanting with us in a loud voice
-saying.

كل جسدٍ حي ونسمة:
يجئُ الآن ويهنينا:
بأي لغة وأي نغمة:
بصوتٍ عالٍ يناغينا.

+ *Hail to you Mother of Mercy:*
While your servants help us:
Blessed are you full of grace:
Intercede for us to your beloved Son .

السلام لك يا أم الرحمة:
نحن عبيدك جيرينا:
طوباك يا مملوءة نعمة:
عند ابنك الحبيب اشفعي
فينا .

FIRST EXPLANATION BY GABRIEL EL-KAI
القطعة الاولى من نظم المعلم غبريال

I start with the name of God the
-Father:
And the Son and the Holy Spirit:
One God Lord of Lords:
Holy is the living Lord of Hosts.

أبدي باسم الله الآب:
والإبن والروح القدس الثالوث:
إله واحد رب الأرباب:
قدوس الحي رب الصاباؤوت.

Holy is the living Lord of hosts:
Holy is the living and immortal:
Holy is He who raised us from
-death:
And saved us from straying.

قدوس الحي رب الصاباؤوت:
قدوس الحي بغير زوال:
قدوس مَن أحيانا من الموت:
وأزَالَ عنّا كل ضلال.

And saved us from straying:

وأزَالَ عنّا كل ضلال:

He incarnated from a pure -Virgin: The undefiled pride of -generations: Mary the lady of mankind.	وتجسد من بكر نقية: الغير دنسة فخر الأجيال: مريم سيدة البشرية.
Mary the lady of mankind: About her the righteous fathers -witnessed: That Moses the prophet in the -wilderness: Saw a bush burning with fire.	مريم سيدة البشرية: عنها شهد الآباء الأبرار: موسى النبي في البرية: عاين عوسج في قلبه نار.
Saw a bush burning with fire: With a high flame: But it did not consume the bush: To confirm the vision of Ezekiel.	عاين عوسج في قلبه نار: بلهيب صاعد يشعل إشعال: وما مسَّ العليقة أضرار: وصدق في رؤياه حزقيال.
To confirm the vision of Ezekiel: Who said that I have seen a door -to the east: Through it the exalted King -entered: And came out while it was sealed.	وصدق في رؤياه حزقيال: قال إني رأيت في المشرق باب: وفيه دخل الملك المُتعال: وخرج وعليه مسبول حجاب.
And came out while it was sealed: Like the pure Virgin: Who carried Jesus the Lord of -Lords: While she is still a virgin.	وخرج وعليه مسبول حجاب: مثال بتول بكر نقية: حمَلت يسوع رب الأرباب: وهي عذراء ببكورية.

32

While she is still a virgin:	وهي عذراء ببكورية:
She carried our Lord Christ:	حملت سيدنا بخرستوس:
She is exalted above all humans:	وفاقت طبع البشرية:
And all the righteous and saints.	نيم ني إثمي نيم ني ذيكيئوس.

And all the righteous and saints:	نيم ني إثمي نيم ني ذيكيئوس:
And all the illuminous ranks:	وكل طقوس نورانية:
And all the choirs of angels:	وجميع طغمات ني أنجيلوس:
And all the heavenly hosts.	وكل أجناد سمائية.

And all the heavenly hosts:	وكل أجناد سمائية:
They kneel to Who is carried on	تسجد للمحمول بين يديك:
-your hands:	ونحن نصيح بالكلية:
And we all proclaim saying:	السلام لكِ ثم السلام إليك.
Hail to you and hail to you.	

Hail to you and hail to you:	السلام لك ثم السلام إليك:
We ask you mother of the Beloved:	ونسألك يا أم المحبوب:
To accommodate us in the	أن تحظينا في مظال آبائك:
tabernacles of your fathers:	إبراهيم وإسحق ويعقوب.
Abraham, Isaac and Jacob.	

THE FIRST EXPLANATION BY AMBA MORCOS

القطعة الاولى من نظم البطريرك انبا مرقس -

I start with the name of the Holy
-God:
Creator of all ages and times:
To Him all the ranks praise:
Our Saviour the judging King.

أبدي بأسم الله القدوس:
الخالق كل دهور وأزمان:
له تسبح سائر كل طقوس:
مخلصنا الملك الديان.

Created Adam and established
-paradise:
Raised high without pillars:
In it dwell all souls:
Who pleased Him with faith and
-works.

خلق آدم وأنشأ الفردوس:
عال مرفوع بغير عمدان:
تسكن فيه جميع النفوس:
من كان يرضيه بأعمال
وإيمان.

Made in it all planted trees:
Giving different sorts of fruits:
All this was made by the holy
-Lord:
For Adam his servant.

وجعل فيه كل شجر مغروس:
يطرح أثمار أصناف وألوان:
هذا صنعه الرب القدوس:
لأجل آدم عبده الإنسان.

He created for him Eve as a
-companion:
Of whom Adam was pleased:
She was created of his left rib:
While he was asleep.

وخلق له حواء فصار بها
مأنوس:
بها آدم صار فرحان:
قد خلقت من ضلعه
الملموس:
الأيسر لما كان نعسان.

He has commanded them from -His holy mouth: Said to Adam I command you O -man: From all the trees from paradise -you can eat: And this is the tree of -disobedience.	وأوصاهما من فمه القدوس: وقال لآدم أنا أوصيك يا إنسان: كل من جميع أشجار الفردوس: وهذه شجرة العصيان.

Walk away from it in particular: If you eat of it you will be naked: And you will certainly die: You and Eve will be in grief.	إبعد عنها دون كل غروس: لا تأكل منها لئلا تصير عريان: وتموتا أجساداً ونفوس: أنت وحواء تصيران في أحزان.

Hail to you o the Lady of virgins: *O Mary the Virgin*: *In whose womb*: *Came and dwelt our Saviour Jesus Christ.*	السلام لك يا ست الأبكار: يا مريم تى بارثينوس: يا من حل في أحشائك وصار: مخلصنا ايسوس بى اخريستوس.

Second Part of the Saturday Theotokia -
ثيؤطوكية السبت القطعه الثانية

The Second Part:	Пιϲⲛⲁⲩ:	:القطعة الثانية
* We are elated by your greatness, O	* Ϫⲉⲛⲉⲣⲙⲁⲕⲁⲣⲓⲍⲓⲛ ⲛ̀ⲧ-	*نغبط عظمتك. أيتها العذراء الحكيمه.

prudent Virgin, and send unto you greetings, with Gabriel the angel.	ⲉⲙⲉⲧⲛⲓϣϯ: ⲱ̀ ϯⲡⲁⲣⲑⲉ-ⲛⲟⲥ ⲛ̀ⲥⲁⲃⲏ: ⲧⲉⲛϯ ⲛⲉ ⲙ̀ⲡⲓⲭⲉⲣⲉⲧⲓⲥⲙⲟⲥ: ⲛⲉⲙ Ⲅⲁⲃⲣⲓⲏⲗ ⲡⲓⲁⲅⲅⲉⲗⲟⲥ.	ونعطيك السلام. مع غبريال الملاك.
For through your fruit, salvation came to our race, and God has reconciled with us once again, through His goodness.	Ⲭⲉ ⲉ̀ⲃⲟⲗϩⲓⲧⲉⲛ ⲡⲉⲕ-ⲁⲣⲡⲟⲥ: ⲁ ⲡⲓⲟⲩϫⲁⲓ ⲧⲁϩⲉ ⲡⲉⲛⲅⲉⲛⲟⲥ: ⲁ Ⲫϯ ϩⲟⲧ-ⲡⲉⲛ ⲉ̀ⲣⲟϥ ⲛ̀ⲕⲉⲥⲟⲡ: ϩⲓⲧⲉⲛ ⲧⲉϥⲙⲉⲧⲁ̀ⲅⲁⲑⲟⲥ.	لأن من قبل ثمرتك. أدرك الخلاص جنسنا. وأصلحنا الله مره أخرى. من قبل صلاحه.
* Hail to you O full of grace, hail to you who has found grace, hail to you who has given birth to Christ, the Lord is with you.	* Ⲭⲉⲣⲉ ⲑⲏⲉⲑⲙⲉϩ ⲛ̀ϩ̀-ⲙⲟⲧ: ⲭⲉⲣⲉ ⲑⲏⲉ̀ⲧⲁⲥϫⲉⲙ ϩ̀ⲙⲟⲧ: ⲭⲉⲣⲉ ⲑⲏⲉ̀ⲧⲁⲥⲙⲉⲥ Ⲡⲭ̅ⲥ̅: ⲟⲩⲟϩ Ⲡⲟ̅ⲥ̅ ϣⲟⲡ ⲛⲉⲙⲉ.	*السلام لك يا ممتلئة نعمة. السلام لك يا من وجدت نعمة. السلام لك يا من ولدت المسيح. الرب معك.

SECOND EXPLANATION BY ABU EL-SAAD

القطعة الثانية من نظم المعلم ابو السعد ـ

I open my mouth with proverbs:
Proclaim morning and evening:
With your glory Mary:
Isaiah said in his prophesy.

انا افتح بالأمثال:
وأنطق كل مساء وصباح:
بمجدك يا مريم قد قال:
أشعياء في السفر وباح.

A Virgin in the fullness of time:
Will give birth to the Good
-Shepherd of His people:
And He sent to you with Gabriel:
Hail, blessing and joy.

بكر في عقب الاجيال:
تلد الراعي أصل كل صلاح:
وهو ارسل لكِ مع غبريال:
السلام والطوبي والافراح.

Because through the One who is
-born:
From your womb O Virgin:
Adam was restored :
Back to the paradise.

لانَّ من قبل المولود:
من احشاكِ ايتها العذراء:
رجع آدم الاول مردود:
الي الفردوس دفعة اخري.

Reconciliation happened through
-your Son:
Between God and the world:
And He completed His mystery:
Which was promised by His
-prophets.

وصار الصلح بك الموجود:
بين العلم وصاحب القدرة:
وأكمل سره المعهود:
علي السنة اصحاب البشري.

You are great and revered:	عظيمة انتِ ومحترمة:
Because you became the mother	لأنك صرتِ ام بارينا:
-of our Creator:	لأن بإبنك زالت النقمة:
And through your Son the wrath	عن العالم وانعتقنا.
-of God:	
Was removed from the world and	
-we became free.	

Hail to you Mother of Mercy: السلام لك يا أم الرحمة:

While your servants help us: نحن عبيدك جيرينا:

Blessed are you full of grace: طوباك يا مملوءة نعمة:

Intercede for us to your beloved Son.   عند ابنك الحبيب اشفعي فينا.

SECOND EXPLANATION BY GABRIEL EL-KAI

القطعة الثانية من نظم المعلم غبريال -

All ranks magnify you:	تعظمك كل الطغمات:
And all generations bless you:	وتطوبكِ كل الاجيال:
And all the Heavenly Powers with	وكل المراتب والقوَّات:
-the Hosts:	نعطيك السلام مع غبريال.
Give you hail with Gabriel.	

Give you hail with Gabriel: نعطيك السلام مع غبريال:

The great Archangel:

When the Lord fulfilled His -promise: The gracious Father sent his angel.	بي نيشتي إن أرشي انجيلوس: حين تم الاله وعده بكمال: آف اؤ أورب انجى افيوت بي أغاثوس.
The gracious Father sent His angel: To a virgin called Mary: Announcing to her the birth of -Jesus: His dwelling in her in great -mystery.	آف اؤ أورب انجى افيوت بي أغاثوس: الي عذراء تدعي مريم: يبشرها بحلول إيسوس: وميلاده بالسر الأعظم.
Dwelling in her in great mystery: He came to her saying blessed are -you: Your Lord sent me to you: He chose you since your childhood.	وميلاده بالسر الأعظم: أتاها قائلاً طوباكِ: ربكِ ارسلني لك بسلام: واختارك من سن صباك.
He chose you since your childhood: It was His will to dwell in you: He who created you: Accepted to be carried on your -arms.	واختارك من سن صباك: شاءَ وأراد ان يسكن فيكِ: الذي خلقكِ وأنشاكِ: يصير محمولاً علي ذراعيكِ.
Accepted to be carried on your -arms: He who is sitting on the Cherubim: Looked to your relative: The barren Elizabeth.	يصير محمولاً علي ذراعيكِ: الجالس فوق الحيوانات: ومن تدعي بالنسب إليك: العاقر أليصابات.

The barren Elizabeth:
Today she is pregnant with a great
-child:
It has been now six months for her
-pregnancy:
For with God nothing is impossible.

For with God nothing is
-impossible:
Whatever God wants will be:
Believe me and accept my
-announcing:
So Mary answered him wisely.

So Mary answered him wisely:
Saying behold I am a servant of the
-Lord:
Let it be to me according to your
-saying:
For this is the will of the Lord.

For this is the will of the Lord:
And we all proclaim for you:
Blessed are you the adornment of
-all ranks:
Hail to you and hail to you.

Hail to you and hail to you:
We ask you mother of the Beloved:
To accommodate us in the

العاقر أليصابات:
اليوم حُبلي بغلام شهير:
لها ستة اشهر بثبات:
وليس عند الله امر عسير.

وليس عند الله امر عسير:
ومهما اراد الرب يكون:
صدِّقي واقبلي مني التبشير:
فجاوبته مريم باتزان.

فجاوبته مريم باتزان:
قائلة هأنذا عبدة الرب:
كقولك لي يا رسول يكون:
لهذا أراد الرب وأحبَّ.

لهذا أراد الرب وأحبَّ:
ونحن الكل نحييك:
طوباك يا زين كل رتب:
السلام لكِ ثم السلام إليك.

السلام لك ثم السلام إليك:
ونسألك يا أم المحبوب:
أن تأخذينا في مظال آبائك:

tabernacles of your fathers:
Abraham, Isaac and Jacob.

إبراهيم واسحق ويعقوب.

THE SECOND EXPLANATION BY AMBA MORCOS

القطعة الثانية من نظم البطريرك انبا مرقس

All ranks magnify you:
O Mary the Virgin:
All honours befit you:
Because you have been exalted
-above the angels.

تعظمكِ كل الطغمات:
يا مريم تي بارثينوس:
قد نلت كل الكرامات:
وفقت رتب ني أنجيلوس.

Adam was commanded by the Lord
-of Hosts:
About a tree that was in paradise:
He disobeyed His Lord and
-transgressed:
By the deceit of the wicked devil.

آدم اوصاه رب القوات:
عن شجرة كانت في الفردوس:
خالف ربه وصنع الزلات:
بغواية من الشيطان المنجوس.

The devil dwelt in the serpent:
And put his deceit in it:
It started speaking with language:
And tricked Eve with lies.

سكن في الحية بخداعات:
كانت في الخلقة كالطاووس:
فصارت تتكلم بكل اللغات:
وطغت حواء بحيل وعكوس.

41

It said that God the Lord of
-heavens:

Has commanded you from His Holy
-mouth:

Not to eat from the tree:

And this is not a true saying.

قالت الإله رب السموات:

اوصاكما من فمه القدوس:

لا تأكلوا من الشجرة ثمرات:

وهذا كلام عنكم مدسوس.

I can confirm to you saying:

Go and eat from this tree:

You and Adam will become gods:

Exactly like the Holy Lord.

وأنا أقول لكِ حقًا بثبات:

أمضوا وكلوا من تلك الغروس:

تصيري أنت وآدم آلهه:

شبيهه بالرب القدوس.

Eve was happy with these words:

From the mouth of the evil serpent:

She went to the tree deceived:

And with Adam they willingly ate
-with lust.

فرحت حواء بهذا الكلمات:

من فم الثعبان الملبوس:

ومضت إلي الشجرة وطغت:

وأكلوا الثمر بشهوات النفوس.

Hail to you o the Lady of virgins:

O Mary the Virgin:

In whose womb:

*Came and dwelt our Saviour Jesus
Christ.*

السلام لك يا ست الأبكار:

يا مريم تى بارثينوس:

يا من حل في أحشائك وصار:

مخلصنا ايسوس بى اخر
يستوس.

Third Part of the Saturday Theotokia
ثيؤطوكية السبت القطعه الثالثة ـ

The Third Part:	Πιϣομτ:	:القطعة الثالثة
Like a bride without blemish, the Holy Spirit came upon you, and the power of the Most High, overshadowed you O Mary.	Ϩⲱⲥ ⲙⲁⲛϣⲉⲗⲉⲧ ⲛ̀ⲁⲧ-ⲧⲁⲕⲟ: ⲁ ⲡⲓⲠⲛⲁ ⲉⲑⲩ ⲓ̀ ⲉϫⲱ: ⲟⲩϫⲟⲙ ⲛ̀ⲧⲉ ⲫⲏⲉⲧϬⲟⲥⲓ: ⲉⲑⲛⲉⲁⲣϧⲏⲓⲃⲓ ⲉ̀ⲣⲟ Ⲙⲁⲣⲓⲁ̀.	كخدر بغير فساد. الروح القدس حل عليك. وقوه العلى. ظللتك يا مريم.
* For you have given birth, to the true Word, the Son of the ever-existing Father, who came and redeemed us from our sins.	* Ϫⲉ ⲁⲣⲉϫ̀ⲫⲟ ⲙ̀ⲡⲓ-ⲁⲗⲏⲑⲓⲛⲟⲥ: ⲛ̀ⲗⲟⲅⲟⲥ ⲛ̀ϣⲏⲣⲓ ⲛ̀ⲧⲉ Ⲫⲓⲱⲧ: ⲉⲑⲙⲏⲛ ⲉ̀ⲃⲟⲗ ϣⲁ ⲉ̀ⲛⲉϩ: ⲁϥⲓ̀ ⲁϥⲥⲟⲧⲧⲉⲛ ϧⲉⲛ ⲛⲉⲛⲛⲟⲃⲓ.	*لانك ولدت. الكلمه الحقيقى أبن الاب. الدائم الى الابد. أتى وخلصنا من خطايانا.

| Hail to you O full of grace, hail to you who has found grace, hail to you who has given birth to Christ, the Lord is with you. | Ⲭⲉⲣⲉ ⲑⲏⲉⲑⲙⲉϩ ̀ⲛ̀ϩⲙⲟⲧ: Ⲭⲉⲣⲉ ⲑⲏ̀ⲉⲧⲁⲥϫⲉⲙ ̀ϩⲙⲟⲧ: ⲭⲉⲣⲉ ⲑⲏ̀ⲉⲧⲁⲥⲙⲉⲥ Ⲡⲭ̅ⲥ̅: ⲟⲩⲟϩ Ⲡ⳽ⲟⲥ ϣⲟⲡ ⲛⲉⲙⲉ. | السلام لك يا ممتلئة نعمة. السلام لك يا من وجدت نعمة. السلام لك يا من ولدت المسيح. الرب معك. |

THE THIRD EXPLANATION BY ABU EL-SAAD - القطعة الثالثة من نظم المعلم ابو السعد

Like a bride without coition:
You accepted the Holy Spirit:
He Wo has power willed:
To be carried in your arms.

مثل عروسة بغير فساد:
قبلت الروح القدس إليكِ:
اله القدرة شاء وأراد:
ان يكون محمولاً علي ذراعيكِ.

He took flesh like ours:
And was nursed by you:
After His birth you remained:
A virgin and the prophecies were -fulfilled.

اتحد جسداً مثل الاجساد:
وصار يرضع من لبن ثدييَكِ:
وصرت من بعد الميلاد:
بتولاً وتم القول عليك.

For you gave birth to God's Son:
Born before all ages:

لأنك ولدتِ وحيد الآب:
المولود من كل الدهور:

44

Who is eternal:
God of true God and Light out of
-Light.

الدائم علي آخر الاحقاب:
اله من اله حق نور من نور.

Come and see all you people:
How the Unseen was seen:
And how the Great, Graceful and
-Feared:
Was carried in her womb for nine
-months.

تعالوا انظروا يا ذوي الألباب:
كيف ظهر منك الغير منظور:
وكيف العجيب العزيز المهاب:
حَمَلَتهُ مريم البكر تسعة
شهور.

Come and let us ask the God of
-glory:
To give us from His goodness:
A peaceful and joyful life:
And to protect us from our enemies
-hands.

تعلوا نسأل اله العظمة:
من عظم جوده ان يعطينا:
حياةً هنيئة وسالمة:
ومن كيد الاعداء ينجينا.

Hail to you Mother of Mercy:
While your servants help us:
Blessed are you full of grace:
Intercede for us to your beloved Son.

السلام لك يا أم الرحمة:
نحن عبيدك جيرينا:
طوباك يا مملوءة نعمة:
عند ابنك الحبيب اشفعي فينا.

THE THIRD EXPLANATION BY GABRIEL EL-KAI

القطعة الثالثة من نظم المعلم غبريال -

Like a chosen bride:
The Groom seeing her awesome
-beauty:
He came to her in purity:
He who created her.

مثل عروسة مختارة:
و العريس عاين عظم بهاها:
واليها أقبل بطهارة:
وهو الذي قد أنشاها.

He who created her:
And chose her above everyone:
He came and dwelt in her womb:
And was born of her in the image of
-man.

وهو الذي قد أنشاها:
وفضَّلها عن كل الناس:
أتي وسكن في احشاءها:
وولد منها إبن الانسان.

And was born of her in the image of
-man:
As they witnessed about her:
And prophecised from ancient days:
And what David has said was
-fulfilled.

وولد منها إبن الانسان:
كما شهدت عنها الاسفار:
وتنبأت من قدم الازمان:
وكَمُلَ ما قال داود البار.

And what David has said was
-fulfilled:
Saying the King has desired your
-beauty:
And what was said was fulfilled:
The God of gods became your Son.

وكَمُلَ ما قال داود البار:
ان الملك قد اشتهي حسنكِ:
وتمّ القول في وضح النهار:
اله الالهه صار ابنك.

The God of gods became your Son:
Who sustained His people in the
-desert:
 You gave birth to Him and gave
-Him milk:
Who is the Sustainer of all creation.

اله الالهه صار ابنك:
مَن عالَ شعبه في البرية:
ولدتِيه ورضع لبنك:
مدبر كل البشرية.

Who is the Sustainer of all creation:
Born before all ages:
You O pure Virgin carried Him:
Who dwells in the bosom of the
-Father.

مدبر كل البشرية:
المولود ازلياً قبل الاحقاب:
حملته يا بكر نقية:
وهو كائن في حضن الآب.

Who dwells in the bosom of the
-Father:
One hypostasis of the Trinity:
 Was concealed in your womb:
 The Divinity united with the
-Humanity.

وهو كائن في حضن الآب:
اقنوم واحد من ثالوث:
صار في بطنك مستور
بحجاب:
واتَّحَد اللاهوت بالناسوت.

The Divinity united with the
-Humanity:
 Became a child and was named
-Jesus:
And made us heirs of His Kingdom:
Through His baptism from the
-Baptiser.

واتَّحَد اللاهوت بالناسوت:
وصار مولود وسمي إيسوس:
تفضَّلَ وأورثنا الملكوت:
بعمادة من بي ابروذروموس.

Through His baptism from the
-Baptiser:
He ransomed us:

بعمادة من بي ابروذروموس:
قد جاء علينا بالعربون:
صام وصلي وأكمل الناموس:

47

He fasted, prayed and fulfilled the -law:
And broke Satan's snare.

وكسر عنًّا فخ الاركون.

And broke Satan's snare:
And we were counted as His:
We say with all Christians:
Hail to you and hail to you.

وكسر عنًّا فخ الاركون:
وصرنا محسوبين عليكِ:
ونقول مع كل المسيحيين:
السلام لكِ ثم السلام إليك.

Hail to you and hail to you:
We ask you mother of the Beloved:
To accommodate us in the tabernacles of your fathers:
Abraham, Isaac and Jacob.

السلام لك ثم السلام إليكِ:
ونسألك يا أم المحبوب: أن
تأخذينا في مظال آبائك:
إبراهيم واسحق ويعقوب.

THE THIRD EXPLANATION BY AMBA MORCOS
القطعة الثالثة من نظم البطريرك انبا مرقس -

You became a bride O Virgin:
For the King of Glory:
To Him all power and dominion:
He came to us with a human body.

صرت عروسة يا عذراء:
لملك المجد الوحداني:
له كل السلطان والقدرة:
أتانا بجسد إنساني.

Adam disobeyed and ate the fruit:
He became naked and in shame:
Was kicked out of paradise:
To the land of toil and suffering.

آدم خالف وأكل الثمرة:
فخرج مطروداً عريان:
من الفردوس إلي برا:
لأرض الشقاء والهوان.

Crying in grief and sorrow:
Bound under the authority of the
-devil:
Who took him and threw him down:
With him to the bottom of Hades.

حزيناً يبكي في حسرة:
مأسوراً في رق الشيطان:
قد أخذه ورماه في حفرة:
في قاع الجحيم موضع
النيران.

A severe and painful punishment:
Came to him and all humans:
All his descendants after him:
Were humiliated with sorrows.

وعذاب أليم كله مرارة:
صار له ولجميع كل إنسان:
ونسله قد صاروا عِبرة:
مذلولين بالأحزان.

The mighty Lord has made His plan:
To restore Adam to Paradise:
So He sent Gabriel with the tidings:
To Mary the pride of mankind.

دبر تدبيره رب القدرة:
ليرده للفردوس ثاني:
فأرسل غبريال بالبشري:
لمريم فخر الأكوان.

He gave her his hail joyfully:
Talked to her peacefully:
Saying the Lord be with you o Virgin:
You will accept a spiritual pregnancy.

وأعطاك السلام والنعمة:
وخاطبك بفمه ولسانه:
قال الرب معكِ يا عذراء:
تقبلين حبلاً روحاني.

Mary answered him politely:
Saying I have not known a man:
Gabriel explained to her the mystery:
Of the Only Begotten Son who will
-dwell in her.

جاوبته مريم في الحضرة:
قالت ليس لي معرفة
بإنسان:
غبريال أعطاها الخبرة:
بحلول الإبن الوحداني.

Hail to you o the Lady of virgins: O Mary the Virgin: In whose womb: Came and dwelt our Saviour Jesus Christ.	السلام لك يا ست الأبكار: يا مريم تى بارثينوس: يا من حل في أحشائك وصار: مخلصنا ايسوس بى اخريستوس.

Fourth Part of the Saturday Theotokia - ثيؤطوكية السبت القطعه الرابعة

The Fourth Part:	Πιϥτοογ:	:القطعة الرابعة
* You are the offspring, and root of David, who has given birth for us according to the flesh, our Savior Jesus Christ.	* Ἡθο γαρ πε πιγενος: νεμ Ϯνογνι ̀ντε Δαγιδ: ̀αρεμιϲι ναν κατα ϲαρξ: ̀μΠενϲωτηρ Ιηϲ Π̅χ̅ϲ̅.	*أنت هى جنس. وأصل داود. ولدت لنا جسديا. مخلصنا يسوع المسيح.
The Only Begotten of the Father, before all ages, emptied Himself and took the form of a servant,	Πιμονογενηϲ ̀εβολϧεν Ⲫιωτ: ϧαχωογ ̀ννιὲων τηρογ: αϥϣογωϥ ̀εβολ	الوحيد من الاب. قبل كل الدهور. أخلى ذاته وأخذ شكل عبد. منكِ لأجل خلاصنا.

from you for our salvation.	ὰμιν ὰμοϥ ⲁϥϭⲓ ⲛ̀ⲟⲩⲙⲟⲣⲫⲏ ⲙ̀ⲃⲱⲕ ⲛ̀ϧⲏⲧ: ⲉⲑⲃⲉ ⲡⲉⲛⲟⲩϫⲁⲓ.	
* Hail to you O full of grace, hail to you who has found grace, hail to you who has given birth to Christ, the Lord is with you.	* Ⲭⲉⲣⲉ ⲑⲏⲉⲑⲙⲉⲏ ⲛ̀ϩⲙⲟⲧ: ⲭⲉⲣⲉ ⲑⲏⲉ̀ⲧⲁⲥϫⲉⲙ ϩ̀ⲙⲟⲧ: ⲭⲉⲣⲉ ⲑⲏⲉ̀ⲧⲁⲥⲙⲉⲥ Ⲡ̄ⲭ̅ⲥ̅: ⲟⲩⲟϩ Ⲡⲟ̅ⲥ̅ ϣⲟⲡ ⲛⲉⲙⲉ.	*السلام لك يا ممتلئة نعمة. السلام لك يا من وجدت نعمة. السلام لك يا من ولدت المسيح. الرب معك.

FOURTH EXPLANATION BY ABU EL-SAAD

القطعة الرابعة من نظم المعلم ابو السعد ـ

You are well known: Descendant from the tribe of David: Through your Son's reconciliation: The promised covenant was fulfilled.	انت هي الجنس المعروف: من أصل قبيلة داود: وصار الصلح بكِ مكشوف: وبكِ تمَّ الوعد الموعود.
As rain falls on wool: So did the Only Begotten Son: His servants thousands and ten	مثل مطر ينزل علي الصوف:

-thousands:
Kneeling before Him with reverence.

اعني هو الابن المولود:
وخُدامه ربوات والوف:
تخر أمام وجهة بسجود.

The Only Begotten of the Father:
Descended and took a body to save us:
He promised and fulfilled His promise:
Was born from Mary and came to us.

وحيد الآب نزَلَ وأخذ:
جسداً حتي نجانا:
وعد وأراد يتم الوعد:
ووُلدَ من مريم وأتانا.

He humbled Himself and took the
-form of a servant:
And suffered for our sins:
He was called the second Adam and
-restored:
The first Adam our father.

تواضعَ وأخذَ شكل العبد:
وتألم لأجل خطايانا:
وسُميَّ آدم الثاني وردَّ:
آدم الاول أبانا.

Through His blessings we received
-Holy Communion:
O Mary you chose us:
And we the gathered congregation:
Magnify you O Mother of our Creator.

من اجل بركة تلك القسمة:
وأنت قد اخترتينا:
ونحن الجموع الملتئمة:
نعظمكِ يا أم بارينا.

Hail to you Mother of Mercy:
While your servants help us:
Blessed are you full of grace:
Intercede for us to your beloved Son.

السلام لكِ يا أم الرحمة:
نحن عبيدك جيرينا:
طوباك يا مملوءة نعمة:
عند ابنك الحبيب اشفعي
فينا.

FOURTH EXPLANATION BY GABRIEL EL-KAI

القطعة الرابعة من نظم المعلم غبريال -

The honoured and chosen daughter:
From a pure and blessed tribe:
The daughter of David the righteous:
The sweet Psalmist with his beautiful
-voice.

يا نسل مكرم مختار:
من سبط نقي طاهر
مغبوط:
يا ابنة داود البار:
حسن التراتيل وشجي
الصوت.

The sweet psalmist with his beautiful
-voice:
Who praised your beauty:
Saying, the Lord of hosts:
Loved the gates of Zion.

حسن التراتيل وشجي
الصوت:
المادح في حسنكِ بفنون:
يقول رب الصاباؤوت:
شاء وأحب ابواب
صهيون.

Loved the gates of Zion:
More than the dwellings of Jacob:
And adorned you with the Hidden
-Mystery:
And what was prophecised about you
-was fulfilled.

شاء وأحب ابواب
صهيون:
عن كل مساكن آل يعقوب:
وزانكِ بالسر المكنون:
وكَمُلَ عنكِ ما هو مكتوب.

And what was prophecised about you
-was fulfilled:
What was prophesied by the righteous

وكَمُلَ عنكِ ما هو مكتوب:
وما تنبأ به الآباء الابرار:
عن تدبير الملك

-fathers:
About the plan of the Fearful King:
And His appearance in the fullness of
-time.

المرهوب:
وظهوره في عقب لاجيال.

And His appearance in the fullness of
-time:
They spoke with firm witness:
About your birth and adornment:
Your pregnancy for a complete nine
-months.

وظهوره من عقب
الاجيال:
نطقوا بشهادات موجودة:
عن حَبَلِكِ يا زين الابكار:
تسعة شهور معدودة.

Your pregnancy for a complete nine
-months:
You carried the worshiped King:
Isaiah the prophet said:
Behold a Virgin will conceive and give
-birth to a Son.

تسعة شهور معدودة:
حبلتِ بالملك المعبود:
اشعياء النبي قال ها
هوذا:
عذراء تحبل وتلد مولد

Behold a Virgin will conceive and give
-birth to a Son:
His name will be called Emmanuel:
Which means God is with us:
Saviour of His people Israel.

عذراء تحبل وتلد مولد:
يدعي اسمه عمانوئيل:
الله معنا حاضر موجود:
مخلص شعبه اسرائيل

Saviour of His people Israel:
From the wickedness of the devils:
What was said was fulfilled:
And through you we became joyful.

مخلص شعبه اسرائيل:
من كيد الاعداء الشياطين:
وتَّم القول وكَمُلَ ما قيل:
ونحن بكِ صرنا فرحين

And through you we became joyful:
We the Christians:
The gathered people:
We magnify you Mother of the Holy.

ونحن بكِ صرنا فرحين:
انون خاني إخر
يستيانوس:
ونحن الشعوب
المجتمعين:
نعظمك يا ام القدوس.

We magnify you Mother of the Holy:
We bow to you in reverence:
Proclaiming and saying:
Hail to you and hail to you.

نعظمك يا ام القدوس:
وننحني بين يديكِ:
إنوش إقول إنجو إموس:
السلام لكِ ثم السلام إليك

Hail to you and hail to you:
We ask you mother of the Beloved:
To accommodate us in the tabernacles
of your fathers:
Abraham, Isaac and Jacob.

السلام لك ثم السلام إليك:
ونسألك يا أم المحبوب:
أن تأخذينا في مظال
آبائك:
إبراهيم واسحق ويعقوب

THE FOURTH EXPLANATION BY AMBA
MORCOS -
القطعة الرابعة من نظم البطريرك انبا مرقس

You are the elect race:
From the house of the blessed
-David:
Through you the purest of virgins:
Adam became happy.

أنت هي الجنس المختار:
من بيت داود الطوباني:
بوجودك يا طهر الأطهار:
أدم بك قد صار فرحان.

The Eternal and Mighty dwelt in
-you:
The Only Begotten Son the Logos:
You carried Him O our Lady:
Nine complete months.

يسكن فيكِ الأزلي الجبار:
الإبن الكلمة الوحداني:
وحملته يا ست الأبكار:
تسعة أشهر من غير نقصان.

Gave birth to Him in Bethlehem:
A small naked child:
And put Him in a manger:
Wrapped with swaddling cloth like
-a human.

وولدته في بيت لحم اجهار:
طفلاً صغيراً عريان:
ووضعته في مزود الأبقار:
ملفوف بخرق كإنسان.

Salome was attending with the
-Carpenter:
The blessed elder Joseph:
The shepherds came to Him
-joyfully:
And knelt before Him in reverence.

بحضور سالومة والنجار:
الشيخ يوسف الطوباني:
وأتوا إليه بفرح ووقار:
وسجد له الرعيان.

His star appeared clearly:
In the east with bright splendour:
And the people there saw it:
And the wise men came to Him
-honestly.

وظهر نجمه يشعل كالنار:
في المشرق زاهي نوراني:
ونظروه في تلك الأقطار:
مجوس وقصدوا إليه في
أمان.

Carrying precious gifts:
Gold, myrrh and frankincense:
And the star is moving day and
-night:
Before them guiding them.

ومعهم هدايا غالية المقدار:
ذهباً ومراً ولباناً:
والنجم يسير ليلاً ونهار:
ومعهم يرشدهم أعيان.

To where the Almighty the Creator:
Who was born before all ages:
And they knelt unto Him with joy
-and reverence:
And got forgiveness from Him.

Hail to you o the Lady of virgins:
O Mary the Virgin:
In whose womb:
Came and dwelt our Saviour Jesus
Christ.

إلى حيث كان عالم الأسرار:
المولود خالق الأزمان:
وسجدوا له بفرح ووقار:
ونالوا منه الغفران.

السلام لك يا ست الأبكار:
يا مريم تى بارثينوس:
يا من حل في أحشائك
وصار:
مخلصنا ايسوس بى اخر
يستوس.

Fifth Part of the Saturday Theotokia

ثيؤطوكية السبت القطعه الخامسة ـ

The Fifth Part:

You became a second
heaven, on earth O
Mother of God, for
out of you the Sun of
Righteousness, shone
upon us.

Пієтіоот:

Ⲁⲣⲉϣⲱⲡⲓ ⲛ̀ⲟⲩⲙⲁⲥ̀ⲥⲛⲟⲩϯ
ⲙ̀ⲫⲉ: ⲥⲓϫⲉⲛ ⲡⲓⲕⲁϩⲓ ⲱ̀
ϯⲙⲁⲥⲛⲟⲩϯ: ϫⲉ ⲁϥϣⲁⲓ
ⲛⲁⲛ ⲉ̀ⲃⲟⲗ ⲛ̀ϧⲏⲧ: ⲛ̀ϫⲉ

:القطعة الخامسة

صرت سماء ثانيه.
على الارض يا
والده الاله. لأنه
أشرق لنا منك.
شمس البر.

	ⲡⲓⲣⲏ ⲛ̀ⲧⲉ ϯⲇⲓⲕⲉⲟⲥⲩⲛⲏ.	
* You gave birth to Him according to the prophecies, without seed or corruption, for He is the Creator, and the Word of the Father.	* Ⲁⲣⲉϫⲫⲟϥ ⲥⲓⲧⲉⲛ ⲟⲩⲡ̀ⲣⲟⲫⲏⲧⲓⲁ̀: ⲁϭⲛⲉ ϫ̀ⲣⲟϫ ⲛ̀ⲁⲧ-ⲧⲁⲕⲟ: ϩⲟⲥ ⳪ⲙⲓⲟⲩⲣⲅⲟⲥ: ⲟⲩⲟϩ ⲛ̀ⲗⲟⲅⲟⲥ ⲛ̀ⲧⲉ Ⲫⲓⲱⲧ.	*ولدته كالنبوه. بغير زرع ولا فساد. وهو الخالق. وكلمه الاب.
Hail to you O full of grace, hail to you who has found grace, hail to you who has given birth to Christ, the Lord is with you.	Ⲭⲉⲣⲉ ⲑⲏⲉⲑⲙⲉϩ ⲛ̀ϩ̀ⲙⲟⲧ: ⲭⲉⲣⲉ ⲑⲏⲉ̀ⲧⲁⲥϫⲉⲙ ϩ̀ⲙⲟⲧ: ⲭⲉⲣⲉ ⲑⲏⲉ̀ⲧⲁⲥⲙⲉⲥ Ⲡⲭ̅ⲥ̅: ⲟⲩⲟϩ Ⲡⲟ̅ⲥ̅ ϣⲟⲡ ⲛⲉⲙⲉ.	السلام لك يا ممتلئة نعمة. السلام لك يا من وجدت نعمة. السلام لك يا من ولدت المسيح. الرب معك.

FIFTH EXPLANATION BY ABU EL-SAAD
القطعة الخامسة من نظم المعلم ابو السعد –

Mary the Virgin: Who was chosen: Became a Second Heaven on Earth: And our Intercessor.	السماء الثانية التي صارت: علي الارض فهي ايضاً: مريم العذراء التي اختيرت: وصارت وسيطة لنا الرضي.

All creation rejoiced in her:	كل البرية بها استنارت:
And from her the Son of	ومنها شمس البر أضاء:
-righteousness:	وبهذا التحقيق أشارت:
Shone fulfilling all promises:	شيوخ الزمان الذي قد
Which was given to our fathers since	مضي.
-the beginning.	

You gave birth to Him according to -the prophecy:
Saying that He will be born without -human seed:
Without any defile for her who -carried Him:
Nine complete months.

ولدته كالنبوة التي شهدت:
انه يولد من غير زرع بشر:
ومن غير فساد حملته مدة:
تسعة شهور ثم اشتهر.

All creation rejoices with the -promise:
And kneels before He who is born:
And cry hail to her who found:
All grace before the Lover of -mankind.

تسر الخليقة بما قد وُعدت:
وتسجد أمام الذي قد ظهر:
وتعطي السلام للتي قد وجدت:
كل نعمة امام محب البشر.

How can I call you O Vine:
From whose wine we drink:
And you became our intercessor:
And pleader for all our needs.

بماذا أدعوك أيتها الكرمة:
عصيرك منة سقيتينا:
وصرت وسيلة ومهتمة:
بنا ولسائر مالنا.

Hail to you Mother of Mercy:
While your servants help us:
Blessed are you full of grace:

السلام لك يا أم الرحمة:
نحن عبيدك جيرينا:
طوباك يا مملوءة نعمة:

Intercede for us to your beloved Son.　　عند ابنك الحبيب اشفعي فينا.

FIFTH EXPLANATION BY GABRIEL EL-KAI
القطعة الخامسة من نظم المعلم غبريال -

You have been called the Second
-Heaven on Earth:
O dome of lights:
The intellectual Son of Righteousness:
Whose light shone upon all.

سماء ثانية جسدانية:
دعيت يا قبة الانوار:
شمس البر العظيمة:
ضياؤها اشرق في الاقطار.

Whose light shone upon all:
On Earth and in Heaven:
Blessed are you the adornment of
-virgins:
You carried God the Lord of hosts.

ضياؤها اشرق في الاقطار:
علي الارض وفي السموات:
طوباك يا زينة الابكار:
حملت الاله رب القوات.

You carried God the Lord of hosts:
You became our intercessor:
As the fathers witnessed:
The elders of all generations.

حملت الاله رب القوات:
وصرتِ وسيطة لنا بالرضي:
كما شهد علي الآيات:
شيوخ الزمان الذي قد مضي.

The elders of all generations:
Spoke with witnesses and prophesies:
Said God will forgive His people:
And come in the fullness of time.

شيوخ الزمان الذي قد مضي:
نطقوا بشهادات وأمثال:
وقالوا سوف يُبدَّل غضبُه بالرضي:
ويأتي في عقب الاجيال.

And come in the fullness of time:
Who is born from a pure Virgin:
His name was called Emmanuel:
Saviour of the whole world.

ويأتي في عقب الاجيال:
المولود من بكر بتول تيبارثينوس:
افموتي إبيفران جي إمانوئيل:
إبسوتي إمبي كوسموس

Saviour of the whole world:
Our true God:
Our Good Savior:
Who came and saved us.

إبسوتي إمبي كوسموس:
بيننوتي إن أليثينوس:
بينسوتير إنآغاثوس:
في إتاف إ افسوتي إممون.

Who came and saved us:
Through His birth:
He granted us the covenant:
Through the washing of the second -birth.

في إتاف إ افسوتي إممون:
بميلاده الإنساني:
قد جاد علينا بالعربون:
بحميم الميلاد الثاني.

Through the washing of the second
-birth:
We the Christians:
Cry with hymns and praises:
Proclaiming and saying.

بحميم الميلاد الثاني:
انون خاني ان
اخريستيانوس:
ونحن نصيح بتراتيل
وألحان:
انوش إفول إنجو
إمموس.

Proclaiming and saying:
And we ask you the flower of the
-garden:
To ask Him to open Paradise:
And save us from the fire of hell.

انوش إفول إنجو
إمموس:
ونسألك يا زهرة
الاطياب:
إفتحي لنا باب
الفردوس:
وجيرينا من النار
وعذاب.

And save us from the fire of hell:
We praise you saying:
Blessed are you the Mother of the Only
-Begotten:
Hail to you and hail to you.

وجيرينا من النار
وعذاب:
لأننا محسوبين عليك:
طوباك يا أم وحيد الآب:
السلام لكِ ثم السلام
إليك.

Hail to you and hail to you:
We ask you mother of the Beloved:
To accommodate us in the tabernacles of
your fathers:

السلام لك ثم السلام
إليك:
ونسألك يا أم المحبوب:

Abraham, Isaac and Jacob.

أن تأخذنا في مظال آبائك: إبراهيم واسحق ويعقوب.

THE FIFTH EXPLANATION BY AMBA MORCOS
القطعة الخامسة من نظم البطريرك انبا مرقس -

You became truly a Second
-Heaven:
Carrying the Lord of Hosts:
O Mary the pride of women:
He truly dwelt in you.

صرت سماء حقاً ثاني:
حملت رب الصباؤوت:
يا مريم فخر الأكوان:
سكن فيك حقاً بثبوت.

And appeared as a human from
-you:
A hypostasis of the Trinity:
Was fed from you:
And from the devil He hid His
-divinity.

وظهر فيك بجسد إنسان:
اقنوماً واحدا من الثالوث:
ورضع من لبن ثدييك:
وعن الشيطان أخفى اللاهوت.

Herod the king was confused:
From his fear he ordered the death:
Of all the baby boys:
Living in and around Bethlehem.

وهيرودس قد صار حيران:
من أجله قد أمر بالموت:
لجميع الأطفال الصبيان:
سكان بيت لحم وكل البيوت.

And the angel of the Lord:
Went to Joseph and spoke with
-him:

وملاك الرب الروحاني:
مضى ليوسف وناداه

In a vision while sleeping and said:
Hasten and arise quickly.

بالصوت:
في النوم قائلاً له يا إنسان:
قم بسرعة لما الليل يفوت.

Take the Child and flee:
You and His mother will be saved
-from death:
From Herod the dishonest king:
Go and stay in the land of Egypt.

خذ الطفل واهرب في أمان:
أنت وأمه تنجو من الموت:
من هيرودس الملك الخوان:
وكن إلى ارض مصر مبعوث.

Remain in this country:
Until this king perishes:
And then return:
To Jerusalem after his death.

وأمضى إلى تلك البلدان:
لما يفنى ملكه ويموت:
تعال وارجع بالثاني:
لما يهلك ذلك الممقوت.

Joseph was not hesitant:
He took his donkey:
And put the Virgin on it:
With the Child who is the Creator.

ويوسف كان غيركسلان:
بسرعة جاب أتانا كان مربوط:
وركَّب العذراء على الأتان:
على يديها من يعطى القوت.

Hail to you o the Lady of virgins:
O Mary the Virgin:
In whose womb:
Came and dwelt our Saviour Jesus
Christ.

السلام لك يا ست الأبكار:
يا مريم تى بارثينوس:
يا من حل في أحشائك وصار:
مخلصنا ايسوس بى اخر يستوس.

Sixth Part of the Saturday Theotokia -
ثيؤطوكية السبت القطعه السادسة

The Sixth Part:

* The tabernacle which is called, the Holy of Holies, which contains the Ark, overlaid roundabout with gold.

Wherein are the Tablets, of the Covenant, and the golden pot, wherein the manna was hidden.

* This is a symbol of the Son of God, who came and dwelt in Mary, the undefiled Virgin, and was incarnate from her.

Ⲡⲓⲥⲟⲟⲩ:

* Ϯⲥⲕⲏⲛⲏ ⲑⲏⲉⲧⲟⲩⲙⲟⲩϯ ⲉⲣⲟⲥ: ϫⲉ ⲑⲏⲉⲑⲩ ⲛⲧⲉ ⲛⲏⲉⲑⲟⲩⲁⲃ: ⲉⲣⲉ ϯⲕⲓⲃⲱⲧⲟⲥ ⲛϧⲏⲧⲥ: ⲉⲧⲟϣϫ ⲛⲛⲟⲩⲃ ⲛⲥⲁⲥⲁ ⲛⲓⲃⲉⲛ.

Ⲑⲏ ⲉⲣⲉ ⲛⲓⲡⲗⲁⲝ ⲛϧⲏⲧⲥ: ⲛⲧⲉ ϯⲆⲓⲁⲑⲏⲕⲏ: ⲛⲉⲙ ⲡⲓⲥⲧⲁⲙⲛⲟⲥ ⲛⲛⲟⲩⲃ: ⲉⲣⲉ ⲡⲓⲙⲁⲛⲛⲁ ⲥⲏⲡ ⲛϧⲏⲧϥ.

* Ϭⲟⲓ ⲛⲧⲩⲡⲟⲥ ⲙⲠϣⲏⲣⲓ ⲙⲪϯ: ⲉⲧⲁϥⲓ̀ ⲁϥϣⲱⲡⲓ ϧⲉⲛ Ⲙⲁⲣⲓⲁ̀: ϯⲠⲁⲣⲑⲉⲛⲟⲥ ⲛⲁⲧⲑⲱ-

---

:القطعة السادسة

*القبه التى تدعى. قدس الاقداس. التى فيها التابوت. المصفح بالذهب من كل ناحيه.

التى فيها. لوحا العهد. والقسط الذهبى. المخفى فيه المن.

*هو مثال لابن الله. الذى أتى وحل فى مريم. العذراء غير الدنسه. وتجسد منها.

65

ⲗⲉⲃ: ⲁϥϭⲓⲥⲁⲣⲝ ⲉⲃⲟⲗ ⲛ̀ϧⲏⲧⲥ.

She gave birth to Him unto the world, in unity without separation, for He is the King of Glory, who came and saved us.

Ⲁⲥϫⲫⲟϥ ⲉ̀ⲡⲓⲕⲟⲥⲙⲟⲥ: ϧⲉⲛ ⲟⲩⲙⲉⲧⲟⲩⲁⲓ ⲛ̀ⲁⲧϥ-ⲱⲣⲝ: ⲁⲗⲗⲁ ⲛ̀ⲑⲟϥ ⲡⲉ Ⲡⲟⲩⲣⲟ ⲛ̀ⲧⲉ ⲡ̀ⲱⲟⲩ: ⲁϥⲓ̀ ⲟⲩⲟⲟⲉ ⲁϥⲥⲱϯ ⲙ̀ⲙⲟⲛ.

ولدته للعالم. باتحاد بغير أفتراق. أذ هو ملك المجد. أتى وخلصنا.

* Paradise rejoiced, at the coming of the Lamb, the Word the Son of the ever existing Father, who came and redeemed us from our sins.

* Ⲡⲓⲡⲁⲣⲁⲇⲓⲥⲟⲥ ⲉ̀ϣ̀-ⲏⲗⲟⲓ̀: ϫⲉ ⲁϥⲓ̀ ⲛ̀ϫⲉ ⲡⲓⲟ̀ⲓⲏⲃ: ⲛ̀ⲗⲟⲅⲟⲥ ⲛ̀ϣⲏⲣⲓ ⲛ̀ⲧⲉ Ⲫⲓⲱⲧ ⲉⲑⲙⲏⲛ ⲉ̀ⲃⲟⲗ ϣⲁ ⲉ̀ⲛⲉⲟ: ⲁϥⲓ̀ ⲁϥⲥⲟⲧⲧⲉⲛ ϧⲉⲛ ⲛⲉⲛⲛⲟⲃⲓ.

*يتهلل الفردوس. بمجيء الحمل الكلمه. أبن الاب الدائم الى الابد. ليخلصنا من خطايانا.

Hail to you O full of grace, hail to you who has found grace, hail to you who has given birth to Christ, the Lord is with you.

Ⲭⲉⲣⲉ ⲑⲏⲉⲑⲙⲉⲟ ⲛ̀ϩⲙⲟⲧ: Ⲭⲉⲣⲉ ⲑⲏⲉ̀ⲧⲁⲥϫⲉⲙ ϩ̀ⲙⲟⲧ: Ⲭⲉⲣⲉ ⲑⲏⲉ̀ⲧⲁⲥⲙⲉⲥ Ⲡⲭⲥ̄:

السلام لك يا ممتلئة نعمة. السلام لك يا من وجدت نعمة. السلام لك يا من

oⲩⲟϩ Ⲡⲟ̅ⲥ̅ ϣⲟⲡ ⲛⲉⲙⲉ.	ولدت المسيح. الرب معك.

SIXTH EXPLANATION BY ABU EL-SAAD
القطعة السادس من نظم المعلم ابو السعد –

The dome and its vessels:
Moses has completed:
And the Ark placed inside it:
Covered with pure gold.

القبة وأوانيها:
موسي كملها تطريز:
والتابوت موضوع فيها:
مطلي بالذهب الإبريز.

And the two tablets:
And the vessels containing the
-manna:
Concerning it's meaning:
The wise people interpreted it.

والألواح وما فيها:
القسط وفيه المن عزيز:
وعن تفسير معانيها:
إحتاروا أهل التمييز.

The true dome:
Is Mary the Virgin:
She is exalted above all humans:
Inside her was the Greatest
-Mystery.

القبة الحقيقية:
أعني هي العذراء مريم:
فاقت طبع البشرية:
وقد حوت السر الأعظم.

All the high ranks:
Could not comprehend:
And all human tongues:

والطغمات العلوية:
تكل ولم تقدر تفهم:

Kept silent.

جميع ألسنة البشرية:
فهي تصمت لم تتكلم.

Mary is the pride of all mankind:
And she is our intercessor:
Caring for us:
Through her we reach the
-harbor.

مريم هي فخر الأمة:
وهي في العالم تحمينا:
سفينة وصارت مهتمة بنا:
توصلنا إلي المينا.

Hail to you Mother of Mercy:
While your servants help us:
Blessed are you full of grace:
Intercede for us to your beloved
Son.

السلام لك يا أم الرحمة:
نحن عبيدك جيرينا:
طوباك يا مملوءة نعمة:
عند ابنك الحبيب اشفعي فينا.

SIXTH EXPLANATION BY GABRIEL
EL-KAI - القطعة السادسة من نظم المعلم غبريال

The dome which was made:
By human hands:
And the vessels in it:
Was adorned with splendor.

القبة المصنوعة:
صناعة أيادي بشرية:
وأواني فيها موضوعة:
زينها بأشكال بهية.

Was adorned with splendor:
It was adorned in different ways:

زينها بأشكال بهية:
وطرزها بأصناف وألوان:

68

By Moses the prophet:
Having the Ark of Testimony.

موسي النبي في البرية:
فيها تابوت الرب الديان.

Having the Ark of testimony:
And the two tablets of the
-Commandments:
And the pure golden vessel:
Carrying the manna in it.

فيها تابوت الرب الديان:
وألواح العهد وما تحويه:
وقسط ذهب غالي الأثمان:
والمن العقلي مخفي فيه.

Carrying the manna in it:
Resembling the hidden mystery:
Who is in the bosom of His Father:
Descended with His divinity in Zion.

والمن العقلي مخفي فيه:
إشارة إلي السر المكتوب:
من هو محجوب في حضن إبيه:
حل بلاهوته في صهيون.

Descended with His divinity in Zion:
I mean the true dome:
About which they prophesied:
With cymbals and witnesses.

حل بلاهوته في صهيون:
أعني القبة الحقيقية:
كما تنبأ عنها المتنبئون:
برموز وشهادات نبوية.

With cymbals and witnesses:
I mean the dome and its meanings:
Symbol of a pure Virgin:
And the Divinity dwelling in her.

برموز وشهادات نبوية:
اعني القبة ومعانيها:
مثال عذراء بكر نقية:
بحلول سر اللاهوت فيها.

And the Divinity dwelling in her:
With a wondrous and great mystery:
A Virgin carried between her hands:

بحلول سر اللاهوت فيها:
بأمر عجيب وسر عظيم:
عذراء حملت بين يديها:

He who is worshiped by the -Seraphim.

من تسجد له السيرافيم.

He who is worshiped by the -Seraphim:
They cannot look to Him:
You carried Him O Mary:
And as a child You nourished Him.

من تسجد له السيرافيم:
ولا يستطيعون النظر إليه:
حملتهِ يا م ر ي م:
وكمثل غلام قد ربيتيه.

And as a child you nourished Him:
He is the Mighty Creator of all:
Who restored Adam and his children:
To the paradise once more.

وكمثل غلام قد ربيتيه:
مُكون الأكوان بالقدرة:
رد آدم وبنيه:
إلي الفردوس دفعة أخري.

To the paradise once more:
And we all proclaim saying:
Blessed are you O Virgin:
Hail to you and hail to you.

إلي الفردوس دفعة أخري:
ونحن الكل نطوبك:
ونقول طوباكِ يا عذراء:
السلام لكِ ثم السلام إليك.

Hail to you and hail to you:
We ask you mother of the Beloved:
To accommodate us in the tabernacles
of your fathers:
Abraham, Isaac and Jacob.

السلام لك ثم السلام إليكِ:
ونسألك يا أم المحبوب:
أن تأخذينا في مظال
آبائك:
إبراهيم واسحق ويعقوب.

THE SIXTH EXPLANATION BY AMBA MORCOS
القطعة السادسة من نظم البطريرك انبا مرقس ـ

The prophetic dome:	القبة النبوية:
Moses adorned with many colours:	زينها موسى بكل الألوان:
Covered it with gold:	وجعلها بذهب مطلية:
And put in it seven oil lamps.	وسبعة سُرُج فيها ينيرون.

And the two tablets:	والألواح العهدية:
Written by the finger of God:	مكتوبة بأصبع الديان:
And the luminous lampstand:	وجعل فيها منارة مضيئة:
And the golden vessel containing the -manna.	وقسط ذهب فيه المن بيان.

These all are witnesses:	على بنى الإسرائيلية:
To the people of Israel:	شهادة نصب الميزان:
Because they have all been symbols:	وذلك إشارة رمزية:
For you the sanctuary of God.	عليك يا هيكل منصان.

O you the pure Virgin Mary:	يا مريم يا بكر نقية:
You became a dome of forgiveness:	قد صرت قبة للغفران:
Adorned with the splendid lights:	وزينك بأنوار بهية:
God the Creator of the Universe.	الإله منشئ الأكوان.

Joseph took you:	وإلى الديار المصرية:
To the land of Egypt:	مضى بك يوسف الإنسان:
And with you the Creator of all:	ومعك خالق كل البرية:
As a Child on your hands.	

طفلاً محمولاً على اليدين.

All the idols fell:
Before Him everywhere:
And the land of Egypt became
-blessed:
And the worship of idols was
-destroyed.

بادت الأصنام بالكلية:
من قدامه في كل مكان:
وصارت ارض مصر
محمية:
وبادت منها عبادة
الأوثان.

Hail to you o the Lady of virgins:
O Mary the Virgin:
In whose womb:
Came and dwelt our Saviour Jesus
Christ.

السلام لك يا ست الأبكار:
يا مريم تى بارثينوس:
يا من حل في أحشائك
وصار:
مخلصنا ايسوس بى اخر
يستوس.

Seventh Part of the Saturday Theotokia
ثيؤطوكية السبت القطعه السابعة ـ

The Seventh Part:	Пɪϣⲁϣϥ:	:القطعة السابعة
* You are called the Mother of God, the true King, and after He was born from	* Ⲁⲩⲙⲟⲩϯ ⲉⲣⲟ ϫⲉ ⲑⲙⲁⲩ ⲙ̀Ⲫϯ: ⲡⲓⲟⲩⲣⲟ ⲙ̀ⲙⲏⲓ ⲙⲉⲛⲉⲛⲥⲁ ⲑ̀ⲣⲉⲙ-	*دعيتِ ام الله. الملك الحقيقى. وبعد ما ولدته. بقيت

you, miraculously you remained a virgin.	ⲁⲥϥ: ⲁⲣⲉⲟ̀ϩⲓ ⲉ̀ⲣⲉⲟⲓ ⲙ̀ⲡⲁⲣⲑⲉⲛⲟⲥ: ϧⲉⲛ ⲟⲩ- ⲱⲃ ⲙ̀ⲡⲁⲣⲁⲇⲟⲝⲟⲛ.	عذراء بأمر عجيب.
Emmanuel whom you have born, has kept you, without corruption, and your virginity remained sealed.	Ⲉⲙⲙⲁⲛⲟⲩⲏⲗ ⲫⲏⲉ̀- ⲧⲁⲣⲉⲝ̀ϥⲟϥ: ⲉⲑⲃⲉ ⲫⲁⲓ ⲁϥⲁⲣⲉϩ ⲉ̀ⲣⲟ: ⲉ̀ⲣⲉⲟⲓ ⲛ̀ⲁⲧⲧⲁⲕⲟ: ⲉⲥⲧⲟⲃ ⲛ̀ϫⲉ ⲧⲉⲡⲁⲣⲑⲉⲛⲓⲁ̀.	عمانوئيل الذى ولدته. هو حفظك. بغير فساد. وبتوليتك مختومه.
* Hail to you O full of grace, hail to you who has found grace, hail to you who has given birth to Christ, the Lord is with you.	* Ⲭⲉⲣⲉ ⲑⲏⲉⲑⲙⲉϩ ⲛ̀ϩ- ⲙⲟⲧ: ⲭⲉⲣⲉ ⲑⲏⲉ̀ⲧⲁⲥ- ϫⲉⲙ ϩ̀ⲙⲟⲧ: ⲭⲉⲣⲉ ⲑⲏⲉ̀ⲧⲁⲥⲙⲉⲥ Ⲡⲭⲥ: ⲟⲩⲟϩ Ⲡⲟⲥ ϣⲟⲡ ⲛⲉⲙⲉ.	*السلام لك يا ممتلئة نعمة. السلام لك يا من وجدت نعمة. السلام لك يا من ولدت المسيح. الرب معك.

SEVENTH EXPLANATION BY ABU EL-SAAD - القطعة السابعة من نظم المعلم ابو السعد -

You have been called the mother of -God:	دعيت أم الله وأي:
Who among humans can proclaim:	لسان بشري ينطق بقليل:
Of the mysteries of the Son of the -living God:	من أسرار إبن الله الحى:
Who is your Son Emmanuel.	وهو إبنك عمانوئيل.

You have given birth to Him while -still a virgin:	ولدته وأنت بتول لكي:
That the prophesies would be -fulfilled:	يتم قول الأنبياء وما قيل:
For everything they have said:	لأنهم لم يقولوا شيئ:
Has a meaning and symbol.	إلا وله معني وتأويل.

Emmanuel to whom you gave birth:	عمانوئيل الذي ولدته
In purity without defile:	: من غير فساد بل
He exalted you from His elect:	بطهارة:
Because you are a chosen Virgin.	وفضَّلك عن مختاريه:
	لأنك مصطفاه ومختاره.

You are like the throne of heaven:	تشبهت بالسماء كرسيه:
Many symbols describe you:	وكم لك من رمز وإشارة:
Like the vessel containing the manna:	كالقسط والمن مخفي فيه:
Also the censor, the Ark and the -lampstand.	شورية وتابوت ومنارة.

74

The people of prophesy and wisdom:
Realised that the Lord will come to
-us:
And destroy the council of the
-enemies:
And save us from perishing.

Hail to you Mother of Mercy:
While your servants help us:
Blessed are you full of grace:
Intercede for us to your beloved Son.

أهل النبوة والحكمة:
علموا أن الرب الإله
يأتينا:
ويهلك مؤامرة الأثمة:
ومن الهلاك ينجينا.

السلام لك يا أم الرحمة:
نحن عبيدك جيرينا:
طوباك يا مملوءة نعمة:
عند ابنك الحبيب اشفعي
فينا.

SEVENTH EXPLANATION BY GABRIEL EL-KAI
القطعة السابعة من نظم المعلم غبريال -

You have been called a mother of
-your Creator:
And what tongue can speak:
About your honour and purity :
And the Great Mystery hidden in
-you.

And the Great Mystery hidden in
-you:
Who is sitting on His throne:
Chose you O Mary:

دعيت أما لمن أنشاك:
وأى لسان يقدر يتكلم:
بوصفك وشرف معناك:
وقبولك للسر الأعظم .

وقبولك للسر الأعظم:
الجالس فوق بيف
اثرونوس:

75

According to the saying of the -Psalmist.	قد اختار حسنك يا مريم: كاتا إبصاجي إمبي هيمنودوس.

According to the saying of the -Psalmist: David the King of Israel: Prophesied about the birth of Jesus: As Gabriel announced to you.	كاتا إبصاجي إمبي هيمنودوس: دافيد إب أورو امبيسرائيل: تنبأ عن ميلاد إيسوس: كما بشرك جبرائيل.

As Gabriel announced to you: The great Archangel said: The most high King will come: Who is the Son of God the Logos.	كما بشرك جبرائيل: بينيشتي إن أرشي انجيلوس: وقال سوف يأتي الملك المتعال: إبشيري إم افنوتي بي لوغوس.

Who is the Son of God the Logos: Emmanuel to whom you gave birth: From your womb O bride and -Virgin: And on your arms you carried Him.	إبشيري إم افنوتي بي لوغوس: عمانوئيل الذي ولدته: من أحشاك يا بكر وعروس: وفوق ذراعيك حملته.

And on your arms you carried Him: You are likened to the Cherubim: Like a son you nourished Him: And fed Him from your chest.	وفوق ذراعيك حملته: وتشبهت بالكاروبيم: وكمثل غلام قد ربيتيه:

76

رضع ثدييك كالفطيم.

And fed Him from your chest:
Heaven and Earth cannot contain
-Him:
As He is a compassionate God and
-merciful Lord:
He humbly took the shape of a
-servant.

رضع ثدييك كالفطيم:
من لا تسعه السماء
والأرض:
إله رؤوف ورب رحيم:
تواضع وأخذ شكل العبد.

He humbly took the shape of a
-servant:
He fulfilled all the Law:
And was called the Second Adam:
And restored the first Adam to
-paradise.

تواضع وأخذ شكل العبد:
وأكمل تعليم الناموس:
وسمي آدم الثاني ورد:
آدم الاول إلي الفردوس.

And restored the first Adam to
-paradise:
After he was cast out:
Your Son Christ returned him:
To his original rank.

آدم الاول إلي الفردوس:
من بعد أن كان مطروداً
مدحوراً:
رده ابنك بي خريستوس:
إلي رتبته دفعة أخري.

To his original rank:
And he rejoiced with happiness:
Being filled with grace and joy:
Hail to you O Lamp of light.

إلي رتبته دفعة أخري:
وصار يتهني بفرح وسرور:
وبهجة ونعيم ومسرة:
السلام لك يا مصباح النور.

Hail to you O Lamp of light:

السلام لك يا مصباح النور:

To you the Lord came O Mary:
The medicine for the broken
-hearted:
Hail to you and hail to you.

يا من اشتياق الرب إليك:
يا مرهم لدوا المكسور:
السلام لكِ ثم السلام إليك.

Hail to you and hail to you:
We ask you mother of the Beloved:
To accommodate us in the
tabernacles of your fathers:
Abraham, Isaac and Jacob.

السلام لك ثم السلام إليك:
ونسألك يا أم المحبوب:
أن تأخذينا في مظال آبائك:
إبراهيم واسحق ويعقوب.

THE SEVENTH EXPLANATION BY AMBA
MORCOS- القطعة السابعة من نظم البطريرك انبا مرقس

You have been called mother of God
-our creator:
O Mary daughter of Zion:
He incarnated from you and made us
-free:
From Satan's prison.

دعيت أم الله خالقنا:
يا مريم ابنة صهيون:
تجسد منك وعتقنا:
من أسر الشيطان الملعون.

Emmanuel, God with us:
God who knows everything:
You fed Him O our intercessor:
From your chest like a human.

عمانوئيل هو صار معنا:
إلهاً عالماً بما سيكون:
ورضعتيه يا شفيعتنا:
من لبنك كسائر البشريين.

He came to save us:
Took our full humanity:

لأنه أتى ليخلصنا: وفعل
كما فعل كل البشريون:

78

But without sin:
The King of heaven.

وليس كفعل الخطية:
ابؤرو ان إبورانيون.

He humbled Himself to teach us:
Made us a people unto Him:
And in the Jordon was baptized:
By John and fulfilled our covenant.

تواضع كي يعلمنا:
ويجعلنا شعباً وبنين:
وفى الأردن من يوحنا:
تعمد وأعطانا العربون.

He accepted to be crucified for our
-sake:
To save those in prison:
And took our human nature:
And was crucified at Golgotha.

وجاء ليصلب عنا:
ويخلص كل من كان
مسجون:
واخذ شكل طبيعتنا:
وصلب عند الإقرانيون.

And accepted the curse from His
-people:
The unbelieving Jewish nation:
They slapped Him and pierced His
-side:
And they mocked Him.

ومن شعبه قبل اللعنة:
وهم اليهود الجاحدون:
وجعلوا فى جنبه الطعنة:
وهم به يستهزئون.

He delivered up His Spirit:
His blood to Adam was a chrism:
Now He is with us:
He resurrected us and gave us joy.

وأسلم روحه سيدنا:
ونزف دمه لآدم ميرون:
وهو الآن كائن معنا:
دائماً وبه صرنا فرحين.

Hail to you o the Lady of virgins:
O Mary the Virgin:

السلام لك يا ست الأبكار:
يا مريم تى بارثينوس:

79

In whose womb: *Came and dwelt our Saviour Jesus* *Christ.*	يا من حل في أحشائك وصار: مخلصنا ايسوس بى اخر يستوس.

Eighth Part of the Saturday Theotokia -
ثيؤطوكية السبت القطعه الثامنة

The Eighth Part:	Πιϣⲙⲏⲛ:	:القطعة الثامنة
You were likened to the ladder, which Jacob saw, rising up to heaven, with the awesome God standing above it.	Ⲁⲣⲉⲧⲉⲛⲑⲱⲛⲧ ⲉ̀ⲙⲟ-ⲧⲕⲓ: ⲑⲏⲉⲧⲁ Ⲓⲁⲕⲱⲃ ⲛⲁⲩ ⲉ̀ⲣⲟⲥ: ⲉⲥⲃⲟⲥⲓ ϣⲁ ⲉ̀ϩⲣⲏⲓ ⲉ̀ⲧⲫⲉ: ⲉⲣⲉ Ⲡⲟ̅ⲥ̅ ϩⲓⲭⲱⲥ ϧⲉⲛ ⲟⲩϩⲟϯ.	شبهت بالسلم. الذى رآه يعقوب. مرتفعا الى السماء. والرب المخوف عليه.
* We hail the one who did, accept the Uncircumscript in her womb, and her virginity, was sealed	* Ⲭⲉⲣⲉ ⲛⲉ ⲉ̀ⲃⲟⲗϩⲓ-ⲧⲟⲧⲉⲛ: ⲱ̀ ⲑⲏⲉⲧⲁⲥϣⲱⲡ ⲉ̀ⲣⲟⲥ ⲙ̀ⲡⲓⲁ̀ⲭⲱⲣⲓⲧⲟⲥ: ϧⲉⲛ ⲧⲉⲥⲙⲏⲧⲣⲁ ⲙ̀ⲡⲁ-	*سلامنا الى من قبلت. غير المحوى فى بطنها. وبتوليتها مختومة. من كل ناحية.

from all sides.	ⲣⲑⲉⲛⲓⲕⲏ: ⲟⲩⲟⲅ ⲉⲥϣⲟⲧⲉⲙ ⲛ̀ⲥⲁⲥⲁ ⲛⲓⲃⲉⲛ.	

You have become our intercessor, before God our Savior, who became incarnate of you, for our salvation.

Ⲁⲣⲉϣⲱⲡⲓ ⲛⲁⲛ ⲛ̀ⲟⲩⲡ̀ⲣⲟⲥⲧⲁⲧⲏⲥ: ⲛⲁⲅⲣⲉⲛ Ⲫ̀ⲧ ⲡⲉⲛⲣⲉϥⲥⲱⲧ: ⲫⲏⲉⲧⲁϥϭⲓⲥⲁⲣⲝ ⲉ̀ⲃⲟⲗⲛ̀ⲅⲏⲧ: ⲉⲑⲃⲉ ⲡⲉⲛⲟⲩ̀ⲝⲁⲓ.

صرت لنا شفيعه. أمام الله مخلصنا. الذى تجسد منك. لآجل خلاصنا.

* Hail to you O full of grace, hail to you who has found grace, hail to you who has given birth to Christ, the Lord is with you.

* Ⲭⲉⲣⲉ ⲑⲏⲉⲑⲙⲉⲅ ⲛ̀ⲅⲙⲟⲧ: ⲭⲉⲣⲉ ⲑⲏⲉ̀ⲧⲁⲥⲭⲉⲙ ⲅ̀ⲙⲟⲧ: ⲭⲉⲣⲉ ⲑⲏⲉ̀ⲧⲁⲥⲙⲉⲥ Ⲡ̅ⲭ̅ⲥ̅: ⲟⲩⲟⲅ Ⲡⲟ̅ⲥ̅ ϣⲟⲡ ⲛⲉⲙⲉ.

*السلام لك يا ممتلئة نعمة. السلام لك يا من وجدت نعمة. السلام لك يا من ولدت المسيح. الرب معك.

EIGHTH EXPLANATION BY ABU EL-SAAD

القطعة الثامن من نظم المعلم ابو السعد -

Our father Jacob saw a ladder:	سلم رآه الآب يعقوب:
And the Lord of Hosts was on its -top:	ومن فوقه رب القوات:
And the ladder stood on Earth:	علي الأرض إذ هو منصوب:
And was raised up to Heaven.	ومرتفعاً إلي السموات.

He was confused and frightened:	فتحير وهو مرعوب:
From the reverence of the Mighty:	من هيبة ذي الهيبات:
And said the Mighty God will -come:	وقال سيجئ الرب المرهوب:
And be incarnated in the fullness of -time.	ويتجسد في عقب الأوقات.

Who is wise in understanding:	أي حكيم العقل علم:
To realise the honour of this -mystery:	شرف هذا السر وما يحويه:
Truly I am ignorant:	حقاً إن عقلي مظلم:
And all my life I have been -confused.	وطول دهري متحير فيه.

Mary you are the ladder:	مريم أنت هي السلم:
And you carried the God of gods:	وإله الآلهه أنت حملتيه:
According to the saying of the -Father:	كقول الاب المتكلم:
In the vision of Jacob.	في الرؤيا يعقوب أبيه.

We have been immersed in
-darkness:
While the devil had dominion over
-us:
And we were made free:
By the descending of the Son of
-God in your womb.

كُنّا في بحر الظلمة:
والشيطان متحكم فينا:
بحلول إبن الله الكلمة:
في أحشائك انعتقنا.

Hail to you Mother of Mercy:
While your servants help us:
Blessed are you full of grace:
Intercede for us to your beloved
Son.

السلام لك يا أم الرحمة:
نحن عبيدك جيرينا:
طوباك يا مملوءة نعمة:
عند ابنك الحبيب اشفعي فينا.

EIGHTH EXPLANATION BY GABRIEL EL-KAI -
القطعة الثامنة من نظم المعلم غبريال

Who is like you and what can I call
-you:
And proclaim about you:
You are blessed by all the fathers:
Throughout all generations.

بمن أشبهكِ وبمن أدعوكِ:
وأنطق وأتكلم بأقوال:
يا من كل الآباء أعطوكِ:
الطوبي في كل الاجيال.

Throughout all generations:
And at all times:
They have said proverbs about
-you:
And many of them saw visions.

الطوبي في كل الاجيال:
وكل الأزمان والأوقات:
وكم ضربوا عنكِ أمثال:
وكم نظر الآباء رؤيات.

And many of them saw visions:
A luminous ladder seen by Jacob:
Reaching up to heaven:
And placed on earth.

وكم نظر الآباء رؤيات:
سلم نوراني رآه يعقوب:
متصلاً بأعلي السموات:
وعلي الأرض إذ هو منصوب.

And placed on earth:
The heavenly ranks are descending
-on it:
And moving up to the Divine
-throne:
Where angels are kneeling around
-it.

وعلي الأرض إذ هو منصوب:
وطقوس السماء نازلين عليه:
وصاعدين للعرش المحجوب:
وملائكته ساجدين حواليه.

Where angels are kneeling around
-it:
Thousands and thousands with ten
-thousands:
And he was confused in describing
-its meaning:
And said the Mighty God will
-come.

وملائكته ساجدين حواليه:
ألوف ألوف مع ربوات:
تتحير في وصف معانيه:
وقال سيجئ ذي الهيبات.

The Mighty God will come:
He will appear in human flesh:
And incarnate in the fullness of
-time:
And will be born as a human.

وقال سيجئ ذي الهيبات:
ويظهر بجسد إنساني:
ويتجسد في عقب الأوقات:
ويولد الميلاد الجسداني.

And will be born as a human:
He dwelt in your womb and was

ويولد الميلاد الجسداني:
سكن في أحشاكِ وولدتيه:

-born:
According to the saying of the
-blessed father:
Jacob in his vision.

كقول الآب الطوباني:
في الرؤيا يعقوب أبيه.

Jacob in his vision:
Mary you are the ladder:
And the God of god's you carried:
He renewed us from oblivion.

في الرؤيا يعقوب أبيه:
لأنك أنت هي السلم:
وإله الآلهه قد حملته:
وجددنا من بعد عدم.

He renewed us from oblivion:
And made us a redeemed people:
And chose you the adornment of
-the world:
Who carried the unseen Creator.

وجددنا من بعد عدم:
وصيرانا له شعباً مبرور:
واختارك يا زين كل الأمم:
وحملت الحي غير المنظور.

Who carried the unseen Creator:
And we all proclaim to you saying:
Blessed are you Mother of Light:
Hail to you and hail to you.

وحملت الحي غير المنظور:
ونحن الكل نطوِّبك:
ونقول طوباك يا أم النور:
السلام لكِ ثم السلام إليك.

Hail to you and hail to you:
We ask you mother of the Beloved:
To accommodate us in the
tabernacles of your fathers:
Abraham, Isaac and Jacob.

السلام لك ثم السلام إليك:
ونسألك يا أم المحبوب:
أن تأخذينا في مظال آبائك:
إبراهيم واسحق ويعقوب.

THE EIGHTH EXPLANATION BY AMBA
MORCOS - القطعة الثامنة من نظم البطريرك انبا مرقس

The ladder was seen by father -Jacob: Truly in the vision: Placed on earth: And raised up to heaven.	سلم نوراني رآه يعقوب: في الرؤيا حقاً بثبات: مرتفعاً عالياً منصوب: من الأرض إلى السماوات.
The angels of the Mighty God: Descending on it in thousands: And flying up to the divine Throne: Where the Lord of Hosts is sitting.	وملائكة الرب المرهوب: نازلين عليه ألوف مع ربوات: وصاعدين للعرش المحجوب: وعليه جالس رب القوات.
He became confused in the vision: Knew that it was a symbol: About Mary as it was written: With different sayings and -prophesies.	وقد صار من رؤياه مرعوب: وهذا رمزاً وإشارات: عن مريم قد تم المكتوب: بكل أقوال ونبوات.
She carried the Forgiver of all sins: Who is worshiped by all ranks: He accepted to be crucified: And placed in the tomb with the -dead.	هي حملت غافر كل ذنوب: وله تسجد كل الطغمات: بتدبيره قد صار مصلوب: ودفن في قبر مع الأموات.

And on the third day:
Our Mighty Master arose:
And saved all who were imprisoned:
In Hades with crying and grief.

وفى ثالث يوم محسوب:
قام سيدنا صاحب الهيبات:
وخلص من كان متعوب:
في نار جحيم بكاء
وحسرات.

Adam and his children:
Were happy and saved from Hades:
While Satan became conquered and
-imprisoned:
Placed in the darkness of Hades.

آدم وبنوه بلغوا المطلوب:
وخلصوا من تلك الويلات:
والشيطان صار مسجوناً
مغلوب:
موضعه في تلك الظلمات.

Hail to you o the Lady of virgins:
O Mary the Virgin:
In whose womb:
Came and dwelt our Saviour Jesus
Christ.

السلام لك يا ست الأبكار:
يا مريم تى بارثينوس:
يا من حل في أحشائك
وصار:
مخلصنا ايسوس بى اخر
يستوس.

9th Part of the Saturday Theotokia -
ثيؤطوكية السبت القطعه التاسعة

The Ninth Part:	Πιϣϯιτ:	:القطعة التاسعة
Behold the Lord came out of you, O blessed and perfect one, to save the world which He has created, according to His many tender mercies.	Ⲋⲏⲡⲡⲉ ⲓⲥ Ⲡⲟⲥ ⲁϥⲓ ⲉⲃⲟⲗ ⲛ̀ϧⲏⲧ: ⲱ̀ ⲑⲏⲉⲧⲥ̀ⲙⲁⲙⲁⲧ ⲉⲧϫⲏⲕ ⲉ̀ⲃⲟⲗ: ⲉ̀ⲛⲟϩⲉⲙ ⲙ̀ⲡⲓⲕⲟⲥⲙⲟⲥ ⲉ̀ⲧⲁϥⲑⲁⲙ-ⲓⲟϥ: ⲉⲑⲃⲉ ⲛⲉϥⲙⲉⲧϣⲉⲛ-ⲋⲏⲧ ⲉⲧⲟϣ.	هوذا الرب خرج منك. ايتها المباركه الكامله. ليخلص العالم الذى خلقه. حسب كثره رأفاته.
* We praise and glorify Him, and exalt Him above all, as a Good One and Lover of man, have mercy on us according to Your great mercy.	* Ⲧⲉⲛϩⲱⲥ ⲉ̀ⲣⲟϥ ⲧⲉⲛ-ϯⲱⲟⲩ ⲛⲁϥ: ⲧⲉⲛⲉⲣϩⲟⲩⲟ̀ ϭⲓⲥⲓ ⲙ̀ⲙⲟϥ: ϩⲱⲥ ⲁⲅⲁⲑⲟⲥ ⲟⲩⲟϩ ⲙ̀ⲙⲁⲓⲣⲱⲙⲓ: ⲛⲁⲓ ⲛⲁⲛ ⲕⲁⲧⲁ ⲡⲉⲕⲛⲓϣϯ ⲛ̀ⲛⲁⲓ.	*نسبحه ونمجده. ونزيده علوا. كصالح ومحب البشر. ارحمنا كعظيم رحمتك.
Hail to you O full of	Ⲭⲉⲣⲉ ⲑⲏⲉⲑⲙⲉϩ ⲛ̀ϩⲙⲟⲧ:	السلام لك يا ممتلئة

88

| grace, hail to you who has found grace, hail to you who has given birth to Christ, the Lord is with you. | ϫⲉⲣⲉ ⲑⲏⲉⲧⲁⲥϫⲉⲙ ϩ̀ⲙ- ⲟⲧ: ϫⲉⲣⲉ ⲑⲏⲉⲧⲁⲥⲙⲉⲥ Ⲡⲭ̅ⲥ̅: ⲟⲩⲟϩ Ⲡⲟ̅ⲥ̅ ϣⲟⲡ ⲛⲉⲙⲉ. | نعمة. السلام لك يا من وجدت نعمة. السلام لك يا من ولدت المسيح. الرب معك. |

NINTH EXPLANATION BY ABU EL-SAAD

القطعة التاسعه من نظم المعلم ابو السعد -

| Behold the Lord incarnated from you:
And saved the world He created:
From the prison of Satan the cursed:
Whom the Lord threw in the bottom
-of Hades. | هوذا الرب أتى منك:
وخلّص العالم الذي خلقة:
من أسر الشيطان اللعين:
وفي جوف الجحيم سحقه. |

| And made us to Him a saved people:
And broke the bonds of our sins:
And saved our father Adam:
Who was imprisoned in the bottom of
-Hades. | وصيرنا له شعباً مبرور:
وكتاب العبودية مزقه:
وآدم أبونا الذي كان مأسور:
من قديم في جوف الجحيم عتقه. |

| We praise and glorify Him:
And exalt Him forever:
As a Good Lover of mankind with His
-Father: | نسبح له ونمجد إباه:
ونزيده علواً إلي الآباد:
كصالح محب البشر مع |

And the Holy Spirit the consubstantial.

أبيه:
والروح القدس الذي به اتحد.

I am with you beloved of God:
Who is praying this praise:
Let us ask the Compassionate:
To grant salvation for everybody.

أنا معكم يا محبي الإله:
أبو السعد سقيم الروح والجسد:
تعالوا نسأل طويل الأناة:
أن يهب الخلاص لكل أحد.

For He has planned salvation:
Through baptism He redeems us:
On the day of the resurrection:
To place us on His right.

لأنه أعطانا رسماً رسمه:
بالمعمودية يحيينا:
ويوم القيامة في الزحمة:
من عن يمينه يوقفنا.

Hail to you Mother of Mercy:
While your servants help us:
Blessed are you full of grace:
Intercede for us to your beloved Son.

السلام لك يا أم الرحمة:
نحن عبيدك جيرينا:
طوباك يا مملوءة نعمة:
عند ابنك الحبيب اشفعي فينا.

NINTH EXPLANATION BY GABRIEL EL-KAI
القطعة التاسعة من نظم المعلم غبريال -

Behold God willed and loved:
And wanted to fulfill His promise:

هوذا الرب شاء وأحب:
وأراد وفاء وعد بكمال:

And perfect all His sayings:	وما وعد به الرب وهب:
And remove all the sins of His people.	ومحا عن شعبه كل ضلال.

And remove all the sins of His people:	ومحا عن شعبه كل ضلال:
He revealed to us the mystery of His -divinity:	وعرفنا سر اللاهوت:
You carried Him and He fulfilled the -sayings:	وحملتيه وأكمل الأقوال:
And baptised us in the name of the Trinity.	وعمدنا باسم الثالوث.

And baptised us in the name of the -Trinity:	وعمدنا باسم الثالوث:
His light shone after darkness:	وأشرق نوره من بعد ظلام:
And granted us the Kingdom:	وجاد علينا بالملكوت:
Forgiving all our sins.	ومحا عنا كل الآثام.

Forgiving all our sins:	ومحا عنا كل الآثام:
We praise and glorify Him:	نسبح له ونمجد إياه:
To Him all glory and honour with His -Father:	له المجد الدائم والإكرام:
As a Good Lover of mankind.	كصالح محب البشر مع آبيه.

As a Good Lover of mankind:	كصالح محب البشر مع آبيه:
And the consubstantial Holy Spirit:	والروح القدس أزلي موجود:
One God and none like Him:	إله واحد لا رب سواه:
Existing with us and forever.	

دائم باقي حاضر موجود.

Existing with us and forever:
Creator, generous and granting all:
He chose you O Daughter of David:
And the Lord of lords dwelt in your
-womb.

دائم باقي حاضر موجود:
خالق رازق عاطي
وهاب:
إختاركِ يا إبنة داود:
وسكن في أحشاك رب
الأرباب.

And the Lord of lords dwelt in your
-womb:
You gave birth and fed Him from your
-chest:
While He is existing in the glory of His
-Father:
This He did for the sake of your
-parents.

وسكن في أحشاك رب
الأرباب:
وولدتيه ورضع من
ثدييك:
وهو كائن في مجد الآب:
من أجل أمك وأبيك.

This He did for the sake of your
-parents:
After they were grieved and sorrowful:
You whom the Lord came to you:
Save us from the devils snares.

من أجل أمك وأبيك:
بعد أن كانوا في ضيق
وأحزان:
يا من تاق الرب إليك:
نجينا من شر الشيطان.

Save us from the devils snares:
For we are your children:
And your servant who wrote this:
I am a sinner asking your prayers.

نجينا من شر الشيطان:
لأننا محسوبين عليك:
والعبد الناظم ذي
الأوزان:

خاطئ وتقدمت إليك

I am a sinner asking your prayers:
I confess my sins to your Son:
Hoping that through your prayers:
O Mary my refuge.

خاطئ وتقدمت إليك:
معترفاً لك بضعفي:
ومتعشم بمديحي فيك:
يا مريم أنت ملجأي.

O Mary my refuge:
You will help me on that fearful day:
I am Gabriel your servant:
Pleading and asking your intercessions.

يا مريم أنت ملجأي:
أترجاكِ في اليوم
المرهوب:
أنا غبريال عبدك من
قاي:
متوسل بكِ وعليك
محسوب.

Pleading and asking your intercessions:
I am sure that you will never neglect
-me:
I am the sinful servant:
I always praise saying hail to you.

متوسل بك و عليك
محسوب:
فلا تفوتي من حسب
عليك:
عبدك في الرق المكتوب:
بالجهد يقول السلام اليك.

Hail to you and hail to you:
We ask you mother of the Beloved:
*To accommodate us in the tabernacles of
your fathers*:
 Abraham, Isaac and Jacob.

بالجهد يقول السلام إليك:
ونسألك يا أم المحبوب:
أن تأخذينا في مظال
آبائك:
إبراهيم واسحق
ويعقوب.

THE NINTH EXPLANATION BY AMBA MORCOS

القطعة التاسعة من نظم البطريرك انبا مرقس -

Behold the Lord appeared from you:
O Mary the Virgin:
And chose you for your purity:
Our good Saviour.

هوذا الرب ظهر منك:
يا مريم تى بارثينوس:
واختار حسن طهارتك:
بين سوتير ان اغاثوس.

Blessed are you who became:
A mother to the Holy God:
The salvation of Adam was:
Through your birth of my Lord Jesus.

طوباك يا من صرت:
أماً للإله القدوس:
خلاص آدم قد ظهر منك:
بحملك بباشويس إيسوس.

He took full humanity from you:
Saved Adam who was imprisoned:
Crying in the bottom of Hades:
Captured by the Devil.

أخذ جسداً كاملاً منك:
خلص به آدم الذي كان محبوس:
في قاع الجحيم كان فيه يبكي:
مسبياً مع ذيافولوس.

He poured His precious blood:
Pilate washed his hands of Him:
In your womb O Mary you carried:
The Salvation of all Christians.

بسفكه عنا دماً زكى:
صار منه بريئاً بيلاطس:
في أحشاكِ يا مريم حملت:
خلاص ان نى اخرستيانوس.

Hail to you who ate:
Bread from the hands of angels:
And on your lap they brought Him:
O Mary the Virgin and bride.

السلام لك يا من أكلت:
خبزاً من يد نى اجيلوس:
وفى بى إرفى جابوه لك:
يا مريم بكر وعروس.

I ask and plead your intersession:
I the sinful servant Marcos:
And for all the congregation contributing:
In spirit, body and soul.

أسال واطلب شفاعتك:
أنا الخاطئ عبدك مرقس:
عن كل الشعب المشترك:
في الإيمان بالابن القدوس.

That they may be protected by you:
By faith in the Holy Son:
And the church be protected:
With its servants, deacons and priests.

يكونون محفوظين بك:
أرواحاً وأجساداً ونفوس:
والبيعة تكون في طمأنينة:
وخدامها قمامصة وشمامسة وقسوس.

Hail to you o the Lady of virgins:
O Mary the Virgin:
In whose womb:
Came and dwelt our Saviour Jesus Christ.

السلام لك يا ست الأبكار:
يا مريم تى بارثينوس:
يا من حل في أحشائك وصار:
مخلصنا ايسوس بى اخر يستوس.

The Sherat - Saturday Lobsh - **Ⲭⲉⲣⲉ**

ⲑⲏⲉ̀ⲑⲙⲉϩ ⲛ̀ϩ̀ⲙⲟⲧ - الشيرات

Hail to you O full of grace, the undefiled Virgin, the chosen vessel, for all the world.	Ⲭⲉⲣⲉ ⲑⲏⲉⲑⲙⲉϩ ⲛ̀ϩ̀ⲙⲟⲧ: ϯⲡⲁⲣⲑⲉⲛⲟⲥ ⲛ̀ⲁⲧⲑⲱⲗⲉⲃ: ⲡⲓⲕⲩⲙⲓⲗⲗⲓⲟⲛ ⲉⲧⲥⲱⲧⲡ: ⲛ̀ⲧⲉ ϯⲟⲓⲕⲟⲩⲙⲉⲛⲏ ⲧⲏⲣⲥ.	السلام لك يا ممتلئة. نعمة العذراء غير الدنسة. الإناء المختار. لكل المسكونة.
***The unextinguished lamp, the pride of virginity, the indestructible altar, and the scepter of the faith.**	*Ⲡⲓⲗⲁⲙⲡⲁⲥ ⲛ̀ⲁⲧϭⲉⲛⲟ: ⲡ̀ϣⲟⲩϣⲟⲩ ⲛ̀ⲧⲉ ϯⲡⲁⲣⲑⲉⲛⲓⲁ̀: ⲡⲓⲉⲣⲫⲉⲓ ⲛ̀ⲁⲧⲃⲱⲗ ⲉ̀ⲃⲟⲗ: ⲟⲩⲟϩ ⲡⲓϣ̀ⲃⲱⲧ ⲛ̀ⲧⲉ ⲡⲓⲛⲁϩϯ.	*المصباح غير المُطفأ. فخر البتولية. الهيكل غير المُنقض. وقضيب الإيمان.
Ask of Him whom you have born, our good Savior, to take away our troubles,	Ⲙⲁϯϩⲟ ⲙ̀ⲫⲏⲉ̀ⲧⲁⲣⲉⲙⲁⲥϥ: Ⲡⲉⲛⲥⲱⲧⲏⲣ ⲛ̀ⲁ̀ⲅⲁⲑⲟⲥ: ⲛ̀ⲧⲉϥⲱ̀ⲗⲓ ⲛ̀ⲛⲁ-	اسألى الذى ولدته. مخلصنا الصالح. أن يرفع عنا هذه

and grant us His peace.	ⲓϭⲓⲥⲓ ⲉⲃⲟⲗϩⲁⲣⲟⲛ: ⲛ̀- ⲧⲉϥⲥⲉⲙⲛⲓ ⲛⲁⲛ ⲛ̀ⲧⲉϥϩ- ⲓⲣⲏⲛⲏ.	الأتعاب. ويقرر لنا سلامه.
*Hail to you O full of grace, the pure lampstand, the bearer of the Lamp, the fire of the divinity.	*Ⲭⲉⲣⲉ ⲑⲏⲉⲑⲙⲉϩ ⲛ̀ϩⲙ- ⲟⲧ: ϯⲗⲩⲭⲛⲓⲁ ⲛ̀ⲕⲁ- ⲑⲁⲣⲟⲥ: ⲑⲏⲉⲧⲁⲥϥⲁⲓ ϧⲁ ⲡⲓⲗⲁ-ⲙⲡⲁⲥ: ⲡⲓⲭⲣⲱⲙ ⲛ̀ⲧⲉ ϯⲙⲉⲑⲛⲟⲩϯ.	*إفرحي يا ممتلئة نعمة. المنارة النقية. حاملة المصباح. نار اللاهوت.
Rejoice O hope of salvation, for all the creation, for through you we have been freed, from the curse of Eve.	Ⲭⲉⲣⲉ ϯϩⲉⲗⲡⲓⲥ ⲛ̀ⲟⲩϫⲁⲓ: ⲛ̀ⲧⲉ ϯⲟⲓⲕⲟⲩⲙⲉⲛⲏ ⲧⲏⲣⲥ: ⲉⲑⲃⲏϯ ⲅⲁⲣ ⲁⲛⲉⲣⲣⲉⲙϩⲉ: ⲉ̀ⲃⲟⲗϩⲁ ⲡⲓⲥⲁϩⲟⲩⲓ ⲛ̀ⲧⲉ Ⲉⲣⲁ̀.	إفرحى يا رجاء خلاص. كل المسكونة. لأننا من أجلك. عُتقنا من لعنة حواء.
*Because of you also we became, a dwelling for the Holy Spirit, who came upon you, and	*Ⲉⲑⲃⲏϯ ⲟⲛ ⲁⲛⲉⲣⲙⲁ- ⲛ̀ϣⲱⲡⲓ: ⲙ̀ⲡⲓⲠⲛⲉⲩⲙⲁ ⲉ̅ⲑ̅ⲩ̅: ⲫⲁⲓ ⲉ̀ⲧⲁϥⲓ̀ ⲉ̀ϩⲣⲏⲓ ⲉϫⲱ: ⲁϥⲉⲣⲁⲅⲓⲁⲍⲓⲛ ⲙ̀ⲙⲟ.	*ومن أجلك أيضاً. صرنا مسكناً للروح القدس. الذى حل عليكِ. وقدسك.

97

sanctified you.

Hail to the one, whom Gabriel greeted saying, "Hail to you O full of grace, the Lord is with you."	Ⲭⲉⲣⲉ ⲑⲏⲉⲧⲁ Ⲅⲁⲃⲣⲓⲏⲗ: ⲉⲣⲭⲉⲣⲉⲧⲓⲍⲓⲛ ⲙ̀ⲙⲟⲥ: ⲭⲉ ⲭⲉⲣⲉ ⲑⲏⲉⲑⲙⲉⲥ ⲛ̀ϩ̀ⲙⲟⲧ: ⲟⲩⲟϩ Ⲡ̄ⲟ̅ⲥ̄ ϣⲟⲡ ⲛⲉⲙⲉ.	السلام للتى أقرأها. غبريال السلام قائلا. السلام لك يا ممتلئة نعمة. الرب معكِ.
*The joy of the Father, was in your conception, and the appearance of the Son, was in your womb.	*Ⲁⲡ̀ϯⲙⲁϯ ⲅⲁⲣ ⲙ̀Ⲫⲓⲱⲧ: ϣⲱⲡⲓ ϧⲉⲛ ⲡⲉⲭⲓⲛⲉⲣⲃⲟⲕⲓ: ⲁ ⲧ̀ⲡⲁⲣⲟⲩⲥⲓⲁ ⲙ̀Ⲡⲓϣⲏⲣⲓ: ϣⲱⲡⲓ ⲛ̀ϩ̀ⲣⲏⲓ ϧⲉⲛ ⲧⲉⲙⲏⲧⲣⲁ.	*لأن مسرة الآب. كانت فى حبلك. وظهور الإبن. كان فى أحشائك.
The Holy Spirit, filled every part of you, your soul and your body, O Mary the Mother of God.	ⲀⲡⲓⲠ̀ⲛⲉⲩⲙⲁ ⲉⲑⲩ̅: ⲙⲟϩ ⲙ̀ⲙⲁⲓ ⲛⲓⲃⲉⲛ ⲛ̀ⲧⲉ: ⲧⲉⲯⲩⲭⲏ ⲛⲉⲙ ⲡⲉⲥⲱⲙⲁ: ⲱ̀ Ⲙⲁⲣⲓⲁ ⲑ̀ⲙⲁⲩ ⲙ̀Ⲫϯ.	والروح القدس. ملأ كل موضع منكِ. نفسك وجسدك. يا مريم أم الله.
*Therefore we too	*Ⲉⲑⲃⲉ ⲫⲁⲓ ⲧⲉⲛⲉⲣϣⲁⲓ	*لأجل هذا نعيد نحن

98

celebrate, both a spiritual, and prophetic feast, proclaiming with king David.	ϩⲱⲛ: ϧⲉⲛ ⲟⲩϣⲁⲓ ⳉⲡⲛⲁⲧⲓⲕⲟⲛ: ⲟⲩⲟϩ ⳉⲡⲣⲟⲫⲏⲧⲓⲕⲟⲛ ⲉⲧⲥⲟⲡ: ⲉⲛⲱϣ ⲉⲃⲟⲗ ⲛⲉⲙ ⳉⲟⲩⲣⲟ Ⲇⲁⲩⲓⲇ.	أيضاً. عيداً روحياً. ونبوياً معاً. صارخين مع الملك داود.
"Arise O Lord to Your rest, You and the Ark, of Your sanctuary, which is you O Mary.	Ϫⲉ ⲧⲱⲛⲕ Ⲡ̅ⲟ̅ⲥ̅ ⲉⲡⲉⲕⲙⲧⲟⲛ: ⲛ̀ⲑⲟⲕ ⲛⲉⲙ ⳦ⲕⲓⲃⲱⲧⲟⲥ: ⲛ̀ⲧⲉ ⲡⲓⲙⲁ ⲉⲑⲩ ⲛ̀ⲧⲁⲕ: ⲉⲧⲉ ⲛ̀ⲑⲟ ⲧⲉ ⲱ̀ Ⲙⲁⲣⲓⲁ̀.	قائلين " قم يا رب. إلى راحتك. أنتَ وتابوت قدسك. الذى هو أنتِ يا مريم.
*We ask you to remember us, O our trusted advocate, before our Lord Jesus Christ, that He may forgive us our sins.	*Ⲧⲉⲛϯϩⲟ ⲁ̀ⲣⲓⲡⲉⲛⲙⲉⲩⲓ̀: ⲱ̀ ϯⲡⲣⲟⲥⲧⲁⲧⲏⲥ ⲉ̀ⲧⲉⲛϩⲟⲧ: ⲛⲁϩⲣⲉⲛ Ⲡⲉⲛⲟ̅ⲥ̅ Ⲓ̅ⲏ̅ⲥ̅ Ⲡ̅ⲭ̅ⲥ̅: ⲛ̀ⲧⲉϥⲭⲁ ⲛⲉⲛⲛⲟⲃⲓ ⲛⲁⲛ ⲉ̀ⲃⲟⲗ.	*نسألك أن تذكرينا. أيتها الشفيعة الأمينة. أمام ربنا يسوع المسيح. ليغفر لنا خطايانا.

The Second Sherat:		:الشيرات الثانية.
Hail to you O full of grace, the undefiled Virgin, the tabernacle not made by hands, the treasure of righteousness.	Ⲭⲉⲣⲉ ⲑⲏⲉⲑⲙⲉϩ ⲛ̀ϩⲙⲟⲧ: ϯⲡⲁⲣⲑⲉⲛⲟⲥ ⲛ̀ⲁⲧⲑⲱⲗⲉⲃ: ϯ̀ⲥⲕⲏⲛⲏ ⲛ̀ⲁⲑⲙⲟⲩⲛⲕ ⲛ̀ϫⲓϫ: ⲡⲓⲁ̀ϩⲟ ⲛ̀ⲧⲉ ϯⲙⲉⲑⲙⲏⲓ.	السلام للممتلئة نعمة. العذراء غير الدنسة. القبة غير المصنوعة. بالأيدى كنز البر.
*Hail to you O beautiful dove, who declared to us, the peace of God, toward mankind.	*Ⲭⲉⲣⲉ ϯϭⲣⲟⲙⲡⲓ ⲉⲑⲛⲉⲥⲱⲥ: ⲑⲏⲉⲧⲁⲥϩⲓϣ̀-ⲛⲛⲟⲩϥⲓ ⲛⲁⲛ: ⲛ̀ϯϩⲓⲣⲏⲛⲏ ⲛ̀ⲧⲉ Ⲫϯ: ⲑⲏⲉ̀ⲧⲁⲥϣⲱⲡⲓ ϣⲁ ⲛⲓⲣⲱⲙⲓ.	*السلام للحمامة الحسنة. التى بشرتنا. بسلام الله. الذى صار للبشر.
Hail to the Mother of the Incarnated, of His own free will, and the goodness of His Father, and the Holy Spirit.	Ⲭⲉⲣⲉ ⲑ̀ⲙⲁⲩ ⲙ̀ⲫⲏⲉⲧ-ⲁϥⲉⲣⲣⲱⲙⲓ: ϧⲉⲛ ⲡⲉϥⲟ-ⲩⲱϣ ⲙ̀ⲙⲓⲛ ⲙ̀ⲙⲟϥ: ⲛⲉⲙ ⲡ̀ϯⲙⲁϯ ⲙ̀Ⲡⲉϥ-ⲓⲱⲧ: ⲛⲉⲙ ⲡⲓⲠ̅Ⲛ̅Ⲁ̅ ⲉⲑ̅ⲩ̅.	السلام لأم المتأنس. بإرادته وحده. ومسرة أبيه. والروح القدس.

*Hail to you O golden vessel, wherein the Manna was hidden, and the almond wooden rod, with which Moses hit the rock.	*Ⲭⲉⲣⲉ ⲡⲓⲥⲧⲁⲙⲛⲟⲥ ⲛ̀ⲛⲟⲩⲃ: ⲉ̀ⲣⲉ ⲡⲓⲙⲁⲛⲛⲁ ϩⲏⲡ ⲛ̀ϧⲏⲧϥ: ⲛⲉⲙ ⲡⲓϣ̀ⲃⲱⲧ ⲛ̀ϣⲉ ⲙ̀ⲡⲉⲣ-ⲕⲓⲛⲱⲛ : ⲉⲧⲁ Ⲙⲱⲩ̀ⲥⲏⲥ ⲙⲉϣ ϯⲡⲉⲧⲣⲁ ⲛ̀ϧⲏⲧϥ.	*السلام للقسط الذهبى. المخفى فيه المن. وعصا الخشب اللوزى. التى ضرب بها موسى الصخرة.
Hail to you O full of grace, O the spiritual table, that gives life to everyone, who eats from it.	Ⲭⲉⲣⲉ ⲕⲉⲭⲁⲣⲓⲧⲱⲙⲉⲛⲏ: ⲱ̀ ϯⲧⲣⲁⲡⲉⲍⲁ ⲙ̀ⲡ̅ⲛ̅ⲁ̅ⲧⲓⲕⲏ: ⲉⲧϯ ⲙ̀ⲡⲱⲛϧ ⲛ̀ⲟⲩⲟⲛ ⲛⲓⲃⲉⲛ: ⲉⲑⲛⲁⲟⲩⲱⲙ ⲉ̀ⲃⲟ-ⲗⲛ̀ϧⲏⲧⲥ.	السلام للممتلئة نعمة. المائدة الروحية. التى تعطى الحياة. لكل من يأكل منها.
*Hail to you O incorrupt vessel, of the divinity, which heals everyone, who drinks from it.	*Ⲭⲉⲣⲉ ⲡⲓⲕⲩⲙⲓⲗⲗⲓⲟⲛ: ⲛ̀ⲁⲫⲑⲁⲣⲧⲟⲛ ⲛ̀ⲧⲉ ϯⲙⲉ-ⲑⲛⲟⲩϯ: ⲉⲧⲉⲣⲫⲁϧⲣⲓ ⲛ̀ⲟ-ⲩⲟⲛ ⲛⲓⲃⲉⲛ: ⲉⲑⲛⲁⲥⲱ ⲉ̀ⲃⲟⲗⲛ̀ϧⲏⲧϥ.	*السلام للإناء غير الفاسد. الذى للاهوت. المعطى الشفاء. لكل من يشرب منه.

I begin eagerly to move, the strings of my tongue, and speak of the honor of this Virgin, together with her analogies.	Ⲁⲓⲛⲁⲉⲣϩⲏⲧⲥ ϧⲉⲛ ⲟⲩϭⲓϣϣⲱⲟⲩ: ⲛ̀ⲧⲁⲕⲓⲙ ⲙ̀ⲡⲟⲣⲅⲁⲛⲟⲛ ⲙ̀ⲡⲁⲗⲁⲥ: ⲛ̀ⲧⲁϫⲱ ⲙ̀ⲡ̀ⲧⲁⲓⲟ ⲛ̀ⲧⲉ ⲧⲁⲓⲡⲁⲣⲑⲉⲛⲟⲥ: ⲛⲉⲙ ⲛⲉⲥ-ⲥⲩⲥⲥⲱⲙⲓⲟⲛ ⲉⲩⲥⲟⲡ.	أبدأ باشتياق. محركاً أرغن لسانى. وأتحدث بكرامة. هذه العذراء ومدائحها معاً.
*For she is our pride, our hope and confirmation, in the second coming of our God, our Lord Jesus Christ.	*Ϫⲉ ⲛ̀ⲑⲟⲥ ⲅⲁⲣ ⲡⲉ ⲡⲉⲛϣⲟⲩϣⲟⲩ: ⲛⲉⲙ ⲧⲉⲛ-ϩⲉⲗⲡⲓⲥ ⲛⲉⲙ ⲡⲉⲛⲧⲁϫⲣⲟ: ϧⲉⲛ ⲧ̀ⲡⲁⲣⲟⲩⲥⲓⲁ ⲙ̀ⲡⲉ-ⲛⲛⲟⲩϯ: Ⲡⲉⲛⲟ̅ⲥ̅ Ⲓⲏ̅ⲥ̅ Ⲡ̅ⲭ̅ⲥ̅.	*لأنها فخرنا. ورجاؤنا وثباتنا. فى ظهور إلهنا. ربنا يسوع المسيح.
We magnify you worthily, with Eliza-beth your cousin, saying "Blessed are you among women, and blessed is the fruit of your womb."	Ⲧⲉⲛϭⲓⲥⲓ ⲙ̀ⲙⲟ ϧⲉⲛ ⲟⲩⲉⲙⲡ̀ϣⲁ: ⲛⲉⲙ Ⲉ̀ⲗⲓ-ⲥⲁⲃⲉⲧ ⲧⲉⲥⲩⲥⲅⲉⲛⲏⲥ: ϫⲉ ⲧⲉⲥⲙⲁⲣⲱⲟⲩⲧ ⲛ̀ⲑⲟ ϧⲉⲛ ⲛⲓϩⲓⲟⲙⲓ: ϥ̀ⲥⲙⲁⲣⲱⲟⲩⲧ ⲛ̀ϫⲉ ⲡ̀ⲟⲩⲧⲁϩ ⲛ̀ⲧⲉ	نعظمك باستحقاق. مع اليصابات نسيبتك قائلين. مباركة أنتِ فى النساء. ومباركة هي ثمرة بطنك.

	ⲦⲈⲚⲈⲜ̀Ⲓ.	
*We send unto you greeting, with Gabriel the Angel saying, "Hail to you O full of grace, the Lord is with you."	*ϮⲈⲚϮ ⲚⲈ ⲙ̀ⲡⲓⲬⲉ-ⲣⲈⲦⲓⲤⲙⲟⲤ: ⲚⲈⲙ Ⲅ̀ⲁⲂⲣⲓⲎⲗ ⲡⲓⲀⲅⲅⲈⲗⲟⲤ: ⲭⲉ Ⲭⲉⲣⲉ ⲕⲉⲬⲁⲣⲓⲦⲱⲙⲈⲚⲎ: ⲟⲔ̀ⲣ-ⲣⲓⲟⲤ ⲙⲈⲦⲀ ⲤⲟⲨ.	*نعطيك السلام. مع غبريال الملاك قائلين. "السلام لك يا ممتلئة نعمة. الرب معكِ. "
Hail to you O Virgin, the very and true queen, hail to the pride of our race, who gave birth to Emmanuel.	Ⲭⲉⲣⲉ ⲚⲈ ⲱ̀ ϮⲠⲀⲣⲐⲈⲚⲟⲤ: ϮⲟⲨⲣⲱ ⲙ̀ⲙⲎⲓ Ⲛ̀ⲀⲗⲎⲐⲒⲚⲎ: Ⲭⲉⲣⲉ ⲡ̀ⲱ̀ⲟⲨⲱⲟⲨ Ⲛ̀ⲦⲈ ⲡⲈⲚⲄⲈⲚⲟⲤ: ⲁ̀ⲣⲈⲜⲫⲟ ⲚⲀⲚ Ⲛ̀ⲈⲙⲙⲁⲚⲟⲎⲗ.	السلام لك أيتها العذراء. الملكة الحقيقية الحقانية. السلام لفخر جنسنا. ولدت لنا عمانوئيل.
*We ask you to remember us, O our trusted advocate, before our Lord Jesus Christ, that He may forgive us our sins.	*ϮⲈⲚϮ̀Ⲏⲟ ⲁ̀ⲣⲓⲡⲈⲚⲙⲈⲨⲓ̀: ⲱ̀ Ϯ̀ⲡ̀ⲣⲟⲤⲦⲀⲦⲎⲤ ⲈⲦⲈ-ⲚⲂⲟⲨ: ⲚⲀ̀ⲀⲣⲈⲚ ⲠⲈⲚⲟⲤ Ⲓ̅Ⲏ̅Ⲥ̅ Ⲡ̅Ⲭ̅Ⲥ̅: Ⲛ̀ⲦⲈϥⲬⲁ ⲚⲈⲚⲚⲟⲂⲒ ⲚⲀⲚ Ⲉ̀Ⲃⲟⲗ.	*نسألك أن تذكرينا. أيتها الشفيعة الأمينة. أمام ربنا يسوع المسيح. ليغفر لنا خطايانا.

103

Exposition of the First Week - طرح للإسبوع الأول

There was in the days of Herod, the king of Judea, a certain priest named Zacharias of the division of Abijah. His wife was of the daughters of Aaron, and her name was Elizabeth.

And they were both righteous before God, walking in all the commandments and ordinances of the Lord blameless. But they had no child, because Elizabeth was barren, and they were both well advanced in years.

So it was, that while he was serving as priest before God in the order of his division, according to the custom of the priesthood, his lot fell to burn incense when he went into the temple of the Lord. And the whole multitude of the people was

كان في أيام هيرودس ملك اليهود كاهن اسمه زكريا، من خدمة أبيا وامرأته من بنات هرون واسمها أليصابات.

وكان الاثنان بارَّان أمام الله سالكين في جميع وصايا الرب وأحكامه بلا لوم. ولم يكن لهما ولد إذ كانت أليصابات عاقر وكانا كلاهما متقدمين في أيامها.

فحدث بينما يكهن في نوبة فرقته أمام الله حسب عادة الكهنوت إصابته القرعة إن يرفع بخورا فدخل إلى هيكل الرب. وكان كل جمهور الشعب

praying outside at the hour of incense.

Then an angel of the Lord appeared to him, standing on the right side of the altar of incense. And when Zacharias saw him, he was troubled, and fear fell upon him. But the angel said to him, "Do not be afraid, Zacharias, for your prayer is heard; and your wife Elizabeth will bear you a son, and you shall call his name John.

And you will have joy and gladness, and many will rejoice at his birth. For he will be great in the sight of the Lord, and shall drink neither wine nor strong drink. He will also be filled with the Holy Spirit, even from his mother's womb. And he will turn many of the children of Israel to the Lord their God.

He will also go before Him in the spirit and power of Elijah, 'to turn the hearts of the fathers to the children,' and the disobedient to the

يصلون خارجا وقت البخور .

فظهر له ملاك الرب واقفا عن يمين مذبح البخور. فلما رآه زكريا اضطرب ووقع عليه خوف. فقال له الملاك لا تخف يا زكريا لان طلبتك قد سمعت وامرأتك لأليصابات ستحبل وستلد لك ابناً وتسميه يوحنا،

لأنه سيكون عظيما أمام الرب وسيكون لك فرح وابتهاج وكثيرون سيفرحون بولادته. لأنه سيكون عظيما أمام الرب. وخمرا مسكر ا لا يشرب. وهو في بطن أمه سيمتلىء من الروح القدس. ويرد كثيرين من بنى إسرائيل إلى الرب إلههم.

ويتقدم أمامه بروح إيليا وقوته ليرد قلوب الآباء إلى أبنائهم

wisdom of the just, to make ready a people prepared for the Lord." And Zacharias said to the angel, "How shall I know this? For I am an old man, and my wife is well advanced in years."

And the angel answered and said to him, "I am Gabriel, who stands in the presence of God, and was sent to speak to you and bring you these glad tidings. But behold, you will be mute and not able to speak until the day these things take place, because you did not believe my words which will be fulfilled in their own time."

And the people waited for Zacharias, and marveled that he lingered so long in the temple. But when he came out, he could not speak to them; and they perceived that he had seen a vision in the temple, for he beckoned to them and remained speechless.

And so it was, as soon as the days of his service were completed, that he

العصاه إلى فكر الأبرار لكي يهيئ للرب شعبا مبررا. فقال زكريا للملاك بماذا أعلم هذا لأني أنا شيخ وامرأتي طعنت في أيامها.

فأجاب الملاك وقال له أنا جبرائيل الواقف أمام الله وأرسلت لأكلمك وأبشرك بهذا. وها أنت ستكون صامتا ولا تقدر أن تتكلم إلى اليوم الذي يكون فيه هذا لأنك لم تؤمن بكلامي هذا الذي سيتم في حينه.

وكان جميع الشعب منتظرين زكريا ومتعجبين من إبطائه في الهيكل. فلما خرج لم يقدر أن يكلمهم فعلموا انه قد رأى رؤيا في الهيكل. فكان يشير إليهم بيده وبقى صامتا.

departed to his own house. Now after those days his wife Elizabeth conceived; and she hid herself five months, saying, "Thus the Lord has dealt with me, in the days when He looked on me, to take away my reproach among people." (Luke 1:5-25)

ولما كملت أيام خدمته مضى إلى بيته. وبعد تلك الأيام حبلت أليصابات امرأته وأخفت حبلها خمسة أشهر قائلة. هكذا قد فعل بي الرب في الأيام التي فيها نظر إلى لينزع عاري من بين الناس.

لوقا (25-5:1)

Exposition of the Second Week ـ طرح للإسبوع الثاني

Now in the sixth month the angel Gabriel was sent by God to a city of Galilee, named Nazareth, to a virgin betrothed to a man whose name was Joseph, of the house of David.

وفى الشهر السادس أرسل جبرائيل الملاك من الله إلى مدينة من الجليل: اسمها الناصرة. إلى عذراء مخطوبة لرجل اسمه

107

The virgin's name was Mary. And having come in, the angel said to her, "Rejoice, highly favored one, the Lord is with you; blessed are you among women!" But when she saw him, she was troubled at his saying, and considered what manner of greeting this was. Then the angel said to her, "Do not be afraid, Mary, for you have found favor with God.

And behold, you will conceive in your womb and bring forth a Son, and shall call His name Jesus. He will be great, and will be called the Son of the Highest; and the Lord God will give Him the throne of His father David. And He will reign over the house of Jacob forever, and of His kingdom there will be no end."

Then Mary said to the angel, "How can this be, since I do not know a man?" And the angel answered and said to her, "The

يوسف من بيت داود:

فدخل إليها. واسم العذراء مريم. الملاك وقال سلام لك أيتها الممتلئة نعمة الرب معك مباركة أنت في النساء. فلما رأته اضطربت من كلامه وفكرت في نفسها قائلة ما عسى أن يكون هذا السلام. فقال لها الملاك لا تخافي يا مريم لأنك قد وجدت نعمة عند الله.

وها هوذا آنت ستحبلين وتلدين ابنا وتسمينه يسوع. هذا يكون عظيما وابن العلى يدعى ويعطيه الرب الإله كرسى داود أبيه. ويملك على بيت يعقوب إلى الأبد ولا يكون لملكه نهاية.

فقالت مريم للملاك كيف يكون لي هذا وأنا لست اعرف رجلاً. فأجاب الملاك وقال الروح القدس

Holy Spirit will come upon you, and the power of the Highest will overshadow you; therefore, also, that Holy One who is to be born will be called the Son of God.

Now indeed, Elizabeth your relative has also conceived a son in her old age; and this is now the sixth month for her who was called barren. For with God nothing will be impossible." Then Mary said, "Behold the maidservant of the Lord! Let it be to me according to your word." And the angel departed from her. (Luke 1:26-38)

And from that time, the pure Virgin Mary was pregnant. We send unto you greeting with Gabriel the angel saying, "Hail to you O fall of grace, the Lord is with you."

يحل عليك وقوة العلى تظللك فلذلك الذي يولد منك قدوس ويدعى ابن الله.

وهوذا أليصابات نسيبتك هي أيضا. حبلى بابن في شيخوختها وهذا هو الشهر السادس لتلك المدعوة عاقر لأنه ليس شيء غير ممكن عند الله. فقالت مريم للملاك هاأنذا أنا أمة الرب ليكن لي كقولك. فمضى من عندها الملاك الطاهر.

(لوقا ٢٦:١ـ٣٨)

ومن ذلك الوقت حبلت العذراء مريم الطاهرة. نعطيك السلام مع غبريال الملاك قائلين: افرحي يا ممتلئة نعمة الرب معك.

Exposition of the Third Week - طرح للإسبوع الثالث

Now Mary arose in those days and went into the hill country with haste, to a city of Judah, and entered the house of Zacharias and greeted Elizabeth. And it happened, when Elizabeth heard the greeting of Mary, that the babe leaped in her womb; and Elizabeth was filled with the Holy Spirit. Then she spoke out with a loud voice and said, "Blessed are you among women, and blessed is the fruit of your womb! But why is this granted to me, that the mother of my Lord should come to me?

For indeed, as soon as the voice of your greeting sounded in my ears, the babe leaped in my womb for joy. Blessed is she who believed, for

فقامت مريم في تلك الأيام ومضت مسرعة إلى الجبل إلى مدينة يهوذا. ودخلت بيت زكريا وسلمت على أليصابات. فلما سمعت أليصابات سلام مريم. تحرك الجنين في بطنها وامتلأت أليصابات من الروح القدس.

وصرخت بصوت عظيم وقالت مباركة أنت في النساء ومباركة هي ثمرة بطنك. فمن أين لي هذا أن تأتى أم ربى إليّ.

لأنه هوذا حين صار صوت سلامك في أذني ارتكض الجنين بتهليل في بطني. فطوبى للتي آمنت أن يتم ما قيل لها من قبل

there will be a fulfillment of those things which were told her from the Lord." And Mary said: "My soul magnifies the Lord, and my spirit has rejoiced in God my Savior.

For He has regarded the lowly state of His maidservant; For behold, henceforth all generations will call me blessed. For He who is mighty has done great things for me, and holy is His name. And His mercy is on those who fear Him from generation to generation.

He has shown strength with His arm; He has scattered the proud in the imagination of their hearts. He has put down the mighty from their thrones, and exalted the lowly. He has filled the hungry with good things, and the rich He has sent away empty.

He has helped His servant Israel, in remembrance of His mercy, as He spoke to our fathers, to Abraham

الرب. فقالت مريم تعظم نفسي الرب وتبتهج روحي بالله مخلصي.

لأنه نظر إلى تواضع أمته. فهوذا منذ الآن جميع الأجيال تطوبني. لان القدير قد صنع بي عظائم واسمه قدوس. ورحمته إلى جيل الأجيال للذين يتقونه صنع قوة بذراعه بدد المستكبرين بفكر قلوبهم. انزل الأعزاء عن الكراسي ورفع المتواضعين. اشبع الجياع خيرات وصرف الأغنياء فارغين.

عضد إسرائيل فتاة ليذكر رحمته كما تكلم مع آباءنا. إبراهيم ونسله إلى الأبد. فمكثت مريم عندها نحو ثلاثة أشهر ثم عادت إلى بيتها ممجدة الرب الإله ونعظمك باستحقاق يا من صرت محلا للكلمة الأزلية. (لوقا

(١:٣٩_٥٦)

and to his seed forever." And Mary remained with her about three months, and returned to her house. (Luke 1:39-56)

Exposition of the Fourth Week - طرح للإسبوع الرابع

Now Elizabeth's full time came for her to be delivered, and she brought forth a son. When her neighbors and relatives heard how the Lord had shown great mercy to her, they rejoiced with her.

So it was, on the eighth day, that they came to circumcise the child; and they would have called him by the name of his father, Zacharias. His mother answered and said, "No; he shall be called John." But they said to her, "There is no one

فلما تم زمان أليصابات لتلد فولدت أبنا. وسمع جيرانها وأقرباؤها أن الرب قد عظم رحمته لها ففرحوا معها.

فلما كان في اليوم الثامن جاءوا ليختنوا الصبي وسموه باسم أبيه زكريا. فأجابت أمه وقالت لا بل يسمى يوحنا. فقالوا لها ليس أحد في جنسك تسمى بهذا الاسم. ثم اومأوا

among your relatives who is called by this name." So they made signs to his father, what he would have him called.

And he asked for a writing tablet, and wrote, saying, "His name is John." So they all marveled. Immediately his mouth was opened and his tongue loosed, and he spoke, praising God. Then fear came on all who dwelt around them; and all these sayings were discussed throughout all the hill country of Judea.

And all those who heard them kept them in their hearts, saying, "What kind of child will this be?" And the hand of the Lord was with him. Now his father Zacharias was filled with the Holy Spirit, and prophesied, saying:

"Blessed is the Lord God of Israel, for He has visited and redeemed His people, and has raised up a horn of salvation for us in the house

إلى أبيه ماذا تريد أن يسمى.

فطلب لوحا وكتب قائلا اسمه يوحنا فتعجب الجميع. وفى الحال انفتح فاه ولسانه تكلم وبارك الله. فوقع خوف على كل جيرانهم وتحدث بهذه الأمور جميعها في كل جبال اليهودية.

وفكر جميع السامعين في قلوبهم قائلين. أترى ماذا يكون هذا الصبي. وكانت يد الرب معه. وامتلأ زكريا أبوه من الروح القدس وتنبأ قائلا.

مبارك الرب اله إسرائيل لأنه افتقد وصنع فداء لشعبه. وأقام لنا قرن خلاص من بيت داود فتاة كما تكلم بأفواه أنبيائه القديسين الذين هم منذ الدهر. خلاص من أعدائنا ومن أيدي

of His servant David, as He spoke by the mouth of His holy prophets, who have been since the world began, that we should be saved from our enemies and from the hand of all who hate us, to perform the mercy promised to our fathers and to remember His holy covenant, the oath which He swore to our father Abraham: To grant us that we, being delivered from the hand of our enemies, might serve Him without fear, in holiness and righteousness before Him all the days of our life and you, child, will be called the prophet of the Highest; For you will go before the face of the Lord to prepare His ways, to give knowledge of salvation to His people by the remission of their sins, through the tender mercy of our God, with which the Dayspring from on high has visited us; To give light to those who sit in darkness and the shadow of death, to guide our feet into the

جميع مبغضينا. ليصنع رحمة مع آبائنا ويذكر عهده المقدس.

القسم الذي اقسم به لإبراهيم أبينا أن يعطينا. إننا بلا خوف منقذين من أيدي أعدائنا نخدمه ببر وعدل وقداسة جميع أيام حياتنا. وأنت أيها الصبي نبي العلى تدعى لأنك تتقدم أمام وجه الرب لتعد طرقه. لتعطى شعبه معرفة الخلاص بمغفرة خطاياهم. من اجل تحنن رحمه إلهنا التي بها افتقدنا المشرق من العلاء ليضيء على الجالسين في الظلمة وظلال الموت لتقسيم أقدامنا في طريق السلام.

أما الصبي فكان ينمو ويتقوى بالروح. وكان في البراري إلى يوم ظهوره لإسرائيل.

لوقا: ٥٧ ـ ٨٠ : ١

way of peace."

So the child grew and became strong in spirit, and was in the deserts till the day of his manifestation to Israel. (Luke 1:57-80)

The Conclusion of Watos

Theotokeias - Ⲱ ⲡⲉⲛⲟⲥ Ⲓⲏⲥ Ⲡ̅ⲭ̅ⲥ

ختام الثؤطوكيات الواطس -

O our Lord Jesus Christ, who carries the sin of the world, count us with Your sheep, those who are to Your right.	Ⲱ ⲡⲉⲛⲟⲥ Ⲓⲏⲥ Ⲡ̅ⲭ̅ⲥ: ⲫⲏⲉⲧⲱ̀ⲗⲓ ⲙ̀ⲫⲛⲟⲃⲓ ⲙ̀ⲡ̀ⲕⲟⲥⲙⲟⲥ: ⲟⲡⲧⲉⲛ ⲉ̀ⲱⲛ ⲛⲉⲙ ⲛⲉⲕⲉⲥⲏⲃ: ⲛ̀ⲁⲓ ⲉⲧⲥ̀ⲁⲟⲩⲓ̀ⲛⲁⲙ ⲙ̀ⲙⲟⲕ.	يا ربنا يسوع المسيح. حامل خطيه العالم. أحسبنا مع خرافك. الذين عن يمينك.
*And when You come again, in Your second fearful appearance, may we never fearfully hear, You say I do not know you.	*Ⲁⲕϣⲁⲛⲓ̀ ϧⲉⲛ ⲧⲉⲕⲙⲁ̀ⲉ̀ⲥⲛⲟⲩ†: ⲙ̀ⲡⲁⲣⲟⲩⲥⲓⲁ ⲉⲧⲟⲓ ⲛ̀ⲉⲟⲩ†: ⲙ̀ⲡⲉⲛⲟ̀ⲣⲉⲛⲥⲱⲧⲉⲙ ϧⲉⲛ ⲟⲩⲥ̀ⲑⲟⲉⲣⲧⲉⲣ: ϫⲉ †ⲥⲱⲟⲩⲛ ⲙ̀ⲙⲱⲧⲉⲛ ⲁⲛ.	*عند ظهورك الثانى. المخوف لا نسمع. برعده اننى. لست أعرفكم.

But rather may we be made worthy, to hear the voice full of joy, of Your tender mercies, proclaiming and saying.	Ⲁⲗⲗⲁ ⲙⲁⲣⲉⲛⲉⲣⲡⲉⲙⲡϣⲁ ⲛ̀ⲥⲱⲧⲉⲙ: ⲉ̀ϯⲥⲙⲏ ⲉⲑⲙⲉϩ ⲛ̀ⲣⲁϣⲓ: ⲛ̀ⲧⲉ ⲛⲉⲕⲙⲉⲧϣⲁⲛⲁ̀ⲑⲏϥ: ⲉⲥⲱϣ ⲉ̀ⲃⲟⲗ ⲉⲥϫⲱ ⲙ̀ⲙⲟⲥ.	بل نكون مستحقين. لسماع صوتك الحنون. الممتلئ فرحا. يصرخ قائلا.
*"Come unto Me, O blessed of My Father, and inherit the Life, that endures forever."	*Ϫⲉ ⲁ̀ⲙⲱⲓⲛⲓ ϩⲁⲣⲟⲓ: ⲛⲏⲉⲧⲥ̀ⲙⲁⲣⲱⲟⲩⲧ ⲛ̀ⲧⲉ Ⲡⲁⲓⲱⲧ: ⲁ̀ⲣⲓⲕⲗⲏⲣⲟⲛⲟⲙⲓⲛ ⲙ̀ⲡⲓⲱⲛϧ: ⲉⲑⲙⲏⲛ ⲉ̀ⲃⲟⲗ ϣⲁ ⲉ̀ⲛⲉϩ.	*تعالوا الىّ. يا مباركى أبى. رثوا الحياة الدائمة. الى الابد.
The martyrs will come, bearing their afflictions, and the righteous will come, bearing their virtues.	Ⲥⲉⲛⲁⲓ̀ ⲛ̀ϫⲉ ⲛⲓⲙⲁⲣⲧⲩⲣⲟⲥ: ⲉⲩϥⲁⲓ ϧⲁ ⲛⲟⲩⲃⲁⲥⲁⲛⲟⲥ: ⲥⲉⲛⲁⲓ̀ ⲛ̀ϫⲉ ⲛⲓⲇⲓⲕⲉⲟⲥ: ⲉⲩϥⲁⲓ ϧⲁ ⲛⲟⲩⲡⲟⲗⲏⲧⲓⲁ.	يأتى الشهداء. حاملين عذاباتهم. ويأتى الصديقيون. حاملين فضائلهم.
*The Son of God shall come in His	*ϥⲛⲁⲓ̀ ⲛ̀ϫⲉ Ⲡϣⲏⲣⲓ	*يأتى ابن الله. فى مجده ومجد

glory, and His Father's glory, to give unto everyone, according to his deeds which he has done.	`ⲙ̀Ⲫϯ: ⲇⲉⲛ ⲡⲉϥⲱⲟⲩ ⲛⲉⲙ ⲫⲁ Ⲡⲉϥⲓⲱⲧ: ϥ̀ⲛⲁϯ ⲙ̀ⲡⲓⲟⲩⲁⲓ ⲡⲓⲟⲩⲁⲓ: ⲕⲁⲧⲁ ⲛⲉϥ̀ⲉ̀ⲃⲏⲟⲩⲓ̀ ⲉ̀ⲧⲁϥⲁⲓⲧⲟⲩ.`	أبيه. ويجازى كل واحد. كأعماله التى عملها.
O Christ the Word of the Father, the Only Begotten God, grant us Your peace, that is full of joy.	`Ⲡⲭ̅ⲥ̅ ⲡⲓⲖⲟⲅⲟⲥ ⲛ̀ⲧⲉ Ⲫⲓⲱⲧ: ⲡⲓⲙⲟⲛⲟⲅⲉⲛⲏⲥ ⲛ̀ⲛⲟⲩϯ: ⲉⲕⲉ̀ϯ ⲛⲁⲛ ⲛ̀ⲧⲉⲕⲉⲓⲣⲏⲛⲏ: ⲑⲁⲓ ⲉⲑⲙⲉⲉⲣ ⲛ̀ⲣⲁϣⲓ ⲛⲓⲃⲉⲛ.`	أيها المسيح كلمه الاب. الإله الوحيد. أعطنا سلامك. المملوء فرحا.
*As You have given, to Your saintly apostles, likewise also say to us, "My peace I give to You."	`*Ⲕⲁⲧⲁ ⲫ̀ⲣⲏϯ ⲉ̀ⲧⲁⲕⲧⲏⲓⲥ: ⲛ̀ⲛⲉⲕⲁⲅⲓⲟⲥ ⲛ̀ⲁ̀ⲡⲟⲥⲧⲟⲗⲟⲥ: ⲉⲕⲉ̀ϫⲟⲥ ⲛⲁⲛ ⲙ̀ⲡⲟⲩⲣⲏϯ: ϫⲉ ⲧⲁⲉⲓⲣⲏⲛⲏ ϯϯ ⲙ̀ⲙⲟⲥ ⲛⲱⲧⲉⲛ.`	*كما أعطيته. لرسلك القديسين. قل لنا مثلهم. أنى أعطيكم سلامى.
"My peace which I have taken, from My Father, I leave unto you, both now and	`Ⲧⲁⲉⲓⲣⲏⲛⲏ ⲁ̀ⲛⲟⲕ: ⲑⲏⲉⲧⲁⲓϭⲓⲧⲥ ⲉⲓⲧⲉⲛ Ⲡⲁⲓⲱⲧ:`	سلامى أنا. الذى أخذته من أبى. أنا أتركه معكم. من

forever."	ⲀⲚⲞⲔ ϮⲬⲰ ⲘⲘⲞⲤ ⲚⲈⲘⲰⲦⲈⲚ: ⲒⲤⲬⲈⲚ ϮⲚⲞⲨ ⲚⲈⲘ ϢⲀ ⲈⲚⲈϨ.	الان وإلى الابد.
*O the angel of this day, flying up with this hymn, remember us before the Lord, that he may forgive us our sins.	*Ⲡⲓⲁⲅⲅⲉⲗⲟⲥ ⲚⲦⲈ ⲡⲀⲒⲈϨⲞⲞⲨ: ⲈⲦϨⲎⲖ ⲈⲠϬⲒⲤⲒ ⲚⲈⲘ ⲠⲀⲒϨⲨⲘⲚⲞⲤ: ⲀⲣⲒ- ⲠⲈⲚⲘⲈⲨⲒ ϦⲀⲦϨⲎ ⲘⲠⲞⲤ: ⲚⲦⲈϤⲬⲀ ⲚⲈⲚⲚⲞⲂⲒ ⲚⲀⲚ ⲈⲂⲞⲖ.	*يا ملاك هذه اليوم. الطائر الى العلو بهذه التسبحة. أذكرنا لدى الرب. ليغفر لنا خطايانا.
The sick heal them, those who have slept O Lord repose them, and all of our brothers in distress, help us my Lord and all of them.	ⲚⲏⲉⲧϢⲰⲚⲒ ⲘⲀⲦⲀⲖ- ϬⲰⲞⲨ: ⲚⲎⲈⲦⲀⲨⲈⲚⲔⲞⲦ Ⲡⲟⲥ ⲘⲀⲘⲦⲞⲚ ⲚⲰⲞⲨ: ⲚⲈⲚⲤⲚⲎⲞⲨ ⲈⲦⲬⲎ ϦⲈⲚ ϨⲞⲬϨⲈⲬ ⲚⲒⲂⲈⲚ: Ⲡⲁⲟⲥ ⲀⲣⲒⲂⲞⲎⲐⲒⲚ ⲈⲣⲞⲚ ⲚⲈⲘ- ⲰⲞⲨ.	المرضى أشفهم. الذين رقدوا يا رب نيحهم. وأخواتنا الذين فى كل شدة. يا ربى أعنا وإياهم.
*May God bless us,	*Ⲉϥⲉⲥⲙⲟⲩ ⲈⲣⲟⲚ ⲚⲬⲈ	*يباركنا الله.

119

and let us bless His holy name, and may His praise continually be, always upon our mouths.

Ⲫϯ: ⲧⲉⲛⲛⲁⲥⲙⲟⲩ ⲉⲡⲉϥⲣⲁⲛ ⲉⲑⲩ: ⲛ̀ⲥⲏⲟⲩ ⲛⲓⲃⲉⲛ ⲉⲣⲉ ⲡⲉϥⲥⲙⲟⲩ: ⲛⲁϣⲱⲡⲓ ⲉϥⲙⲏⲛ ⲉ̀ⲃⲟⲗ ϧⲉⲛ ⲣⲱⲛ.

ولنبارك أسمه القدوس. فى كل حين تسبحته. دائمة فى أفواهنا.

For blessed is the Father and the Son, and the Holy Spirit, the perfect Trinity, we worship and glorify Him.

Ⲭⲉ ϥ̀ⲥⲙⲁⲣⲱⲟⲩⲧ ⲛ̀ϫⲉ Ⲫⲓⲱⲧ ⲛⲉⲙ ⲡ̀ϣⲏⲣⲓ: ⲛⲉⲙ ⲡⲓⲠ̅ⲛⲉⲩⲙⲁ ⲉ̅ⲑ̅ⲩ̅: ϯⲦⲣⲓⲁⲥ ⲉⲧϫⲏⲕ ⲉ̀ⲃⲟⲗ: ⲧⲉⲛⲟⲩⲱϣⲧ ⲙ̀ⲙⲟⲥ ⲧⲉⲛϯⲱⲟⲩ ⲛⲁⲥ.

مبارك الاب والابن. والروح القدس. الثالوث الكامل. نسجد له ونمجده.

THE KIAHK

PSALMODY

FOR

SUNDAY

Arise, O Children - Ⲧⲉⲛ ⲑⲏⲛⲟⲩ – قوموا يا بنى

Arise, O children of the Light, let us praise the Lord of hosts.	Ⲧⲉⲛⲑⲏⲛⲟⲩ ⲉ̀ⲡϣⲱⲓ ⲛⲓ-ϣⲏⲣⲓ ⲛ̀ⲧⲉ ⲡⲓⲟⲩⲱⲓⲛⲓ ⲛ̀-ⲧⲉⲛϩⲱⲥ ⲉ̀Ⲡϭⲟⲓⲥ ⲛ̀ⲧⲉ ⲛⲓϫⲟⲙ.	قوموا يا بنى النور لنسبح رب القوات.
*That He may grant us the salvation of our souls.	*Ϩⲟⲡⲱⲥ ⲛ̀ⲧⲉϥⲉⲣϩⲙ-ⲟⲧ ⲛⲁⲛ ⲙ̀ⲡⲥⲱⲧ ⲛ̀ⲧⲉ ⲛⲉⲛⲯⲩⲭⲏ.	*لكى ينعم لنا بخلاص نفوسنا.
Whenever we stand before You in the flesh.	Ϧⲉⲛ ⲡ̀ϫⲓⲛⲑⲣⲉⲛⲟϩⲓ ⲉ̀ⲣ-ⲁⲧⲉⲛ ⲙ̀ⲡⲉⲕⲙ̀ⲑⲟ ⲥⲱ-ⲙⲁⲧⲓⲕⲱⲥ.	عندما نقف أمامك جسدياً.
*Cast away from our minds the slumber of sleep.	*Ⲁⲗⲓⲟⲩⲓ̀ ⲉ̀ⲃⲟⲗ ϩⲓⲧⲉⲛ ⲡⲉⲛⲛⲟⲩⲥ ⲙ̀ⲡⲓϩⲩⲛⲓⲙ ⲛ̀ⲧⲉ ϯⲉⲃϣⲓ.	*إنزع عن عقولنا نوم الغفلة.
Grant us sobriety, O Lord, that we may know how to stand before You at	Ⲙⲟⲓ ⲛⲁⲛ Ⲡϭⲟⲓⲥ ⲛ̀ⲟⲩ-ⲙⲉⲧⲣⲉϥⲉⲣⲛⲩⲙⲫⲓⲛ ϩⲟ-ⲡⲱⲥ ⲛ̀ⲧⲉⲛⲕⲁϯ ⲛ̀ⲧⲉⲛⲟϩⲓ	اعطنا يا رب يقظة لكى نفهم أن نقف أمامك وقت الصلاة.

times of prayer.	ⲉ̀ⲣⲁ ⲧⲉⲛ ⲙ̀ⲡⲉⲕⲙ̀ⲑⲟ ⲙ̀ⲫ̀ⲛⲁⲩⲛ̀ⲧⲉ ϯⲡⲣⲟⲥⲉⲩⲭⲏ.	
*And ascribe unto You the befitting glorification and win the forgiveness of our many sins: *Glory be to You, O Lover of mankind.*	*Ⲟⲩⲟϩ ⲛ̀ⲧⲉⲟⲩⲱⲣⲡ ⲛⲁⲕ ⲉ̀ⲡ̀ϣⲱⲓ ⲛ̀ϯⲇⲟⲝⲟ-ⲗⲟⲅⲓⲁ̀ ⲉⲧⲉⲣⲡ̀ⲣⲉⲡⲓ ⲟⲩⲟϩ ⲛ̀ⲧⲉⲛϣⲁϣⲛⲓ ⲉ̀ⲡ̀ⲭⲱ ⲉ̀ⲃⲟⲗ ⲛ̀ⲧⲉ ⲛⲉⲛⲛⲟⲃⲓ ⲉⲧⲟϣ ⲇⲟⲝⲁ ⲥⲓ ⲫⲓⲗⲁⲛⲑⲣⲱⲡⲉ.	*ونرسل لك إلى فوق التمجيد اللائق. ونفوز بغفران خطايانا الكثيرة. المجد لك يامحب البشر.
Behold bless the Lord, all you servants of the Lord: *Glory...*	Ϩⲏⲡⲡⲉ ⲇⲉ ⲥ̀ⲙⲟⲩ ⲉ̀Ⲡ̀ϭⲟⲓⲥ ⲛⲓⲉ̀ⲃⲓⲁⲓⲕ ⲛ̀ⲧⲉ Ⲡ̀ϭⲟⲓⲥ: ⲇⲟ...	ها باركوا الرب يا عبيد الرب. المجد ..
*You who stand in the house of the Lord, in the courts of the house of our God: *Glory be to You, O Lover of mankind.*	*Ⲛⲏⲉⲧⲟ̀ϩⲓ ⲉ̀ⲣⲁⲧⲟⲩ ϧⲉⲛ ⲡ̀ⲏⲓ ⲙ̀Ⲡ̀ϭⲟⲓⲥ: ϧⲉⲛ ⲛⲓⲁⲩⲗⲏⲟⲩ ⲛ̀ⲧⲉ ⲡ̀ⲏⲓ ⲙ̀-Ⲡⲉⲛⲛⲟⲩϯ: ⲇⲟ...	*القائمين فى بيت الرب. فى ديار بيت إلهنا. المجد..
By night lift up your hands, O you saints	Ⲛ̀ϩⲣⲏⲓ ϧⲉⲛ ⲛⲓⲉ̀ϫⲱⲣϩ	بالليالى إرفعوا أيديكم إلى فوق

123

and bless the Lord: *Glory...*	ϥⲁⲓ ⲛ̀ⲛⲉⲧⲉⲛϫⲓϫ ⲉ̀ⲡϣⲱⲓ ⲛⲏⲉ̀ⲑⲟⲩⲁⲃ ⲥ̀ⲙⲟⲩ ⲉ̀Ⲡϭⲟⲓⲥ: Ⲇⲟ...	أيها القديسون باركوا الرب. المجد ..
*The Lord bless you from Zion, who created heaven and earth: *Glory...*	*Ⲡϭⲟⲓⲥ ⲉϥⲉ̀ⲥⲙⲟⲩ ⲉ̀ⲣⲟⲕ ⲉ̀ⲃⲟⲗ ϧⲉⲛ Ⲥⲓⲱⲛ: ⲫⲏⲉ̀ⲧⲁϥⲑⲁⲙⲓⲟ ⲛ̀ⲧⲫⲉ ⲛⲉⲙ ⲡ̀ⲕⲁϩⲓ: Ⲇⲟ...	*يباركك الرب من صهيون الذى خلق السماء والأرض. المجد ..
Let my cry come near before You, O Lord, give me understanding according to Your word: *Glory be to You, O Lover of mankind.*	Ⲙⲁⲣⲉ ⲡⲁϯϩⲟ ϧⲱⲛⲧ ⲙ̀ⲡⲉⲕⲙ̀ⲑⲟ Ⲡϭⲟⲓⲥ : ⲙⲁⲕⲁϯ ⲛⲏⲓ ⲕⲁⲧⲁ ⲡⲉⲕⲥⲁϫⲓ: Ⲇⲟ...	فلتدن وسيلتى قدامك يارب.كقولك فهمنى. المجد ..
*Let my supplication come before You, deliver me according to Your word: *Glory...*	*Ⲉϥⲉ̀ⲓ ⲉ̀ϧⲟⲩⲛ ⲙ̀ⲡⲉⲕⲙ̀ⲑⲟ ⲛ̀ϫⲉ ⲡⲁⲁⲝⲓⲱⲙⲁ : ⲕⲁⲧⲁ ⲡⲉⲕⲥⲁϫⲓ ⲙⲁⲧ-ⲁⲛϧⲟⲓ: Ⲇⲟ...	*ليدخل إبتهالى أمامك. ككلمتك أحينى. المجد ..
My lips shall	Ⲉⲣⲉ ⲛⲁⲥⲫⲟⲧⲟⲩ ⲃⲉ-	تفيض شفتاى

overflow with praise, when You have taught me Your statutes: *Glory...*	Ⲃⲓ ⲛ̀ⲟⲩⲥⲙⲟⲩ ⲉ̀ϣⲱⲡ ⲁⲕϣⲁⲛ̀ⲧⲥⲁⲃⲟⲓ ⲉ̀ⲛⲉⲕⲙⲉⲑⲙⲏⲓ: Ⲇⲟ...	السبح إذا ما علمتنى حقوقك. المجد ..
*My tongue shall speak of Your words, for all Your commandments are righteous: *Glory ....*	*Ⲡⲁⲗⲁⲥ ⲉϥⲉ̀ⲉⲣⲟⲩⲱ̀ ϧⲉⲛ ⲛⲉⲕⲥⲁϫⲓ : ϫⲉ ⲛⲉⲕⲉⲛⲧⲟⲗⲏ ⲧⲏⲣⲟⲩ ϩⲁⲛⲙⲉⲑⲙⲏⲓ ⲛⲉ: Ⲇⲟ...	*لسانى يجيب بأقوالك. لأن جميع وصاياك هى حق. المجد ..
Let Your hand help me, for I have chosen Your precepts: *Glory...*	Ⲙⲁⲣⲉⲥϣⲱⲡⲓ ⲛ̀ϫⲉ ⲧⲉⲕϫⲓϫ ⲉ̀ϥⲛⲁϩⲙⲉⲧ : ϫⲉ ⲛⲉⲕⲉⲛⲧⲟⲗⲏ ⲁⲓⲉⲣⲉ̀ⲡⲓⲑⲩⲙⲓⲛ ⲉ̀ⲣⲱⲟⲩ: Ⲇⲟ...	لتكن يدك لتخلصنى لأنى اشتهيت وصاياك. المجد ..
*I have longed for Your salvation, O Lord, and Your law is my delight: *Glory...*	*Ⲁⲓϭⲓϣϣⲱⲟⲩ ⲙ̀ⲡⲉⲕⲟⲩϫⲁⲓ Ⲡ̀ϭⲟⲓⲥ : ⲟⲩⲟϩ ⲡⲉⲕⲛⲟⲙⲟⲥ ⲡⲉ ⲧⲁⲙⲉⲗⲉⲧⲏ: Ⲇⲟ...	*اشتقت إلى خلاصك يارب و ناموسك هو تلاوتى. المجد ..
Let my soul live, and it shall praise You, and let Your	Ⲉⲥⲉ̀ⲱⲛϧ ⲛ̀ϫⲉ ⲧⲁⲯⲩⲭⲏ ⲟⲩⲟϩ ⲉⲥⲉ̀ⲥⲙ-	تحيا نفسى و تسبحك و أحكامك

judgments help me: *Glory …*	ⲟⲩ ⲉⲣⲟⲕ : ⲟⲩⲟⲟ ⲛⲉⲕϩⲁⲡ ⲉⲩⲉⲉⲣⲃⲟⲏⲑ-ⲓⲛ ⲉⲣⲟⲓ: Ⲇⲟ...	تعينني. المجد ..
*I have gone astray like a lost sheep, seek Your servant for I do not forget Your commandments: *Glory...*	*Ⲁⲓⲥⲱⲣⲉⲙ ⲙ̇ⲫⲣⲏϯ ⲛ̇-ⲟⲩⲉⲥⲱⲟⲩ ⲉⲁϥⲧⲁⲕⲟ : ⲕⲱϯ ⲛ̇ⲥⲁ ⲡⲉⲕⲃⲱⲕ ϫⲉ ⲛⲉⲕⲉⲛⲧⲟⲗⲏ ⲙ̇ⲡⲓⲉⲣⲡⲟⲩ ⲱⲃϣ: Ⲇⲟ...	*ضللت مثل الخروف الضال فاطلب عبدك فإني لوصاياك لم أنس. المجد ..
Glory be to the Father, the Son and the Holy Spirit: *Glory...*	Ⲇⲟⲝⲁ Ⲡⲁⲧⲣⲓ ⲕⲉ Ⲩⲓⲱ ⲕⲉ ⲁ̇ⲅⲓⲱ Ⲡⲛⲉⲩⲙⲁⲧⲓ : Ⲇⲟ...	المجد للآب والأبن والروح القدس. المجد ..
*Now and forever and unto the ages of ages, Amen: *Glory...*	*Ⲕⲉ ⲛⲩⲛ ⲕⲉ ⲁ̇ⲓ ⲕⲉ ⲓⲥ ⲧⲟⲩⲥ ⲉ̇ⲱⲛⲁⲥ ⲧⲱⲛ ⲉ̇ⲱ-ⲛⲱⲛ ⲁ̇ⲙⲏⲛ: Ⲇⲟ...	*الآن وكل أوان وإلى دهر الداهرين آمين. المجد ..
Glory be to the Father, the Son and the Holy Spirit, now and forever and ever, Amen: *Glory*	Ⲡⲓⲱⲟⲩ ⲙ̇Ⲫⲓⲱⲧ ⲛⲉⲙ Ⲡ̇-ϣⲏⲣⲓ ⲛⲉⲙ Ⲡⲓⲡⲛⲉⲩ-ⲙⲁ ⲉ̇ⲑⲟⲩⲁⲃ : ⲓⲥϫⲉⲛ ϯⲛⲟⲩ ⲛⲉⲙ ϣⲁ ⲉⲛⲉⲟ ⲛ̇ⲧⲉ	المجد للآب والابن والروح القدس منذ الآن وإلى أبد الآبدين كلها

be to You, O Lover of mankind.	ⲛⲓⲉⲛⲉϩ ⲧⲏⲣⲟⲩ ⲁⲙⲏⲛ: Ⲇⲟ...	آمين. المجد ..
Glory be to You, O Good One, the Lover of mankind. Hail to Your Mother, the Virgin, and all Your saints: Glory...	*Ⲡⲓⲱⲟⲩ ⲛⲁⲕ ⲡⲓⲙⲁⲓⲣⲱⲙⲓ ⲛ̀ⲁⲅⲁⲑⲟⲥ: ⲡⲓⲱⲟⲩ ⲛ̀ⲧⲉⲕⲙⲁⲩ ⲙ̀ⲡⲁⲣⲑⲉⲛⲟⲥ ⲛⲉⲙ ⲛⲏⲉ̀ⲑⲟⲩⲁⲃ ⲧⲏⲣⲟⲩ ⲛ̀ⲧⲁⲕ: Ⲇⲟ...	*المجد لك يامحب البشر الصالح. المجد لأمك العذراء وجميع قديسيك. المجد ..
Glory be to You, O Only-Begotten One, O Holy Trinity, have mercy upon us: Glory...	Ⲇⲟⲍⲁ ⲥⲓ ⲟ̀ⲙⲟⲛⲟⲩⲉⲛⲏⲥ: ⲁ̀ⲅⲓⲁ Ⲧⲣⲓⲁⲥ ⲉⲗⲉ̀ⲏⲥⲟⲛ ⲏ̀ⲙⲁⲥ: Ⲇⲟ...	المجد لك أيها الوحيد. أيها الثالوث المقدس ارحمنا. المجد..
Let God arise and let all His enemies be scattered and let all that hate His Holy Name flee from before His face: Glory…	*Ⲙⲁⲣⲉϥⲧⲱⲛϥ ⲛ̀ϫⲉ Ⲫϯ : ⲙⲁⲣⲟⲩϫⲱⲣ ⲉ̀ⲃⲟⲗ ⲛ̀ϫⲉ ⲛⲉϥϫⲁϫⲓ ⲧⲏⲣⲟⲩ : ⲙⲁⲣⲟⲩⲫⲱⲧ ⲉ̀ⲃⲟⲗ ϧⲁⲧϩⲏ ⲙ̀ⲡⲉϥϩⲟ ⲛ̀ϫⲉ ⲟⲩⲟⲛ ⲛⲓⲃⲉⲛ ⲉⲑⲙⲟⲥϯ ⲙ̀ⲡⲉϥⲣⲁⲛ ⲉ̀ⲑⲟⲩⲁⲃ : Ⲇⲟ...	*ليقم الله . وليتبدد جميع أعدائه . وليهرب من قدام وجهه كل مبغضى اسمه القدوس. المجد ..

As for Your people let them be blessed, a thousand thousand fold and ten thousand ten thousand fold, doing Your will.

Ⲡⲉⲕⲗⲁⲟⲥ ⲇⲉ ⲙⲁⲣⲉϥ-ϣⲱⲡⲓ ϧⲉⲛ ⲡⲓⲥⲙⲟⲩ: ⲉϩⲁ-ⲛⲁⲛϣⲟ ⲛ̀ϣⲟ ⲛⲉⲙ ϩⲁⲛ-ⲑ̀ⲃⲁ ⲛ̀ⲑⲃⲁ ⲉⲩⲓⲣⲓ ⲙ̀ⲡⲉⲕⲟⲩⲱϣ.

وأما شعبك فليكن بالبركة ألوف ألوف وربوات ربوات يصنعون إرادتك.

*O Lord, open my lips and my mouth will declare Your praise.

*Ⲡ̀ϭⲟⲓⲥ ⲉⲕⲉ̀ⲁⲟⲩⲱⲛ ⲛ̀ⲛ-ⲁⲥⲫⲟⲧⲟⲩ: ⲟⲩⲟϩ ⲉ̀ⲣⲉ ⲣⲱⲓ ⲭⲱ ⲙ̀ⲡⲉⲕⲥ̀ⲙⲟⲩ.

*يارب افتح شفتى . ولينطق فمى بتسبحتك .

The Kiahk's Ode - Hⲱⲥ ⲉ̀Ⲡϭ̄ⲟⲓⲥ

الهوس الكيهكى -

O sing unto the Lord a new song, sing unto the Lord all the earth. Declare among the heathen His glory, and among all people His wonders. For great is the Lord and greatly to be praised. He is to be feared above all gods. Alleluia.

Ⲑⲱⲥ ⲉ̀Ⲡϭ̄ⲟⲓⲥ ϧⲉⲛ ⲟⲩ- ⲑⲱⲥ ⲛ̀ⲃⲉⲣⲓ: Ⲑⲱⲥ ⲉ̀- Ⲡϭ̄ⲟⲓⲥ ⲡ̀ⲕⲁϩⲓ ⲧⲏⲣϥ: Ⲑⲱⲥ ⲉ̀Ⲡϭ̄ⲟⲓⲥ ⲥ̀ⲙⲟⲩ ⲉ̀ⲡⲉϥⲣⲁⲛ : ϩⲓϣⲉⲛⲛⲟⲩϥⲓ ⲙ̀ⲡⲉϥⲟⲩⲝⲁⲓ ⲛ̀ⲉ̀ϩⲟⲟⲩ ϧⲁ ⲧ̀ϣⲓ ⲛ̀ⲉ̀ϩⲟⲟⲩ: ⲥⲁϫⲓ ⲙ̀ⲡⲉϥⲱⲟⲩ ϧⲉⲛ ⲛⲓⲉⲑⲛⲟⲥ ⲛⲉⲙ ⲛⲉϥϣ̀ⲫⲏⲣⲓ ϧⲉⲛ ⲛⲓⲗⲁⲟⲥ ⲧⲏⲣⲟⲩ: ϫⲉ ⲟⲩⲛⲓϣϯ ⲡⲉ Ⲡϭ̄ⲟⲓⲥ ⲟⲩⲟϩ ϥ̀ⲥⲙⲁⲣⲱⲟⲩⲧ ⲉ̀ⲙⲁϣⲱ: ϥ̀ⲟⲓ ⲛ̀ϩⲟϯ ⲉ̀ϫⲉⲛ ⲛⲓⲛⲟⲩϯ ⲧⲏⲣⲟⲩ: Ⲁⲗ- ⲗⲏⲟⲩⲓⲁ.

سبحوا الرب تسبيحاً جديداً: سبحى الرب أيتها الأرض كلها: سبحوا الرب وباركوا اسمه: بشروا بخلاصه يوماً فيوم: وأخبروا بمجده فى الأمم وبعجائبه فى جميع الشعوب: لأن الرب عظيم ومبارك جداً: ومخوف على كل الآلهة. الليلويا.

I will bless the Lord at all times. His praise shall continually be in my mouth. My soul shall make her boast in the Lord, the humble shall hear of it, and be glad. O magnify the Lord with me, and let us exalt His Name together. Alleluia.

أبارك الرب فى كل حين. وفى كل أوان تسبحته موجودة فى فمى. بالرب تفتخر نفسى وليسمع أهل الدعة و يفرحون. عظموا الرب معى و لنرفعن اسمه معا. الليلويا.

You dwell between the Cherubim, shine forth. Before Ephraim and Benjamin and Manasseh stir up Your strength, and come and save us. Turn us again, O God, and cause Your face to shine, and we shall be saved. Alleluia.

أيها الجالس على الشاروبيم أظهر امام إفرايم وبنيامين ومنسى. أنهض قوتك وهلم لخلاصنا. اللهم أرددنا ولينر وجهك علينا فنخلص. الليلويا.

He bowed the heavens also, and came down, and darkness was under His feet, and He rode upon a Cherub, and did fly; yes, He did fly upon the wings of the wind. He made darkness His secret place: His pavilion round about Him. Alleluia.

طأطأ السماء ونزل والضباب تحت رجليه. وركب على الشاروبيم وطار. طار على أجنحة الرياح وجعل الظلمة له حجاباً تحوط به مظلته. الليلويا.

The wings of a dove are covered with silver, and her feathers with yellow gold. When the Almighty scattered kings in it, it was as white as snow in Salmon. Alleluia.

أجنحة حمامة مغشاة بحلىّ الفضة ومنكباها بصفرة الذهب. وعندما يرسم السماوى عليها ممالكاً فيبيضون مثل الثلج فى سلمون. الليلويا.

The hill of God is as the hill of Bashan, a high hill as the hill of Bashan. Why leap you, you high hills? This is the hill, which God desires to dwell in; the Lord will dwell in it forever. Alleluia.

جبل الله الجبل الدسم. الجبل المتجمد الجبل الدسم. ما بالكم تظنون جبالاً مجبنة الجبل الذى سُر الله أن يسكن فيه. فإن الرب يسكن فيه الى الأنقضاء. الليلويا.

At Your right hand stood the queen, arrayed in vesture of unwoven gold, adorned in varied colors. Alleluia.

قامت الملكة عن يمينك مشتملة بلباس موشى بالذهب مزينة بأنواع كثيرة. الليلويا.

Hearken, O daughter, and see, and incline your ear, and forget your own people and your father's house. And the king shall greatly desire your beauty, for He,

اسمعى يا ابنتى وانظرى وأميلى بسمعك. وانسى شعبك وكل بيت أبيك فإن الملك قد اشتهى حسنك. لأنه هو ربك . الليلويا.

Himself, is your Lord. Alleluia.

The daughters of Tyre shall worship Him with gifts; the rich of the people of the land shall supplicate His favor. Alleluia.

تسجد له بنات صور. يتلقون وجهك بالهدايا أغنياء شعوب الارض. الليلويا.

All the glory of the daughter of the king is within, with gold-ringed garments is she arrayed, adorned in varied colors. The virgins that follow after her are brought unto You. They shall be brought with gladness and rejoicing. They shall be brought into the temple of the King. Alleluia.

كل مجد ابنة الملك من داخل مشتملة بأذيال موشاة بالذهب. مزينة بأشكال كثيرة. يدخلن إلى الملك عذارى خلفها . يدخلن صاحباتها جميعاً. يدخلن بالفرح والتهليل . يدخلن إلى هيكل الملك. الليلويا.

Great is the Lord, and greatly to be praised in the City of our God, in the mountain of His holiness. Beautiful is its situation, the joy of the whole earth, in Mount Zion, on the sides of the north the city of the great King. Alleluia.

عظيم هو الرب ومبارك جداً فى مدينة إلهنا على جبله المقدس. تتسع كل الأرض بالتهليل جبال صهيون جوانب الشمال مدينة الملك العظيم. الليلويا.

His foundation is in the holy

أساساته فى الجبال المقدسة.

mountains. The Lord loves the gates of Zion more than all the dwellings of Jacob. Glorious things are spoken of You, O City of God. Alleluia.

الرب أحب أبواب صهيون أفضل من جميع مساكن يعقوب أعمال كريمة قيلت من أجلك يامدينة الله . الليلويا.

And of Zion it shall be said: This and that man was born in her, and the Highest Himself established her. Alleluia.

الأم صهيون تقول ان انسانأ وانسانأ حل فيها. وهو العلى الذى أسسها الى الأبد. الليلويا.

The angel of the Lord encamps round about them that fear Him, and delivers them. O taste and see that the Lord is good. Blessed is the man that trusts in Him. Alleluia.

ملاك الرب يحوط بكل خائفيه وينجيهم. ذوقوا وانظروا ما أطيب الرب. طوبى للرجل المتوكل عليه. الليلويا.

Who makes His angels spirits. His ministers a flaming fire. Alleluia.

الذى خلق ملائكته أرواحأ وخدامه نارأ تتقد. الليلويا.

Who makes the clouds His chariot. Who walks upon the wings of the wind. Alleluia.

الذى جعل مسالكه على السحاب. الماشى على أجنحة الرياح. الليلويا.

Bless the Lord, you His angels who excel in strength, who do His commandments. Bless you the Lord, all His hosts, you ministers of His, who do His pleasure. Bless the LORD from the heavens; Bless Him in the heights. Alleluia.

باركوا الرب يا جميع ملائكته. الأشداء فى قوتهم الصانعين قوله. سبحوه يا جميع جنوده خدامه الصانعين إرادته. باركوا الرب من السموات. باركوه فى الأعالى. الليلويا.

Before the angels I will praise, I will worship Your holy temple. Alleluia.

أمام الملائكة أرتل لك واسجد نحو هيكلك المقدس. الليلويا.

The heavens declare the glory of God and the firmament shows His great work. Day unto day utters speech and night unto night shows knowledge. There is neither speech nor language. Alleluia.

السموات تنطق بمجد الله والفلك يخبر بعمل يديه يوماً يقول كلاماً ليوم. وليلا يظهر علماً لليل. ليس من قول ولا من كلام. الليلويا.

Where their voice is not heard, their line is gone out through all the earth and their words to the end of the world. Alleluia.

الذين لم يسمع لهم صوت. خرجت أصواتهم على الأرض كلها وبلغ كلامهم الى أقطار المسكونة. الليلويا.

The Lord gave the word, great was

الرب يعطى كلمة للمبشرين

the company of those that published it. The King of armies is the Beloved. Alleluia.

بعظم قوة. وملك القوات هو الحبيب. الليلويا.

Give thanks unto the Lord, call upon His Name, make known His deeds among the people, talk you of all His wondrous works. Glory you in His Holy Name. Alleluia.

اعترفوا للرب وادعوا باسمه. وبشروا بأعماله فى الأمم. أخبروا بجميع عجائبه. افتخروا باسمه القدوس. الليلويا.

Precious in the sight of the Lord is the death of His saints. O Lord, I am Your servant, and the son of Your handmaid: You have loosed my bonds. I will offer to You the sacrifice of thanksgiving. I will pay my vows unto the Lord now in the presence of all His people, in the courts of the Lord's house, in the midst of you, O Jerusalem. Alleluia.

كريم أمام الرب موت أصفيائه. يارب أنا عبدك وابن أمتك. حللت وثاقى فلك أذبح ذبيحة التسبيح. وأوفى للرب نذورى فى ديار بيت إلهنا قدام جميع الشعب فى وسط أورشليم. الليلويا.

God is greatly to be feared in the assembly of the saints. He is the God of Israel. He will give strength unto His people. Let the

عجيب هو الله فى قديسيه. إله اسرائيل هو يعطى قوة وعزاء لشعبه. الصديقون يفرحون ويتهللون أمام الله.

135

righteous be glad, let them rejoice before God. Yes, let them exceedingly rejoice before God, yes, let them exceedingly rejoice. Blessed be the Lord God. Alleluia.

ويتنعمون بسرور. مبارك الرب الإله. الليلويا.

Gird Your sword upon Your thigh, O most Mighty. With Your glory and Your majesty ride prosperously. Alleluia.

تقلد سيفك على فخذك أيها الجبار بحداثتك وبهائك امتد وسر واملك. الليلويا.

You shall tread upon the lion and serpent, the young lion and the dragon shall You trample underfoot. Because he has set His love upon Me, therefore will I deliver him. I will set him on high because he has known My Name. Alleluia.

تطأ الأفعى وملك الحيات. وتكسر الأسد والتنين. لانه إياى ترجى فأخلصه. وأستره لأنه قد عرف اسمى. الليلويا.

The salvation of the righteous is of the Lord. He is their strength in the time of trouble. And the Lord shall help them and save them from the wicked because they trust in Him. Alleluia.

خلاص الأبرار من عند الرب. وهو ناصرهم فى زمن الشدائد. الرب يعينهم وينقذهم من الخطاة. لأنهم توكلوا عليه. الليلويا.

Let the righteous rejoice with joy. They cried and the Lord heard them and He delivered them out of all their distress. The Lord is near to them that are of a contrite heart and He will save the humble of spirit. Alleluia.

Many are the afflictions of the righteous, but the Lord delivers him out of them all. He keeps all his bones, not one of them is broken. Alleluia.

Light is sown for the righteous and gladness for the upright in heart. Rejoice in the Lord, you righteous! Give thanks at the remembrance of His holiness. Alleluia.

The righteous shall flourish like the palm tree. He shall grow like a cedar in Lebanon. Those that are planted in the house of the Lord shall flourish in the courts of our

فليفرح الأبرار بالفرح . والصديقون صرخوا إلى الرب فسمع لهم ونجاهم من جميع شدائدهم. قريب الرب من مستقيمى القلوب والمتواضعى الأرواح يخلصهم. الليلويا.

كثيرة هى أحزان الصديقين. والرب يخلصهم من جميعها. الرب يحفظ جميع عظامهم. وواحدة منها لا تنكسر. الليلويا.

نور أشرق للصديقين. وفرح للمستقيمى القلوب. افرحوا أيها الصديقون بالرب. واعترفوا لذكر قدسه. الليلويا.

البار يعلوا مثل النخلة ويكثر مثل أرز لبنان. المغروسون فى بيت الرب يزهرون فى ديار بيت إلهنا الليلويا.

137

God. Alleluia.

The mouth of the righteous speaks wisdom and his tongue talks of judgment. The law of his God is in his heart; none of his steps shall slide. Alleluia.

فم البار يتلو الحكمة ولسانه ينطق بالحكم ناموس الله كائن فى قلبه. وخطواته لا تزل. الليلويا.

Your saints shall speak of the glory of Your kingdom, and talk of Your power. He will fulfill the desire of them that fear Him. He also will hear their cry and will save them. The Lord preserves all them that love Him. Alleluia.

قديسوك يباركونك وينطقون بمجد ملكوتك. يصنع إرادة خائفيه ويسمع تضرعهم ويخلصهم. الرب يحفظ كل محبيه. الليلويا.

Be glad in the Lord and rejoice, you righteous. Shout for joy, all you that are upright in heart. For this, shall everyone that is godly pray unto You in a time when You may be found. Alleluia.

افرحوا بالرب وتهللوا ايها الابرار. افتخروا يا جميع مستقيمى القلوب فلهذا يصلى لك كل الابرار فى زمان مستقيم. الليلويا.

Let Your tender mercies come speedily to meet us because we have been brought very low. Help

فلتسبق وتدركنا سريعاً رأفتك لأننا قد تمسكنا جداً. أعنا يالله مخلصنا. من أجل مجد اسمك

us, O God of our salvation, for the glory of Your Name. O Lord, save us and forgive us our sins for the glory of Your Name. Alleluia.

يارب تخلصنا. وتغفر لنا خطايانا من أجل اسمك القدوس. الليلويا.

Let them exalt Him in the church of His people and praise Him in the seat of the elders, for He has made His families like a flock of sheep, that the upright may see and rejoice. Alleluia.

فليرفعوه فى كنيسة شعبه. وليباركوه على منابر الشيوخ. لأنه جعل الابوة مثل الخراف. ينظر المستقيمون ويفرحون. الليلويا.

The Lord has sworn and will not relent. You are a priest forever according the order of Melchizedek. Alleluia.

أقسم الرب ولن يندم أنك أنت الكاهن إلى الأبد على طقس ملشيصاداق. الليلويا.

God be merciful to us, bless us, cause His face to shine upon us, and have mercy upon us. Alleluia.

الله يتراءف علينا ويباركنا ويشرق وجهه علينا ويرحمنا. الليلويا.

Save Your people, bless Your inheritance, shepherd them, and raise them up forever. Alleluia.

يارب خلص شعبك بارك ميراثك ارعهم وارفعهم إلى الأبد. الليلويا.

Whoever is wise will observe these things, and they will understand the loving-kindness of the LORD. Alleluia. Bless me. Lo, the metania. Forgive me. O my fathers and my brethren pray for me. In love, I ask you to remember me.

Ⲛⲓⲙ ⲡⲉ ⲡⲓⲥⲁⲃⲉ ⲟⲩⲟϩ ⲛ̀ⲧⲉϥ̀ⲁⲣⲉϩ ⲉ̀ⲛⲁⲓ ⲟⲩⲟϩ ⲛ̀ⲥⲉⲕⲁϯ ⲉ̀ⲛⲓⲛⲁⲓ ⲛ̀ⲧⲉ Ⲡϭⲟⲓⲥ ⲇ Ⲁⲗⲗⲏⲗⲟⲩⲓⲁ̀. Ⲥⲙⲟⲩ ⲉ̀ⲣⲟⲓ ⲇ ⲓⲥ ϯⲙⲉ-ⲧⲁ̀ⲛⲟⲓⲁ̀ ⲭⲱ ⲛⲏⲓ ⲉ̀ⲃⲟⲗ ⲇ ⲛⲁⲓⲟϯ ⲛⲉⲙ ⲛⲁⲥⲛⲏ-ⲟⲩ ϣ̀ⲗⲏⲗ ⲉ̀ϩⲣⲏⲓ ⲉ̀ϫⲱⲓ ⲇ ϧⲉⲛ ⲟⲩⲁ̀ⲅⲁⲡⲏ ϯϯ-ϩⲟ ⲉ̀ⲣⲱⲧⲉⲛ ⲁ̀ⲣⲓⲡⲁⲙⲉⲩⲓ

من هو الحكيم فيحفظ هذه ويتفهم مراحم الرب. الليلويا. باركوا على. ها مطانية اغفروا لى يا آبائى واخوتى صلوا علي. بالمحبة اسالكم اذكرونى.

Glory to the Father and to the Son and to the Holy Spirit, now and ever and unto the ages of ages. Amin Alleluia. Lord have mercy, Lord have mercy, Lord have mercy.

Ⲇⲟⲝⲁ Ⲡⲁⲧⲣⲓ ⲕⲉ Ⲩ̀ⲓⲱ ⲕⲉ ⲁ̀ⲅⲓⲱ ` Ⲡ̀ⲛⲉⲩⲙⲁⲧⲓⲇ ⲕⲉ ⲛⲩⲛ ⲕⲉ ⲁ̀ⲓ ⲕⲉ ⲓⲥⲧⲟⲩⲥ ⲉ̀ⲱⲛⲁⲥ ⲧⲱⲛ ⲉ̀ⲱⲛ-ⲱⲛⲇ ⲁⲙⲏⲛ ⲁⲗ. Ⲕⲉ ⲕ̅ⲉ̅ ⲕⲉ.

المجد للاب والابن والروح القدس الان وكل أوان وإلي دهر الدهور. آمين الليلويا كيرياليسون كيرياليسون كيرياليسون

Agios O Theos   اجيؤس اوثيئوس

Agios O Theos	آجيوس أوثيئوس
Agios Ees-sheros	آجيوس إس شيروس
Agios Athanatos	أجيوس أثاناطوس
Amen Alleluia	آمين الليلويا

Holy God Holy	قدوس الله قدوس
Mighty in His glory	قدوس القوي قدوس
Holy is the Living God	قدوس الحيّ الله
Amen Alleluia	آمين الليلويا

By the help of Mighty God	بمعونة رب قدير
The great Lord of lords	إله عظيم خبير
I'll explain the meaning of	أشرح معنى تفسير
Amen Alleluia	آمين الليلويا

How beautiful is its meaning	معناه ياما أحلاه
There is none but our God	ليس غير الله إله
We praise Him high in His heaven	نسبحه فوق أعلى سماه
Amen Alleluia	آمين الليلويا

Michael and Gabriel	ميخائيل وغبريال
Raphael and Souriel	رافائيل وسوريال
All praising Him saying	يتلون تسابيح وأقوال
Amen Alleluia	آمين الليلويا

141

The heavenly Cherubim	تسبحه الشيروبيم
And the mighty Seraphim	وأيضاً السيرافيم
They also glorify Him	قائلين بصوت عظيم
Amen Alleluia	آمين الليلويا
Heavenly hosts of light	أجناد نورانية
And all the spiritual ranks	وطغمات روحانية
Continuously praise Him	يصيحون علانية
Amen Alleluia	آمين الليلويا
Myriads of myriads	ربوات ربوات وألوف
Ranks around the Throne	من حول العرش صفوف
Proclaiming before the Lord	يقولون وهم وقوف
Amen Alleluia	أمين الليلويا
The four Living Creatures	والأربعة الكائنات
Around the Throne of God	من تحت العرش ثبات
Pleading on our behalf	يتلون كل الأوقات
Amen Alleluia	آمين الليلويا
The first is like a lion	الأول شبه أسد
A figure without a body	صورة من غير جسد
And innumerable eyes	وأعين بلا عدد
Amen Alleluia	آمين الليلويا
The second is like a calf	الثانى شبه الثور
A sign of sacrifice	وهو منظر من نور

Proclaiming unceasingly	يصيح بلا فتور
Amen Alleluia	آمين الليلويا

The third is like an eagle	الثالث شبه عقاب
Soaring in the heavens	يسأل عن الطير بإيجاب
Pleading before the Only-Begotten	أمام وحيد الآب
Amen Alleluia	آمين الليلويا

The fourth has a face of a man	الرابع شبه إنسان
Asking forgiveness on our behalf	يسأل عنا الغفران
Before the Lord our God	أمام الله الديان
Amen Alleluia	آمين الليلويا

A scene encountered with light	منظر بالنور مكسى
They praise God who is seated	يسبحون فى ات هيمسى
High above on His throne	من فوق أعلى الكرسى
Amen Alleluia	آمين الليلويا

Scenes with diversities	منظر بانواع شتى
Seraphim with six wings	سيرافيم باجنحة ستة
Praising continuously	يصيحون بلا سكتة
Amen Alleluia	آمين الليلويا

The Twenty-Four Elders	والأربعة والعشرون
Priests of the high order	قسيس
Chanting in holy reverace	كهنة بمقام نفيس
Amen Alleluia	يصيحون بالتقديس
	آمين الليلويا

The stars and the galaxies	وتسبحه الأفلاك
Praise Him while orbiting	الذين سلكوا الأسلاك
Up high in the heavens	من فوق أعلى السموات
Amen Alleluia	آمين الليلويا
Satanael has become	سطانائيل قد صار
A devil through his pride	شيطانا بالاستكبار
When he ceased to say	لما بطل هذا التذكار
Amen Alleluia	آمين الليلويا
Pitiful is the one who hears it	مسكين من يسمعها
In the midst of the congregation	فى حضرة قائلها
And does not sing with them	ولايتلو معها
Amen Alleluia	آمين الليلويا
Alleluia is praise	الليلويا تسبيح
Hymns and songs	وترتيل ومديح
We cry out saying	بها نصرخ ونصيح
Amen Alleluia	آمين الليلويا
Alleluia is glorification	الليلويا تمجيد
For a mighty Lord	لاله عظيم مجيد
It's a unique and great memorial	وهو تذكار عظيم فريد
Amen Alleluia	آمين الليلويا
Alleluia is pleasure	الليلويا تنزيه
And it gives satisfaction	وقائلها يكفيه

Chant it whole-heartedly	يقول بملء فيه
Amen Alleluia	آمين الليلويا
Alleluia is joy	الليلويا بهجة
And it is a sweet language	وهى أحلى لهجة
It saves from damage	وقائلها ينجى
Amen Alleluia	آمين الليلويا
Alleluia is exaltation	الليلويا تعظيم
For a merciful God	لإله رؤوف رحيم
Who is generous for generations	خفى الألطاف كريم
Amen Alleluia	آمين الليلويا
Alleluia is a memorial	الليلويا تذكار
For the great God of Wonders	لإله عظيم ستار
We praise in great numbers	يجب له التذكار
Amen Alleluia	آمين الليلويا
Alleluia is a hymn	الليلويا ترتيل
A praise and rejoicing	وتسبيح وتهليل
And it is the best chanting	وهى أفضل ما قيل
Amen Alleluia	آمين الليلويا
Blessed is the Creator	سبحانه مكون ماكان
Existent before the ages	كائن قبل الأكوان
Filling all places	ما يخلى منه مكان
Amen Alleluia	آمين الليلويا

Blessed is the Mighty	سبحانه جل ثناه
Unseen and incomprehensible	خفى لاعين تراه
The only One to be worshipped	ولامعبود سواه
Amen Alleluia	آمين الليلويا

He created the waters	سبحانه خلق من الماء
The fire and the earth's ground	ناراً وأرضاً صماء
He made it from nothing	أوجدها من العدماء
Amen Alleluia	آمين الليلويا

Blessed is the zealous Lord	سبحانه رب غيور
Merciful and forgiving	رؤوف رحيم غفور
All deeds He is covering	على كل فعل ستور
Amen Alleluia	آمين الليلويا

Through Alleluia was fulfilled	بالليلويا قد صار
Purity for the righteous	تحقيق بر الأبرار
Let us all say together	قولوا يا ذا الحضار
Amen Alleluia	آمين الليلويا

King David prophesied	داود بها تنبأ
And by it glorified	وبفضلها أنبأ
Words which are divinely inspired	بأقاويل تتلألأ
Amen Alleluia	آمين الليلويا

In the book of the Psalms	فى شرح سفر المزامير
The hundred and fifty one psalms	المائة واحد والخمسين
And at the end of every psalm	مزمور:

146

Amen Alleluia	وفى آخر كل مزمور
	آمين الليلويا
It is prayed at all times	تقرأ سائر الأوقات
To the Creator of the heavens	إلى خالق السموات
And is explained in the canticles	وفى شرح الهوسات
Amen Alleluia	آمين الليلويا
A fraction for the Korban	وقسمة للقربان
Hippe Evshe Neman	هيبى إفكى نيمان
In it the faith is clear	وفيها شرح الإيمان
Amen Alleluia	آمين الليلويا
David the pure proclaimed	مدح داود البار
Praised Mary the Virgin	مريم ست الأبكار
On the ten strings of his harp	على العشرة الأوتار
Amen Alleluia	آمين الليلويا
With the organ and the harp	بالأرغن والقيثار
The cymbals and the strings	والصنوج والأوتار
The timbrel and chorus	والدف مع المزمار
Amen Alleluia	آمين الليلويا
He said, "O daughter of Zion	قال ياإبنة ربك
Your Lord loved and chose you	اختارك وأحبك
Listen and incline your ears"	أصغى وانسى شعبك
Amen Alleluia	آمين الليلويا

For her he also said	وعنها أيضاً قال
"She is the high mountain of God	هى جبل الله العال
Above all other types"	أعلى من كل مثال
Amen Alleluia	آمين الليلويا
He called her Zion	وسماها صهيون
And said she is the chosen one	وقال سوف يكون
From whom God will be human	اله سره مكنون
Amen Alleluia	آمين الليلويا
Again he named her	وسماها بالجملة
The Queen who is	الملكة المشتملة
Embraced by light	بالنور والحلة
Amen Alleluia	آمين الليلويا
He called all the nations	وقال جميع الأمم
To clap hands and praise	تصفق بتراتيل وهمم
Singing hymns and praises	يتلون تسابيح بنغم
Amen Alleluia	آمين الليلويا
He said, "Blessed is the man	وقال طوبى للإنسان
Who is adorned with mercy	المتعطف بالإحسان
For the poor and the down	على البائس والمهان
-trodden":	آمين الليلويا
Amen Alleluia	
"For God will save him	إن الرب ينجيه
And grant him many benefits	ومن الخيرات يعطيه

To satisfy him for many years."
Amen Alleluia

ما يكفيه ويعافيه
آمين الليلويا

Lord, we ask of You
Keep Pope Shenouda the Great
Our Patriarch and grant him
-wisdom:
Amen Alleluia

يارب إليك نسأل
إحفظ البابا (شنوده)
الأمثل بطريركاً واعطه
الاقبال آمين الليلويا

Also keep in safety
The ones who watch over us
Our metropolitans and bishops
Amen Alleluia

يارب طمنا على
الساهرين عنا
مطرانتنا واساقفتنا
آمين الليلويا

And keep O Lord of lords
All the beloved ones
Who are present and absent
Amen Alleluia

واحفظ يارب الأرباب
سائر كل الأحباب
الحضّار والغياب
آمين الليلويا

And also protect the reader
Who said it to the audience
And living it in abundance
Amen Alleluia

وأحفظ قاريها
والشارح لمعانيها
والعامل بما فيها
آمين الليلويا

First Hoos – Πιϩⲱⲥ

Ⲛ̀ϨⲞⲨ̀ⲒⲦ – الهوس الأول

Then Moses and the children of Israel sang this song to the Lord and spoke saying, "I will sing to the Lord for He has triumphed gloriously."	Ⲧⲟⲧⲉ ⲁϥϩⲱⲥ ⲛ̀ⲭⲉ Ⲙⲱⲩ̀ⲥⲏⲥ ⲛⲉⲙ ⲛⲉⲛ-ϣⲏⲣⲓ ⲙ̀Ⲡⲓⲥⲣⲁⲏⲗ ⲉ̀ⲧⲁⲓ ϩⲱⲇⲏ ⲛ̀ⲧⲉ Ⲡϭⲟⲓⲥ ⲟⲩⲟϩ ⲁϥϫⲟⲥ ⲉⲑⲣⲟⲩϫⲟⲥ: ϫⲉ ⲙⲁⲣⲉⲛϩⲱⲥ ⲉ̀Ⲡϭⲟⲓⲥ: ϫⲉ ϧⲉⲛ ⲟⲩⲱ̀ⲟⲩ ⲅⲁⲣ ⲁϥϭ̀ⲓⲱⲟⲩ.	حينئذ سبح موسى وبنو إسرائيل بهذه التسبحة للرب و قالوا. فلنسبح للرب لانه بالمجد قد تمجد.
*The horse and its rider He has thrown into the sea. The Lord is my strength and song and He has become my salvation.	*Ⲟⲩϩⲑⲟ ⲛⲉⲙ ⲟⲩⲃⲁⲥⲓϩⲑⲟ ⲁϥⲃⲉⲣⲃⲱⲣⲟⲩ ⲉ̀ⲫⲓⲟⲙ: ⲟⲩ-ⲃⲟⲏⲑⲟⲥ ⲛⲉⲙ ⲟⲩⲣⲉϥϩⲱⲃⲥ ⲉ̀ⲃⲟⲗ ϩⲓϫⲱⲓ: ⲁϥϣⲱⲡⲓ ⲛⲏⲓ ⲛ̀ⲟⲩⲥⲱⲧⲏⲣⲓⲁ.	*الفرس وراكبه طرحهما فى البحر. معينى وساترى صار لى خلاصاً.

He is my God and I will glorify Him, my father's God and I will exalt Him.	Ⲫⲁⲓ ⲡⲉ Ⲡⲁⲛⲟⲩϯ ϯⲛⲁ-ϯⲱⲟⲩ ⲛⲁϥ: Ⲫϯ ⲙ̀ⲡⲁⲓⲱⲧ ϯⲛⲁϭⲁⲥϥ.	هذا هو إلهى فأمجده. إله أبى فأرفعه.
*The Lord is a Man of war, the Lord is His name. Pharaoh's chariots and his army He has cast into the sea.	*Ⲡϭ︤ⲥ︥ ⲡⲉⲧϧⲟⲙϧⲉⲙ ⲛ̀ⲛⲓ-ⲃⲱⲧⲥ: Ⲡϭ︤ⲥ︥ ⲡⲉ ⲡⲉϥⲣⲁⲛ: ⲛⲓⲃⲉⲣⲉϭⲱⲟⲩⲧⲥ ⲛ̀ⲧⲉ Ⲫⲁⲣ-ⲁⲱ ⲛⲉⲙ ⲧⲉϥϫⲟⲙ ⲧⲏⲣⲥ ⲁϥⲃⲉⲣⲃⲱⲣⲟⲩ ⲉ̀ⲫⲓⲟⲙ.	*الرب مكسر الحروب الرب اسمه. مركبات فرعون وكل قوته طرحهما فى البحر.
His chosen captains also are drowned in the Red Sea.	Ⳅⲁⲛⲥⲱⲧⲡ ⲛ̀ⲁⲛⲁⲃⲁⲧ-ⲏⲥ ⲛ̀ⲧⲣⲓⲥⲧⲁⲧⲏⲥ ⲁϥϫ-ⲟⲗⲕⲟⲩ ϧⲉⲛ ⲫⲓⲟⲙ ⲛ̀ϣⲁⲣⲓ.	ركباناً منتخبين ذى ثلاث جنبات. غرّقهم فى البحر الأحمر.
*The depths have covered them; they sank to the bottom as a stone.	*Ⲁϥϩⲱⲃⲥ ⲉ̀ϧⲣⲏⲓ ⲉϫ-ⲱⲟⲩ ⲛ̀ϫⲉ ⲡⲓⲙⲱⲟⲩ : ⲁⲩⲱⲙⲥ ⲉ̀ϧⲣⲏⲓ ⲉⲡⲉⲧϣⲏⲕ ⲙ̀ⲫⲣⲏϯ ⲛⲟⲩⲱⲛⲓ.	*غطاهم الماء. انغمسوا إلى العمق مثل الحجر.
Your right hand, O Lord, has become glorious in power.	Ⲧⲉⲕⲟⲩⲓⲛⲁⲙ Ⲡϭ︤ⲥ︥ ⲁⲥϭ-ⲓⲱⲟⲩ ϧⲉⲛ ⲟⲩϫⲟⲙ: ⲧⲉⲕ-	يمينك يا رب تمجدت بالقوة. يدك اليمنى يا

Your right hand, O Lord, has dashed the enemy in pieces.	ϫⲓϫ ⲛ̀ⲟⲩⲓⲛⲁⲙ Ⲡⲁⲛⲟⲩϯ ⲁⲥⲧⲁⲕⲉ ⲛⲉⲕϫⲁϫⲓ.	إلهي أهلكت أعداءك.
*And in the greatness of Your excellence, You have overthrown those who rose up against You. You sent forth Your wrath, it consumed them like stubble.	*Ϧⲉⲛ ⲡ̀ⲁϣⲁⲓ ⲛ̀ⲧⲉ ⲡⲉⲕⲱⲟⲩ ⲁⲕϭⲟⲙϭⲉⲙ ⲛ̀ⲛⲏⲉⲧϯⲟⲩⲃⲏⲛ: ⲁⲕⲟⲩⲱⲣⲡ ⲙ̀ⲡⲉⲕϫⲱⲛⲧ ⲁϥⲟⲩⲟⲙⲟⲩ ⲙ̀ⲫ̀ⲣⲏϯ ⲛ̀ⲉ̀ⲁⲛⲣ ⲱⲟⲩⲓ.	*بكثرة مجدك سحقت الذين يقاوموننا. ارسلت غضبك فأكلهم مثل الهشيم.
And with the blast of Your nostrils the waters were gathered together, the flood stood upright like a wall, and the depths were congealed in the heart of the sea.	Ⲉ̀ⲃⲟⲗϩⲓⲧⲉⲛ ⲡⲓⲡ̀ⲛⲉⲩⲙⲁ ⲛ̀ⲧⲉ ⲡⲉⲕⲙ̀ⲃⲟⲛ ⲁϥⲟ̀ϩⲓ `ⲉ̀ⲣⲁⲧϥ ⲛ̀ϫⲉ ⲡⲓⲙⲱⲟⲩ: ⲁⲩϭⲓⲥⲓ ⲛ̀ϫⲉ ⲛⲓⲙⲱⲟⲩ ⲙ̀ⲫ̀ⲣⲏϯ ⲛ̀ⲟⲩⲥⲟⲃⲧ: ⲁⲩϭⲱⲥ ⲛ̀ϫⲉ ⲛⲓϫⲟⲗ ϧⲉⲛ ⲑ̀ⲙⲏϯ ⲙ̀ⲫⲓⲟⲙ.	وبروح غضبك وقف الماء و ارتفعت المياه مثل السور. و جمدت الأمواج في وسط البحر.

*The enemy said, "I will pursue, I will overtake, I will divide the spoil, my lust shall be satisfied upon them, I will draw my sword, and my hand shall destroy them."	*Ⲁϥϫⲟⲥ ⲅⲁⲣ ⲛ̀ϫⲉ ⲡⲓϫⲁϫⲓ: ϫⲉ ϯⲛⲁϭⲟϫⲓ ⲛ̀ⲧⲁⲧⲁϩⲟ: ⲛ̀ⲧⲁϥⲱϣ ⲛ̀ϩⲁⲛϣⲱⲗ: ⲛ̀ⲧⲁⲧ̀ⲥⲓⲟ ⲛ̀ⲧⲁⲯⲩⲭⲏ: ⲛ̀ⲧⲁϧⲱⲧⲉⲃ ϧⲉⲛ ⲧⲁⲥⲏϥⲓ: ⲛ̀ⲧⲉ ⲧⲁϫⲓϫ ⲉⲣϭⲟⲓⲥ.	*قال العدو اسرع وادرك واقسم كل الغنائم واشبع نفسى وسيفى ويدى تملك دائم.
You blew with Your wind, the sea covered them, they sank like lead in the mighty waters.	Ⲁⲕⲟⲩⲱⲣⲡ ⲙ̀ⲡⲉⲕⲡ̀ⲛⲉⲩⲙⲁ ⲁϥϩⲟⲃⲥⲟⲩ ⲛ̀ϫⲉ ⲫ̀ⲓⲟⲙ: ⲁⲩⲱⲙⲥ ⲉ̀ⲡⲉⲥⲏⲧ ⲙ̀ⲫ̀ⲣⲏϯ ⲛ̀ⲟⲩⲧⲁⲧϩ ϧⲉⲛ ϩⲁⲛⲙⲱⲟⲩ ⲉⲧⲟϣ.	ارسلت روحك فغطاهم البحر. وغطسوا إلى أسفل كالرصاص فى مياه كثيرة.
*Who is like You, O Lord, among the gods? Who is like You, glorified in his saints, amazing in glory, performing wonders?	*Ⲛⲓⲙ ⲉⲧⲟ̀ⲛⲓ ⲙ̀ⲙⲟⲕ ϧⲉⲛ ⲛⲓⲛⲟⲩϯ Ⲡ̀ϭⲟⲓⲥ: ⲛⲓⲙ ⲉⲧⲟ̀ⲛⲓ ⲙ̀ⲙⲟⲕ: ⲉⲁⲩϯⲱⲟⲩ ⲛⲁⲕ ϧⲉⲛ ⲛⲏⲉⲑⲟⲩⲁⲃ ⲛ̀ⲧⲁⲕ: ⲉⲩⲉⲣ̀ϣ̀ⲫⲏⲣⲓ ⲙ̀ⲙⲟⲕ ϧⲉⲛ ⲟⲩⲱⲟⲩ : ⲉⲕⲓⲣⲓ ⲛ̀ϩⲁⲛϣⲫⲏⲣⲓ.	*من يشبهك فى الآلهة يارب من يشبهك. ممجداً فى قديسيك متعجباً منك بالمجد صانعاً عجائب.

You stretched out Your right hand, the earth swallowed them. You, in Your mercy, have led forth the people whom You have redeemed. You have guided them, in Your strength, to Your holy habitation.	Ⲁⲕⲥⲟⲩⲧⲉⲛ ⲧⲉⲕⲟⲩⲓⲛⲁⲙ ⲉⲃⲟⲗ ⲁϥⲟⲙⲕⲟⲩ ⲛϫⲉ ⲡ̅-ⲕⲁϩⲓ꞉ ⲁⲕϭⲓⲙⲱⲓⲧ ϧⲁϫⲱϥ ⲙⲡⲉⲕⲗⲁⲟⲥ ϧⲉⲛ ⲟⲩⲙⲉⲑ-ⲙⲏ꞉ ⲫⲁⲓ ⲉⲧⲁⲕⲥⲟⲧⲡϥ ꞉ ⲁⲕϯϫⲟⲙ ⲛⲁϥ ϧⲉⲛ ⲧⲉⲕⲛⲟⲙϯ ⲉⲩⲙⲁ ⲛⲉⲙⲧⲟⲛ ⲉϥⲟⲩⲁⲃ ⲛⲁⲕ.	مددت يمينك فابتلعتهم الأرض هديت شعبك بالحقيقة. هذا الذى اخترته وقويته بتعزيتك إلى موضع راحة قدسك.
*The people will hear and be afraid, sorrow will take hold of the inhabitants of Palestine.	*Ⲁⲩⲥⲱⲧⲉⲙ ⲛϫⲉ ϩⲁⲛ-ⲉⲑⲛⲟⲥ ⲟⲩⲟϩ ⲁϥϫⲱⲛⲧ꞉ ϩⲁⲛⲛⲁⲕϩⲓ ⲁⲩϭⲓ ⲛⲛⲏ-ⲧⲱⲟⲡ ϧⲉⲛ Ⲛⲓⲫⲩⲗⲓⲥⲧⲓⲙ.	*الامم سمعوا وغضبوا واخذهم طلق عظيم وأهل فلسطين هربوا وشملهم حزن عظيم.
Then the dukes of Edom will be amazed, the mighty men of Moab, trembling will take hold of them.	Ⲧⲟⲧⲉ ⲁⲩⲏⲥ ⲙⲙⲱⲟⲩ ⲛϫⲉ ⲛⲓϩⲏⲅⲉⲙⲱⲛ ⲛⲧⲉ Ⲉⲇⲟⲙ꞉ ⲛⲓⲁⲣⲭⲱⲛ ⲛⲧⲉ Ⲛⲓⲙⲱⲁⲃ-ⲓⲧⲏⲥ ⲟⲩⲥⲑⲉⲣⲧⲉⲣ ⲡⲉ ⲉⲧⲁ-ϥϭⲓⲧⲟⲩ.	حينئذ أسرع ولاة أدوم. ورؤساء المؤابين أخذتهم الرعدة.

*All the inhabitants of Canaan will melt away, fear and dread will fall on them.	*Ⲁⲩⲃⲱⲗ ⲉ̀ⲃⲟⲗ ⲛ̀ϫⲉ ⲟⲩⲟⲛ ⲛⲓⲃⲉⲛ ⲉⲧϣⲟⲡ ϧⲉⲛ Ⲭⲁⲛⲁⲁⲛ: ⲁϥⲓ̀ ⲉ̀ϩ̀ⲣⲏⲓ ⲉ̀ϫⲱⲟⲩ ⲛ̀ϫⲉ ⲟⲩⲥ̀ⲑⲉⲣⲧⲉⲣ ⲛⲉⲙ ⲟⲩϩⲟ†.	*ذاب كل سكان كنعان. وأتت عليهم الرعدة والخوف.
By the greatness of Your arm, they will be as still as a stone, till Your people pass over, O Lord, till Your people pass over whom You have purchased.	ϧⲉⲛ ⲡ̀ⲁ̀ϣⲁⲓ ⲛ̀ⲧⲉ ⲡⲉⲕⲭ̀ϥⲟⲓ ⲙⲁⲣⲟⲩⲉⲣⲱⲛⲓ : ϣⲁⲧⲉϥⲥⲓⲛⲓ ⲛ̀ϫⲉ ⲡⲉⲕⲗⲁⲟⲥ Ⲡ̀ϭⲟⲓⲥ ϣⲁⲧⲉϥⲥⲓⲛⲓ ⲛ̀ϫⲉ ⲡⲉⲕⲗⲁⲟⲥ ⲫⲁⲓ ⲉ̀ⲧⲁⲕⲭ̀ⲫⲟϥ.	بكثرة ساعدك فليصيروا كالحجر. حتى يجتاز شعبك يارب حتى يجتاز شعبك هذا الذى اقتنيته.
*You will bring them in, and plant them in the mountain of Your inheritance, in the place, O Lord, which You have made for You to dwell in.	*Ⲁⲛⲓⲧⲟⲩ ⲉ̀ϧⲟⲩⲛ ⲧⲟϫⲟⲩ ϩⲓϫⲉⲛ ⲟⲩⲧⲱⲟⲩ ⲛ̀ⲧⲉ ⲧⲉⲕⲕ̀ⲗⲏⲣⲟⲛⲟⲙⲓⲁ̀: ⲛⲉⲙ ⲉ̀ϧⲟⲩⲛ ⲉ̀ⲡⲉⲕⲙⲁⲛϣⲱⲡⲓ ⲉⲧⲥⲉⲃⲧⲱⲧ: ⲫⲁⲓ ⲉⲧⲁⲕⲉⲣϩⲱⲃ ⲉ̀ⲣⲟϥ Ⲡ̀ϭⲟⲓⲥ.	*ادخلهم و اغرسهم على جبل ميراثك. وفى مسكنك المعد هذا الذى صنعته يارب.

In Your sanctuary, O Lord, which Your hands have established, the Lord shall reign forever and ever.	Πεκμα εθοναβ Πδοιс φηεταντсεβτωτϥ ̀νхε νεκхιх : Πδοιс εκοι ̀νονρο ϣα ̀ενεϩ νεμ ιс-хεν ̀πενεϩ ονοϩ ετι.	موضعك المقدس يارب الذى أعددته يداك. يارب تملك منذ الازل والآن وإلى الابد.
*For the horses of Pharaoh went with his chariots and his horsemen into the sea.	*Хε αϥі ̀εϧονν ̀εφ-ιομ ̀νхε νιϩθωρ ̀ντε Φαραὼ νεμ νεϥβε-ρεδωνтс νεμ νεϥδα-сιϩθο.	*لانه قد دخل إلى البحر خيل فرعون ومركباته وفرسانه.
And the Lord brought back the waters of the sea on them, but the children of Israel went on dry land in the midst of the sea.	Ⲁ̀Πδοιс εν πιμωον ̀ντε φιομ ὲϩρηι ὲхωον: νενϣηρι δε ̀μΠιсрαηλ ναντμοϣι δεν πετϣο-ρϣον δεν ̀θμηϯ ̀μφιομ.	والرب غمرهم بماء البحر. أما بنو اسرائيل فكانوا يمشون على اليابسة فى وسط البحر .
*And Miriam the prophetess, the sis-	*Ⲁсδі δε νας ̀νхε Ⲙαριαμ ϯπροφητ-	*فاخذت مريم النبيه اخت

ter of Aaron, took a timbrel in her hand, and all the women went out after her with timbrels and with praises.	нс ⲧⲥⲱⲛⲓ ⲛ̀Ⲁ̀ⲣⲱⲛ ⲙ̀ⲡⲓ ⲕⲉⲙⲕⲉⲙ ϧⲉⲛ ⲛⲉⲥϫⲓϫ: ⲟⲩⲟϩ ⲁⲩⲓ ⲉ̀ⲃⲟⲗ ⲥⲁⲙⲉⲛ- ⲥⲏⲥ ⲛ̀ϫⲉ ⲛⲓϩⲓⲟⲙⲓ ⲧⲏⲣⲟⲩ ϧⲉⲛ ϩⲁⲛⲕⲉⲙⲕⲉⲙ ⲛⲉⲙ ϩⲁⲛϩⲱⲥ.	هرون الدف بيديها. وخرج فى إثرها جميع النسوة بالدفوف والتسابيح.
And Miriam answered them saying, " Sing to the Lord for He has triumphed gloriously".	Ⲁⲥⲉⲣϩⲏⲧⲥ ⲇⲉ ϧⲁⲝ- ⲱⲟⲩ ⲛ̀ϫⲉ Ⲙⲁⲣⲓⲁⲙ ⲉⲥ- ϫⲱ ⲙ̀ⲙⲟⲥ: ϫⲉ ⲙⲁⲣ- ⲉⲛϩⲱⲥ ⲉ̀Ⲡϭⲟⲓⲥ: ϫⲉ ϧⲉⲛ ⲟⲩⲱⲟⲩ ⲅⲁⲣ ⲁϥϭⲓ̀ⲱⲟⲩ.	وبدأت مريم فى مقدمتهن تقول. فلنسبح الرب لانه بالمجد قد تمجد.
*The horse and its rider, He has thrown into the sea, "Let us sing to the Lord for He has triumphed gloriously."	*Ⲟⲩϩⲑⲟ ⲛⲉⲙ ⲟⲩϭⲁⲥⲓ- ϩⲑⲟ ⲁϥⲃⲉⲣⲃⲱⲣⲟⲩ ⲉ̀ⲫ- ⲓⲟⲙ: ϫⲉ ⲙⲁⲣⲉⲛϩⲱⲥ ⲉ̀Ⲡ- ϭⲟⲓⲥ: ϫⲉ ϧⲉⲛ ⲟⲩⲱⲟⲩ ⲅⲁⲣ ⲁϥϭⲓ̀ⲱⲟⲩ.	*الفرس وراكب الفرس طرحهما فى البحر. فلنسبح الرب لانه بالمجد قد تمجد

(Psali Adam)	(Ⲯⲁⲗⲓ Ⲁⲇⲁⲙ)	(مديح آدام)
With the split the waters of the sea split, and the very deep became a walkway.	Ϧⲉⲛ ⲟⲩϣⲱⲧ ⲁϥϣⲱⲧ: ⲛ̀ϫⲉ ⲡⲓⲙⲱⲟⲩ ⲛ̀ⲧⲉ ⲫⲓⲟⲙ : ⲟⲩⲟ̅ϩ̅ ⲫⲛⲟⲩⲛ ⲉⲧϣⲏⲕ : ⲁϥϣⲱⲡⲓ ⲛ̀ⲟⲩⲙⲁⲙ̀ⲙⲟϣⲓ.	قطعاً إنقطع ماء البحر. والعمق العميق صار مسلكاً.
*A hidden earth, was shone upon by the sun, and an untrodden road was walked upon.	*Ⲟⲩⲕⲁϩⲓ ⲛ̀ⲁⲑⲟⲩⲱⲛϩ : ⲁ ⲫⲣⲏ ϣⲁⲓ ϩⲓϫⲱϥ : ⲟⲩⲙⲱⲓⲧ ⲛ̀ⲁⲧⲥⲓⲛⲓ : ⲁⲩⲙⲟϣⲓ ϩⲓⲱⲧϥ.	*أرض غير ظاهرة أشرقت الشمس عليها. وطريق غير مسلوكه مشوا عليها.
The flowing water, stood still, by a miraculous, act of wonder.	Ⲟⲩⲙⲱⲟⲩ ⲉϥⲃⲏⲗ ⲉ̀ⲃⲟⲗ : ⲁϥⲟ̅ϩ̅ⲓ ⲉ̀ⲣⲁⲧϥ : ϧⲉⲛ ⲟⲩϩⲱⲃ ⲛ̀ϣ̀ⲫⲏⲣⲓ : ⲙ̀ⲡⲁⲣⲁⲇⲟⲍⲟⲛ.	ماء منحل وقف بفعل عجيب معجز.
*Pharaoh and his	*Ⲫⲁⲣⲁⲱ̀ ⲛⲉⲙ ⲛⲉϥϩⲁ-	*غرق فرعون

chariots, were drowned, and the children of Israel, crossed the sea.	ⲣⲙⲁ : ⲁⲩⲱⲙⲥ ⲉⲡⲉⲥⲏⲧ: ⲛⲉⲛϣⲏⲣⲓ ⲙⲡⲓⲥⲣⲁⲏⲗ : ⲁⲩⲉⲣⲭⲓⲛⲓⲟⲣ ⲙⲫⲓⲟⲙ.	ومركباته وعبر بنو اسرئيل البحر.
And in front of them was Moses the prophet praising, until he brought them, to the wilderness of Sinai.	Ⲉⲛⲁⲩϩⲱⲥ ϧⲁϫⲱⲟⲩ ⲡⲉ : ⲛ̀ϫⲉ Ⲙⲱ̀ⲩⲥⲏⲥ ⲡⲓⲡ̀ⲣⲟⲫⲏⲧⲏⲥ : ϣⲁⲛⲧⲉϥϭⲓⲧⲟⲩ ⲉ̀ϧⲟⲩⲛ : ϩⲓ ⲡ̀ϣⲁϥⲉ ⲛ̀Ⲥⲓⲛⲁ.	وكان موسى النبى يسبح قدامهم حتى ادخلهم برية سيناء.
*And they were praising God, with this new psalmody, saying "Let us sing to the Lord, for He has triumphed gloriously."	*Ⲉⲛⲁⲩϩⲱⲥ ⲉ̀Ⲫ̀ϯ : ϧⲉⲛ ⲧⲁⲓϩⲱⲇⲉ ⲙ̀ⲃⲉⲣⲓ : ϫⲉ ⲙⲁⲣⲉⲛϩⲱⲥ ⲉ̀Ⲡϭⲟⲓⲥ : ϫⲉ ϧⲉⲛ ⲟⲩⲱ̀ⲟⲩ ⲅⲁⲣ ⲁϥϭ̀ⲓⲱⲟⲩ.	*وكانوا يسبحون الله بهذه التسبحة الجديدة فلنسبح الرب لانه بالمجد قد تمجد.
Through the prayers of Moses the Archprophet, O Lord grant us the forgiveness of our	Ϩⲓⲧⲉⲛ ⲛⲓⲉⲩⲭⲏ ⲛ̀ⲧⲉ Ⲙⲱ̀ⲩⲥⲏⲥ ⲡⲓⲁⲣⲭⲏⲡⲣⲟⲫⲏⲧⲏⲥ: Ⲡϭⲟⲓⲥ ⲁⲣⲓ̀ϩ̀ⲙⲟⲧ ⲛⲁⲛ : ⲙ̀ⲡⲓⲭⲱ ⲉ̀	بصلوات موسى رئيس الأنبياء يارب أنعم لنا بمغفرة خطايانا.

sins.	Ⲃⲟⲗ ⲛ̀ⲧⲉ ⲛⲉⲛⲛⲟⲃⲓ	
*Through the inter-cessions, of the Mother of God Saint Mary, O Lord grant us, the forgiveness of our sins.	*Ϩⲓⲧⲉⲛ ⲛⲓⲡⲣⲉⲥⲃⲓⲁ̀ ⲛ̀ⲧⲉ ϯⲑⲉⲟ̀ⲧⲟⲕⲟⲥ ⲉ̀ⲑⲟⲩⲁⲃ Ⲙⲁⲣⲓⲁ̀ · Ⲡ̀ϭⲟⲓⲥ ⲁⲣⲓϩ̀-ⲙⲟⲧ ⲛⲁⲛ ⲙ̀ⲡⲓⲭⲱ ⲉ̀-ⲃⲟⲗ ⲛ̀ⲧⲉ ⲛⲉⲛⲛⲟⲃⲓ.	*بشفـاعات والدة الاله القديسة مريم يارب انعم لنا بمغفرة خطايانا.
We worship You, O Christ, with Your Good Father and the Holy Spirit, for You have come and saved us.	Ⲧⲉⲛⲟⲩⲱϣⲧ ⲙ̀ⲙⲟⲕ ⲱ̀-Ⲡⲓⲭ̀ⲣⲓⲥⲧⲟⲥ· ⲛⲉⲙ Ⲡⲉⲕ-ⲓⲱⲧ ⲛ̀ⲁ̀ⲅⲁⲑⲟⲥ· ⲛⲉⲙ Ⲡⲓⲡ̀ⲛⲉⲩⲙⲁ ⲉ̀ⲑⲟⲩⲁⲃ · ϫⲉ ⲁⲕⲓ̀ⲁⲕⲥⲱϯ ⲙ̀ⲙⲟⲛ.	نسجد لك أيها المسيح مع أبيك الصالح والروح القدس لانك أتيت وخلصتنا.

Hymn After the 1st Hoos

مديح يقال بعد لبش الهوس الأول

The Lord said to Moses,	قال الرب لموسى
Tell your people to depart	قل لشعبك هو يرحل
Lift up your rod over the sea	اضرب البحر بالعصا
And they shall find an entrance	ينفتح لك فيه مدخل.
So Moses rose at night	فقام موسي بالليل
Hit the sea with the rod	وضرب البحر بسرعة
And Israel went on dry ground	فانفتح فيه درب طويل
Through the midst of the sea	وطريق متسعة.
The sea was divided in half	فانشق البحر نصفين
And they departed together	وعبروا جملة سوية
And they walked on ground	وصاروا فيه ماشيين
At the bottom of the sea	علي الأرض السفلية.
The pillar of fire was a guide	وعامود النور دليل
Throughout the way	للطريق يدل بهم
Before the children of Israel	من قدام آل اسرائيل
To illuminate their path	وبنوره شاملهم.

161

They walked on ground and -rocks :	داسوا علي الباج والصخور
In the midst of the sea	في وسط قاع البحر
And the waters were a high wall	والمياه كمثل السور
On their right hand and their left	العالى يمين ويسار.

Pharaoh dared to enter	دخل فرعون وتجاسر
With his horses after them	بخيوله في أثرهم
His chariots and horsemen	ومعه كل عساكر
Were chasing them	بعبيده قاطرهم.

The pillar of cloud went before -them.	فأتاهم عامود الغمام
And separated the two camps	وحجز بين الصفين
And Pharaoh was in darkness	فبقي فرعون في ظلام
And his servants could not see	وعبيده مطموسين.

The Egyptians said	قال المصريون
Let us flee from them	نحن نهرب منهم
Before the children of Israel	من قدام آل إسرائيل
For the Lord fights for them	الرب يحارب عنهم.

The Lord said to Moses	قال الرب لموسى
Stretch your hand over the sea	اضرب البحر رده
That the waters may come again	فضرب البحر بالعصا
Upon the Egyptians	رجع الماء إلي أصله.

The chariots of Pharaoh	فانقلبت بكرات فرعون
Drowned in the midst of the sea	وغطسوا في وسط المياه
And his servants died	وعبيده ينطمسون
And the darkness blocked their	وعمتهم الظلمة.
-sight	

A vicious storm began	فثار عاصف بعجاجه
In the midst of the high sea	في وسط البحر هاجه
The waves and tides relapsed	وانطبقت أمواجه
And the waters returned and	ورجع الماء إلى باجه.
-closed	

Pharaoh surely drowned	غطس فرعون وغاص
Along with all his horsemen	وعساكره الكل معاه
None remained of them	وصاروا الجميع كالرصاص
They settled at the bottom of the	ورسخوا في قاع المياه.
-sea.	

The sun shined at that time	أشرقت الشمس تلك الساعة
When this monster drowned	حين غرق ذاك الجبار
And Israel was courageous	واسرائيل صار في شجاعة
They crossed the sea and walked	عبر البحر وسار.

Joyfully they crossed the sea	جازوا البحر بسرور
Walking on ground and rocks	ماشيين علي الباج
They almost flew like eagles	والصخور:
And descended on the mountain.	وطاروا مثل النسور

163

ونزلوا علي أعلى الطور.

Then Moses praised the Lord
Along with the children of Israel
With all the ranks and chiefs
Singing a joyful song.

حينئذ سبح موسى
وجماعة اسرائيل
ومعه كل الرؤساء
بالتسابيح والتهليل.

Moses and the Israelites
Spoke in one tongue saying
Let us sing to the Lord
For He has triumphed gloriously.

وكان موسى والشعب
يقولون بفم واحد
تعالوا نسبح الرب
لأنه بالمجد تمجد.

The horsemen and the chariots
Were thrown in the Red Sea
And Israel was saved
From shame and humiliation.

الخيل وركاب الخيل
طرحهم في البحر الأحمر
وخلص اسرائيل
من الذلة والعار.

This is the Lord my God
I glorify His Great Name
This is the Lord my God
Maker of all great things.

هذا هو إلهى
أمجد اسمه دائم
هذا هو إله آبائى
صانع كل عظائم.

He abolished the army by His
-might:
The Lord God is honored

حطم الجيش بجبروته
الرب اسمه مكرم
فرعون وقواته

Pharaoh and his horsemen Drowned in the sea.	آف فير فورو إفيوم.
The best of his horsemen Drowned in the midst of the sea And all his warriors At the bottom of the sea settled.	خيار فرسانه الثلاثية في وسط البحر غطست وعساكره الحربية في قاع المياه رسخت.
The waters covered them And they were taken to the -depths Like cast stones And the waters shut them in and -closed.	وغطتهم المياه وغطسوا في الأعماق مثل حجر ورماه والبحر عليهم ضاق.
Your mighty right hand, O Lord Is glorified by Its actions Your Mighty Right Hand, O Lord Destroyed all its enemies.	يمينك ياربى تمجدت بقواها يمينك يا إلهى هلكت كل أعداها.
O God in Your great glory You destroyed the evil enemy You sent forth Your wrath It consumed them like stubble.	ياربى بكثرة مجدك سحقت العدو الاثيم وارسلت روح غضبك فأكلهم مثل الهشيم.
You sent forth Your wrath	من قبل روح غضبك

And the water stood upright like -a wall:	وقف الماء كسور ملموم
The waves ceased and froze In the heart of the sea.	وصمت الموج وحبك خين اثميتى امفيوم.
The enemy said I will pursue, I will -overtake:	قال العدو اسرع وادرك
I will divide the spoil	واقسم كل غنائم
My lust shall be satisfied, I will draw -my sword	واشبع نفسى وسيفى
My hand shall destroy them.	ويدى تملك دائم.
You sent forth Your wind	ارسلت روحك غطسوا
And they drowned	فى بحر مالوش قرار
And settled at the bottom of the -sea	فى اسفل قاعه رسخوا
Like lead in water.	كالرصاص فى مياه غزار.
Who is like You O God	من يشبهك في الآلهة
Among the other gods	ياربي من مثلك
You are glorified in Your saints	ممجد في قديسيك
Who marvel at You.	يتعجبون منك.
You have stretched Your hands	بسطت يدك
And the sea swallowed them	والأرض ابتلعتهم
You led Your people by Your -justice	وبالعدل هديت شعبك
To the place of rest.	إلى موضع راحتهم.

The nations heard and were
-angered
 And became infuriated
And the Philistines fled away
And sorrow took hold of them.

الامم سمعوا وغضبوا
واخذهم طلق عظيم
وأهل فلسطين هربوا
وشملهم حزن جسيم.

Then the Chiefs of Edom
Were troubled and confused
All the mighty men trembled
When they heard the news.

فانصرعت رؤساء أدوم
وقلق موأب واحتار
وفزعت كل التخوم
لما سمعوا الاخبار.

The inhabitants of Canaan were
-scattered
 And were trembling with fear
Fear and sadness overtook them
And they could not move.

انحلت سكان كنعان
والرعدة اخذتهم
ولحقهم خوف واحزان
وبطلت حركتهم.

By the greatness of Your arm
They will be as still as stone
Until your people pass over
Whom You have purchased.

بقوة ذراعيك
يصيروا كالاحجار
حتى يجوز شعبك
يجوز شعبك المختار.

You will bring them in and plant
-them:
 In the mountain of Your
-inferitance:

ادخلهم جبل ميراثك
واغرسهم فى ذاك الدار
فى مسكنك ومحلك

In the place O Lord Which You made for the -rightuous.	الذى اعددته للاطهار.
To You only is the Kingdom And power and the glory Pharaoh stood against You With his soldiers and horses.	الملك لك وحدك والعظمه والسلطان دخل فرعون ضدك بالعسكر والفرسان.
They entered into he sea And all of them walked in the -middle of it With their chariots and soldiers They entered into the sea.	لأنهم دخلوا فى البحر ومشوا الكل فى وسطه بمراكب وعساكر نيم نيف اتشاس اهثو.
Our Lord ordered the sea to -cover Pharoaoh's army with all its -horses While Israel walked on dry land In the midst of the sea.	الرب جاء بالماء وكبس على الخيول وكل القوم واسرائيل مشى على اليابس: خين اثميتى امفيوم.
Miriam Aaron's sister Took a timbrel in her hand And all the women went out after -her With timbrels and dances.	أخذت مريم أخت هارون الدف بايديها والنسوة معها يغنون بطبولهن حواليها.

Miriam the prophetess	فبدأت مريم النبية
Sang before them all	تغني قدام وتقول
And the women along with her	والنسوة معها سوية
Playing the timbrels and cymbals.	يدقوا صنوج و طبول.

Singing a joyful song	يغنون بغناء يطرب
Saying in one voice	ويقولون بفم واحد
"Let us praise the Lord	تعالوا نسبح الرب
For He triumphed gloriously"	لأنه بالمجد تمجد.

The chariots and the horsemen	الخيل وركاب الخيل
Were drowned in the Red Sea	طرحهم في البحر الأحمر
What a great joy for Israel	يافرحة اسرائيل
For their salvation from the	بخلاصه من الكفار.
-Egyptians.	

The waters of the sea split	بالقطع انقطع ماء البحر
And the very deep became a	والأعماق صارت مسلك
-walkway	وموسى فيها خطر
And Moses passed through it	والعدو سقط في مهلك.
While the enemy was destroyed.	

A hidden earth	أرض غير منظورة
Was shone upon by the sun	أشرقت الشمس عليها
And an untrodden road	وطريق مستورة
Was walked upon.	

اف موشي هي أوتف.

The liquid water stood
Before Moses and Aaron
In a spectacular way
Miraculously.

الماء المحلول وقف
قدام موسى وهارون
بعجب لا يوصف
أووه أمباراذوكسون.

Pharaoh and his horsemen
Drowned in the bottom of the sea
And the children of Israel
Crossed through the Red Sea.

فرعون ومراكبه غطسوا
أسفل في القاع في اليم
وبنوا اسرائيل عبروا
ناف جين يور ام فيوم.

And Moses praised before them
Till they reached the harbor
In peace and happiness
In the wilderness of Sinai.

وكان موسى يسبح قدام
وطلعوا من المينا
إلي حين وصلوا بسلام
هي ابشا في انسينا.

Praise Before Monday Theotokia
مديح على ثيؤطوكية يوم الأثنين

Be strengthened in faith	تقوَ بالإيمان
O you who believe in Christ	يا من تؤمن بايسوس
And praise the joy of the world	وامدح بهجة الأكوان
Maria- Ti Parthenos	ماريا تى بارثينوس
Begin by signing yourself	بادر وارشم ذاتك
With the sign of the Cross	بعلامة بى استافروس
And praise at all times	وامدح كل أوقاتك
Maria- Ti Parthenos	ماريا تى بارثينوس
Repent from doing evil	تب عن فعل الزلات
And obey the Laws	وتمسك بالناموس
And praise at all times	وأمدح كل الأوقات
Maria- Ti Parthenos	ماريا تى بارثينوس
Gabriel who was sent came	جبرائيل أتي مرسول
From the Holy Father	من عند الآب القدوس
He announced to the Virgin	بشر عذراء وبتول
Maria- Ti Parthenos	ماريا تى بارثينوس

171

When he told her she accepted	حين بشرها قبلت
The tidings of the angel	بشارة بي أنجيلوس
And with the Spirit of God she conceived	وبروح الله حملت
Maria-Ti Parthenos.	ماريا تى بارثينوس

The salvation of the human race	خلاص البشرية
And of the entire world	وسائر بي كوسموس
From the pure Virgin	من بكر نقية
Maria- Ti Parthenos	ماريا تى بارثينوس

They called you many names	دعوكِ ذو الألباب
You are called righteous	سيموتى إيروذيكيئوس
O you the holy saint	اوثي إثؤاب
Maria- Ti Parthenos	ماريا تى بارثينوس

The Lord of Glory chose you	رب المجد اختارك
According to the Psalmist	كاتا إبساجي إم بي
With His Holy Spirit adorned you	هيمنودوس
Maria-Ti Parthenos	وبروح قدسه زانك
	ماريا تى بارثينوس

The Divine Light adorned you	زانك نور اللاهوت
With the dwelling of my Lord	بحلول باشويس إيسوس

Jesus The One from the Trinity	الواحد من الثالوث
Maria-Ti Parthenos	ماريا تى بارثينوس
They called you the censer	سموك تي شوري
Made of pure gold	إننوب انكاثاروس
And a famous tabernacle	وقبة مشهورة
Maria-Ti Parthenos	ماريا تى بارثينوس
You bore the Son of Righteousness	شمس البر حملتِ
In your womb O Virgin and bride	في أحشاكِ يابكر عروس
Who received what you received	من نال شبه ما نلتِ
Maria-Ti Parthenos	ماريا تى بارثينوس
Zephaniah proclaimed	صوفونيوس خبر
About the birth of Christ	عن ميلاد بي إخرستوس
That He will descend as dew and	انه ينزل كندي ومطر
-rain	ماريا تى بارثينوس
Maria-Ti Parthenos	
The Pantocrator	ضابط كل الأكوان
The Life-giver of all people	ومحيي كل النفوس
You gave birth to the Son of Man	حملتِه شبه انسان
Maria-Ti Parthenos	ماريا تى بارثينوس

Blessed are you O Mother of God	طوباك يا أم المعبود
Blessed are you O Mother of The -Holy	طوباك ياأم القدوس
You are of the seed of David	يانسل الأب داود
Maria- Ti Parthenos	ماريا تى بارثينوس

From you the Divine appeared	ظهر منك اللاهوت
Christ the King of glory	ملك المجد بى اخريستوس
United with humanity	متحدا بالناسوت
Maria- Ti Parthenos	ماريا تى بارثينوس

On you we have hoped	عليك توكلنا ونسألك يا أم
And we ask you O Mother of -Jesus	ايسوس لا تتخلى عنا
Do not forsake us	ماريا تى بارثينوس
Maria- Ti Parthenos	

Your praise is precious and -pleasant	غلى مدحك وحلي
Above the whole world	عن سائر بي كسموس
Your honor increased greatly	وقدرك زاد وعلي
Maria- Ti Parthenos	ماريا تى بارثينوس

You are exceedingly higher	فقت الآباء والأبرار

Than the righteous fathers	ني إثمي نيم ني ذيكيئوس
And surpassed all measures	وعليت فوق المقدار
Maria- Ti Parthenos	ماريا تى بارثينوس

Everlasting and worshipped	قديم أزلي معبود
Unique in essence and Holy	واحد بالذات قدوس
He chose the daughter of David	اختار ابنة داود
Maria-Ti Parthenos	ماريا تى بارثينوس

You are the Mother of Christ	كوني لي يا أم ايسوس
And to all the world	ولسائر بي كوسموس
You are truly declared	عند الصوت المسموع
Maria- Ti Parthenos	ماريا تي بارثينوس

Without you who could have	لولاك من كان يقدر
Witnessed the glory of Christ	يعاين مجد ايسوس
When He appeared in the world	بين العالم منذ ظهر
Maria- Ti Parthenos	ماريا تى بارثينوس

Moses desired to see Him	موسي قصد أن يري
The face of the Holy God	وجه الرب القدوس
He couldn't see a glance of His -Light	فما طاق من نوره ثقب
Maria- Ti Parthenos	إبرة ماريا تى بارثينوس

We ask you to guide us	نسألك أن تهدينا
To please the Holy Lord	إلي رضا الرب القدوس
So He may lead us to the city	ليوصلنا إلي المينا
Maria- Ti Parthenos	ماريا تى بارثينوس
You became a pure sanctuary	هيكلاً طاهر صرتِ
For the dwelling of my Lord Jesus	لحلول باشويس ايسوس
And in your womb you did carry	وفي أحشاكِ حملتِ
-Him	ماريا تى بارثينوس
Maria- Ti Parthenos	
He drank milk from your chest	ورضع من لبن ثدييك
The Creator of all lives	محيى كل النفوس
You carried Him in your bosom	وحملتيه بين يديك
Maria- Ti Parthenos	ماريا تى بارثينوس
Do not forget O Mary	لا تنسى يا مريم
The Christian people	شعب إن ني
Before the Great God	إخريستيانوس:
Maria- Ti Parthenos	بالميلاد الأعظم
	ماريا تى بارثينوس
O Mary help us	يا مريم أعينينا

Before Jesus Christ	نرجوك قدام إيسوس
To lead us to the harbor	أن يوصلنا إلي المينا
Maria- Ti Parthenos	ماريا تى بارثينوس
Hail to the Virgin Mary	وسلامي إلى العذراً
Mother of Jesus Christ	إثماف إن إيسوس
Through her we gain victory	بخرستوس:
Maria- Ti Parthenos	وبها نلنا النصرة
	ماريا تى بارثينوس
Hail to Saint Mary	وسلامي إلى مريم
Ti Theotokos	تى ثيؤطوكوس
The pride of the whole world	فخر جميع العالم
Maria- Ti Parthenos	ماريا تى بارثينوس
Peace be to the people	وسلامى إلى الحضار
Who are present with us	ومن فى الجمع جلوس
To be saved and redeemed	ينجون من حر النار
Maria- Ti Parthenos	بصلاة تى بارثينوس
I conclude my words with	وأختم قولي يااخوة
Praising the mother of God	بمدح تى ثيؤطوكوس
Mary the gate of Heaven	مريم باب السما
Maria- Ti Parthenos	ماريا تى بارثينوس

Praise Before Tuesday Theotokia
مديح على ثيؤطوكية يوم الثلاثاء

O Mary, I'm your servant	يا مريم أنا عبدك
Baptized in the name of your Son	موسوم باسم ولدك
You gave me a promise	وعدتيني بوعدك
I ask you to fulfill	وبحقك توّفيني
O Mary, by your prayers	يا مريم بحياتك
And your chaste purity	وحسن طهارتك
And your virtuous life	أنقليني بصلاتك
Put me in Paradise	إلي موضع يرضيني
O Mary, you are my crown	يا مريم تاج رأسي
My honor among the crowd	ياعزى بين ناسى
Praising you among my guests	مدحك بين جلاسي
Cools and quenches me	كزلال ماء يرويني
O Mary, I'm carrying	يا مريم ثقل حملى
A heavy burden	من فوق رأسى وعلى
My trust is in you	لكن ما خاب أملي فيك
To help me O my pride	ياعمدة ديني

178

I am running out of time	يامريم دهري فات
Unaware and forgetting	وأنا تائه في غفلات
While Satan is offering	وإبليس حسن لي آفات
Many attractive traps	وحلاها في عيني
O Mary, I've seen his deeds	يا مريم رأيت شغله
Attractive and very sweet	كأنه شهد بعسله
He tempts me to sin	وبلغ في أمله
Yet I haven't yet lost hope	أنا ما خاب يقيني
O Mary, I am concerned	يا مريم زاد همي
With this heavy load	من فوق رأسي وعلي
Do not let me stray	ورجعت إلي الندم
I want to repent and live	هل ندمي يحيني
O Mary, your mystery	يا مريم سرك بان
Declared the hidden secrets	والمخفي صار معلن
The Judge dwelt in your womb	وسكن فيك الديان
And He freed the oppressed	وعتق المسكين
My hope is you, O Mary	يا مريم ظني فيك
Intercede to your Holy Son	شفاعة عند ابنك
To grant me forgiveness	طول عمري أرجوك

And let Jesus strengthen me	عند يسوع تقويني
O Mary, I request of you	يا مريم طالبوني
To clear me of my dues	بوفاء ثقل ديوني
For you are my medicine	وأنت طب عيوني
Your prayers cure me	بصلاتك غيريني
O Mary, you are an ointment	يامريم أنت مرهم
To heal the greatest wounds	يبرئ الجرح الأعظم
You are always favored	وجميلك متقدم
For you enlightened my heart	حين نورت عيني
O Mary, I plead with you to keep	يا مريم أوفي الميعاد
Your promise and guide me	جئتك مشمول برشاد
For the time is at hand	ودنا الوقت وعاد
To reach the harbor in peace	حتي نصل المينا
Abraham, Isaac and Jacob	ابراهيم واسحق
All desired the Lord	ويعقوب لهم مشتاق
His covenant was from you	أخذ منك الميثاق
A mystery now revealed	سر خفي صار مجهر
This is my happiness	هذا كان من سعدى
To rejoice in fulfilling my promise	أفرح بوفاء وعدى

For your praise is an enjoyment	فإن مدحك عندى
As a medicine which heals	يحييني كدواء شافى

The fathers and the brethren	والآباء والإخوة
The pious and religious	أهل الدين والتقوى
Save them from tribulation	خلصيهم من بلوى
And help my abject self	وأنا عبدك نجينى

Our Pope the Patriarch	والأب بطريركنا
A good and honest shepherd	راعي صالح وأمين
Grant him a long life	أعطيه يارب سنين
For his honor pleases me	دا مقامه يرضينى

Psali Adam on the 2ⁿᵈ Hoos
ابصالية آدم على الهوس الثانى -

My heart and my tongue, praise the Trinity. O Holy Trinity, have mercy on us.	Ⲁⲡⲁϩⲏⲧ ⲛⲉⲙ ⲡⲁⲗⲁⲥ: ϩⲱⲥ ⲉ̀ϯⲧⲣⲓⲁⲥ: ⲁ̀ⲅⲓⲁ ⲧ̀ⲣⲓⲁⲥ: ⲉ̀ⲗⲉ̀ⲏⲥⲟⲛ ⲏ̀ⲙⲁⲥ.	قلبى ولسانى. الثالوث يسبحان. أيها الثالوث القدوس أرحمنا.
Everyone praises You, and worships You, O Holy Trinity, have mercy on us.	Ⲃⲟⲛ ⲛⲓⲃⲉⲛ ⲥⲉϩⲱⲥ ⲛⲁⲕ: ⲟⲩⲟϩ ⲥⲉⲉⲣⲃⲱⲕ ⲛⲁⲕ: ⲁ̀ⲅⲓⲁ ⲧ̀ⲣⲓⲁⲥ: ⲉ̀ⲗⲉ̀ⲏⲥⲟⲛ ⲏ̀ⲙⲁⲥ.	كل أحد يسبحك. ويتعبد لك. أيها الثالوث القدوس أرحمنا.
*For You are our God, and our Great Savior, O Holy Trinity, have mercy on us.	*Ϫⲉ ⲅⲁⲣ ⲛ̀ⲑⲟⲕ ⲡⲉⲛⲛⲟⲩϯ Ⲡⲉⲛⲥⲱⲧⲏⲣ ⲟⲩⲟϩ ⲡⲓⲛⲓϣϯ: ⲁ̀ⲅⲓⲁ ⲧ̀ⲣⲓⲁⲥ: ⲉ̀ⲗⲉ̀ⲏⲥⲟⲛ ⲏ̀ⲙⲁⲥ.	*لأنك أنت إلهنا. ومخلصنا العظيم. أيها الثالوث القدوس أرحمنا.

*The Master Lord, He came and saved us, O Holy Trinity, have mercy on us.	*Ⲇⲉⲥⲡⲟⲧⲉ ⲕⲩⲣⲓⲟⲛ : ⲁϥⲓ ⲁϥⲥⲱϯ ⲙ̅ⲙⲟⲛ : ⲁ̀ⲅⲓⲁ ϯⲣⲓⲁⲥ : ⲉ̀ⲗⲉⲏⲥⲟⲛ ⲏ̀ⲙⲁⲥ.	*السيد الرب. أتى وخلصنا. أيها الثالوث القدوس أرحمنا.
For the sake of Your true judgments, teach me Your justice, O Holy Trinity, have mercy on us.	Ⲉⲑⲃⲉ ⲛⲉⲕ̅ϩⲁⲡ ⲙ̅ⲙⲏⲓ : ⲙⲁ̀ⲧⲥⲁⲃⲟⲓ ⲉⲛⲉⲕⲙⲉⲑ ⲙⲏⲓ ⲁ̀ⲅⲓⲁ ϯⲣⲓⲁⲥ : ⲉ̀ⲗⲉⲏⲥⲟⲛ ⲏ̀ⲙⲁⲥ.	من أجل أحكامك الحقيقية. علمنى عدلك. أيها الثالوث القدوس أرحمنا.
Many are Your mercies, grant us Your salvation, O Holy Trinity, have mercy on us.	Ⲍⲉⲟϣ ⲡⲉ ⲡⲉⲕⲛⲁⲓ : ⲭⲉⲙ ⲡⲉⲛϣⲓⲛⲓ ⲃ̀ⲉⲛ ⲡⲉⲕⲟⲩⲭⲁⲓ : ⲁ̀ⲅⲓⲁ ϯⲣⲓⲁⲥ : ⲉ̀ⲗⲉⲏⲥⲟⲛ ⲏ̀ⲙⲁⲥ.	كثيرة هى رحمتك. تعهدنا بخلاصك. أيها الثالوث القدوس أرحمنا.
*I am here before You, I took refuge in You, O Holy Trinity, have mercy on us.	*Ⲏⲥ ϩⲏⲡⲡⲉ ⲁ̀ⲛⲟⲕ : ⲉⲓⲉ̀ⲫⲱⲧ ϩⲁⲣⲟⲕ : ⲁ̀ⲅⲓⲁ ϯⲣⲓⲁⲥ : ⲉ̀ⲗⲉⲏⲥⲟⲛ ⲏ̀ⲙⲁⲥ.	*هوذا أنا. التجأت إليك. أيها الثالوث القدوس أرحمنا.

*Yours is the power and glory, O King of glory, O Holy Trinity, have mercy on us.	*Ⲑⲱⲕ ⲧⲉ ϯϫⲟⲙ ⲛⲉⲙ ⲡⲓⲱⲟⲩ: ⲱ ⲡⲓⲟⲩⲣⲟ ⲛ̀ⲧⲉ ⲡⲱⲟⲩ: ⲁ̀ⲅⲓⲁ ⲧ̀ⲣⲓⲁⲥ : ⲉ̀ⲗⲉⲏⲥⲟⲛ ⲏ̀ⲙⲁⲥ.	*لك القوة والمجد. يا ملك المجد. أيها الثالوث القدوس أرحمنا.
Jesus is our hope, in our tribulations, O Holy Trinity, have mercy on us.	Ⲓⲏⲥⲟⲩⲥ ⲡⲉ ⲧⲉⲛϩⲉⲗⲡⲓⲥ: ϧⲉⲛ ⲛⲉⲛⲑ̀ⲗⲩⲯⲓⲥ : ⲁ̀ⲅⲓⲁ ⲧ̀ⲣⲓⲁⲥ : ⲉ̀ⲗⲉⲏⲥⲟⲛ ⲏ̀ⲙⲁⲥ.	يسوع هو رجاؤنا. في شدائدنا. أيها الثالوث القدوس أرحمنا.
You are blessed O Son of God, deliver us from temptations, O Holy Trinity, have mercy on us.	Ⲕ̀ⲥⲙⲁⲣⲱⲟⲩⲧ ⲱ Ⲩⲓⲟⲥ Ⲑⲉⲟⲥ : ⲛⲁϩⲙⲉⲛ ϧⲉⲛ ⲛⲓⲡⲓⲣⲁⲥⲙⲟⲥ: ⲁ̀ⲅⲓⲁ ⲧ̀ⲣⲓⲁⲥ : ⲉ̀ⲗⲉⲏⲥⲟⲛ ⲏ̀ⲙⲁⲥ.	تباركت يابن الله. نجنا من التجارب. أيها الثالوث القدوس أرحمنا.
*All nations praise You, O Christ the King, O Holy Trinity, have mercy on us.	*Ⲗⲁⲟⲥ ⲛⲓⲃⲉⲛ ⲥⲉϩⲱⲥ ⲛⲁⲕ: ⲱ ⲡ̀ⲟⲩⲣⲟ Ⲡⲓⲭ̀-ⲣⲓⲥⲧⲟⲥ: ⲁ̀ⲅⲓⲁ ⲧ̀ⲣⲓⲁⲥ : ⲉ̀ⲗⲉⲏⲥⲟⲛ ⲏ̀ⲙⲁⲥ.	*كل الشعوب تسبحك. أيها الملك المسيح. أيها الثالوث القدوس أرحمنا.

*Grant us Your peace, heal our sickness, O Holy Trinity, have mercy on us.	*Ⲙⲟⲓ ⲛⲁⲛ ⲛ̀ⲧⲉⲕⲥⲓⲣⲏⲛⲏ ⲝ ⲙⲁⲧⲁⲗϬⲟ ⲛ̀ⲛⲉⲛϣⲱⲛⲓ ⲝ ⲁ̀ⲅⲓⲁ Ⲧⲣⲓⲁⲥ ⲝ ⲉ̀ⲗⲉ̀ⲏⲥⲟⲛ ⲏ̀ⲙⲁⲥ.	*أعطينا سلامك.ا شف أمراضنا. أيها الثالوث القدوس أرحمنا.
You are the compassionate, and You are the Merciful, O Holy Trinity, have mercy on us.	Ⲛ̀ⲑⲟⲕ ⲟⲩⲣⲉϥϣⲉⲛϩⲏⲧⲝ ⲟⲩⲟϩ ⲛ̀ⲛⲁⲏⲧ ⲝ ⲁ̀ⲅⲓⲁ Ⲧⲣⲓⲁⲥⲝⲉ̀ⲗⲉ̀ⲏⲥⲟⲛ ⲏ̀ⲙⲁⲥ.	انت المتحنن. وانت الرحوم. أيها الثالوث القدوس أرحمنا.
You are blessed, we praise and bless You, O Holy Trinity, have mercy on us.	Ⲍ̀ⲙⲁⲣⲱⲟⲩⲧ ⲛ̀ⲑⲟⲕⲝ ⲧⲉⲛϩⲱⲥ ⲛⲁⲕ ⲥ̀ⲙⲟⲩ ⲉ̀ⲣⲟⲕ ⲝ ⲁ̀ⲅⲓⲁ Ⲧⲣⲓⲁⲥ ⲝ ⲉ̀ⲗⲉ̀ⲏⲥⲟⲛ ⲏ̀ⲙⲁⲥ.	تباركت أنت. نسبحك ونباركك. أيها الثالوث القدوس أرحمنا.
*Truly great, is the Just Judge, O Holy Trinity, have mercy on us.	*Ⲟⲩⲛⲓϣϯ ⲛ̀ⲧⲁⲫⲙⲏⲓⲝ ⲡⲓⲣⲉϥϯϩⲁⲡ ⲙ̀ⲙⲏⲓ ⲁ̀ⲅⲓⲁ Ⲧⲣⲓⲁⲥⲝⲉ̀ⲗⲉ̀ⲏⲥⲟⲛ ⲏ̀ⲙⲁⲥ.	*عظيم بالحقيقة. الديان العادل. أيها الثالوث القدوس أرحمنا.

*Your Name is blessed, O the True Logos (Word), O Holy Trinity, have mercy on us.	*Ⲡⲉⲕⲣⲁⲛ ⲉⲧⲥⲙⲁⲣⲱⲟⲩⲧ : ⲱ̅ ⲡⲓⲗⲟⲅⲟⲥ ⲛ̀ⲧⲁⲫⲙⲏⲓ : ⲁ̀ⲅⲓ̀ⲁ ⲧⲣⲓⲁⲥ : ⲉ̀ⲗⲉⲏⲥⲟⲛ ⲏ̀ⲙⲁⲥ.	*اسمك مبارك. أيها الكلمة الحقيقي. أيها الثالوث القدوس أرحمنا.
Guard us O Christ, with Your Goodness, O Holy Trinity, have mercy on us.	Ⲣⲱⲓⲥ ⲉ̀ⲣⲟⲛ ⲱ̅ Ⲡⲓⲭ̅ⲣ̅ⲓⲥⲧⲟⲥ : ϧⲉⲛ ⲧⲉⲕⲙⲉⲧⲁ̀ⲅⲁⲑⲟⲥ : ⲁ̀ⲅⲓ̀ⲁ ⲧⲣⲓⲁⲥ : ⲉ̀ⲗⲉⲏⲥⲟⲛ ⲏ̀ⲙⲁⲥ.	أحرسنا أيها المسيح. بصلاحك. أيها الثالوث القدوس أرحمنا.
Hearken unto the sinners, in their tribulations, O Holy Trinity, have mercy on us.	Ⲥⲱⲧⲉⲙ ⲉ̀ⲛⲓⲣⲉϥⲉⲣⲛⲟⲃⲓ : ϧⲉⲛ ⲛⲟⲩⲁ̀ⲛⲁⲅⲕⲏ : ⲁ̀ⲅⲓ̀ⲁ ⲧⲣⲓⲁⲥ : ⲉ̀ⲗⲉⲏⲥⲟⲛ ⲏ̀ⲙⲁⲥ.	اسمع للخطاة. فى شدائدهم. أيها الثالوث القدوس أرحمنا.
*My soul and my mind, lift them up to heaven, O Holy Trinity, have mercy on us.	*Ⲧⲁⲯⲩⲭⲏ ⲛⲉⲙ ⲡⲁⲛⲟⲩⲥ : ⲱ̀ⲗⲟⲩ ⲉ̀ⲟⲩⲣⲁⲛⲟⲥ : ⲁ̀ⲅⲓ̀ⲁ ⲧⲣⲓⲁⲥ : ⲉ̀ⲗⲉⲏⲥⲟⲛ ⲏ̀ⲙⲁⲥ.	*نفسي وعقلى. إرفعهما الى السماء. أيها الثالوث القدوس

أرحمنا.

*O Son of our God, grant us Your salvation, O Holy Trinity, have mercy on us.	*Ⲩⲓⲟⲥ Ⲑⲉⲟⲥ Ⲡⲉⲛⲛⲟⲩ† : ⲙⲟⲓ ⲛⲁⲛ ⲛ̀ⲟⲩⲥⲱϯ : ⲁ̀ⲅⲓⲁ ⲧ̀ⲣⲓⲁⲥ : ⲉ̀ⲗⲉⲏⲥⲟⲛ ⲏ̀ⲙⲁⲥ.	*يا ابن الله. إلهنا أعطنا خلاصاً. أيها الثالوث القدوس أرحمنا.
God the Merciful, the long-suffering, O Holy Trinity, have mercy on us.	Ⲫ† ⲡⲓⲛⲁⲏⲧ: ⲡⲓⲣⲉϥ- ⲱⲟⲩⲛ̀ⲏⲧ: ⲁ̀ⲅⲓⲁ ⲧ̀ⲣⲓ ⲁⲥ:ⲉ̀ⲗⲉⲏⲥⲟⲛ ⲏ̀ⲙⲁⲥ.	الله الرحوم. طويل الآناة. أيها الثالوث القدوس أرحمنا.
Holy, Holy, Holy, O Son of the Holy, O Holy Trinity, have mercy on us.	Ⲭⲟⲩⲁⲃ ⲭ̀ⲟⲩⲁⲃ ⲭ̀ⲟ- ⲩⲁⲃ: ⲡ̀ϣⲏⲣⲓ ⲙ̀Ⲫⲏⲉⲑ- ⲟⲩⲁⲃ: ⲁ̀ⲅⲓⲁ ⲧ̀ⲣⲓⲁⲥ :ⲉ̀ⲗⲉⲏⲥⲟⲛ ⲏ̀ⲙⲁⲥ.	قدوس قدوس قدوس. يا ابن القدوس. أيها الثالوث القدوس أرحمنا.
*The souls of our fathers, give rest to them O Savior, O Holy Trinity, have	*Ⲯⲩⲭⲏ ⲛ̀ⲛⲉⲛⲓⲟ† : ⲙⲁ̀ⲙⲧⲟⲛ ⲛⲱⲟⲩ ⲱ̀ ⲡⲓⲣⲉϥⲥⲱ† : ⲁ̀ⲅⲓⲁ ⲧ̀ⲣⲓⲁⲥ	*آباؤنا الراقدون. نيحهم. أيها المخلص

mercy on us.	**⳾ⲉⲗⲉⲏⲥⲟⲛ ⲏⲙⲁⲥ.**	أيها الثالوث القدوس أرحمنا.
*O our Master remember us, in Your heavenly kingdom, O Holy Trinity, have mercy on us.	* **Ⲱ ⲡⲉⲛⲛⲏⲃ ⲁ̀ⲣⲓⲡⲉⲛⲙⲉⲩⲓ̀ ⳾ ϧⲉⲛ ⲧⲉⲕⲙⲉⲧⲟⲩⲣⲟ ⲛ̀ⲛⲁ ⲛⲓⲫⲏⲟⲩⲓ̀ ⳾ ⲁ̀ⲅⲓⲁ ⳨ⲣⲓⲁⲥ ⳾ ⲉ̀ⲗⲉⲏⲥⲟⲛ ⲏⲙⲁⲥ.**	*ياملكنا اذكرنا. فى ملكوتك السمائية. أيها الثالوث القدوس أرحمنا.

188

Second Hoos – Πⲓϩⲱⲥ

ⲙⲙⲁϩ ⲃ   الهوس الثاني

*O give thanks to the Lord for He is good: <u>Alleluia, His mercy endures forever.</u>	*Ⲟⲩⲱⲛϩ ⲉ̀ⲃⲟⲗ ⲙ̀Ⲡ̀ϭⲟⲓⲥ ϫⲉ ⲟⲩⲭⲣⲏⲥⲧⲟⲥ ⲟⲩⲁ̀ⲅⲁⲑⲟⲥ ⲡⲉ ⲁⲗⲗⲏⲗⲟⲩⲓ̀ⲁ : ϫⲉ ⲡⲉϥⲛⲁⲓ ϣⲟⲡ ϣⲁ ⲉ̀ⲛⲉϩ.	*اشكروا الرب لأنّه صالح وخيّر الليلويا. لأن إلى الأبد رحمته.
O give thanks to the God of gods: Alleluia, His mercy endures forever.	Ⲟⲩⲱⲛϩ ⲉ̀ⲃⲟⲗ ⲙ̀Ⲫ̀ⲛⲟⲩϯ ⲛ̀ⲧⲉ ⲛⲓⲛⲟⲩϯ ⲁ̅ⲗ̅: ϫⲉ ⲡⲉϥⲛⲁⲓ ϣⲟⲡ ϣⲁ ⲉ̀ⲛⲉϩ.	اشكروا إله الآلهة الليلويا. لأن إلى الأبد رحمته.
*O give thanks to the Lord of lords: Alleluia, His mercy endures forever.	*Ⲟⲩⲱⲛϩ ⲉ̀ⲃⲟⲗ ⲙ̀Ⲡ̀ϭⲟⲓⲥ ⲛ̀ⲧⲉ ⲛⲓϭⲟⲓⲥ ⲁ̅ⲗ̅: ϫⲉ ⲡⲉϥⲛⲁⲓ ϣⲟⲡ ϣⲁ ⲉ̀ⲛⲉϩ.	*اشكروا رب الارباب الليلويا. لأن إلى الأبد رحمته.
To Him who alone	Ⲫⲏⲉⲧⲓⲣⲓ ⲛ̀ϩⲁⲛⲛⲓϣϯ	الصانع العجائب

does great wonders: Alleluia, His mercy endures forever.	ⲛ̀ϣⲫⲏⲣⲓ ⲙ̀ⲙⲁⲩⲁⲧϥ ⲁ̅ⲗ̅ : ϫⲉ ⲡⲉϥⲛⲁⲓ ϣⲟⲡ ϣⲁ ⲉ̀ⲛⲉϩ.	العظام وحده الليلويا. لأن إلى الأبد رحمته.
*To Him who by wisdom made the heavens: Alleluia, His mercy endures forever.	*Ⲫⲏⲉⲧⲁϥⲑⲁⲙⲓⲟ ⲛ̀ⲛⲓⲫⲏⲟⲩⲓ̀ ϧⲉⲛ ⲟⲩⲕⲁϯ ⲁ̅ⲗ̅ : ϫⲉ ⲡⲉϥⲛⲁⲓ ϣⲟⲡ ϣⲁ ⲉ̀ⲛⲉϩ.	*الذي خلق السموات بفهم الليلويا. لأن إلى الأبد رحمته.
To Him who stretched out the Earth above the waters: Alleluia, His mercy endures forever.	Ⲫⲏⲉⲧⲁϥⲧⲁϫⲣⲟ ⲙ̀ⲡⲓⲕⲁϩⲓ ϩⲓϫⲉⲛ ⲛⲓⲙⲱⲟⲩ ⲁ̅ⲗ̅ : ϫⲉ ⲡⲉϥⲛⲁⲓ ϣⲟⲡ ϣⲁ ⲉ̀ⲛⲉϩ.	الذى ثبت الأرض على المياه الليلويا. لأن إلى الأبد رحمته.
*To Him who made great lights: Alleluia, His mercy endures forever.	*Ⲫⲏⲉⲧⲁϥⲑⲁⲙⲓⲟ ⲛ̀ϩⲁⲛⲛⲓϣϯ ⲛ̀ⲣⲉϥⲉⲣⲟⲩⲱⲓⲛⲓ ⲙ̀ⲙⲁⲩⲁⲧϥ ⲁ̅ⲗ̅ : ϫⲉ ⲡⲉϥⲛⲁⲓ ϣⲟⲡ ϣⲁ ⲉ̀ⲛⲉϩ	*الذي خلق نيرين عظيمين وحده الليلويا. لأن إلى الأبد رحمته.
The sun to rule by day: Alleluia, His	Ⲫⲣⲏ ⲉ̀ⲟⲩⲉⲣϣⲓϣⲓ ⲛ̀ⲧⲉ	الشمس لحكم النهار الليلويا.

mercy endures forever.	ⲡⲓⲉϩⲟⲟⲩ $\overline{ⲁⲗ}$ ⲉ ⲡⲉϥⲛⲁⲓ ϣⲟⲡ ϣⲁ ⲉⲛⲉϩ	لأن إلى الأبد رحمته.
*The moon and stars to rule by night: Alleluia, His mercy endures forever.	*Ⲡⲓⲟϩ ⲛⲉⲙ ⲛⲓⲥⲓⲟⲩ ⲉⲩⲉⲝⲟⲩⲥⲓⲁ ⲛ̀ⲧⲉ ⲡⲓⲉ̀ⲭⲱⲣϩ $\overline{ⲁⲗ}$ ⲉ ⲡⲉϥⲛⲁⲓ ϣⲟⲡ ϣⲁ ⲉ̀ⲛⲉϩ.	*القمر والنجوم لحكم الليل الليلويا. لأن إلى الأبد رحمته.
To Him who smote Egypt in their firstborn: Alleluia, His mercy endures forever.	Ⲫⲏⲉ̀ⲧⲁϥϣⲁⲣⲓ ⲉ̀ⲛⲁⲭⲏⲙⲓ ⲛⲉⲙ ⲛⲟⲩϣⲁⲙⲓⲥⲓ $\overline{ⲁⲗ}$ ⲉ ⲡⲉϥⲛⲁⲓ ϣⲟⲡ ϣⲁ ⲉ̀ⲛⲉϩ.	الذى ضرب المصريين مع ابكارهم الليلويا. لأن إلى الأبد رحمته.
*And brought out Israel from among them: Alleluia, His mercy endures forever.	*Ⲟⲩⲟϩ ⲁϥⲓⲛⲓ ⲙ̀ⲡ̀Ⲓⲥⲣⲁⲏⲗ ⲉ̀ⲃⲟⲗ ϧⲉⲛ ⲧⲟⲩⲙⲏϯ $\overline{ⲁⲗ}$ ⲉ ⲡⲉϥⲛⲁⲓ ϣⲟⲡ ϣⲁ ⲉ̀ⲛⲉϩ.	*وأخرج إسرائيل في وسطه الليلويا. لأن إلى الأبد رحمته.
With a strong hand and with a stretched out arm: Alleluia, His mercy endures	Ϧⲉⲛ ⲟⲩϫⲓϫ ⲉⲥⲁ̀ⲙⲁϩⲓ ⲛⲉⲙ ⲟⲩϣⲱⲃϣ ⲉϥϭⲟⲥⲓ $\overline{ⲁⲗ}$ ⲉ ⲡⲉϥⲛⲁⲓ ϣⲟⲡ	بيد عزيزة وذراع عالية الليلويا. لأن إلى الأبد رحمته.

forever.	ϣⲁ ⲉⲛⲉϩ.	
*To Him who divided the Red Sea into parts: Alleluia, His mercy endures forever.	*Ⲫⲏⲉⲧⲁϥⲫⲱⲣϫ ⳙ-ⲫⲓⲟⲙ ⳹ⲛϣⲁⲣⲓ ϧⲉⲛ ϩⲁⲛⲫⲱⲣϫ ⲁⲗ꞉ ϫⲉ ⲡⲉϥⲛⲁⲓ ϣⲟⲡ ϣⲁ ⲉⲛⲉϩ	*الذى شق البحر الأحمر إلى أقسام الليلويا. لأن إلى الأبد رحمته.
And made Israel pass through the midst of it: Alleluia, His mercy endures forever.	Ⲟⲩⲟϩ ⲁϥⲓⲛⲓ ⳙⲠⲓⲥⲣ-ⲁⲏⲗ ⲉⲙⲏⲣ ϧⲉⲛ ⲧⲉϥⲙⲏϯ ⲁⲗ ꞉ ϫⲉ ⲡⲉϥⲛⲁⲓ ϣⲟⲡ ϣⲁ ⲉⲛⲉϩ	وأجاز إسرائيل فى وسطه الليلويا. لأن إلى الأبد رحمته.
*But overthrew pharaoh and his hosts in the Red Sea: Alleluia, His mercy endures forever.	*Ⲟⲩⲟϩ ⲁϥⲃⲟⲣⲃⲉⲣ ⳙ-Ⲫⲁⲣⲁⲱ ⲛⲉⲙ ⲧⲉϥϫ-ⲟⲙ ⲧⲏⲣⲥ ⲉⲫⲓⲟ-ⲙ ⳹ⲛϣⲁⲣⲓ ⲁⲗ ꞉ ϫⲉ ⲡⲉϥⲛⲁⲓ ϣⲟⲡ ϣⲁ ⲉⲛⲉϩ	*وطرح فرعون وكل قوته فى البحر الأحمر الليلويا. لأن إلى الأبد رحمته.
To Him who led His people through the wilderness: Alleluia, His mercy endures	Ⲫⲏⲉⲧⲁϥⲓⲛⲓ ⳙⲡⲉϥⲗ-ⲁⲟⲥ ⲉⲃⲟⲗ ⳹ⲛϩⲣⲏⲓ ϩⲓ ⲡϣⲁϥⲉ ⲁⲗ꞉ ϫⲉ	الذى أخرج شعبه إلى البرية الليلويا. لأن إلى الأبد

forever.	ⲡⲉϥⲛⲁⲓ ϣⲟⲡ ϣⲁ ⲉ̀-ⲛⲉϩ.	رحمته.
*To Him who retrieved water from a rock: Alleluia, His mercy endures forever.	*Ⲫⲏⲉⲧⲁϥ̀ⲓⲛⲓ ⳿ⲛⲟⲩⲙⲱⲟⲩ ⲉ̀ⲃⲟⲗ ϧⲉⲛ ⲟⲩⲡⲉⲧⲣⲁ ⳿ⲛⲕⲟϩ ⳿ⲛϣⲱⲧ ⲁ̅ⲗ̅: ϫⲉ ⲡⲉϥⲛⲁⲓ ϣⲟⲡ ϣⲁ ⲉ̀ⲛⲉϩ.	*الذى أخرج ماء من صخرة صماء الليلويا. لأن إلى الأبد رحمته.
To Him who smote great kings: Alleluia, His mercy endures forever.	Ⲫⲏⲉⲧⲁϥϣⲁⲣⲓ ⲉ̀ϩⲁⲛⲛⲓϣϯ ⳿ⲛⲟⲩⲣⲱⲟⲩ ⲁ̅ⲗ̅: ϫⲉ ⲡⲉϥⲛⲁⲓ ϣⲟⲡ ϣⲁ ⲉ̀ⲛⲉϩ.	الذى ضرب ملوكاً عظماء الليلويا. لأن إلى الأبد رحمته.
*And slew famous kings: Alleluia, His mercy endures forever.	*Ⲟⲩⲟϩ ⲁϥϧⲱⲧⲉⲃ ⳿ⲛϩⲁⲛⲟⲩⲣⲱⲟⲩ ⲉⲩⲟⲓ ⳿ⲛϣⲫⲏⲣⲓ ⲁ̅ⲗ̅: ϫⲉ ⲡⲉϥⲛⲁⲓ ϣⲟⲡ ϣⲁ ⲉ̀ⲛⲉϩ.	*وقتل ملوكاً عجيبين الليلويا. لأن إلى الأبد رحمته.
Sihon the king of the Amorites: Alleluia, His mercy endures forever.	Ⲥⲏⲱⲛ ⳿ⲡⲟⲩⲣⲟ ⳿ⲛⲧⲉ Ⲛⲓⲁⲙⲟⲣⲣⲉⲟⲥ ⲁ̅ⲗ̅: ϫⲉ ⲡⲉϥⲛⲁⲓ ϣⲟⲡ ϣⲁ ⲉ̀ⲛⲉϩ	سيحون ملك الأموريين الليلويا. لأن إلى الأبد رحمته.

193

*And Og the king of Bashan: Alleluia, His mercy endures forever.	*Ⲛⲉⲙ Ⲱⲅ ⲡⲟⲩⲣⲟ ⲛⲧⲉ Ⲑⲃⲁⲥⲁⲛ ⲁ̅ⲗ̅ : ϫⲉ ⲡⲉϥⲛⲁⲓ ϣⲟⲡ ϣⲁ ⲉⲛⲉϩ.	*وعوج ملك باشان الليلويا. لأن إلى الأبد رحمته.
And gave their lands for a heritage: Alleluia, His mercy endures forever.	Ⲁϥϯ ⲙⲡⲟⲩⲕⲁϩⲓ ⲉⲩⲕⲗⲏⲣⲟⲛⲟⲙⲓⲁ ⲁ̅ⲗ̅ : ϫⲉ ⲡⲉϥⲛⲁⲓ ϣⲟⲡ ϣⲁ ⲉⲛⲉϩ.	اعطى أرضهم ميراثاً الليلويا. لأن إلى الأبد رحمته.
*A heritage unto Israel His servant: Alleluia, His mercy endures forever.	*Ⲉⲩⲕⲗⲏⲣⲟⲛⲟⲙⲓⲁ ⲙ̅ⲡⲉϥⲃⲱⲕ Ⲡⲓⲥⲣⲁⲏⲗ: ϫⲉ ⲡⲉϥⲛⲁⲓ ϣⲟⲡ ϣⲁ ⲉⲛⲉϩ.	*ميراثاً لعبده اسرائيل الليلويا. لأن إلى الأبد رحمته.
Who remembered us in our lowly estate: Alleluia, His mercy endures forever.	Ⲛ̅ϧⲣⲏⲓ ϧⲉⲛ ⲡⲉⲛⲑⲉⲃⲓⲟ ⲁϥⲉⲣⲡⲉⲛⲙⲉⲩⲓ ⲛ̅ϫⲉ Ⲡ̅ϭⲟⲓⲥ ⲁ̅ⲗ̅ : ϫⲉ ⲡⲉϥⲛⲁⲓ ϣⲟⲡ ϣⲁ ⲉⲛⲉϩ.	فى تواضعنا ذكرنا الرب الليلويا. لأن إلى الأبد رحمته.
*And has redeemed us from our enemies: Alleluia, His mercy	*Ⲟⲩⲟϩ ⲁϥⲥⲟⲧⲧⲉⲛ ⲉ̅ⲃⲟⲗ ϧⲉⲛ ⲛⲉⲛϫⲓϫ ⲛⲧⲉ	*و خلصنا من أيدى أعدائنا الليلويا. لأن إلى

endures forever.	ⲛⲉⲛϫⲁϫⲓ ⲁ̅ⲗ̅ ⳾ ϫⲉ ⲡⲉϥⲛⲁⲓ ϣⲟⲡ ϣⲁ ⲉ̀ⲛⲉϩ	الأبد رحمته.
Who gives food to all flesh: Alleluia, His mercy endures fore- ver.	Ⲫⲏⲉⲧϯ ϧ̀ⲣⲉ ⲛ̀ⲥⲁⲣⲝ ⲛⲓⲃⲉⲛ ⲉⲧⲟⲛϧ ⲁ̅ⲗ̅ ⳾ ϫⲉ ⲡⲉϥⲛⲁⲓ ϣⲟⲡ ϣⲁ ⲉ̀ⲛⲉϩ	الذى يعطى طعاماً لكل جسد حي الليلويا. لأن إلى الأبد رحمته.
*O give thanks to the God of heaven: Alleluia, His mercy endures forever.	*Ⲟⲩⲱⲛϩ ⲉ̀ⲃⲟⲗ ⲙ̀- Ⲫϯ ⲛ̀ⲧⲉ ⲧ̀ⲫⲉ ⲁ̅ⲗ̅ ⳾ ϫⲉ ⲡⲉϥⲛⲁⲓ ϣⲟⲡ ϣⲁ ⲉ̀ⲛⲉϩ	*احمدوا إله السماء الليلويا. لأن إلى الأبد رحمته.
O give thanks to the Lord of lords for He is good: Alleluia, His mercy endures fore- ver.	Ⲟⲩⲱⲛϩ ⲉ̀ⲃⲟⲗ ⲙ̀Ⲡϭⲟ- ⲓⲥ ⲛ̀ⲧⲉ ⲛⲓϭⲟⲓⲥ ϫⲉ ⲟⲩⲭ̅ⲣ̅ⲏⲥⲧⲟⲥ ⲟⲩⲁ̀ⲅ- ⲁⲑⲟⲥ ⲡⲉ ⲁ̅ⲗ̅⳾ ϫⲉ ⲡⲉϥⲛⲁⲓ ϣⲟⲡ ϣⲁ ⲉ̀- ⲛⲉϩ.	احمدوا رب الأرباب لأنه طيب وصالح الليلويا. لأن إلى الأبد رحمته.

Psali Adam	Ⲯⲁⲗⲓ Ⲁⲇⲁⲙ	لبش الهوس الثانى
*Let us give thanks, to Christ our God, with David the prophet, and psalmist.	*Ⲙⲁⲣⲉⲛⲟⲩⲱⲛϩ ⲉ̀ⲃⲟⲗ : ⲙ̀Ⲡⲓⲭⲣⲓⲥⲧⲟⲥ Ⲡⲉⲛⲛⲟⲩϯ : ⲛⲉⲙ ⲡⲓⲉⲣⲟⲯⲁⲗⲧⲏⲥ: Ⲇⲁⲩⲓⲇ ⲡⲓ̀ⲡⲣⲟⲫⲏⲧⲏⲥ.	*فلنشكر المسيح إلهنا مع المرتل داود النبي.
For He has made the heavens, and all its hosts, and established the earth, on the waters.	Ⲭⲉ ⲁϥⲑⲁⲙⲓⲟ̀ ⲛ̀ⲛⲓⲫⲏⲟⲩⲓ̀ : ⲛⲉⲙ ⲛⲟⲩⲆⲩⲛⲁⲙⲓⲥ : ⲁϥϩⲓⲥⲉⲛ ⲧ̀ ⲙ̀ⲡⲓⲕⲁϩⲓ : ⲉ̀ⲉ̀ϩⲣⲏⲓ ϩⲓⲭⲉⲛ ⲛⲓⲙⲱⲟⲩ.	لأنه خلق السموات وجنودها وأسس الأرض على المياه.
*These two great stars, the sun and the moon, He has made to enlighten, the firmament.	*Ⲛⲁⲓ ⲛⲓϣϯ ⲙ̀ⲫⲱⲥⲧⲏⲣ : ⲡⲓⲣⲏ ⲛⲉⲙ ⲡⲓⲟϩ : ⲁϥⲭⲁⲩ ⲉⲩⲉⲣⲟⲩⲱⲓⲛⲓ : ϧⲉⲛ ⲡⲓⲥⲧⲉⲣⲉⲱ̀ⲙⲁ.	*هذان الكوكبان العظيمان الشمس والقمر جعلهما ينيران في الفلك.

He brought forth the winds, out of His treasure box, He breathed unto the trees, and they blossomed.	Ⲁϥⲓⲛⲓ ⲛ̅ϩⲁⲛⲑⲏⲟⲩ : ⲉ̀ⲃⲟⲗ ϧⲉⲛ ⲛⲉϥⲁϩⲱⲣ : ⲁϥⲛⲓϥⲓ ⲛ̅ⲥⲁ ⲛⲓ̀ϣϣⲏⲛ : ϣⲁⲛ̀ⲧⲟⲩⲫⲓⲣⲓ ⲉ̀ⲃⲟⲗ.	أخرج الرياح من خباياها. نفخ في الأشجار حتى ازهرت.
*He caused the rain to fall, upon the face of the earth, and it sprouted, and gave its fruit.	*Ⲁϥϩⲱⲟⲩ ⲛ̅ⲟⲩⲙⲟⲩⲛ ϩⲱⲟⲩ : ϩⲓϫⲉⲛ ⲡ̅- ϩⲟ ⲙ̅ⲡⲕⲁϩⲓ : ϣⲁⲛ̅ⲧ- ⲉϥⲣⲱⲧ ⲉ̀ⲡ̀ϣⲱⲓ : ⲛ̅ⲧⲉ- ϥϯ ⲙ̅ⲡⲉϥⲟⲩⲧⲁϩ.	*أمطر مطراً على وجه الأرض حتى انبتت وأعطت ثمرها.
He brought forth water, out of a rock, and gave it to His people, in the wilderness.	Ⲁϥⲓⲛⲓ ⲛ̅ⲟⲩⲙⲱⲟⲩ: ⲉ̀- ⲃⲟⲗ ϧⲉⲛ ⲟⲩⲡⲉⲧⲣⲁ : ⲁϥⲧ̀ⲥⲟ ⲙ̅ⲡⲉϥⲗⲁⲟⲥ : ⲛ̀ϩ̀ⲣⲏⲓ ϩⲓ ⲡ̀ϣⲁϥⲉ.	أخرج ماء من صخرة وسقى شعبه في البرية.
*He made man, in His image, and His likeness, that he may praise Him.	*Ⲁϥⲑⲁⲙⲓⲟ ⲙ̅ⲡⲓⲣⲱⲙⲓ : ⲕⲁⲧⲁ ⲡⲉϥⲓⲛⲓ : ⲛⲉⲙ ⲧⲉϥϩⲓⲕⲱⲛ : ⲉⲑⲣⲉϥ- ⲥⲙⲟⲩ ⲉ̀ⲣⲟϥ.	*صنع الإنسان كشبهه وصورته لكى يباركه.

Let us praise Him, and exalt His name, and give thanks to Him, His mercy endures forever.	Ⲙⲁⲣⲉⲛϩⲱⲥ ⲉⲣⲟϥ : ⲧⲉⲛϭⲓⲥⲓ ⲙ̅ⲡⲉϥⲣⲁⲛ : ⲧⲉⲛⲟⲩⲱⲛϩ ⲛⲁϥ ⲉⲃⲟⲗ : ϫⲉ ⲡⲉϥⲛⲁⲓ ϣⲟⲡ ϣⲁ ⲉⲛⲉϩ	فلنسبحه ونرفع اسمه ونشكره لأن رحمته كائنة إلى الأبد.
*Through the prayers, of David the psalmist, O Lord grant us, the forgiveness of our sins.	*Ϩⲓⲧⲉⲛ ⲛⲓⲉⲩⲭⲏ: ⲛ̅ⲧⲉ ⲡⲓⲉⲣⲟⲯⲁⲗⲧⲏⲥ Ⲇⲁⲩⲓⲇ: Ⲡϭⲟⲓⲥ ⲁⲣⲓ ϩⲙⲟⲧ ⲛⲁⲛ : ⲙ̅ⲡⲓ ⲭⲱ ⲉⲃⲟⲗ ⲛ̅ⲧⲉ ⲛⲉⲛⲛⲟⲃⲓ.	*بصلوات المرتل داود يارب أنعم لنا بمغفرة خطايانا.
Through the intercessions, of the Mother of God Saint Mary, O Lord, grant us, the forgiveness of our sins.	Ϩⲓⲧⲉⲛ ⲛⲓⲡⲣⲉⲥⲃⲓⲁ : ⲛ̅ⲧⲉ ϯⲑⲉⲟⲧⲟⲕⲟⲥ ⲉⲑⲟⲩⲁⲃ Ⲙⲁⲣⲓⲁ : Ⲡϭⲟⲓⲥ ⲁⲣⲓϩⲙⲟⲧ ⲛⲁⲛ : ⲙ̅ⲡⲓⲭⲱ ⲉⲃⲟⲗ ⲛ̅ⲧⲉ ⲛⲉⲛⲛⲟⲃⲓ.	بشفاعات والدة الاله القديسة مريم يارب انعم لنا بمغفرة خطايانا.
*Through the intercessions, of all the	*Ϩⲓⲧⲉⲛ ⲛⲓⲡⲣⲉⲥⲃ	*بشفاعات كل صفوف

| heavenly hosts, O Lord, grant us, the forgiveness of our sins. | ⲓⲁ̈: ⲛ̅ⲧⲉ ⲡ̅ⲭⲟⲣⲟⲥ ⲧⲏⲣϥ ⲛ̅ⲧⲉ ⲛⲓⲁⲅ- ⲅⲉⲗⲟⲥ : Ⲡ̅ⲟⲓⲥ ⲁⲣⲓ- ϩⲙⲟⲧ ⲛⲁⲛ ⲙ̅ⲡⲓ- ⲭⲱ ⲉ̇ⲃⲟⲗ ⲛ̅ⲧⲉ ⲛⲉⲛⲛⲟⲃⲓ. | الملائكة يارب انعم لنا بمغفرة خطايانا. |
| Blessed are You indeed, with your Good Father, and the Holy Spirit, for You have come and saved us. | `Ⲕ̇ⲥⲙⲁⲣⲱⲟⲩⲧ ⲁⲗⲏ- ⲑⲱⲥ : ⲛⲉⲙ Ⲡⲉⲕ- ⲓⲱⲧ ⲛ̇ⲁⲅⲁⲑⲟⲥ : ⲛⲉⲙ Ⲡⲓ̅ⲡⲛⲉⲩⲙⲁ ⲉ̇ⲟⲟⲩⲁⲃ : ⲭⲉ ⲁⲕⲓ̀ ⲁⲕⲥⲱ- ⲧ̇ ⲙ̇ⲙⲟⲛ. | مبارك أنت بالحقيقة مع أبيك الصالح والروح القدس لأنك أتيت وخلصتنا. |

Hymn after the 2ⁿᵈ Hoos

مديح بعد الهوس الثانى

*Let us sing with David	* فلنرتل مع داود
And thank the graciousness of God	ونشكر فضل الله
For He is merciful and kind	لأنه رحوم وودود
Je pef-nay Shop Sha-eneh	جى بيف ناي شوب شا إينيه
Thank the Lord for He is good	إشكروا الرب فإنه صالح
Sending His rain from heaven above	مرسل غيثه من أعلى سماه
Upon the righteous and the wicked	علي الصالح والطالح
Je pef-nay Shop Sha-eneh	جى بيف ناي شوب شا إينيه
*Thank the God of gods	* اشكروا إله الآلهة
For He is good and long-suffering	فإنه صالح طويل الأناة
To Whom is due glory and honor	له المجد والعظمة
Je pef-nay Shop Sha-eneh	جى بيف ناي شوب شا إينيه
Holy, Holy, Holy	قدوس قدوس قدوس
One and Only God	واحد لا رب سواه
Thank the Lord of lords	اشكروا رب الارباب
Je pef-nay Shop Sha-eneh	جي بيف ناي شوب شا إينيه

*The earth is filled with His glory
As He is glorified in heaven
Maker of all wonders
Je pef-nay Shop Sha-eneh

* ملأ الأرض بمجده
له المجد في علو سماه
صنع العجائب وحده
جي بيف ناي شوب شا إينيه

He created the heavens
And established it by His Word
The stars move in their orbits
Je pef-nay Shop Sha-eneh

صوّر علو السموات
واسسها بكلمة فاه
والنجوم فيها سائرات
جي بيف ناي شوب شا إينيه

*In wisdom He created the earth
And spread it over the waters
He filled it with creatures
Je pef-nay Shop Sha-eneh

*جبل الأرض بالحكمة
وبسطها فوق وجه المياه
وملأها بالخلقة
جي بيف ناي شوب شا إينيه

He created two great stars
To illuminate the heavens
The sun and the moon orbiting
Je pef-nay Shop Sha-eneh

رتب كوكبين عظيمين
ينيران في جو سماه
الشمس والقمر سائرين
جي بيف ناي شوب شا إينيه

*He made the sun for the day
In its celestial sphere
The moon and the stars for the night
Je pef-nay Shop Sha-eneh

*جعل الشمس لسلطان النهار
سائرة في الفلك دائرة
والقمر والنجوم لليل
جي بيف ناي شوب شا إينيه

He poured His wrath on Pharaoh	سكب غضبه علي فرعون
And destroyed all His enemies	وأهلك كامل أعداه
And chose Moses and Aaron	واختار موسي وهرون
Je pef-nay Shop Sha-eneh	جي بيف ناي شوب شا إينيه

*He made miracles for His people	*لشعبه صنع الآيات
In Egypt by His mighty hand	في مصر بذراع ما أعلاه
And struck them with heavy plagues	وضربهم بأشنع الضربات
Je pef-nay Shop Sha-eneh	جي بيف ناي شوب شا إينيه

The Egyptians and their horsemen	المصريون وأبكارهم
Were hit by a Mighty hand	ضربهم بذراع ما أعلاه
He saved His people from them	وخلص شعبه من وسطهم
Je pef-nay Shop Sha-eneh	جي بيف ناي شوب شا إينيه

*The sea was split in half	*شق البحر وفلقه
And Pharaoh was drowned in it	وطرح فرعون جواه
While Israel passed through it	وجاز اسرائيل وسطه
Je pef-nay Shop Sha-eneh	جي بيف ناي شوب شا إينيه

He gave them water from the rock	أنبع الماء من الصخرة
To quenched His people They drank	وروي شعبه وسقاه
water in the dry wilderness	في البرية القفرة
Je pef-nay Shop Sha-eneh	جي بيف ناي شوب شا إينيه

*He sent them to Canaan	* أوصلهم بلاد كنعان

And killed Sihon King of the	وقتل سيحون وفناه
-Amorites	وعوج ملك باشان
And Og king of Bashan	جي بيف ناي شوب شا إينيه
Je pef-nay Shop Sha-eneh	

He gave their lands to Israel	أعطي أرضهم ميراثا
His servant and His only child	لإسرائيل عبده وفتاه
He remembered our humble souls	وذكرنا في تواضعنا
Je pef-nay Shop Sha-eneh	جي بيف ناي شوب شا إينيه

*He saved us from our enemies	*خلصنا من الأعداء المحيطين
He is the comfort of everyone	لكل حي عزاء
Let us profess to the Lord of heaven	اعترفوا لإله السماء
Je pef-nay Shop Sha-eneh	جي بيف ناي شوب شا إينيه

Unto Him is due all honor	يجب له الإكرام
And reverent worship	والسجود عند قدماه
Thank Him for His graciousness	أشكروا فضله على الدوام
Je pef-nay Shop Sha-eneh	جي بيف ناي شوب شا إينيه

*Let us proclaim the Name of Christ	*أعترفوا لأسم المسيح
And thank Him for His grace	واشكروا فضله ورضاه
Praise Him and exalt Him	وزيدوه من التسابيح
Je pef-nay Shop Sha-eneh	جي بيف ناي شوب شا إينيه

He saved us from Satan	خلصنا من إبليس

203

The symbolic Pharaoh was disgraced	فرعون العقلي خزاه
And we crossed the water of baptism	وأجازنا بحر التقديس
Je pef-nay Shop Sha-eneh	جي بيف ناي شوب شا إينيه
*We were baptized in holy water	*أدخلنا بحر العماد
Freed from the bondage of tyranny	وعتقنا من رق الطغيان
And assured of the promised land	ووعدنا بأرض الميعاد
Je pef-nay Shop Sha-eneh	جي بيف ناي شوب شا إينيه
Christ split the sea of Hades	شق المسيح بحر الجحيم
And threw the devil in it	ورمي الشيطان جواه
And lifted us from it in great mystery	وأخرجنا منه بسر عظيم
Je pef-nay Shop Sha-eneh	جي بيف ناي شوب شا إينيه
*He resurrected us with His people	*وأصعدنا مع شعبه
To His heights and happiness	إلي محله وهناه
And called us 'beloved '	ودعانا أحبابه
Je pef-nay Shop Sha-eneh	جي بيف ناي شوب شا إينيه
Instead of manna and quail	عوض المن والسلوى
He gave us His body for food	اعطانا جسده غذاء
And the wonderful Church	وأعطانا البيعة الحلوة
Je pef-nay Shop Sha-eneh	جي بيف ناي شوب شا إينيه
*He sprung water from the rock	*أنبع الماء من الصخرة
And we drank His blood	وأعطانا دمه شربناه

And quenched our weary souls
Je pef-nay Shop Sha-eneh

وأروى نفوسنا القفرة
جي بيف ناي شوب شا إينيه

We reached the promised land
And received the new promise
Which is the Kingdom of heaven
Je pef nay Shop Sha-eneh

وأوصلنا ارض الميعاد
والوعد الجديد نلناه
وهو ملكوت السموات
جي بيف ناي شوب شا إينيه

Hymn Before Wednesday Theotokia
مديح واطس على ثيؤطوكية يوم الأربعاء -

All the hosts of the heaven	كل الطغمات السمائية
And the angelic soldiers	وعساكر ني أنجيلوس
Cry out in beautiful voices	يصيحون بأصوات شجية
Blessed O, Virgin and bride	طوباك يابكر وعروس
In heavenly tunes	بالنغمات العلوية
Everyone says let us praise	الكل يقولون مارين هوس
And proclaim in a wonderful chant	ويصيحون بلغات بهية
Blessed O, Virgin and bride	طوباك يابكر عروس
The Father looked from heaven	تطلع الآب من سماه ولم يجد
-and did not find	من يشبه طهرك في كل
Anyone to match your purity	طقوس:
He sent His Son to take flesh from you	ارسل ابنه تجسد منك
Blessed O, Virgin and bride	طوباك يا بكر وعروس
Came with good tidings	جاء بالبشرى مرسول
Gabriel the Archangel	غبريال بي أرشي أنجيلوس
Greeted you happily without delay	بشرك برضى وقبول
Blessed O, Virgin and bride	طوباك يا بكر وعروس

He dwelt with His Holy Spirit in you	حل بروح قدسه في احشاك
And the Lord Jesus appeared from	وظهر منك باشويس
- you	إيسوس:
You became a Mother to your	وصرت أماً لمن أنشاك
-Creator	طوباك يا بكر وعروس
Blessed O, Virgin and bride	

The salvation of Adam and his race	خلاص آدم وبنيه
And his return to Paradise	ورجوعه إلى الفردوس
Has appeared from an Ever Virgin	ظهر من بكر بتول
Blessed O, Virgin and bride	طوباك يابكر وعروس

You've been called "Best of flowers"	دعيت يازهرة الأطياب
The pure and golden censer	تى شوري إن نوب إنكا
And the holy and blessed flower"	ثاروس:
Blessed O, Virgin and bride	نيم تي إهريري إثؤاب
	طوباك يا بكر وعروس

The Lord of glory chose your beauty	رب المجد اختار حسنك
As the words of the Psalmist	كاتا إبساجي إم بي
The Lord of lords became your Son	هيمنوذوس:
Blessed O, Virgin and bride	إله الآلهة صار إبنك
	طوباك يا بكر وعروس

Ezekiel saw in his vision	رأى فى رؤياه حزقيال
A closed door guarded in the East	باباً مقفولا في المشرق

	محروس:
The High King entered by it	وقد دخله الملك المتعال
Blessed O, Virgin and bride	طوباك يا بكر وعروس

A ladder seen by Jacob	سلم رآه الأب يعقوب
Surrounded by angelic hosts	وحوله طغمات ني أنجيلوس
Worshipping the revered King	سجود للملك المرهوب
Blessed O, Virgin and bride	طوباك يا بكر وعروس

Moses witnessed and prophesied	شهد موسي وتنبا اجهار
And likened you to a planted vineyard	وشبهك بكرم مغروس
A green bush aflame with fire	عوسج أخضر في قلبه نار
Blessed O, Virgin and bride	طوباك يابكر وعروس

Zephaniah said concerning you	صوفونيوس عنك خبر
And prophesied concerning Jesus'	بشهادة عن ميلاد إيسوس
- birth	قال ينزل كندي ومطر
He will come down as rain and dew.	طوباك يا بكر وعروس
Blessed O, Virgin and bride	

Daniel said of his vision	دانيال في رؤياه قال
"I have seen a great Throne	آنوك آي ناف إأوإثرونوس
On it sat the great High King."	وعليه جلس الملك المتعال
Blessed O, Virgin and bride	طوباك يا بكر وعروس

| Moses asked to glimse and see | طلب موسي ينظر نظرة |

As you saw O Mother of the Holy One	كما رأيت يا ام القدوس
And could not bear His Light	فما طاق من نوره ثقب إبرة
Blessed O, Virgin and bride	طوباك يا بكر وعروس

He came from you and fulfilled the - promise:	ظهر منك و أوفيَ الميثاق
To Adam by entering Paradise	لآدم بدخوله إلي الفردوس
And freed his offspring from all ties	وعتق نسله من كل وثاق
Blessed O, Virgin and bride	طوباك يا بكر وعروس

Precious and sweet is your praise	علا مدحك وحلا نظمه
As the sweetness of Paradise	كحلاوة أثمار الفردوس
Who tasted it will not like otherwise	من ذاقه لايسل طعمه
Blessed O, Virgin and bride	طوباك يا بكر وعروس

You are honored and privileged	علا قدرك وحلا ذكرك
Above all the angelic ranks	وزاد رفعة عن كل الطقوس
By having the Creator in your lap	بجلوس الخالق في حجرك
Blessed O, Virgin and bride	طوباك يابكر وعروس

If we make your praise our treasure	من يجعل مدحك رأس ماله
We will gain the Lords favour	وتعشم برضي الرب القدوس
And attain our wishes	فاز ببلوغ آماله
Blessed O, Virgin and bride	طوباك يا بكر وعروس

All my life I wanted	قصدي طول عمري وحياتي

209

To praise you O, Ti-Parthenos	أكون مادح تي بارثينوس
So you will be my help when I depart	لتكون عوني عند مماتي
Blessed O, Virgin and bride	طوباك يا بكر وعروس

Who can explain the honor of Mary	كرامة مريم من يقدر
Or liken it to the moon and the sun	يشبهها بقمر وشموس
She is even greater than the Throne	إن قلنا الكرسي فهي أفخر
Blessed O, Virgin and bride	طوباك يا بكر وعروس

You bore the Lord of glory	رب المجد حملتِ
And became above all the hosts	وقد فقت كل الطقوس
Your rank is elevated and up high	وزدت قدراً وعلوتِ
Blessed O, Virgin and bride	طوباك يا بكر وعروس

Without you O Mother of Light	لولاك ياأم النور
Who could have seen Jesus' glory	من كان يعاين مجد إيسوس
Revealed so clear to the world	ويراه بين العالم مشهور
Blessed O, Virgin and bride	طوباك يابكر وعروس

O Mary who has received what you - have	من نال مانلت يامريم
Or who resembles you O Theotokos	ومن يشبهك يا أم القدوس
Which tongue can actually explain	وأي لسان يقدر يتكلم
Blessed O, Virgin and bride	طوباك يا بكر وعروس

We ask of you O Virgin	نسألك يابكر وبتول

210

Remember me before my Lord Jesus	آرى باميفئى ناهرين
So He may forgive my sins	باشويس إيسوس:
Blessed O, Virgin and bride	هينا إن تين كو إيفول
	طوباك يابكر وعروس
Your servant pleads to you	هوذا عبدك يترجاك
Do not forget me O Mother of Christ	فلا تنسيني يا أم بي
For I ask for your protection	إخرستوس
Blessed O, Virgin and bride	لأني متوسل بحماك
	طوباك يابكر وعروس
The honored father our shepherd	والاب الفاضل راعينا
Abba Shenouda Pi-archi Erevs	أنبا (شنوده) بي ارشي
With his prayers on our behalf	إيريفس بقبول صلواته
Blessed O, Virgin and bride	تعهدينا
	طوباك يابكر وعروس
And his partners in the service	وشركاؤه في الخدمة
Our holy fathers the bishops	الرسولية نين يوتي إثؤاب
Help them O pride of the human race	إن إيبيسكوبوس:
Blessed O, Virgin and bride	أجيريهم يازين البشرية
	طوباك يا بكر وعروس
Do not forget all our priests	لا تنسي سائر كهنتنا
And all the Christians	وجميع إن ني إخريستيانوس
And all the ranks of our Church	وكل رتب بيعتنا

Blessed O, Virgin and bride.	طوباك يا بكر وعروس

O pride of the human race	يازين كل البشرية
The pearl of all the hosts and ranks	زينة الرتب والطقوس
Help the Christian people	أجيري شعب المعمودية
Blessed O, Virgin and bride	طوباك يا بكر وعروس

And the Orthodox believers	وأبناء البيعة الأرثوذكسية
The leaders and the workers	الرئيس منهم والمرءوس
All the seven ranks of the Church	شاشف إن طغما إن إككليسيا
Blessed O, Virgin and bride	طوباك يا بكر وعروس

Hmyn Before Thursday Theotokia

مديح على ثيؤطوكية الخميس العليقة

REFRAIN:

المرد:

The burning bush that was seen
By Moses in the desert
And the fire burning inside it
But never hurting or harming

العليقة التى رآها
موسى النبى فى البرية
والنيران تشعل جواها
ولم تمسسها بأذية

And the bush like St Mary
Carried the flame of Divinity
In her womb for nine months
Even though still a Virgin

مثال ام النور طوباها
حملت جمر اللاهوتية
تسعة أشهر فى احشاها
وهى عذراء ببكورية

I open my mouth revealing
Pronouncing the hidden secrets
About St Mary Mother of Light
Blessed are you Pride of Humanity.

انا أفتح فمى واتكلم
وانطق بأسرار خفية
بكرامة ام النور مريم
طوباك يازين البشرية

Through Your Son, O Pride of
-creation
We became free after slavery
From Satan's grip we were saved

بابنك يازين العالم صرنا
احراراً بعد العبودية
ومن أسر إبليس خلصنا
طوباك يازين البشرية

Blessed are you Pride of Humanity.

The sayings and the prophecies
Of the Old Testament were all fulfilled
That Emmanuel will be born of you
Blessed are you Pride of Humanity.

تمت عنك كل الاقوال
والشهادات النبوية
إثفى إبجين ميسى إن
إممانوئيل طوباك يازين
البشرية

The Archangel Gabriel revealed
That the word of God will dwell in You
O pure St Mary you will carry Your
-Lord
You are the everlasting Virgin

جبرائيل بالبشرى ناداها
بحلول الكلمة الازلية
بكر بتول حملت مولاها
وهى عذراء ببكورية

REFRAIN:

المرد:

The burning bush that was seen
By Moses in the desert
And the fire burning inside it
But never hurting or harming

العليقة التى رآها
موسى النبى فى البرية
والنيران تشعل جواها
ولم تمسسها بأذية

And the bush like St Mary
Carried the flame of Divinity
In her womb for nine months
Even though still a Virgin

مثال ام النور طوباها
حملت جمر اللاهوتية
تسعة أشهر فى احشاها
وهى عذراء ببكورية

The Holy Spirit came upon you

حل بروح قدسه فى احشاكِ

And the Lord took humanity from you

وأخذ منك الناسوتية

A full human your hands carried

بشريّ كامل حملتهُ يداكِ

Blessed are you Pride of Humanity

طوباك يازين البشرية

He saved Adam and his children

خلص آدم وبنيه

And cured him from the deadly venom

وابرأه من سم الحية

And restored him to his rank

والى مرتبته قد رده

Blessed are you Pride of humanity.

طوباك يازين البشرية

David your father spoke about you

داود أبوك قال عنك

Saying prophetical testimonies

ونطق بشهادات نبوية

The God of gods became your Son

إله الآلهة صار ابنك

Blessed are you Pride of humanity.

طوباك يازين البشرية

You have been a mother of your

دعيت أماً لمن أنشاكِ

-Creator

لأجل خلاص البشرية

For the salvation of humans

اتى وسكن فى أحشاكِ

He came and dwelt in your womb

وانت عذراء ببكورية

And your virginity is sealed.

REFRAIN:

المرد:

The burning bush that was seen

العليقة التى رآها

By Moses in the desert

موسى النبى فى البرية

And the fire burning inside it

والنيران تشعل جواها

But never hurting or harming

ولم تمسسها بأذية

And the bush like St Mary   مثال ام النور طوباها
Carried the flame of Divinity   حملت جمر اللاهوتية
In her womb for nine months   تسعة أشهر فى احشاها
Even though still a Virgin   وهى عذراء ببكورية

Lord of glory chose you   رب المجد اختار حسنك
And adorned you with Divinity   وزانك باللاهوتية
He took humanity from You   واخذ طبع الناسوت منك
Blessed are you Pride of Humanity.   طوباك يازين البشرية

A Fruitful plant without seeding   زرع اثمر من غير بذار
Grew without watering   ظهر من غير ماء وسقية
In a pure chosen field   فى حقل نقى طاهر مختار
Blessed are you Pride of Humanity.   طوباك يازين البشرية

The righteous fathers called you   سماك الآباء الابرار
A second heaven but in flesh   سماء ثانية جسدانية
In whom dwelt the Mighty God   سكن فيك المولى الجبار
Blessed are you Pride of Humanity.   طوباك يازين البشرية

Ezekiel the prophet saw you   شهد حزقيال ورآها
A sealed door towards the east   بابا مختوما فى الشرقية
Which God came into and out of   دخل فيه وخرج مولاها
And the door is still sealed tightly.   والباب مصان ببكورية

REFRAIN:

المرد:

The burning bush that was seen
By Moses in the desert
And the fire burning inside it
But never hurting or harming

العليقة التى رآها
موسى النبى فى البرية
والنيران تشعل جواها
ولم تمسسها بأذية

And the bush like St Mary
Carried the flame of Divinity
In her womb for nine months
Even though still a Virgin

مثال ام النور طوباها
حملت جمر اللاهوتية
تسعة أشهر فى احشاها
وهى عذراء ببكورية

Zephaniah explained with prophecies
About the plan of the Divinity saying
Coming down like rain without clouds
Blessed are you Pride of Humanity.

صوفونيوس شرح بكلام
عن تدبير اللاهوتية
قال ينزل كقطر بغير غمام
طوباك يازين البشرية

Daniel saw the throne
Surrounded by ranks of Light
On it sat the Holy King
Blessed are you Pride of Humanity.

دانيال عاين بى إثرونوس
وحوله طغمات نورانية
وعليه جلس الملك القدوس
طوباك يازين البشرية

God shook the heaven of heavens
Descended and took humanity
While He is still in His Father's Bosom
Blessed are you Pride of Humanity.

طأطأ سماء السموات ونزل
واتحد بالناسوتية وهو فى
حضن ابيه لم يزل
طوباك يازين البشرية

217

Many wonders appeared to us	ظهرت عجائب ورأيناها
In the books of Christianity	فى كتب البيعة المسيحية
A pure Virgin carried her Creator	بكر بتول حملت مولاها
And yet she is still a virgin.	وهي عذراء ببكورية

REFRAIN:　　　　　　　　　　　　　　　　المرد:

The burning bush that was seen　　　العليقة التى رآها
By Moses in the desert　　　موسى النبى فى البرية
And the fire burning inside it　　　والنيران تشعل جواها
But never hurting or harming　　　ولم تمسسها بأذية

And the bush like St Mary　　　مثال ام النور طوباها
Carried the flame of Divinity　　　حملت جمر اللاهوتية
In her womb for nine months　　　تسعة أشهر فى احشاها
Even though still a Virgin　　　وهى عذراء ببكورية

Your dignity is above all ranks　　　علا قدرك عن كل الطقوس
And all the heavenly hosts　　　وعن الطغمات العلوية
And all the angelic soldiers　　　وعساكر نى أنجيلوس
Blessed are you Pride of Humanity　　　طوباك يازين البشرية

He who forgives the sins of His people　　　غافر كل خطايا شعبه
And grants them all gifts　　　ومانحهم كل عطية
Took our likeness and loved us　　　تشبه بالعبد وأحبه
Blessed are you Pride of Humanity.　　　طوباك يازين البشرية

You are exalted above the whole world
And all the angelic ranks
And all the saints and righteous
Blessed are you Pride of Humanity.

فقت عن سائر بى
كوسموس:
نيم ني طغما نيم نيستراتيا:
نيم نى إثمى نيم نى
ذيكيئوس:
طوباك يازين البشرية

All of you share with me
Blessing Our Lady St Mary
Who carried God in her womb
Let us ask her prayers and
-intercessions.

قولوا ياأخوة طوباها
أوتين شويس إنيب ماريا
أمام من حملت فى أحشاها
هيتين نى طفه نيم نى
إبريسفيا

REFRAIN:

المرد:

The burning bush that was seen
By Moses in the desert
And the fire burning inside it
But never hurting or harming

العليقة التى رآها
موسى النبى فى البرية
والنيران تشعل جواها
ولم تمسسها بأذية

And the bush like St Mary
Carried the flame of Divinity
In her womb for nine months
Even though still a Virgin

مثال ام النور طوباها
حملت جمر اللاهوتية
تسعة أشهر فى احشاها
وهى عذراء ببكورية

You carried the Lord of Glory

رب المجد قد حملت

Who created all mankind	مصور كل البشرية
So you have been a throne for Him	وبكرسي الآب تشبهت
Blessed are you Pride of Humanity	طوباك يازين البشرية
He took humanity from you	لبس منك طبع الناسوت
And united it to His Divinity	متحداً باللاهوتية
And you carried one of the Trinity	وحملت الواحد من الثالوث
Blessed are you Pride of Humanity.	طوباك يازين البشرية
Who is blessed like you O St Mary?	من نال مانلت يامريم
Among all mankind	فى سائر كل البشرية
And all peoples and nations	وكل الشعوب وكل الامم
Blessed are you Pride of Humanity.	طوباك يازين البشرية
We all bless you	نحن الكل نقول طوباك
With hymns, matins and vespers	ونرتل باكر وعشية
God chose your splendour	لمن اختار حسن بهاك
For the dwelling of His Eternal Word.	لحلول الكلمة الأزلى

REFRAIN: *المرد:*

The burning bush that was seen	العليقة التى رآها
By Moses in the desert	موسى النبى فى البرية
And the fire burning inside it	والنيران تشعل جواها
But never hurting or harming	ولم تمسسها بأذية
And the bush like St Mary	مثال ام النور طوباها

Carried the flame of Divinity	حملت جمر اللاهوتية
In her womb for nine months	تسعة أشهر فى احشاها
Even though still a Virgin	وهى عذراء ببكورية

Prepare to me the means of repentance	هيئى لى التوبة يامريم
-O Mary	قبل ان يدنو الوقت علىّ
Before my end approaches	واستيقظ من غفلة الأيام
And let me awake from my sleep	وانهض من بعد توانىّ
And rise up from my laziness.	

And prepare my oil before departure	واهيئ الزاد قبل السفر
And get my strength to carry the	واجهز للحمل مطية
-burden	ساعدينى فى أرض قفرة
Help me in the wilderness of this world	بصلاتك ياسيدة البشرية
Through your prayers O Lady of	
-humanity.	

Because I am weak and lacking energy	لأنى عاجز وجهدى قليل
My burden is too heavy	وحملى مشطوط علىّ
My time for departure is at hand	وحان وقت السفر والرحيل
And your prayers are my hope.	وليس لي ملجأ الا هي

You are the one who always asks	يامن لانترجى سواها
In matins and vespers	ونسألها باكر وعشية
And we rely on your prayers	ونتعلق فى هدب رداها
And your acceptable intercessions.	وملابسها النورانية

REFRAIN:
المرد:

The burning bush that was seen
العليقة التى رآها

By Moses in the desert
موسى النبى فى البرية

And the fire burning inside it
والنيران تشعل جواها

But never hurting or harming
ولم تمسسها بأذية

And the bush like St Mary
مثال ام النور طوباها

Carried the flame of Divinity
حملت جمر اللاهوتية

In her womb for nine months
تسعة أشهر فى احشاها

Even though still a Virgin
وهى عذراء ببكورية

I send my hail to the Mother of Light
واقرئ سلامى لأم النور

Mary the support of Christianity
عون كل المسيحية

From whom our salvation came
التى منها الخلاص مشهور

For all the children of Baptism.
لجميع شعب المعمودية

Save us from all evils
تنجينا من الشرور

And the disasters of this age
ومن الآفات الزمنية

Help us in all matters
وتساعدنا فى كل الامور

As well as all Christians.
وكل الشعوب المسيحية

Everyone blesses her
يقول الكل طوباها

And asks her at matins and vespers
ويسألونها باكر وعشية

To intercede for us all
قدام من حملت فى أحشاها

Before Whom she carried in her
تشفع فينا الكل سوية
-womb.

222

And the Honoured Father Our Pope
The Head of Our Church
The Shepherd of Shepherds
Who leads us with his wisdom.

والأب الفاضل بطركنا
تاج الملة النصرانية
راعى الرعاة مثبتنا
بحسن سياسته للرعية

REFRAIN:

المرد:

The burning bush that was seen
By Moses in the desert
And the fire burning inside it
But never hurting or harming

العليقة التى رآها
موسى النبى فى البرية
والنيران تشعل جواها
ولم تمسسها بأذية

And the bush like St Mary
Carried the flame of Divinity
In her womb for nine months
Even though still a Virgin

مثال ام النور طوباها
حملت جمر اللاهوتية
تسعة أشهر فى احشاها
وهى عذراء ببكورية

The Father of fathers who inherited
 the priesthood of Melchezedek
With true steadfast faith
And true Orthodox love.

اب الآباء الحبر الوارث
كهنوت ملكيصاداكية
بإيمان صحيح ورجاء ثابت
ومحبة ارثوذكسية

Keeping his sheep from the wolves
And from all devilish snares
Pushing away from them all strange

حافظ غنمهُ من أنياب الديب
ومن كل فخاخ شيطانية
ومبطل عنهم كل أمر غريب

-doctrines And all the heresies.	وكل بدع الاريوسية
Shepherding his people in calmness	راعي شعبة بحنان صوته
Along with his spiritual teachings	وتعاليمة الروحانية
Let him enjoy his priesthood	هنيه يارب بكهنوته
Give him long life and tranquillity	بعمر فسيح وطمأنينة
The father who is keeping the laws	الأب العامل بالناموس
And all the holy commandments	وقوانين الشرطانية
Abba (…….) Pi-archi-Erevs	أنبا (شنوده) بى أرشى
The pillar of Christianity	إيرفس
	عمود دين النصرانية
And our honoured fathers the bishops	والآباء الأفاضل اساقفتنا
His partners in the Apostolic service	شركاؤه فى الخدمة
Accept their prayers so we may	الرسولية بقبول صلواتهم
Become the children of the Kingdom	يجعلنا أبناء الملكوت الأبدية
Install and keep all the presbyters	وثبت سائر كهنتنا
Priests and all the deacons	قسوس وشمامسة سوية
And keep our holy Church	وأدِم عمارة بيعتنا
By offering acceptable sacrifices	برفع قرابين مرضية
REFRAIN:	المرد:
The burning bush that was seen	العليقة التى رآها

By Moses in the desert
And the fire burning inside it
But never hurting or harming

And the bush like St Mary
Carried the flame of Divinity
In her womb for nine months
Even though still a Virgin

موسى النبى فى البرية
والنيران تشعل جواها
ولم تمسسها بأذية

مثال ام النور طوباها
حملت جمر اللاهوتية
تسعة أشهر فى احشاها
وهى عذراء ببكورية

Psali Adam on the Third Hoos
ابصالية آدم على الهوس الثالث

I thank You, O God of Israel, for You had mercy on us according to Your great mercy	Ϯϣⲉⲡ ϩ̀ⲙⲟⲧ ⲛ̀ⲧⲟⲧⲕ: Ⲫϯ ⲙ̀Ⲡⲓⲥⲣⲁⲏⲗ: ϫⲉ ⲁⲕⲓ̀ⲣⲓ ⲛⲉⲙⲁⲛ: ⲕⲁⲧⲁ ⲡⲉⲕⲛⲓϣϯ ⲛ̀ⲛⲁⲓ.	أشكرك يا إله اسرائيل لأنك صنعت معنا كعظيم رحمتك
I thank You, O God of Israel, for You have sent Your Son until He saved us.	Ϯϣⲉⲡ ϩ̀ⲙⲟⲧ ⲛ̀ⲧⲟⲧⲕ: Ⲫϯ ⲙ̀Ⲡⲓⲥⲣⲁⲏⲗ: ϫⲉ ⲁⲕⲟⲩⲱⲣⲡ ⲙ̀ⲡⲉⲕϣⲏⲣⲓ: ϣⲁ ⲛ̀ⲧⲉⲕⲥⲱϯ ⲙ̀ⲙⲟⲛ.	أشكرك يا إله اسرائيل لأنك أرسلت ابنك حتى خلصتنا
*I thank You, O God of Israel, for You were incarnate from Saint Mary.	*Ϯϣⲉⲡ ϩ̀ⲙⲟⲧ ⲛ̀ⲧⲟⲧⲕ: Ⲫϯ ⲙ̀Ⲡⲓⲥⲣⲁⲏⲗ: ϫⲉ ⲁⲕϭⲓⲥⲁⲣⲝ ⲉ̀ⲃⲟⲗ: ϧⲉⲛ ⲑⲏⲉ̀ⲑⲟⲩⲁⲃ Ⲙⲁⲣⲓⲁ̀.	*أشكرك يا إله اسرائيل لأنك تجسدت من القديسة مريم
*I thank You, O God of Israel, for You were born in	*Ϯϣⲉⲡ ϩ̀ⲙⲟⲧ ⲛ̀ⲧⲟⲧⲕ: Ⲫϯ ⲙ̀Ⲡⲓⲥⲣⲁⲏⲗ: ϫⲉ ⲁⲩⲙⲁⲥⲕ	*أشكرك يا إله اسرائيل لأنك ولدت فى بيت

Bethlehem, according to the prophecies.	ϧεν Βηθλεεμ: κατα †πⲣοφητιⲁ.	لحم كالنبوة
I thank You, O God of Israel, for the shepherds beheld Your glory.	Ϯϣεπ ⲉ̀μοτ ⲛ̀τοτⲕ: Ⲫ̀ϯ ⲙ̀Ⲡⲓⲥⲣⲁⲏⲗ : ϫε ⲁⲩⲛⲁⲩ ⲉ̀πεⲕⲱⲟⲩ: ⲛ̀ϫε ⲛⲓⲙⲁⲛⲉ̀ⲥⲱⲟⲩ.	أشكرك ياإله اسرائيل لأن الرعاة نظروا مجدك.
I thank You, O God of Israel, for You revealed to us Your Holy glory.	Ϯϣεπ ⲉ̀μοτ ⲛ̀τοτⲕ : Ⲫ̀ϯ ⲙ̀Ⲡⲓⲥⲣⲁⲏⲗ : ϫε ⲁⲕϣⲁⲓ ⲛⲁⲛ: ϧεν τεⲕμετⲥⲁⲓⲉ̀.	أشكرك ياإله اسرائيل لأنك أشرقت لنا ببهائكَ.
*I thank You, O God of Israel, for You have performed many miracles.	*Ϯϣεπ ⲉ̀μοτ ⲛ̀τοτⲕ: Ⲫ̀ϯ ⲙ̀Ⲡⲓⲥⲣⲁⲏⲗ : ϫε ⲁⲕⲣⲓ ⲛ̀ϩⲁⲛⲙⲏⲓⲛⲓ: ⲛεⲙ ϩⲁⲛ ϣ̀ⲫⲏⲣⲓ ⲉⲩⲟϣ.	*أشكرك ياإله اسرائيل لأنك صنعت آيات ومعجزات كثيرة.
*I thank You, O God of Israel, for the Jews conspired against You.	*Ϯϣεπ ⲉ̀μοτ ⲛ̀τοτⲕ: Ⲫ̀ϯ ⲙ̀Ⲡⲓⲥⲣⲁⲏⲗ: ϫε ⲁⲩⲉⲣ ⲟⲩⲥⲟϭⲛⲓ ⲉ̀ⲣⲟⲕ: ⲛ̀ϫε Ⲛⲓⲓⲟⲩⲇⲁⲓ.	*أشكرك ياإله اسرائيل لأن اليهود تشاورا عليك.

I thank You, O God of Israel, for You were crucified upon the Cross in Golgotha	Ϯϣⲉⲡ ⳉⲙⲟⲧ ⲛ̀ⲧⲟⲧⲕ: Ⲫϯ ⲙ̀Ⲡⲓⲥⲣⲁⲏⲗ : ϫⲉ ⲁⲧⲁϣⲕ ⲉ̀ⲡⲓⲥ̀ⲧⲁⲩⲣⲟⲥ: ϧⲉⲛ ϯⲅⲟⲗⲅⲟⲑⲁ.	أشكرك ياإله اسرائيل لأنك صلبت على الصليب بالجلجثة.
I thank You, O God of Israel, for You were placed in the tomb like those who are dead.	Ϯϣⲉⲡ ⳉⲙⲟⲧ ⲛ̀ⲧⲟⲧⲕ: Ⲫϯ ⲙ̀Ⲡⲓⲥⲣⲁⲏⲗ: ϫⲉ ⲁⲩⲭⲁⲕ ϧⲉⲛ ⲡⲓⲙ̀ⳉⲁⲩ: ⲙ̀ⲫⲣⲏϯ ⲛ̀ⲛⲓⲣⲉϥ-ⲙⲱⲟⲩⲧ.	أشكرك ياإله اسرائيل لأنك وضعت فى القبرمثل الاموات.
*I thank You, O God of Israel, for You have risen from the dead after three days.	*Ϯϣⲉⲡ ⳉⲙⲟⲧ ⲛ̀ⲧⲟⲧⲕ: Ⲫϯ ⲙ̀Ⲡⲓⲥⲣⲁⲏⲗ : ϫⲉ ⲙⲉⲛⲉⲛⲥⲁ ϣⲟⲙⲧ ⲛ̀ⲉ̀ⳉ-ⲟⲟⲩ: ⲁⲕⲧⲱⲛⲕ ⲉ̀ⲃⲟⲗ ϧⲉⲛ ⲛⲏⲉⲑⲙⲱⲟⲩⲧ.	*أشكرك ياإله اسرائيل لأنك قمت من الموت بعد ثلاثة أيام.
*I thank You, O God of Israel, for You have desce-nded into Hades and the abyss.	*Ϯϣⲉⲡ ⳉⲙⲟⲧ ⲛ̀ⲧⲟⲧⲕ: Ⲫϯ ⲙ̀Ⲡⲓⲥⲣⲁⲏⲗ :ϫⲉ ⲁⲕϣⲉⲛⲁⲕ ⲉ̀ⲡⲉⲥⲏⲧ ⲉ̀ⲁ̀ⲙⲉⲛ ϯ: ⲉ̀ϧⲟⲩⲛ ⲉ̀ϯⲡⲣⲟⲛⲓⲁ.	*أشكرك ياإله اسرائيل لأنك نزلت الى الجحيم حيث الهاوية.

I thank You, O God of Israel, for You have saved Adam, and his entire race.	Ϯϣⲉⲡ ⲉ̀ⲙⲟⲧ ⲛ̀ⲧⲟⲧⲕ: Ⲫϯ ⲙ̀Ⲡ̀ⲓⲥⲣⲁⲏⲗ : ϫⲉ ⲁⲕⲛⲟ-ϩⲉⲙ ⲛ̀Ⲁⲇⲁⲙ: ⲛⲉⲙ ⲡⲉϥ-ⲅⲉⲛⲟⲥ ⲧⲏⲣϥ.	أشكرك ياإله اسرائيل لأنك خلصت آدم وكل جنسه.
I thank You, O God of Israel, for You have sent Your apostles.	Ϯϣⲉⲡ ⲉ̀ⲙⲟⲧ ⲛ̀ⲧⲟⲧⲕ: Ⲫϯ ⲙ̀Ⲡ̀ⲓⲥⲣⲁⲏⲗ : ϫⲉ ⲁⲕϩⲟ-ⲛϩⲉⲛ ⲉ̀ⲧⲟⲧⲟⲩ: ⲛ̀ⲛⲉⲕⲁ̀ⲡⲟⲥⲧ ⲟⲗⲟⲥ.	أشكرك ياإله اسرائيل لأنك اوصيت رسلك.
*I thank You, O God of Israel, for You ascended into the highest heavens.	*Ϯϣⲉⲡ ⲉ̀ⲙⲟⲧ ⲛ̀ⲧⲟⲧⲕ: Ⲫϯ ⲙ̀Ⲡ̀ⲓⲥⲣⲁⲏⲗ : ϫⲉ ⲁⲕ-ϣⲉⲛⲁⲕ ⲉ̀ϩⲣⲏⲓ : ⲉ̀ⲡ-ϣⲱⲓ ⲉ̀ⲛⲓⲫⲏⲟⲩⲓ	*أشكرك ياإله اسرائيل لأنك صعدت الى أعلى السموات
*I thank You, O God of Israel, for You sat On the right of the Pantocrator.	*Ϯϣⲉⲡ ⲉ̀ⲙⲟⲧ ⲛ̀ⲧⲟⲧⲕ: Ⲫϯ ⲙ̀Ⲡ̀ⲓⲥⲣⲁⲏⲗ : ϫⲉ ⲁⲕ-ϩⲉⲙⲥⲓ ⲥⲁⲟⲩⲓⲛⲁⲙ: ⲙ̀Ⲡⲓⲡⲁⲛ ⲧⲟⲕⲣⲁⲧⲱⲣ.	*أشكرك ياإله اسرائيل لأنك جلست عن يمين ضابط الكل.
I thank You, O God of Israel, for You shall come	Ϯϣⲉⲡ ⲉ̀ⲙⲟⲧ ⲛ̀ⲧⲟⲧⲕ: Ⲫϯ ⲙ̀Ⲡ̀ⲓⲥⲣⲁⲏⲗ : ϫⲉ ⲉⲕⲉ̀ⲓ ⲉ̀ⲧϩⲁⲡ: ⲉ̀ϯⲟⲓⲕⲟⲩⲙⲉⲛⲏ.	أشكرك ياإله اسرائيل لأنك ستأتى وتدين

and judge the entire world.		المسكونة
I thank You, O God of Israel, Grant unto me mercy and forgiveness.	Ϯϣⲉⲡ ⳉⲙⲟⲧ ⲛ̀ⲧⲟⲧⲕ: Ⲫϯ ⲙ̀Ⲡⲓⲥⲣⲁⲏⲗ : ⲙⲟⲓ ⲛⲏⲓ ⲛ̀ⲟⲩⲛⲁⲓ: ⲛⲉⲙ ⲟⲩⲭⲱ ⲉⲃⲟⲗ.	أشكرك ياإله اسرائيل اعطنى رحمة وغفراناً
*I thank You, O God of Israel, absolve and remit all our trespasses.	*Ϯϣⲉⲡ ⳉⲙⲟⲧ ⲛ̀ⲧⲟⲧⲕ: Ⲫϯ ⲙ̀Ⲡⲓⲥⲣⲁⲏⲗ : ⲁ̀ⲣⲓⲥⲧⲛⲭⲱⲣⲓⲛ : ⲛ̀ⲛⲉⲛⲡⲁⲣⲁⲡⲧⲱⲙⲁ.	*أشكرك ياإله اسرائيل اصفح عن زلاتنا
*I thank You, O God of Israel, we glorify Your Name and we worship You according to Your great mercy.	*Ϯϣⲉⲡ ⳉⲙⲟⲧ ⲛ̀ⲧⲟⲧⲕ: Ⲫϯ ⲙ̀Ⲡⲓⲥⲣⲁⲏⲗ : ϯϯⲱⲟⲩ ⲙ̀ⲡⲉⲕⲣⲁⲛ: ⲟⲩⲟⳉ ⲧⲉⲛ-ⲟⲩⲱϣⲧ ⲙ̀ⲙⲟⲕ: ⲕⲁⲧⲁ ⲡⲉⲕⲛⲓϣϯ ⲛ̀ⲛⲁⲓ.	*أشكرك ياإله اسرائيل و نمجد إسمك و نسجد لك كعظيم رحمتك.

Third Hoos – Пιϩⲱⲥ ⲙⲙⲁϩ $\overline{\Gamma}$

الهوس الثالث

Blessed are You, O Lord, God of our fathers, and exceedingly to be praised, and exalted above all forever.	Ⲕ̀ⲥⲙⲁⲣⲱⲟⲩⲧ Ⲡϭⲟⲓⲥ Ⲫⲛⲟⲩϯ ⲛ̀ⲧⲉ ⲛⲉⲛⲓⲟϯ : ⲕⲉⲣϩⲟⲩⲟ̀ ⲥⲙⲁⲣⲱⲟⲩⲧ ⲕⲉⲣϩⲟⲩⲟ̀ ϭⲓⲥⲓ ϣⲁ ⲛⲓⲉⲛⲉϩ.	مبارك أنت أيها الرب إله آبائنا ومتزايد بركة ومتزايد علواً إلى الآباد.
*Blessed is Your Holy Name and Your glory, and exceedingly to be praised, and exalted above all forever.	*Ⲧ̀ⲥⲙⲁⲣⲱⲟⲩⲧ ⲛ̀ⲝⲉ ⲡⲓⲣⲁⲛ ⲉⲑⲟⲩⲁⲃ ⲛ̀ⲧⲉ ⲡⲉⲕⲱ̀ⲟⲩ : ϥⲉⲣϩⲟⲩⲟ̀ ⲥ̀ⲙⲁⲣⲱⲟⲩⲧ ϥⲉⲣϩⲟⲩⲟ̀ ϭⲓⲥⲓ ϣⲁ ⲛⲓⲉⲛⲉϩ.	*مبارك اسم مجدك القدوس ومتزايد بركة ومتزايد علواً إلى الآباد.
Blessed are You in the holy temple of Your glory, and exceedingly to be praised, and exalted above all forever.	Ⲕ̀ⲥⲙⲁⲣⲱⲟⲩⲧ ϧⲉⲛ ⲡⲓⲉⲣⲫⲉⲓ ⲛ̀ⲧⲉ ⲡⲉⲕⲱ̀ⲟⲩ ⲉⲑⲟⲩⲁⲃ: ⲕⲉⲣϩⲟⲩⲟ̀ ⲥⲙⲁⲣⲱⲟⲩⲧ ⲕⲉⲣϩⲟⲩⲟ̀ ϭⲓⲥⲓ ϣⲁ ⲛⲓⲉⲛⲉϩ.	مبارك أنت فى هيكل مجدك المقدس و متزايد بركة ومتزايد علواً إلى الآباد.

231

*Blessed are You who beholds the depths and sits upon the Cherubim, and exceedingly to be praised, and exalted above all forever.	*K̀ⲥⲙⲁⲣⲱⲟⲩⲧ ⲫⲏⲉⲑ-ⲛⲁⲩ ⲉ̀ⲛⲓⲛⲟⲩⲛ ⲉϥϩⲉⲙⲥⲓ ϩⲓϫⲉⲛ ⲛⲓ ⲭⲉⲣⲟⲩⲃⲓⲙ : ⲕ̀-ⲉⲣϩⲟⲩⲟ̀ ⲥ̀ⲙⲁⲣⲱⲟⲩⲧ ⲕⲉⲣϩⲟⲩⲟ̀ ϭ̀ⲓⲥⲓ ϣⲁ ⲛⲓⲉ̀ⲛⲉϩ.	*مبارك أنت أيها الناظر إلى الأعماق الجالس على الشاروبيم و متزايد بركة ومتزايد علواً إلى الآباد.
Blessed are You on the throne of Your Kingdom, and exce-edingly to be praised, and exalted above all forever.	`K̀ⲥⲙⲁⲣⲱⲟⲩⲧ ϩⲓϫⲉⲛ ⲡⲓⲑⲣⲟⲛⲟⲥ ⲛ̀ⲧⲉ ⲧⲉⲕⲙ-ⲉⲧⲟⲩⲣⲟ : ⲕⲉⲣϩⲟⲩⲟ̀ ⲥ̀ⲙ-ⲁⲣⲱⲟⲩⲧ ⲕⲉⲣϩⲟⲩⲟ̀ ϭ̀ⲓⲥⲓ ϣⲁ ⲛⲓⲉ̀ⲛⲉϩ.	مبارك أنت على عرش مُلكك ومتزايد بركة ومتزايد علواً إلى الآباد.
*Blessed are You in the firmament of heaven, and exce-edingly to be prai-sed, and exalted above all forever.	*K̀ⲥⲙⲁⲣⲱⲟⲩⲧ ϧⲉⲛ ⲡⲓ-ⲥⲧⲉⲣⲉⲱ̀ⲙⲁ ⲛ̀ⲧⲉ ⲧ̀ⲫⲉ : ⲕⲉⲣϩⲟⲩⲟ̀ ⲥ̀ⲙⲁⲣⲱⲟⲩ-ⲧ ⲕⲉⲣϩⲟⲩⲟ̀ ϭ̀ⲓⲥⲓ ϣⲁ ⲛⲓⲉ̀ⲛⲉϩ.	*مبارك أنت فى فلك السماء و متزايد بركة ومتزايد علواً إلى الآباد.
Bless the Lord, O you works of the Lord: Praise Him	`Cⲙⲟⲩ ⲉ̀Ⲡϭⲟⲓⲥ ⲛⲓϩ̀-ⲃⲏⲟⲩⲓ̀ ⲧⲏⲣⲟⲩ ⲛ̀ⲧⲉ Ⲡϭⲟⲓⲥ : ϩⲱⲥ ⲉ̀ⲣⲟϥ	باركى الرب ياجميع أعمال الرب سبّحيه

and exalt Him above all forever.	ⲁⲣⲓϩⲟⲩⲟ̀ ϭⲁⲥϥ ϣⲁ ⲛⲓⲉⲛⲉϩ.	وزيديه علواً إلى الآباد.
*Bless the Lord, O heaven: Praise Him and exalt Him above all forever.	* Ⲥⲙⲟⲩ ⲉ̀Ⲡϭⲟⲓⲥ ⲛⲓⲫⲏ-ⲟⲩⲓ : ϩⲱⲥ ⲉ̀ⲣⲟϥ ⲁⲣⲓ-ϩⲟⲩⲟ̀ ϭⲁⲥϥ ϣⲁ ⲛⲓⲉⲛⲉϩ.	*باركى الرب ايتها السموات سبّحيه وزيديه علواً إلى الآباد.
Bless the Lord, all you angels of the Lord: Praise Him and exalt Him above all forever.	ˋⲤⲙⲟⲩ ⲉ̀Ⲡϭⲟⲓⲥ ⲛⲓⲁⲅ-ⲅⲉⲗⲟⲥ ⲧⲏⲣⲟⲩ ⲛ̀ⲧⲉ Ⲡϭⲟⲓⲥ :ϩⲱⲥ ⲉ̀ⲣⲟϥ ⲁ̀-ⲣⲓϩⲟⲩⲟ̀ ϭⲁⲥϥ ϣⲁ ⲛⲓⲉⲛⲉϩ.	باركوا الرب يا جميع ملائكة الرب سبّحوه وزيدوه علواً إلى الآباد.
*Bless the Lord, all you waters that be above the heaven: Praise Him and exalt Him above all forever.	* Ⲥⲙⲟⲩ ⲉ̀Ⲡϭⲟⲓⲥ ⲛⲓⲙ-ⲱⲟⲩ ⲧⲏⲣⲟⲩ ⲉⲧⲥⲁ ⲡ̀ϣ-ⲱⲓ ⲛ̀ⲧⲫⲉ : ϩⲱⲥ ⲉ̀ⲣⲟϥ ⲁⲣⲓϩⲟⲩⲟ̀ ϭⲁⲥϥ ϣⲁ ⲛⲓⲉⲛⲉϩ.	*باركى الرب يا جميع المياه التي فوق السماء سبّحيـه وزيديه علواً إلى الآباد.
Bless the Lord, all you powers of the	Ⲥⲙⲟⲩ ⲉ̀Ⲡϭⲟⲓⲥ ⲛⲓϫⲟⲙ	باركا الرب ياجميع قوات

Lord: Praise Him and exalt Him above all forever.	ⲧⲏⲣⲟⲩ ⲛ̀ⲧⲉ Ⲡ̀ϭⲟⲓⲥ : ϩⲱⲥ ⲉ̀ⲣⲟϥ ⲁⲣⲓϩⲟⲩⲟ̀ ϭⲁⲥϥϣⲁ ⲛⲓⲉ̀ⲛⲉϩ.	الرب سبّحيه وزيديه علواً إلى الآباد.
*Bless the Lord, O sun and moon: Praise Him and exalt Him above all forever.	*Ⲥⲙⲟⲩ ⲉ̀Ⲡ̀ϭⲟⲓⲥ ⲡⲓⲣⲏ ⲛⲉⲙ ⲡⲓⲓⲟϩ : ϩⲱⲥ ⲉ̀ⲣⲟϥ ⲁⲣⲓϩⲟⲩⲟ̀ ϭⲁⲥϥ ϣⲁ ⲛⲓⲉ̀ⲛⲉϩ.	*باركا الرب أيتها الشمس والقمر سبّحاه وزيداه علواً إلى الآباد.
Bless the Lord, all you stars of heaven: Praise Him and exalt Him above all forever.	` Ⲥⲙⲟⲩ ⲉ̀Ⲡ̀ϭⲟⲓⲥ ⲛⲓⲥⲓⲟⲩ ⲧⲏⲣⲟⲩ ⲛ̀ⲧⲉ ⲧ̀ⲫⲉ : ϩⲱⲥ ⲉ̀ⲣⲟϥ ⲁⲣⲓϩⲟⲩⲟ̀ ϭⲁⲥϥϣⲁ ⲛⲓⲉ̀ⲛⲉϩ.	باركي الرب ياسائر نجوم السماء سبّحيه وزيديه علواً إلى الآباد.
*Bless the Lord, O you rain and dew: Praise Him and exalt Him above all forever.	*Ⲥⲙⲟⲩ ⲉ̀Ⲡ̀ϭⲟⲓⲥ ⲛⲓⲙⲟ-ⲩⲛϩⲱⲟⲩ ⲛⲉⲙ ⲛⲓⲓⲱϯ: ϩⲱⲥ ⲉ̀ⲣⲟϥ ⲁⲣⲓϩⲟⲩⲟ̀ ϭⲁⲥϥϣⲁ ⲛⲓⲉ̀ⲛⲉϩ.	*باركى الرب أيتها الأمطار مع الأنداء سبّحيه وزيديه علواً إلى الآباد.
Bless the Lord, O you clouds and	` Ⲥⲙⲟⲩ ⲉ̀Ⲡ̀ϭⲟⲓⲥ ⲛⲓϭⲏⲡⲓ	باركي الرب أيتها السحب

winds: Praise Him and exalt Him above all forever.	ⲛⲉⲙ ⲛⲓⲑⲏⲟⲩ: ϩⲱⲥ ⲉ̀ⲣⲟϥ ⲁⲣⲓϩⲟⲩⲟ̀ ϭⲁⲥϥ ϣⲁ ⲛⲓⲉⲛⲉϩ.	والرياح سبّحيه وزيديه علواً إلى الآباد.
*Bless the Lord, all you spirits: Praise Him and exalt Him above all forever.	*Ⲥⲙⲟⲩ ⲉ̀Ⲡϭⲟⲓⲥ ⲛⲓⲡ̄ⲛⲉⲩⲙⲁ ⲧⲏⲣⲟⲩ: ϩⲱⲥ ⲉ̀ⲣⲟϥ ⲁⲣⲓϩⲟⲩⲟ̀ ϭⲁⲥϥ ϣⲁ ⲛⲓⲉⲛⲉϩ.	*باركي الرب ياجميع الأرواح سبحيه وزيديه علواً إلى الآباد.
Bless the Lord, O fire and heat: Praise Him and exalt Him above all forever.	̀Ⲥⲙⲟⲩ ⲉ̀Ⲡϭⲟⲓⲥ ⲡⲓⲭⲣⲱⲙ ⲛⲉⲙ ⲡⲓⲕⲁⲩⲙⲁ: ϩⲱⲥ ⲉ̀ⲣⲟϥ ⲁⲣⲓϩⲟⲩⲟ̀ ϭⲁⲥϥ ϣⲁ ⲛⲓⲉⲛⲉϩ.	باركا الرب أيتها النار و الحرارة سبّحاه وزيداه علواً إلى الآباد.
*Bless the Lord, O cold and heat: Praise Him and exalt Him above all forever.	*̀Ⲥⲙⲟⲩ ⲉ̀Ⲡϭⲟⲓⲥ ⲡⲓⲱϫⲉⲃ ⲛⲉⲙ ⲡⲓⲕⲁⲩⲥⲱⲛ : ϩⲱⲥ ⲉ̀ⲣⲟϥ ⲁⲣⲓϩⲟⲩⲟ̀ ϭⲁⲥϥ ϣⲁ ⲛⲓⲉⲛⲉϩ.	*باركا الرب أيها البرد و الحر سبّحاه و زيداه علواً إلى الآباد.
Bless the Lord, O you dew and winds: Praise Him and	̀Ⲥⲙⲟⲩ ⲉ̀Ⲡϭⲟⲓⲥ ⲛⲓⲓⲱϯ ⲛⲉⲙ ⲛⲓⲛⲓϥⲓ : ϩⲱⲥ ⲉ̀ⲣⲟϥ	باركي الرب أيتها الأهوية و الأنداء سبّحيه

exalt Him above all forever.	ⲁⲣⲓϩⲟⲩⲟ̀ ϭⲁⲥϥ ϣⲁ ⲛⲓⲉⲛⲉϩ.	وزيديه علواً إلى الآباد.
*Bless the Lord, O you nights and days: Praise Him and exalt Him above all forever.	* Ⲥⲙⲟⲩ ⲉ̀Ⲡϭⲟⲓⲥ ⲛⲓⲉϫ-ⲱⲣϩ ⲛⲉⲙ ⲛⲓⲉ̀ϩⲟⲟⲩ ⲇ ϩⲱⲥ ⲉ̀ⲣⲟϥ ⲁⲣⲓϩⲟⲩⲟ̀ ϭⲁⲥϥ ϣⲁ ⲛⲓⲉⲛⲉϩ.	*باركي الرب أيتها الليالي والأيام سبّحيه وزيديه علواً إلى الآباد.
Bless the Lord, O light and darkness: Praise Him and exalt Him above all forever.	` Ⲥⲙⲟⲩ ⲉ̀Ⲡϭⲟⲓⲥ ⲡⲓⲟⲩⲱ- ⲓⲛⲓ ⲛⲉⲙ ⲡⲓⲭⲁⲕⲓ ϩ ϩⲱⲥ ⲉ̀ⲣⲟϥ ⲁⲣⲓϩⲟⲩⲟ̀ ϭⲁⲥϥ ϣⲁ ⲛⲓⲉⲛⲉϩ.	باركا الرب أيها النور والظلمة سبّحاه وزيداه علواً إلى الآباد.
*Bless the Lord, O frost and cold: Praise Him and exalt Him above all forever.	*` Ⲥⲙⲟⲩ ⲉ̀Ⲡϭⲟⲓⲥ ⲡⲓϫⲁϥ ⲛⲉⲙ ⲡⲓⲱ̀ϫⲉⲃ ⳥ ϩⲱⲥ ⲉ̀ⲣ- ⲟϥ ⲁⲣⲓϩⲟⲩⲟ̀ ϭⲁⲥϥ ϣⲁ ⲛⲓⲉⲛⲉϩ.	*باركا الرب أيها البرد والصقيع سبّحاه وزيداه علواً إلى الآباد.
Bless the Lord, O snow and ice: Praise Him and exalt Him above all forever.	` Ⲥⲙⲟⲩ ⲉ̀Ⲡϭⲟⲓⲥ ϯⲡⲁⲭⲛⲏ ⲛⲉⲙ ⲡⲓⲭⲓⲱⲛ ⳥ ϩⲱⲥ ⲉⲣⲟϥ ⲁⲣⲓϩⲟⲩⲟ̀ ϭⲁⲥϥ ϣⲁ	باركا الرب أيها الجليد والثلج سبّحاه وزيداه علواً إلى

	ⲛⲓⲉ̀ⲛⲉϩ.	الآباد.
*Bless the Lord, O you lightnings and clouds: Praise Him and exalt Him above all forever.	*Ⲥⲙⲟⲩ ⲉ̀Ⲡϭⲟⲓⲥ ⲛⲓⲥⲉⲧⲉⲃⲣⲏϫ ⲛⲉⲙ ⲛⲓϭⲏⲡⲓ ϩⲱⲥ ⲉ̀ⲣⲟϥ ⲁⲣⲓϩⲟⲩⲟ̀ ϭⲁⲥϥ ϣⲁ ⲛⲓⲉ̀ⲛⲉϩ.	*باركي الرب أيتها البروق والسحب سبّحيه وزيديه علواً إلى الآباد.
Bless the Lord, all the earth: Praise Him and exalt Him above all forever.	Ⲥⲙⲟⲩ ⲉ̀Ⲡϭⲟⲓⲥ ⲡⲓⲕⲁϩⲓ ⲧⲏⲣϥ : ϩⲱⲥ ⲉ̀ⲣⲟϥ ⲁⲣⲓϩⲟⲩⲟ̀ ϭⲁⲥϥ ϣⲁ ⲛⲓⲉ̀ⲛⲉϩ.	باركي الرب أيتها الأرض كلها سبّحيه وزيديه علواً إلى الآباد.
*Bless the Lord, O you mountains and all hills: Praise Him and exalt Him above all forever.	*Ⲥⲙⲟⲩ ⲉ̀Ⲡϭⲟⲓⲥ ⲛⲓⲧⲱⲟⲩ ⲛⲉⲙ ⲛⲓⲕⲁⲗⲁⲙⲫⲱⲟⲩ ⲧⲏⲣⲟⲩ : ϩⲱⲥ ⲉ̀ⲣⲟϥ ⲁⲣⲓϩⲟⲩⲟ̀ ϭⲁⲥϥ ϣⲁ ⲛⲓⲉ̀ⲛⲉϩ.	*باركي الرب أيتها الجبال وجميع الآكام سبّحيه وزيديه علواً إلى الآباد.
Bless the Lord, all you things that spring up on the earth: Praise Him	Ⲥⲙⲟⲩ ⲉ̀Ⲡϭⲟⲓⲥ ⲛⲏ ⲧⲏⲣⲟⲩ ⲉⲧⲣⲏⲧ ϩⲓϫⲉⲛ ⲡ̀ϩⲟ ⲙ̀ⲡⲕⲁϩⲓ: ϩⲱ-	باركى الرب يا جميع ما ينبت على وجه الأرض سبّحه

and exalt Him above all forever.	ⲥ ⲉⲣⲟϥ ⲁⲣⲓϩⲟⲩⲟ ϭⲁⲥϥ ϣⲁ ⲛⲓⲉⲛⲉϩ.	وزيده علواً إلى الآباد.
*Bless the Lord, O you fountains: Praise Him and exalt Him above all forever.	*Ⲥⲙⲟⲩ ⲉⲠϭⲟⲓⲥ ⲛⲓⲙⲟⲩⲙⲓ : ϩⲱⲥ ⲉⲣⲟϥ ⲁⲣⲓϩⲟⲩⲟ ϭⲁⲥϥ ϣⲁ ⲛⲓⲉⲛⲉϩ.	*باركي الرب أيتها الينابيع سبّحيه وزيديه علواً إلى الآباد.
Bless the Lord, O you seas and rivers: Praise Him and exalt Him above all forever.	`Ⲥⲙⲟⲩ ⲉⲠϭⲟⲓⲥ ⲛⲓⲁⲙⲁⲓⲟⲩ ⲛⲉⲙ ⲛⲓⲓⲁⲣⲱⲟⲩ: ϩⲱⲥ ⲉⲣⲟϥ ⲁⲣⲓϩⲟⲩⲟ ϭⲁⲥϥ ϣⲁ ⲛⲓⲉⲛⲉϩ.	باركي الرب أيتها البحار والأنهار سبّحيه وزيديه علواً إلى الآباد.
*Bless the Lord, O you whales and all that moves in the waters: Praise Him and exalt Him above all forever.	*Ⲥⲙⲟⲩ ⲉⲠϭⲟⲓⲥ ⲛⲓⲕⲏⲧⲟⲥ ⲛⲉⲙ ⲉⲛⲭⲁⲓ ⲛⲓⲃⲉⲛ ⲉⲧⲕⲓⲙ ϧⲉⲛ ⲛⲓⲙⲱⲟⲩ : ϩⲱⲥ ⲉⲣⲟϥ ⲁⲣⲓϩⲟⲩⲟ ϭⲁⲥϥ ϣⲁ ⲛⲓⲉⲛⲉϩ.	*باركي الرب أيتها الحيتان وجميع ما يتحرك في المياه سبّحيه وزيديه علواً إلى الآباد.
Bless the Lord, all you birds of the sky: Praise Him and	`Ⲥⲙⲟⲩ ⲉⲠϭⲟⲓⲥ ⲛⲓϩⲁⲗⲁϯ ⲧⲏⲣⲟⲩ ⲛⲧⲉ ⲧⲫⲉ :	باركي الرب يا جميع طيور السماء سبّحيه

exalt Him above all forever.	ϩⲱⲥ ⲉⲣⲟϥ ⲁⲣⲓϩⲟⲩⲟ ϭⲁⲥϥϣⲁ ⲛⲓⲉⲛⲉϩ.	وزيديه علواً إلى الآباد.
*Bless the Lord, all you wild beasts and cattle: Praise Him and exalt Him above all forever.	* Ⲥⲙⲟⲩ ⲉⲠϬ̅ⲟ̅ⲓ̅ⲥ̅ ⲛⲓⲑⲏⲣⲓⲟⲛ ⲛⲉⲙ ⲛⲓⲧⲉⲃⲛⲱⲟⲩⲓ ⲧⲏⲣⲟⲩ : ϩⲱⲥ ⲉⲣⲟϥ ⲁⲣⲓϩⲟⲩⲟ ϭⲁⲥϥ ϣⲁ ⲛⲓⲉⲛⲉϩ.	*باركي الرب أيتها الوحوش وكل البهائم سبّحيه وزيديه علواً إلى الآباد.
Bless the Lord, O you sons of men, worship the Lord: Praise Him and exalt Him above all forever.	Ⲥⲙⲟⲩ ⲉⲠϬ̅ⲟ̅ⲓ̅ⲥ̅ ⲛⲓϣⲏⲣⲓ ⲛ̀ⲧⲉ ⲛⲓⲣⲱⲙⲓ ⲟⲩⲱϣⲧ ⲙ̀Ⲡϭⲟⲓⲥ : ϩⲱⲥ ⲉⲣⲟϥ ⲁⲣⲓϩⲟⲩⲟ ϭⲁⲥϥ ϣⲁ ⲛⲓⲉⲛⲉϩ.	باركوا الرب يا بنى البشر واسجدوا للرب سبّحوه وزيدوه علواً إلى الآباد.
*Bless the Lord, O Israel: Praise Him and exalt Him above all forever.	*Ⲥⲙⲟⲩ ⲉⲠϬ̅ⲟ̅ⲓ̅ⲥ̅ Ⲡⲓⲥⲣⲁⲏⲗ: ϩⲱⲥ ⲉⲣⲟϥ ⲁⲣⲓϩⲟⲩⲟ ϭⲁⲥϥ ϣⲁ ⲛⲓⲉⲛⲉϩ.	*بارك الرب يا اسرائيل سبّحه وزيده علواً إلى الآباد.
Bless the Lord, O	Ⲥⲙⲟⲩ ⲉⲠϬ̅ⲟ̅ⲓ̅ⲥ̅ ⲛⲓⲟⲩ-	باركوا الرب يا

you priests of the Lord: Praise Him and exalt Him above all forever.	ⲏⲃ ⲛ̀ⲧⲉ Ⲡ̅ϭⲟⲓⲥ⳾ ϩⲱⲥ ⲉ̀ⲣⲟϥ ⲁⲣⲓϩⲟⲩ̀ⲟ ϭⲁⲥϥϣⲁ ⲛⲓⲉ̀ⲛⲉϩ.	كهنة الرب سبّحوه وزيدوه علواً إلى الآباد.
*Bless the Lord, O you servants of the Lord: Praise Him and exalt Him above all forever.	*Ⲥⲙⲟⲩ ⲉ̀Ⲡ̅ϭⲟⲓⲥ ⲛⲓⲉ̀ⲃⲓⲁⲓⲕ ⲛ̀ⲧⲉ Ⲡ̅ϭⲟⲓⲥ ⳾ ϩⲱⲥ ⲉ̀ⲣⲟϥ ⲁⲣⲓϩⲟⲩ̀ⲟ ϭⲁⲥϥϣⲁ ⲛⲓⲉ̀ⲛⲉϩ.	*باركوا الرب يا عبيد الرب سبّحوه وزيدوه علواً إلى الآباد.
Bless the Lord, O you spirits and souls of the just: Praise Him and exalt Him above all forever.	Ⲥⲙⲟⲩ ⲉ̀Ⲡ̅ϭⲟⲓⲥ ⲛⲓⲡ̀ⲛⲉⲩⲙⲁ ⲛⲉⲙ ⲛⲓⲯⲩⲭⲏ ⲛ̀ⲧⲉ ⲛⲓⲑⲙⲏⲓ ⳾ ϩⲱⲥ ⲉ̀ⲣⲟϥ ⲁⲣⲓϩⲟⲩ̀ⲟ ϭⲁⲥϥ ϣⲁ ⲛⲓⲉ̀ⲛⲉϩ.	باركوا الرب يا ارواح وانفس الصديقين سبّحوه وزيدوه علواً إلى الآباد.
*Bless the Lord, O you holy and humble of heart: Praise Him and exalt Him above all forever.	* Ⲥⲙⲟⲩ ⲉ̀Ⲡ̅ϭⲟⲓⲥ ⲛⲏⲉⲑⲟⲩⲁⲃ ⲛⲉⲙ ⲛⲏⲉⲧⲑⲉⲃⲓⲏⲟⲩⲧ ϧⲉⲛ ⲡⲟⲩϩⲏⲧ ⳾ ϩⲱⲥ ⲉ̀ⲣⲟϥ ⲁⲣⲓϩⲟⲩ̀ⲟ ϭⲁⲥϥϣⲁ ⲛⲓⲉ̀ⲛⲉϩ.	*باركوا الرب أيها القديسون والمتواضعو القلوب سبّحوه وزيدوه علواً إلى الآباد.
Bless the Lord, O	Ⲥⲙⲟⲩ ⲉ̀Ⲡ̅ϭⲟⲓⲥ Ⲁⲛⲁⲛ-	باركوا الرب

| Hananiah, Azariah, Mishael: Praise Him and exalt Him above all forever. | ⲓⲁⲥ Ⲇⲍⲁⲣⲓⲁⲥ Ⲙⲓⲥⲁⲏⲗ ⲕⲉ Ⲇⲁⲛⲓⲏⲗ : ϩⲱⲥ ⲉⲣⲟϥ ⲁⲣⲓϩⲟⲩⲟ ϭⲁⲥϥ ϣⲁ ⲛⲓⲉⲛⲉϩ. | ياحنانيا و عزاريا و ميصائيل سبّحوه وزيدوه علواً إلى الآباد. |
| *Bless the Lord, O you who worship the Lord, the God of our fathers: Praise Him and exalt Him above all forever. | *Ⲥⲙⲟⲩ ⲉⲠϭⲟⲓⲥ ⲛⲏⲉⲧⲉⲣⲥⲉⲃⲉⲥⲑⲉ ⲙⲠϭⲟⲓⲥ Ⲫϯ ⲛⲧⲉ ⲛⲉⲛⲓⲟϯ : ϩⲱⲥ ⲉⲣⲟϥ ⲁⲣⲓϩⲟⲩⲟ ϭⲁⲥϥ ϣⲁ ⲛⲓⲉⲛⲉϩ. | *باركوا الرب ياعابدي الرب اله آبائنا سبّحوه وزيدوه علواً إلى الآباد. |

Praise of the Three Young Men
ابصالية الثلاثة فتية

O sing unto Him who was crucified, buried and resurrected, Who trampled and abolished death, Praise Him and exalt Him above all.

Take off the old man, and put on the new and superior one, come closer to the Greatness of mercy, Praise Him and exalt Him above all.

*All you Christian people, the priests and the deacons, glorify the Lord for He is worthy, Praise

Ⲁⲣⲓⲯⲁⲗⲓⲛ ⲉⲫⲏⲉⲧ-ⲁⲩⲁϣϥ: ⲉ̀ϩⲣⲏⲓ ⲉ̀ϫⲱⲛ ⲟⲩⲟϩ ⲁⲩⲕⲟⲥϥ: ⲁϥ-ⲱⲛϥ ⲁϥⲕⲱⲣϥ ⲙ̀ⲫⲙⲟⲩ ⲁϥϯ ϣⲟϣϥ: ϩⲱⲥ ⲉ̀ⲣⲟϥ ⲁ̀ⲣⲓϩⲟⲩⲟ̀ ϭⲁⲥϥ.

Ⲃⲱϣ ⲙ̀ⲡⲓⲣⲱⲙⲓ ⲙ̀ⲡⲁ-ⲗⲉⲟⲥ: ⲟⲩⲟϩ ⲭⲱⲗ-ϩ ⲙ̀ⲡⲓⲃⲉⲣⲓ ⲉⲩⲕⲗⲉⲟⲥ: ⲟⲩⲟϩ ⲉ̀ϧⲱⲛⲧ ⲉ̀ⲙⲉⲧⲁ-ⲉⲗⲉⲟⲥ: ϩⲱⲥ ⲉ̀ⲣⲟ-ϥ ⲁ̀ⲣⲓϩⲟⲩⲟ̀ ϭⲁⲥϥ.

*Ⲅⲉⲛⲟⲥ ⲛ̀ⲛⲓⲭⲣⲓⲥⲧⲓ-ⲁⲛⲟⲥ: ⲛ̀ⲛⲓⲡⲣⲉⲥⲃⲩⲧⲉⲣ-ⲟⲥ ⲕⲉ Ⲇⲓⲁⲕⲟⲛⲟⲥ: ⲙⲁ-ⲱⲟⲩ ⲙ̀Ⲡϭⲟⲓⲥ ϫⲉ ⲟⲩ-

رتلوا للذى صلب عنا وقبر وقام. وأبطل الموت وأهانه سبّحوه وزيدوه علواً.

اخلعوا الانسان العتيق والبسوا الجديد الفاخر. واقتربوا إلى عظم الرحمة سبّحوه وزيدوه علواً.

*ياجنس المسيحين القسوس والشمامسة أعطوا مجداً.

Him and exalt Him above all.

*Come to us o three children, whom Christ our God has lifted, and from the devil has delivered, Praise Him and exalt Him above all.

For the sake of your God the Messiah, the giver of all good things, come unto us O Hananiah, Praise Him and exalt Him above all.

O Azariah the Zealot, morning and noon and in the evening, glorify the

ⲇⲓⲕⲁⲛⲟⲥ: ϩⲱⲥ ⲉⲣⲟ-ϥⲁⲣⲓϩⲟⲩⲟ ϭⲁⲥϥ.

*Ⲇⲉⲩⲧⲉ ϩⲁⲣⲟⲛ ⲱ ⲡⲓϣⲟⲙⲧ ⲛⲁⲗⲟⲩ : ⲉⲧⲁ Ⲡⲓⲭⲣⲓⲥⲧⲟⲥ Ⲡⲉⲛⲛⲟⲩϯ ⲟⲗⲟⲩ : ⲁϥⲛⲁϩⲙⲟⲩ ⲉⲃⲟⲗϩⲁ ⲡⲓⲇⲓⲁⲃⲟⲗⲟⲥ : ϩⲱⲥ ⲉⲣⲟϥⲁⲣⲓϩⲟⲩⲟ ϭⲁⲥϥ.

Ⲉⲑⲃⲉ Ⲡⲉⲕⲛⲟⲩϯ Ⲙⲁⲥⲓⲁⲥ: ⲫⲣⲉϥϯ ⲛⲉⲩⲉⲣⲅⲉⲥⲓⲁⲥ: ⲁⲙⲟⲩ ϣⲁⲣⲟⲛ Ⲁⲛⲁⲛⲓⲁⲥ: ϩⲱⲥ ⲉⲣⲟ ϥⲁⲣⲓϩⲟⲩⲟ ϭⲁⲥϥ.

Ⲍⲏⲗⲱⲧⲉ ` Ⲁⲍⲁⲣⲓⲁⲥ ⲉⲥⲡⲉⲣⲁⲥ ⲕⲉ ⲡⲣⲱⲓ ⲕⲉ ⲙⲉⲥⲛⲙⲃⲣⲓⲁⲥ: ⲙⲁⲱⲟⲩ ⲛⲧϫⲟⲙ ⲛϯⲧⲣⲓ-

للرب لانه مستوجب سبّحوه وزيدوه علواً.

*هلمّ إلينا أيها الثلاثة فتية الذين رفعهم المسيح إلهنا. وأنقذهم من ابليس سبّحوه وزيدوه علواً.

من أجل الهك ماسيا المانح الإحسان. هلمّ إلينا ياحنانيا سبّحوه وزيدوه علوا.

يا عزاريا الغيور عشية وبكرة والظهيرة. أعط مجداً لقوة

power of the Trinity, Praise Him and exalt Him above all.

ⲁⲥ: ϩⲱⲥ ⲉⲣⲟϥ ⲁ-ⲣⲓϩⲟⲩ̀ⲟ ϭⲁⲥϥ.

الثالوث. سبّحه وزده علواً.

*Behold Emmanuel our Lord, is now in our midst O Mishael, proclaim with the voice of joy, Praise Him and exalt Him above all.

*Ⲏⲡⲡⲉ ⲅⲁⲣ ⲓⲥ Ⲉⲙⲙ-ⲁⲛⲟⲩⲏⲗ: ϩⲓⲧⲉⲛ ⲙ-ⲏϯ ⲱ̀ Ⲙⲓⲥⲁⲏⲗ: ⲗⲉⲗⲓ ϧⲉⲛ ⲟⲩⲥⲙⲏ ⲛ̀ⲑⲉⲗⲏⲗ: ϩⲱⲥ ⲉⲣⲟϥ ⲁ̀ⲣⲓϩⲟⲩⲟ̀ ϭⲁⲥϥ.

*فها هوذا عمانوئيل فى وسطنا يا ميصائيل تكلم بصوت التهليل. سبّحه وزده علواً.

*Gather now and persevere, and proclaim with the priests, praise the Lord all His works, Praise Him and exalt Him above all.

*Ⲑⲱⲟⲩϯ ϯⲛⲟⲩ ⲕⲁ-ⲧⲁⲭⲓⲛ ⲑⲏⲣⲟⲩ: ⲥⲁϫⲓ ⲛⲉⲙ ⲛⲓⲡⲣⲉⲥⲃⲩⲧⲉ-ⲣⲟⲩ: ⲥ̀ⲙⲟⲩ ⲉ̀Ⲡϭⲟⲓⲥ ⲛⲉϥϩ̀ⲃⲏⲟⲩⲓ̀ ⲑⲏⲣⲟⲩ: ϩⲱⲥ ⲉⲣⲟϥ ⲁ̀ⲣⲓϩⲟⲩⲟ̀ ϭⲁⲥϥ.

*اجتمعوا و ثابروا جميعاً تكلموا مع القسوس. و سبّحى الرب ياجميع أعماله. سبّحوه وزيدوه علواً.

The heavens declare the glory, of God until this day, O you angels whom He has

Ⲓⲥ ⲛⲓⲫⲏⲟⲩⲓ̀ ⲥⲉⲥⲁ-ϫⲓ ⲙ̀ⲡⲱⲟⲩ: ⲙ̀Ⲫⲛⲟⲩϯ ϣⲁ ⲉ̀ϧⲟⲩⲛ ⲙ̀ⲫⲟⲟⲩ: ⲱ̀

ها السموات تنطق بمجد الله الى هذا اليوم. يا أيها الملائكة

made, Praise Him and exalt Him above all.	ⲛⲓⲁⲅⲅⲉⲗⲟⲥ ⲉⲧⲁϥ̄ⲭ̄ⲫⲱⲟⲩ: ⲥⲱⲥ ⲉⲣⲟϥⲁⲣⲓⲥⲟⲩ̀ⲟ ϭⲁⲥϥ.	الذين أنشأهم سبحوه وزيدوه علواً
Now all you powers of the Lord, bless His honored name, O sun and moon and all the stars, Praise Him and exalt Him above all.	Ⲕⲉ ⲛⲧⲛ Ⲇⲩⲛⲁⲙⲓⲥ ⲧⲟⲩ Ⲕⲩⲣⲓⲟⲩ: ⲥ̀ⲙⲟⲩ ⲉ̀ⲡⲉϥⲣⲁⲛ ⲧⲟⲩ ⲧⲓⲙⲓⲟⲩ: ⲡⲓⲣⲏ ⲛⲉⲙ ⲡⲓⲟⲏ ⲛⲉⲙ ⲛⲓⲥⲓⲟⲩ : ⲥⲱⲥ ⲉ̀ⲣⲟϥ ⲁ̀ⲣⲓⲥⲟⲩ̀ⲟ ϭⲁⲥϥ.	والآن ياقوات الرب باركوا أسمه الكريم. أيتها الشمس والقمر والنجوم سبّحيه وزيديه علواً.
*And also you rain and dew, sing praises unto our Savior, for He is the God of our fathers, Praise Him and exalt Him above all.	*Ⲗⲟⲓⲡⲟⲛ ⲛⲓⲙⲟⲩⲛ̀ⲏⲱⲟⲩ ⲛⲉⲙ ⲛⲓⲓⲱϯ: ⲉⲩϥⲏⲙⲓⲥⲁⲧⲉ Ⲡⲉⲛⲣⲉϥⲥⲱⲧ :ⲭⲉ ⲛ̀ⲑⲟϥ ⲡⲉ Ⲫⲛⲟⲩϯ ⲛ̀ⲧⲉ ⲛⲉⲛⲓⲟϯ: ⲥⲱⲥ ⲉ̀ⲣⲟϥ ⲁ̀ⲣⲓⲥⲟⲩ̀ⲟ ϭⲁⲥϥ.	*وأيضا ايتها الأمطار والأنداء امدحى مخلصنا. لأنه هو اله آبائنا سبحيه وزيديه علواً.
*Glorify the Lord O clouds and winds,	*Ⲙⲁⲱⲟⲩ ⲙ̀Ⲡϭⲟⲓⲥ ⲱ̀	*أعطى مجداً أيتها السحب معاً

together with the souls and the spirits, O you cold and fire and heat, Praise Him and exalt Him above all.	ⲛⲓϭⲏⲡⲓ ⲉⲧⲙⲁϩ ⲛⲓⲑⲏⲟⲩ ⲛⲉⲙ ⲛⲓⲛⲓϥⲓ ⲛⲉⲙ ⲛⲓⲡⲛⲉⲩⲙⲁ: ⲡⲓⲭⲁϥ ⲛⲉⲙ ⲡⲓⲭⲣⲱⲙ ⲛⲉⲙ ⲡⲓⲕⲁⲩⲙⲁ: ϩⲱⲥ ⲉ̀ⲣⲟϥⲁ̀ⲣⲓϩⲟⲩⲟ̀ ϭⲁⲥϥ.	والأهوية والنفوس والأرواح. والبرد والنار والحرارة سبّحيه وزيده علوا.
You also O nights and days, light and darkness and lightning, glorify the Lover of mankind, Praise Him and exalt Him above all.	ⲛⲩⲕⲧⲉⲥ ⲕⲉ ⲏ̀ⲙⲉⲣⲉ ⲣⲱ ⲡⲉ: ⲫⲱⲥⲕⲉ ⲥⲕ̀ⲟⲧⲟⲥ ⲕⲉ ⲁⲥⲧⲣⲁⲡⲉ: ⲝⲉ ⲇⲟⲝⲁⲥⲓ ⲫⲓⲗⲁ̀ⲛⲑⲣⲱⲡⲉ: ϩⲱⲥ ⲉ̀ⲣⲟϥⲁ̀ⲣⲓϩⲟⲩⲟ̀ ϭⲁⲥϥ.	ايتها الليالى والأيام أيضاً والنور والظلمة والبروق. قائلة المجد لك يا محب البشر سبّحوه وزيدوه علواً.
You trees and all that springs on the earth, and all that moves in the sea, mountains and the forests, Praise Him and exalt Him above all.	ⲝⲩⲗⲁ ⲕⲉ ⲡⲁⲛⲧⲁ ⲧⲁ ⲫⲩⲟⲙⲉⲛⲁ: ⲉⲛ ⲧⲏ ⲅⲉ ⲕⲉ ⲡⲁⲛⲧⲁ ⲧⲁⲕⲓⲛⲟⲩⲙⲉⲛⲁ: ϩⲓ ⲛⲓⲙⲱⲟⲩ ⲛⲉⲙ ⲛⲓⲧⲱⲟⲩ ⲛⲉⲙ ⲇ̀ⲣⲩⲙⲟⲛⲁ: ϩⲱⲥ ⲉ̀ⲣⲟϥⲁ̀ⲣⲓϩⲟⲩⲟ̀ ϭⲁⲥϥ.	أيتها الاشجار وجميع ما ينبت فى الأرض. وكل ما يتحرّك في المياـه والجبال والغياض سبّحوه وزيدوه علواً.

*Praise without ceasing, the Lord the King of kings, O you rivers and seas, Praise Him and exalt Him above all.

*Oʊⲟⲅ ⲟⲛ ⲥⲙⲟⲩ ⲛ̀ⲁⲧϫⲁⲣⲱⲟⲩⲧ ⲉ̀Ⲡ6ⲟⲓⲥ ⲡ̀ⲟⲩⲣⲟ ⲛ̀ⲧⲉ ⲛⲓⲟⲩⲣⲱⲟⲩⲧ ⲛⲓⲁ̀ⲙⲁⲓⲟⲩ ⲛⲉⲙ ⲛⲓⲓⲁⲣⲱⲟⲩⲧ ⲥⲱⲥ ⲉ̀ⲣⲟϥ ⲁ̀ⲣⲓⲥⲟⲩⲟ6ⲁⲥϥ.

*وأيضاً سبّحى بغير فتور الرب ملك الـملـوك. أيتها البحار والأنهار سبّحيه وزيديه علواً.

*And we also seeing them, let us say with all these things, praise the Lord all you birds, Praise Him and exalt Him above all.

*Ⲡⲁⲓⲣⲏϯ ⲁ̀ⲛⲟⲛ ⲧⲉⲛⲛⲁⲩ ⲉ̀ⲣⲱⲟⲩⲧ ⲙⲁⲣⲉⲛϫⲟⲥ ⲛⲉⲙ ⲛⲁⲓ ⲱⲛ ⲧⲏⲣⲟⲩⲧ ⲥⲙⲟⲩ ⲉ̀Ⲡ6ⲟⲓⲥ ⲛⲓⲥⲁⲗⲁϯ ⲧⲏⲣⲟⲩⲧ ⲥ̀ⲱⲥ ⲉ̀ⲣⲟϥ ⲁ̀ⲣⲓⲥⲟⲩⲟ6ⲁⲥϥ.

*هكذا نحن إذ ننظر اليهم فلنقل مع هذه الموجودات جميعها. باركي الرب يا جميع الطيور سبّحيه وزيديه علواً.

O snow and ice, cattle and wild beasts, bless the Lord of Lords, Praise Him and exalt Him above all.

Ⲣⲱ ⲛ̀ⲛⲓⲡⲁⲭⲛⲏ ⲛⲉⲙ ⲛⲓⲭⲓⲱⲛⲧ ⲕⲉ ⲕ̀ⲧⲏⲛⲱⲛ ⲛⲉⲙ ⲛⲓⲑⲏⲣⲓⲟⲛ ⲥ̀ⲙⲟⲩ ⲉ̀Ⲡ6ⲟⲓⲥ ⲧⲱⲛ ⲕⲩⲣⲓⲱⲛ ⲥⲱⲥ ⲉ̀ⲣⲟϥ ⲁ̀ⲣⲓⲥⲟⲩⲟ6ⲁⲥϥ.

أيها الجليد والثلج والبهائم والوحوش. باركي رب الارباب سبّحيه وزيديه علواً.

247

Bless the Lord as befits Him, and not like the heretics, all you sons of men, Praise Him and exalt Him above all.

Ⲥⲙⲟⲩ ⲉⲠϭⲟⲓⲥ ⲕⲁⲧⲁ ⲫ̅ⲧⲱⲙⲓ ⲉⲣⲟϥ ⲕⲉ ⲟⲩ ⲙⲏ ⲡⲁⲣⲁⲛⲟⲙⲓ ⲱ̅ ⲛⲓϣⲏⲣⲓ ⲛ̀ⲧⲉ ⲛⲓⲣⲱⲙⲓ ⲥ̅ⲙⲟⲩ ⲉⲣⲟϥ ⲁ̀ⲣⲓϩⲟⲩⲟ ϭ̀ⲁⲥϥ.

سبّحوا الرب كما يليق به وليس كالمخالفين. يا أبناء البشر سبّحوه وزيدوه علواً.

*O Israel offer before Him, honor and glory in a joyful voice, all you priests of Emmanuel, Praise Him and exalt Him above all.

*Ⲓⲙⲏ ⲕⲉ Ⲇⲟⲝⲁ ⲱ̅ Ⲡⲓ̀ⲥⲣⲁⲏⲗ ⲓ̀ⲛⲓ ⲛⲁϩ̅ⲣⲁϥ ϧⲉⲛ ⲟⲩⲥⲙⲏ ⲛ̀ⲑⲉⲗⲏⲗ ⲛⲓⲟⲩⲏⲃ ⲛ̀ⲧⲉ Ⲉⲙⲙⲁⲛⲟⲩⲏⲗ ϩⲱⲥ ⲉ̀ⲣⲟϥ ⲁ̀ⲣⲓϩⲟⲩⲟ̀ ϭⲁⲥϥ.

*مجداً وإكراماً قدم أمامه يا اسرائيل بصوت التهليل. يا كهنة عمانوئيل سبّحوه وزيدوه علواً.

*You servants of the true God, the souls of the righteous, and the humble and the charitable, Praise Him and exalt Him above all.

*Ⲧⲏⲣⲉⲧⲱⲛ ⲙ̀Ⲫⲛⲟⲩϯ ⲙ̀ⲙⲏⲓ ⲛⲉⲙ ⲛⲓⲯⲩⲭⲏ ⲛ̀ⲧⲉ ⲛⲓⲟ̀ⲙⲏⲓ ⲛⲏⲉⲧⲑⲉⲃⲓⲏⲟⲩⲧ ⲛ̀ⲣⲉϥⲙⲉⲓ ϩⲱⲥ ⲉ̀ⲣⲟϥ ⲁ̀ⲣⲓϩⲟⲩⲟ̀ ϭⲁⲥϥ.

*يا خدام الله الحقيقي وأنفس الأبرار. المتواضعين المحبين سبّحوه وزيدوه علواً.

God my God is the

Ⲫⲛⲟⲩϯ Ⲡⲁⲛⲟⲩϯ ⲉ̀-

الله إلهى أنا هو

One, who saved you from danger, O Shadrach Meshach and Abednego, Praise Him and exalt Him above all.

ⲅⲱⲑ ⲡⲉⲧⲉⲛⲣⲉϥⲥⲱϯ ⲉⲕ ⲧⲟⲛ ⲁⲅⲱⲑ Ⲥⲉⲇⲣⲁⲭ Ⲙⲓⲥⲁⲭ Ⲇⲃⲇⲉⲛⲁⲅⲱⲑ ⲥⲱⲥ ⲉ̀ⲣⲟϥⲁ̀ⲣⲓⲟⲟⲩ̀ⲟ̀ⲃⲁⲥϥ.

مخلصكم من الخطر. ياسدراك وميساك و أبدناغو. سبّحوه وزيدوه علوا.

Hurry with great haste, O you righteous of the Lord, and all the creatures He has made, Praise Him and exalt Him above all.

Ⲭⲱⲗⲉⲙ ϧⲉⲛ ⲟⲩⲛⲓϣϯ ⲛ̀ϣⲣⲱⲓⲥⲑ ⲱ̀ ⲛⲏⲉⲧⲉⲣⲥⲉⲃⲉⲥⲑⲉ ⲙ̀Ⲡϭⲟⲓⲥ ⲑ ⲛⲉⲙ ⲛⲓⲫⲩⲥⲓⲥ ⲧⲏⲣⲟⲩ ⲉⲧⲁϥⲁⲓⲥⲑ ⲥⲱⲥ ⲉ̀ⲣⲟϥⲁ̀ⲣⲓⲟⲟⲩ̀ⲟ̀ⲃⲁⲥϥ.

أسرعوا بحرص عظيم يا أتقياء الرب. وكل الطبائع التى صنعها سبّحوه وزيدوه علواً.

*Coolness and repose without ceasing, grant unto all of us, that we may joyfully proclaim, Praise Him and exalt Him above all.

*Ⲯⲩⲭⲟⲥ ⲕⲉ ⲁ̀ⲛⲁⲡⲁⲩⲥⲓⲥⲑ ⲙⲟⲓ ⲛⲁⲛ ⲧⲏⲣⲉⲛ ⲭⲱⲣⲓⲥ ⲑ̀ⲣⲁⲩⲥⲓⲥⲑ ⲉⲑⲣⲉⲛⲭⲱ ϧⲉⲛ ⲟⲩⲁ̀ⲡⲟⲗⲁⲩⲥⲓⲥⲑⲥⲱⲥ ⲉ̀ⲣⲟϥⲁ̀ⲣⲓⲟⲟⲩ̀ⲟ̀ⲃⲁⲥϥ.

*برودة ونياحاً أعطنا كلنا بغير انقطاع. لنقول بتمتع سبّحوه وزيدوه علواً.

*And also Your poor servant Sarkis, make

* Ⲙⲥⲁⲩⲧⲱⲥ ⲡⲉⲕⲃ-

*كذلك عبدك المسكين

him without condemnation, that we may join all those and say, Praise Him and exalt Him above all.

ⲱⲕ ⲡⲓⲡⲧⲱⲭⲟⲥ : Ⲥⲁⲣⲕⲓⲥ ⲁ̀ⲣⲓⲧϥ ⲉϥⲟⲓ ⲛ̀ⲉ̀ⲛⲟⲭⲟⲥ ⲉ̀ⲥⲁⲝⲓ ⲛⲉⲙ ⲛⲁⲓ ⲉⲱⲥ ⲙⲉⲧⲟⲭⲟⲥ: ⲉⲱⲥ ⲉ̀ⲣⲟϥ ⲁ̀ⲣⲓⲉ̀ⲟⲩⲟ̀ ϭⲁⲥϥ.

سركيس اجعله بغير دينونة. ليقول مع هؤلاء كشريك سبّحوه وزيدوه علواً.

Hmyn after Praise of the Three Young Men

مديح بعد ابصالية الثلاثة فتية

God existent before the ages
Sent His chosen Angel
To deliver the youths from the furnace
(Hoas Erof Ari-Ho-oo Chasf)

الله الأزلى قبل الأدهار
ارسل ملاكه المختار
نجى الفتية من أتون النار
هوس إيروف آرى
هوؤتشاسف

Nebuchadnezzar the king made
-a golden image:
And told the ministers and all people
When you hear the sound of the
-trumpet
(Hoas Erof Ari-Ho-oo Chasf)

بختنصر الملك أقام صورة من
ذهب. وقال للوزراء وكل
الشعب. إذا ما سمعتم آلات
الطرب. هوس إيروف آرى
هوؤتشاسف

Immediately come out and fall down
To worship the golden image
Or you'll be cast in the furnace
(Hoas Erof Ari-Ho-oo Chasf)

تعالوا لوقتكم مسرعين
ولتلك الصورة ساجدين
وإذا لم تسجدوا تلقون فى
الآتون. هوس إيروف آرى
هوؤتشاسف

Then came forth the Chaldeans
And worshipped before the image
Except for the three saintly youths

تقدم الكلدانيون
لتلك الصورة خروا ساجدين
ماخلا الثلاثة الفتية القديسين

251

(Hoas Erof Ari-Ho-oo Chasf)   هوس إيروف آرى
هوؤتشاسف

O come Ananias and praise   تعال إلينا ياأنانياس
With the voice of salvation   ورتل معنا بصوت الخلاص
And praise your God the Messiah   وسبح إلهك ماسياس
(Hoas Erof Ari-Ho-oo Chasf)   هوس إيروف آرى
هوؤتشاسف

Men came and informed the king   جاء قوم وأعلنوا الملك قائلين
-saying: هاهنا ثلاثة رجال ساكنين
 There are three men in the city   لم يسجدوا للصورة بل
Who do not worship the image   مهملين. هوس إيروف آرى
(Hoas Erof Ari-Ho-oo Chasf)   هوؤتشاسف

The king gathered the leaders   جمع الملك رؤساء الشعب
The authorities and all ranks   وأرباب الدولة وكل الرتب
And ordered the furnace to be hotter   وقال لهم أوقدوا الأتون
(Hoas Erof Ari-Ho-oo Chasf)   بالحطب. هوس إيروف آرى
هوؤتشاسف

They bound the hands of the three   أتوا بالفتية موثقين
-youths: وطرحوهم فى وسط الأتون
And cast them in the midst of the   فصار كندى الياسمين
-furnace: هوس إيروف آرى
But to them it became as dew not heat   هوؤتشاسف

252

(Hoas Erof Ari-Ho-oo Chasf).

The angel of the Lord came unto them	حينئذ ملاك الله جاءهم
And quenched the furnace	أطفأ الأتون وقواهم
-strengthening them:	وفرحوا به لما أتاهم
And they rejoiced when they saw Him	هوس إيروف آرى
(Hoas Erof Ari-Ho-oo Chasf)	هوؤتشاسف

Azariah started to praise and pray	حينئذ صلى عزارياس
Faithfully without defilement	صلاة قوية بغيرأدناس
And gave glory to the power of the	تى اوأوإن إتجوم إن تى
-Trinity:	اترياس.
(Hoas Erof Ari-Ho-oo Chasf)	هوس إيروف آرى
	هوؤتشاسف

Mishael likewise proclaimed	خاصة بالأكثر ميصائيل
With the voice of rejoicing	علَّ صوته بالتهليل
Bless the Name of Emmanuel	اسمو إإ فران إن إممانوئيل
(Hoas Erof Ari-Ho-oo Chasf)	هوس إيروف آرى
	هوؤتشاسف

The king was amazed and surprised	دهش الملك أيضاً واحتار
There were only three in the furnace	أليس ثلاثة ألقوا فى النار
But now there are four walking freely	هوذا أربعة يمشون أجهار
(Hoas Erof Ari-Ho-oo Chasf)	هوس إيروف آرى
	هوؤتشاسف

The king truly saw all of them free	رأى الملك حقاً اجهار
Four men walking in the fire	أربعة رجال يمشون فى النار
And praising with the voice of	ويسبحون ببهجة ووقار
-rejoicing	هوس إيروف آرى
(Hoas Erof Ari-Ho-oo Chasf)	هوؤتشاسف

The king was greatly amazed	زاد عجباً ونطق بفاه
And proclaimed saying	هوذا الرابع يشبه ابن الآله
The fourth looks like the Son of God	فى منظره وفى رؤياه
(Hoas Erof Ari-Ho-oo Chasf)	هوس إيروف آرى
	هوؤتشاسف

Praise our God, O you people	سبحوه أيها السادات
The Angels, the Thrones and the	الملائكة والكراسى والقوات
-Powers	سبحوا رب السموات
Praise the Lord God of heaven	هوس إيروف آرى
(Hoas Erof Ari-Ho-oo Chasf)	هوؤتشاسف

Praise Him and glorify Him	سبحوه ومجدوه
In the congregations exalt Him	فى كنائس شعبه ارفعوه
And above all the elders bless Him	على منابر الشيوخ باركوه
(Hoas Erof Ari-Ho-oo Chasf)	هوس إيروف آرى
	هوؤتشاسف

Praise your God O Shadrach	سبح إلهك ياسدراك وابدناغو
Abednego and the praised Meshach	والممدوح ميساك لأنه نجاكم

For He saved you from destruction
(Hoas Erof Ari-Ho-oo Chasf)

من الهلاك هوس إيروف آرى
هوؤتشاسف

Praise Him all you nations
The free, the slave and the servant
For He saved you from destruction
(Hoas Erof Ari-Ho-oo Chasf)

سبحوه ياجميع الامم
الأحرار والعبيد والخدم
لأنه أنشاكم من العدم
هوس إيروف آرى
هوؤتشاسف

The fiery furnace O Hananiah
Was quenched by your God the
-Messiah
Bless His honored Name
(Hoas Erof Ari-Ho-oo Chasf)

سعير اللهيب ياأناتياس
أطفأه إلهك ماسياس
إسموا إبيفران توديمياس
هوس إيروف آرى
هوؤتشاسف

The youths proclaimed with rejoicing
Bless the Lord young men
Hannaih, Azariah and Mishael
You servants of the exalted God

صاح الفتية بصوت عال
باركوا الرب ايها الفتيان
ياحنانيا وعزاريا وميصائيل
عبيد الله القوى المتعال

An undefiled sacrifice was offered
O Azariah the praised
Praise the honored Name of God
(Hoas Erof Ari-Ho-oo Chasf)

تقدمة قربت بغير أدناس
أيها الممدوح عزارياس
إسمو إإفران توديمياس
هوس إيروف آرى
هوؤتشاسف

Emmanuel quenched the furnace
So rejoice and praise O Mishael
And offer to your God praises
(Hoas Erof Ari-Ho-oo Chasf)

طفى اللهيب عمانوئيل
فسر وسبح ياميصائيل
ورتل لإلهك بالتهليل
هوس إيروف آرى
هوؤتشاسف

The three youths praised with glory
And proclaimed in a joyful voice
Holy is the Beloved Son
(Hoas Erof Ari-Ho-oo Chasf)

ظهروا الفتية بالتمجيد
ورتلوا بصوت لذيذ
إفؤاب إبشيرى إم مينريت
هوس إيروف آرى
هوؤتشاسف

The fire of the furnace rose up
Forty nine full breadths
But the youths did not fear it
(Hoas Erof Ari-Ho-oo Chasf)

عَلَا ايضا لهيب الأتون
تسعة وأربعين ذراعاً كاملون
ولم يرهبوا المجاهدون
هوس إيروف آرى
هوؤتشاسف

The three youths overcame
The fiery furnace
And conquered the enemy saying
(Hoas Erof Ari-Ho-oo Chasf)

غلب الفتية لهيب النار
وقهروا الاعداء الكفار
فصار لهم المديح والتذكار
هوس إيروف آرى
هوؤتشاسف

The king proclaimed in a loud voice
Hananiah, Azariah and Mishael

فصاح الملك بصوت عال
حنانيا وعزاريا وميصائيل

The servants of the Most High God	عبيد الله القوى المتعال
(Hoas Erof Ari-Ho-oo Chasf)	هوس إيروف آرى
	هووتشاسف

Come out from the fiery furnace	فتعالوا اخرجوا من النار
For your God is powerful	لأن إلهكم ذو إقتدار
The performer of wonders	صانع العجائب الكبار
(Hoas Erof Ari-Ho-oo Chasf)	هوس إيروف آرى
	هووتشاسف

Honor and glory O Israel	كرامة ومجداً يا اسرائيل
Offer before God Emmanuel	قدم لإلهك عمانوئيل. تسابيح
The sound of rejoicing and praise	البركة والتهليل. هوس
(Hoas Erof Ari-Ho-oo Chasf)	إيروف آرى هووتشاسف

Before Him all the nations worship	له تسجد كل الاسباط
And all tongues and languages	وكل الألسن واللغات
They praise the Lord of Sabaoth	تسبح رب القوات. هوس
(Hoas Erof Ari-Ho-oo Chasf)	إيروف آرى هووتشاسف

There is no other Lord like You	من يشبهك يارب الأرباب
Who is powerful and feared	إله قوى عزيز مهاب
Your dominion is eternal	سلطانك فى كل الأحقاب
(Hoas Erof Ari-Ho-oo Chasf	هوس إيروف آرى
	هووتشاسف

The furnace became a cool mist	ندى بارد صار الأتون
Therefore the youths proclaimed	فصاح الفتية بصوت حنون
-saying	إسمو إبشويس تون كيريون
Praise the gracious Lord	هوس إيروف آرى
(Hoas Erof Ari-Ho-oo Chasf)	هوؤتشاسف

Rejoice in the God of Jacob	هللوا لإله يعقوب
For He is a powerful and feared God	وابتهجوا بالله القوى
And praise His Holy Name	المرهوب. ورتلوا لإسمه
(Hoas Erof Ari-Ho-oo Chasf)	المحبوب. هوس إيروف آرى
	هوؤتشاسف

Praise Him also with hymns	وسبحوه أيضاً بالألحان
Bless the Lord O you three youths	باركوا الرب أيها الفتيان
Praise the Lord at all times	إفهوس إإفنوتى ان سيو
(Hoas Erof Ari-Ho-oo Chasf)	نيفين. هوس إيروف آرى
	هوؤتشاسف

For the Lord our God is greatly	لأنه عظيم ومبارك جدا
-praised	ومخوف على كل الآلهة
And feared above the other gods	بقدرته نجى الفتية
By His might He delivered the youths	هوس إيروف آرى
(Hoas Erof Ari-Ho-oo Chasf)	هوؤتشاسف

To Him are due glory and worship	يليق كل مديح واغانى
Before the Creator and feared God	ويصيحون باسمه العالى
The Gracious God bestower of	افؤاب ابشيرى انجورى
-Life	هوس إيروف آرى
(Hoas Erof Ari-Ho-oo Chasf)	هوؤتشاسف

Hymn Of Tenen - Ⲧⲉⲛⲉⲛ

لحن تينين -

We therefore present an offering and rational worship, we send unto you this day psalmodies for Your glory O our Savior; Hananiah Azariah and Mishael.

Ⲧⲉⲛⲉⲛ ⲟⲑⲉⲛ ⲟⲩⲥⲓⲁⲛ ⲕⲉ ⲧⲏⲛ ⲗⲟⲅⲓⲕⲏⲛ ⲗⲁⲧⲣⲓⲁⲛ : ⲁⲛⲁⲡⲉⲙⲡⲱⲙⲉⲛ ⲥⲉⲁⲩⲧⲱ ⲥⲏⲙⲉⲣⲟⲛ ⲱ̀ⲗⲁⲥ : ⲡ̀ⲣⲟⲥ ⲇⲟⲝⲁ ⲥⲟⲩ ⲥⲱⲧⲏⲣ ⲛ̀ⲙⲱⲛ :Ⲁⲛⲁⲛⲓⲁⲥ Ⲁⲍⲁⲣⲓⲁⲥ ⲕⲉ Ⲙⲓⲥⲁⲏⲗ.

فمن ثم نقدم الذبيحة والعبادة العقلية . ونرسل لك فى هذا اليوم التسابيح لدى مجدك يا مخلصنا. حنانيا وعزاريا وميصائيل.

When they were raised to take glory in their bodies, the angel came down, stopped the fire and it became cool for Hananiah Azariah and Mishael.

Ⲧ̀ⲣⲓⲟⲛ ⲡⲁⲓⲑⲟⲛ ⲛ̀ϫⲉ ⲙⲉⲗⲓⲛ ⲛⲁⲧⲟⲩ ⲡⲉⲣⲟⲥ ⲇⲟⲝⲁ ⲙ̀ⲡⲥⲁⲧⲉⲧⲟⲩ: ⲥⲱⲙⲁⲧⲟⲥ ⲁⲅⲅⲉⲗⲟⲥ ⲅⲁⲣ ⲥⲉⲛⲁⲥⲉⲗ ⲑⲉⲗⲉ : ⲁⲩⲧⲟⲕⲓⲑⲟⲛ ⲫ̀ⲗⲓⲅⲁⲣⲧⲏⲥ : ⲉ̀ⲗⲉⲩⲥⲉⲱⲛ ⲛ̀ⲙⲱⲛ : Ⲁⲛⲁⲛⲓⲁⲥ Ⲁⲍⲁⲣⲓⲁⲥ

لما رُفعوا ليأخذوا المجد فى أجسادهم انحدر ملاك وأطفأ اللهيب وصيره بارداً عن حنانيا وعزاريا وميصائيل.

	ⲕⲉ Ⲱⲥⲁⲏⲗ.	
They praise and worship God continually.	Ⲉⲩϩⲱⲥ ⲉⲩⲥⲙⲟⲩ ⲉ̀ⲫϯ ⲛ̀ⲥⲏⲟⲩ ⲛⲓⲃⲉⲛ.	يسبحون ويباركون الله فى كل حين.

Psali Batos for the Three Young Men

أبصالية واطس للثلاثة القديسين

We follow You with all our hearts, and we fear You, and we seek Your face, O God do not forsake us.	Ⲧⲉⲛⲟⲩⲉϩ ⲛ̀ⲥⲱⲕ ϧⲉⲛ ⲡⲉⲛϩⲏⲧ ⲧⲏⲣϥ : ⲧⲉⲛⲉⲣϩⲟϯ ϧⲁⲧⲉⲕⲏ : ⲟⲩⲟϩ ⲧⲉⲛⲕⲱϯ ⲛ̀ⲥⲁ ⲡⲉⲕϩⲟ : Ⲫϯ ⲙ̀ⲡⲉⲣϯϣⲓⲡⲓ ⲛⲁⲛ.	نتبعــك بكل قلوبنا و نخافــك و نطلب وجهك يا الله لا تخزنا .
*But rather deal with us, according to Your meekness, and according to Your great mercy, O Lord help us.	*Ⲁⲗⲗⲁ ⲁ̀ⲣⲓⲟⲩⲓ ⲛⲉⲙⲁⲛ : ⲕⲁⲧⲁ ⲧⲉⲕⲙⲉⲧⲉ̀ⲡⲓⲕⲏⲥ : ⲛⲉⲙ ⲕⲁⲧⲁ ⲡ̀ⲁϣⲁⲓ ⲛ̀ⲧⲉ ⲡⲉⲕⲛⲁⲓ : Ⲡϭⲟⲓⲥ ⲁⲣⲓⲃⲟⲏⲑⲓⲛ ⲉ̀ⲣⲟⲛ.	*بل إصنع معنا بحسب دعتــك وكثرة رحمتك يارب أعنّا .
May our prayers ascend to You, O our Master, like burnt offerings of lambs, and fat calves.	Ⲙⲁⲣⲉ ⲧⲉⲛⲡⲣⲟⲥⲉⲩⲭⲏ ⲡⲉⲛⲛⲏⲃ : ⲓ̀ ⲉ̀ⲡϣⲱⲓ ⲙ̀ⲡⲉⲕⲙⲑⲟ : ⲙ̀ⲫⲣⲏϯ ⲛ̀ϩⲁⲛϭⲗⲓⲗ ⲛ̀ⲧⲉ ϩⲁⲛⲱⲓⲗⲓ : ⲛⲉⲙ ϩⲁⲛⲙⲁⲥⲓ ⲉⲩⲕⲉⲛⲓ̀ⲱⲟⲩⲧ.	فلتصعد صلاتنا أمامك يا سيدنا مثـــل محرقات كباش وعجـــول سمان .

*Do not forget the covenant, which You have made with our fathers, Abraham, Isaac, and Jacob, Israel Your saints.	*Ⲙⲡⲉⲣⲉⲣⲡⲱⲃϣ ⲛ̀ϯⲁⲓⲁⲑⲏⲕⲏ : ⲑⲏⲉ̀ⲧⲁⲕⲥⲉⲙⲛⲏⲧⲥ ⲛⲉⲙ ⲛⲉⲛⲓⲟϯ: Ⲁⲃⲣⲁⲁⲙ Ⲓⲥⲁⲁⲕ Ⲓⲁⲕⲱⲃ :Ⲡⲓⲥⲣⲁⲏⲗ ⲡⲉⲉⲑⲟⲩⲁⲃ ⲛ̀ⲧⲁⲕ.	*لا تنـــسَ العهد الذى قطعته مع آبائنا ابراهيم واسحق ويعقوب اسرائيل قديسيك .
Bless the Lord, all you nations, the tribes and all kinds of tongues, Praise Him and glorify Him, above all forever.	Ⲥⲙⲟⲩ ⲉ̀Ⲡϭⲟⲓⲥ ⲛⲓⲗⲁⲟⲥ ⲧⲏⲣⲟⲩ : ⲛⲓⲫⲩⲗⲏ ⲛⲓⲁⲥⲡⲓ ⲛ̀ⲗⲁⲥ : ⲥⲱⲥ ⲉ̀ⲣⲟϥ ⲙⲁⲱⲟⲩ ⲛⲁϥ : ⲁⲣⲓ̀ⲥⲟⲓ̀ⲟ ϭⲁⲥϥϣⲁ ⲛⲓⲉ̀ⲛⲉⲥ.	باركوا الرب ياجميع الشعوب والقبائل ولغات الالسن سبحوه ومجدوه و زيدوه علواً إلى الآباد .
*Pray to the Lord on our behalf, O three saintly children, Shadrach, Meshach and Abednego, that He may forgive us our sins.	*Ⲧⲱⲃⲥ ⲙ̀Ⲡϭⲟⲓ ⲉ̀ⲉ̀ⲣⲏⲓ ⲉ̀ϫⲱⲛ: ⲱ̀ ⲡⲓϣⲟⲙⲧ ⲛ̀ⲁ̀ⲗⲟⲩ ⲛ̀ⲁ̀ⲅⲓⲟⲥ : Ⲥⲉⲇⲣⲁⲕ Ⲙⲓⲥⲁⲕ Ⲁⲃⲇⲉⲛⲁⲅⲱ : ⲛ̀ⲧⲉϥⲭⲁ ⲛⲉⲛⲛⲟⲃⲓ ⲛⲁⲛ ⲉ̀ⲃⲟⲗ.	*أطلبوا من الرب عنا أيها الثلاثة فتية القديسين سدراك وميساك وابدناغو ليغفر لنا خطايانا .

263

The Commemoration- المجمع

Intercede on our behalf, O lady of us all the Mother of God, St. Mary the Mother of our Savior, that He may forgive us our sins.	Ⲁⲣⲓⲡⲣⲉⲥⲃⲉⲧⲓⲛ ⲉ̀ϩⲣⲏⲓ ⲉ̀ ϫⲱⲛ : ⲱ̀ ⲧⲉⲛϭ̅ⲟ̅ⲓ̅ⲥ ⲛ̀ⲛⲏⲃ ⲧⲏⲣⲉⲛ ϯⲑⲉⲟ̀ⲧⲟⲕⲟⲥ: Ⲙⲁⲣⲓ̀ⲁ ⲑ̀ⲙⲁⲩ ⲙ̀Ⲡⲉⲛⲥⲱⲧⲏⲣ : ⲛ̀ⲧⲉϥⲭⲁ ⲛⲉⲛⲛⲟⲃⲓ ⲛⲁⲛ ⲉ̀ⲃⲟⲗ.	إشفعى فينا يا سيدتنا كلنا السيدة والدة الإله مريم ام مخلصنا ليغفرلنا خطايانا.
*Intercede on our behalf, O holy Archangels, Michael and Gabriel, that He may forgive us our sins.	*Ⲁⲣⲓⲡⲣⲉⲥⲃⲉⲧⲓⲛ ⲉ̀ϩⲣⲏⲓ ⲉ̀ϫⲱⲛ: ⲱ̀ ⲛⲓⲁⲣⲭⲏⲁⲅⲅⲉⲗⲟⲥ ⲉ̀ⲑⲟⲩⲁⲃ: Ⲙⲓⲭⲁⲏⲗ ⲛⲉⲙ Ⲅⲁⲃⲣⲓⲏⲗ : ⲛ̀ⲧⲉϥⲭⲁ ⲛⲉⲛⲛⲟⲃⲓ ⲛⲁⲛ ⲉ̀ⲃⲟⲗ.	*إشفعا فينا يارئيسى الملائكة الطاهرّين ميخائيل وغبريال ليغفر لنا خطايانا.
Intercede on our behalf, O holy Archangels, Raphael and Suriel, that He may...	Ⲁⲣⲓⲡ̅ : ⲱ̀ ⲛⲓⲁⲣⲭⲏⲁⲅⲅⲉⲗⲟⲥ ⲉ̀ⲑⲟⲩⲁⲃ : Ⲣⲁ-ⲫⲁⲏⲗ ⲛⲉⲙ Ⲥⲟⲩⲣⲓⲏⲗ : ⲛ̀ⲧⲉϥ...	إشفعا فينا يارئيسى الملائكة الطاهرّين رافائيل وسوريال ليغفر ...

*Intercede: O holy Archangels, Sedakiel, Sarathiel and Ananiel, that He may...	*Ⲁⲣⲓⲡ : ⲱ̀ ⲛⲓⲁⲣⲭⲏ-ⲁⲅⲅⲉⲗⲟⲥ ⲉ̀ⲑⲟⲩⲁⲃ: Ⲥ-ⲉⲇⲁⲕⲓⲏⲗ Ⲥⲁⲣⲁⲑⲓⲏⲗ ⲛⲉⲙ Ⲁⲛⲁⲛⲓⲏⲗ : ⲛ̀ⲧⲉϥ ...	*اشفعوا فينا ياروؤساء الملائكة الأطهار سداكيال وسراتيال وأنانيال ليغفر ...
Intercede: O Thrones, Dominions and Powers, the Cherubim and the Seraphim, that He may...	Ⲁⲣⲓⲡ : ⲛⲓⲑⲣⲟⲛⲟⲥ ⲛⲓ-ⲙⲉⲧϭⲟⲓⲥ ⲛⲓϫⲟⲙ: ⲛⲓⲬⲉ-ⲣⲟⲃⲓⲙ ⲛⲉⲙ ⲛⲓⲤⲉⲣⲁⲫⲓⲙ : ⲛ̀ⲧⲉϥ...	أشفعى فينا أيتها الكراسى والارباب والقوات و الشاروبيم و السيرافيم ليغفر ..
*Intercede on our behalf, O four Incorporeal Beasts, the ministers fervent as fire, that He may...	*Ⲁⲣⲓⲡ: ⲡⲓϥⲧⲟⲩ ⲛ̀ⲍⲱ-ⲟⲛ ⲛ̀ⲁⲥⲱⲙⲁⲧⲟⲥ : ⲛ̀ⲗⲓ-ⲧⲟⲩⲣⲅⲟⲥ ⲛ̀ϣⲁϩ ⲛ̀ⲭⲣⲱⲙ: ⲛ̀ⲧⲉϥ...	*أشفعوا فينا أيها الأربعة الحيوانات غير المتجسدين الخدام الملتهبين ناراً ليغفر ...
Intercede: O priests of the Truth, the Twenty Four Presbyters, that He may...	Ⲁⲣⲓⲡ : ⲛⲓⲟⲩⲏⲃ ⲛ̀ⲧⲉ ϯⲙⲉⲑⲙⲏⲓ : ⲡⲓϫⲟⲩⲧϥ̀ⲧⲟⲩ ⲙ̀ⲡⲣⲉⲥⲃⲩⲧⲏⲣⲟⲥ: ⲛ̀ⲧⲉϥ ...	إشفعوا فينا ياكهنة الحق الأربعة والعشرين قسيساً ليغفر ...

265

*Intercede: O angelic hosts, and all the heavenly multitudes, that He may...	*Ⲁ̅ⲣⲓⲡ︦ⲥ ⲛⲓⲥⲧⲣⲁⲧⲓⲁ ⲛ̀ⲁⲅⲅⲉⲗⲓⲕⲟⲛ ⲛⲉⲙ ⲛⲓⲧⲁⲅⲙⲁ ⲛ̀ⲉⲡⲟⲩⲣⲁⲛⲓⲟⲛ ⲛ̀ⲧⲉϥ...	*إشفعوا فينا أيها العساكر الملائكية والطغمات السمائية ليغفر ...
Pray to the Lord on our behalf, our masters and fathers, the patriarchs, Abraham, Isaac and Jacob, that He may...	Ⲧⲱⲃϩ ⲙ̀Ⲡϭⲟⲓⲥ ⲉ̀ϩ̀ⲣⲏⲓ ⲉ̀ϫⲱⲛ ⲛⲁϭⲟⲓⲥ ⲛ̀ⲓⲟϯ ⲙ̀ⲡⲁⲧⲣⲓⲁⲣⲭⲏⲥ Ⲁⲃⲣⲁⲁⲙ Ⲓⲥⲁⲁⲕ Ⲓⲁⲕⲱⲃ ⲛ̀ⲧⲉϥ ...	إطلبوا من الرب عنا ياسادتى الآباء البطاركة إبراهيم وإسحق ويعقوب ليغفر ...
*Pray to the Lord on our behalf, O perfect man, the righteous and the just Enoch, that He may...	*Ⲧⲱⲃϩ ⲙ̀Ⲡϭⲟⲓⲥ ⲉ̀ϩ̀ⲣⲏⲓ ⲉ̀ϫⲱⲛ ⲱ̀ ⲡⲓⲣⲱⲙⲓ ⲛ̀ⲧⲉⲗⲓⲟⲥ ⲡⲓⲑ̀ⲙⲏⲓ Ⲉ̀ⲛⲱⲭ ⲡⲓⲇⲓⲕⲉⲟⲥ ⲛ̀ⲧⲉϥ...	*إطلب من الرب عنا أيها الرجل الكامل البار أخنوخ الصديق ليغفر ...
Pray to the Lord on our behalf, Elijah the Tishbite, and his disciple Elisha, that He	Ⲧⲱ̄ Ⲏⲗⲓⲁⲥ ⲡⲓⲑⲉⲥⲃⲓⲧⲏⲥ ⲛⲉⲙ Ⲉ̀ⲗⲓⲥⲉⲟⲥ ⲡⲉϥⲙⲁⲑⲏⲧⲏⲥ ⲛ̀ⲧⲉϥ ...	إطلبوا من الرب عنا يا إيليا التسبيتى وآليشع تلميذه ليغفر...

266

may...

*Pray to the Lord on our behalf, O Moses the Archprophet and Isaiah, and Jeremiah, that He may...

| Ⲧⲱ̅ ⲱ̇ Ⲙⲱ̀ⲥⲏⲥ ⲡⲓⲁⲣⲭⲏⲡⲣⲟⲫⲓⲧⲏⲥ: ⲛⲉⲙ Ⲏⲥⲁⲏⲁⲥ: ⲛⲉⲙ Ⲓⲉⲣⲉⲙⲓⲁⲥ: ⲛ̀ⲧⲉϥ... |

*إطلبوا من الرب عنا ياموسى رئيس الأنبياء وأشعياء وأرمياء ليغفر ...

Pray: O David the Psalmist, Ezekiel and Daniel, that He may...

Ⲧⲱ̅ Ⲇⲁⲩⲓⲇ ⲡⲓⲉⲣⲟⲯⲁⲗⲧⲏⲥ: ⲛⲉⲙ Ⲓⲉⲍⲉⲕⲓⲏⲗ ⲛⲉⲙ Ⲇⲁⲛⲓⲏⲗ: ⲛ̀ⲧⲉϥ...

إطلبوا من الرب عنا ياداود المرتل وحزقيال ودانيال ليغفر ...

*Pray: Joachim, Anna and Joseph the Elder, and the righteous Job, Joseph and Nicodemus, that He may...

*Ⲧⲱ̅ Ⲓⲱⲁⲕⲓⲙ ⲛⲉⲙ Ⲁⲛⲛⲁ ⲛⲉⲙ Ⲓⲱⲥⲏⲫ ⲡⲓⲡⲣⲉⲥⲃⲩⲧⲉⲣⲟⲥ: ⲛⲉⲙ ⲡⲓⲑⲙⲏⲓ Ⲓⲱⲃ ⲛⲉⲙ Ⲓⲱⲥⲏⲫ ⲛⲉⲙ Ⲛⲓⲕⲟⲇⲏⲙⲟⲥ: ⲛ̀ⲧⲉϥ...

*إطلبوا من الرب عنا يايواقيم وحنّة ويوسف الشيخ والصديق ايوب ويوسف و نيقوديموس ليغفر...

Pray to the Lord on our behalf, O Melchizedek and Aaron, and Zach-

Ⲧⲱ̅ Ⲙⲉⲗⲭⲓⲥⲉⲇⲉⲕ ⲛⲉⲙ Ⲁ̀ⲁⲣⲱⲛ: ⲛⲉⲙ Ⲍⲁⲭⲁⲣⲓⲁⲥ ⲛⲉⲙ Ⲥⲩⲙⲉⲱⲛ

أطلبوا من الرب عنا ياملشيصادق وهرون وزكريا وسمعان ليغفر ...

267

ariah and Simeon, that He may...	: ⲛ̄ⲧⲉϥ...	
*Pray: O choirs of the prophets, and all the righteous and the just, that He may...	*Ϯⲱ̄ : ⲛⲓⲭⲟⲣⲟⲥ ⲛ̄ⲧⲉ ⲛⲓⲡⲣⲟⲫⲏⲧⲏⲥ : ⲛⲉⲙ ⲛⲓⲑⲙⲏⲓ ⲛⲉⲙ ⲛⲓⲇⲓⲕⲉⲟⲥ : ⲛ̄ⲧⲉϥ •••	*أطلبوا من الرب عنا ياصفوف الأنبياء والأبرار والصديقين ليغفر...
Intercede on our behalf, O fore-runner and bap-tizer, John the Baptist, that he may...	Ⲁⲣⲓⲡ̄ : ⲱ̀ ⲡⲓⲡⲣⲟⲇⲣⲟⲙⲟⲥ ⲙ̀ⲃⲁⲡⲧⲓⲥⲧⲏⲥ : Ⲓⲱⲁⲛⲛⲏⲥ ⲡⲓⲣⲉϥϯⲱⲙⲥ : ⲛ̄ⲧⲉϥ...	إشفع فينا أيها السابق الصابغ يوحنا المعمدان ليغفر ...
*Intercede on our behalf, O the Hundred and For-ty Four Thousand, and the celibate Evangelist, that He may...	*Ⲁⲣⲓⲡ̄ : ⲱ̀ ⲡⲓϣⲉⲃⲙⲉϥⲧⲟⲩ ⲛ̄ϣⲟ : ⲛⲉⲙ ⲡⲓⲡⲁⲣⲑⲉⲛⲟⲥ ⲛ̀ⲉⲩⲁⲅⲅⲉⲗⲓⲥⲧⲏⲥ : ⲛ̄ⲧⲉϥ...	*إشفعوا فينا ايها المئة والأربعة والأربعين الفاً والبتول الانجيلى ليغفر ...
Pray to the Lord on our behalf, our	Ϯⲱ̄ : ⲛⲁϭⲟⲓⲥ ⲛ̄ⲓⲟϯ ⲛ̀ⲁⲡⲟⲥⲧⲟⲗⲟⲥ : ⲛⲉⲙ ⲡ̄ⲥⲉ-	أطلبوا من الرب عنا ياسادتى

masters and fathers, the Apostles, and the rest of the Disciples, that He may…	ⲡⲓ ⲛ̀ⲧⲉ ⲛⲓⲙⲁⲑⲏⲧⲏⲥ: ⲛ̀ⲧⲉϥ…	الآباء الرسل وبقية التلاميذ ليغفر...
*Pray: O blessed arch-deacon, Stephen the first martyr, that He may...	*Ⲧⲱ̅: ⲡⲓⲁⲣⲭⲏⲇⲓⲁ-ⲕⲱⲛ ⲉⲧⲥⲙⲁⲣⲱⲟⲩⲧ: Ⲥⲧⲉⲫⲁⲛⲟⲥ ⲡⲓϣⲟⲣ-ⲡ ⲙ̀ⲙⲁⲣⲧⲩⲣⲟⲥ: ⲛ̀ⲧⲉ-ϥ …	*أطلب من الرب عنا يارئيس الشمامسة المبارك استفانوس الشهيد الاول ليغفر...
Pray to the Lord on our behalf, O beholder of God the Evangelist, Mark the Apostle, that He may...	Ⲧⲱ̅: ⲡⲓⲑⲉⲱⲣⲓⲙⲟⲥ ⲛ̀ⲉ-ⲩⲁⲅⲅⲉⲗⲓⲥⲧⲏⲥ: ⲁⲃⲃⲁ Ⲙⲁⲣⲕⲟⲥ ⲡⲓⲁ̀ⲡⲟⲥⲧⲟⲗⲟⲥ: ⲛ̀ⲧⲉϥ…	أطلب من الرب عنا أيها الناظر الإله الإنجيلى مرقس الرسول ليغفر ...
*Pray: O struggle mantled martyr, my master Prince George, that He may...	*Ⲧⲱ̅: ⲡⲓⲁⲑⲗⲟⲫⲟⲣⲟⲥ ⲙ̀ⲙⲁⲣⲧⲩⲣⲟⲥ: ⲡⲁϭⲟⲓⲥ ⲛ̀ⲟⲩⲣⲟ Ⲅⲉⲱⲣⲅⲓⲟⲥ: ⲛ̀ⲧⲉϥ …	*أطلب من الرب عنا أيها الشهيد المجاهد سيدى الملك جيؤرجيوس ليغفر ...

Pray: Theodorus and Theodorus, Leontius and Panikarus, that he may...	Ϯⲱ : Θⲉⲟⲇⲱⲣⲟⲥ ⲛⲉⲙ Θⲉⲟⲇⲱⲣⲟⲥ : ⲛⲉⲙ Ⲗⲉⲟⲛⲧⲓⲟⲥ ⲛⲉⲙ Ⲡⲁⲛⲓⲕⲁⲣⲟⲥ : ⲛ̀ⲧⲉϥ...	اطلبوا من الرب عنا ياثيؤدوروس وثيؤدوروس ولاونديوس وبانيكاروس ليغفر ...
*Pray to the Lord on our behalf, Philopater Mercurius, and Abba Mina and Abba Victor, that He may...	*Ϯⲱ : Ⲫⲓⲗⲟⲡⲁⲧⲏⲣ Ⲙⲉⲣⲕⲟⲩⲣⲓⲟⲥ : ⲛⲉⲙ ⲁⲡⲁ Ⲙⲏⲛⲁ ⲛⲉⲙ ⲁⲡⲁ Ⲃⲓⲕⲧⲱⲣ : ⲛ̀ⲧⲉϥ...	*اطلبوا من الرب عنا يافيلوباتير مرقوريوس وأبا مينا وأبا بقطر ليغفر ...
Pray: Master Claudius and Theodore, Abba Eskhyron and Abba Isaac, that He may...	Ϯⲱ : ⲕⲩⲣⲓ Ⲕⲗⲁⲩⲇⲓⲟⲥ ⲛⲉⲙ Θⲉⲟⲇⲱⲣⲟⲥ : ⲛⲉⲙ ⲁⲡⲁ Ⲥⲭⲩⲣⲟⲛ ⲛⲉⲙ ⲁⲡⲁ Ⲓⲥⲁⲁⲕ : ⲛ̀ⲧⲉϥ...	اطلبوا من الرب عنا ياسيدى اقلوديوس و ثيئودوروس وأبا سخيرون وأبا اسحق ليغفر ...
*Pray: Basilidis and Eusebius, Macarius and Philotheos, that He may...	*Ϯⲱ : Ⲃⲁⲥⲓⲗⲓⲧⲏⲥ ⲛⲉⲙ Ⲉⲩⲥⲉⲃⲓⲟⲥ : ⲛⲉⲙ Ⲙⲁⲕⲁⲣⲓⲟⲥ ⲛⲉⲙ Ⲫⲓⲗⲟⲑⲉⲟⲥ : ⲛ̀ⲧⲉϥ...	*اطلبوا من الرب عنا ياواسيليدس وأوسابيوس ومقاريوس وفيلوثاؤس ليغفر

Pray to the Lord on our behalf, Abba Pisura and Abba Epshoi, Abba Isi and his sister Thecla, that He may...	Ⲧⲱ̄ : ⲁⲃⲃⲁ Ⲡⲓⲥⲟⲩⲣⲁ ⲛⲉⲙ ⲁⲡⲁ Ⲡϣⲱⲓ : ⲛⲉⲙ ⲁⲡⲁ Ⲏⲥⲓ ⲛⲉⲙ Ⲑⲉⲕⲗⲁ ⲧⲉϥⲥⲱⲛⲓ: ⲛ̀ⲧⲉϥ...	اطلبوا من الرب عنا يأانبا بسوره وأبابشاى و أبايسى وتكلا اخته ليغفر ...
*Pray: O struggle mantled martyrs, Justus, Apali and Theoclia, that He may…	*Ⲧⲱ̄:ⲛⲓⲁⲑⲗⲟⲫⲟⲣⲟⲥ ⲙ̀ⲙⲁⲣⲧⲩⲣⲟⲥ : Ⲓⲟⲩⲥⲧⲟⲥ ⲛⲉⲙ Ⲁ̇ⲡⲁⲗⲓ ⲛⲉⲙ Ⲑⲉⲟⲕⲗⲓⲁ: ⲛ̀ⲧⲉϥ...	*اطلبوا من الرب عنا أيها الشهداء المجاهدون يسطس و آبالى وتاوكليا ليغفر...
Pray: Abba Jacob the Persian, Saint Sergius and Saint Bacchus, that He may...	Ⲧⲱ̄ : ⲁⲃⲃⲁ Ⲓⲁⲕⲱⲃⲟⲥ ⲡⲓϥⲉⲣⲥⲓⲥ : ⲛⲉⲙ ⲡⲓⲁ̀ⲅⲓⲟⲥ Ⲥⲉⲣⲅⲓⲟⲥ ⲛⲉⲙ Ⲃⲁⲭⲟⲥ : ⲛ̀ⲧⲉϥ...	اطلبوا من الرب عنا يأانبا يعقوب الفارسى والقديس سرجيوس و واخس ليغفر ...
*Pray: O struggle mantled martyrs, Cosmas, his brothers and their mother, that He may…	*Ⲧⲱ̄ : ⲛⲓⲁⲑⲗⲟⲫⲟⲣⲟⲥ ⲙ̀ⲙⲁⲣⲧⲩⲣⲟⲥ: Ⲕⲟⲥⲙⲁ ⲛⲉⲙ ⲛⲉϥⲥⲛⲏⲟⲩ ⲛⲉⲙ ⲧⲟⲩⲙⲁⲩ : ⲛ̀ⲧⲉϥ ...	*اطلبوا من الرب عنا أيها الشهداء المجاهدون قزمان واخوته وأمهم ليغفر...

271

Pray: Abba Kir and his brother John, and Barbara and Juliana and Demiana, that He may…	Ⲧⲱ : ⲁⲡⲁ Ⲕⲓⲣ ⲛⲉⲙ Ⲓⲱⲁⲛⲛⲏⲥ ⲡⲉϥⲥⲟⲛ : ⲛⲉⲙ Ⲃⲁⲣⲃⲁⲣⲁ ⲛⲉⲙ Ⲓⲟⲩⲗⲓⲁⲛⲏ ⲛⲉⲙ Ⲇⲩⲙⲓⲁⲛⲏ : ⲛⲧⲉϥ…	اطلبوا من الرب عنا ياباقير و يوحنا أخوه و برباره و يوليانه و دميانه ليغفر …
*Pray: O struggle mantled martyrs, master Apatir and his sister Irae, that He may...	*Ⲧⲱ: ⲛⲓⲁⲑⲗⲟⲫⲟⲣⲟⲥ ⲙ̇ⲙⲁⲣⲧⲩⲣⲟⲥ : ⲕⲩ̇ⲣⲓ Ⲁ̇ⲡⲁⲧⲏⲣ ⲛⲉⲙ Ⲏ̇ⲣⲁ̇ⲏ ⲧⲉϥⲥⲱⲛⲓ: ⲛ̇ⲧⲉϥ…	*اطلبوا من الرب عنا أيها الشهيدان المجاهدان السيد أبادير وإيرائى أخته ليغفر …
Pray to the Lord on our behalf, O struggle mantled martyrs, Julius and those who were with him, that He may...	Ⲧⲱ : ⲛⲓⲁⲑⲗⲟⲫⲟⲣⲟⲥ ⲙ̇ⲙⲁⲣⲧⲩⲣⲟⲥ : Ⲓⲟⲩⲗⲓⲟⲥ ⲛⲉⲙ ⲛⲏⲉⲑⲛⲉⲙⲁϥ : ⲛ̇ⲧⲉϥ …	اطلبوا من الرب عنا أيها الشهداء المجاهدون يوليوس ومن معه ليغفر …
*Pray: O struggle mantled martyrs, Mari Pahnam and his sister Sarah, that He may…	*Ⲧⲱ: ⲛⲓⲁⲑⲗⲟⲫⲟⲣⲟⲥ ⲙ̇ⲙⲁⲣⲧⲩⲣⲟⲥ: ⲙⲁⲣ Ⲡⲁϩⲛⲁⲙ ⲛⲉⲙ Ⲥⲁⲣⲣⲁ ⲧⲉϥⲥⲱⲛⲓ: ⲛ̇ⲧⲉϥ…	*اطلبوا من الرب عنا أيها الشهيدان المجاهدان ماريبهنام وساره أخته ليغفر …

Pray: Abba Sarapamon the Bishop, Psati and Gallinikos, that He may…	Ⲧⲱ̅ : ⲁⲃⲃⲁ Ⲥⲁⲣⲁⲡⲁⲙⲱⲛ ⲡⲓⲉ̇ⲡⲓⲥⲕⲟⲡⲟⲥ : ⲛⲉⲙ Ⲫⲁⲧⲉ ⲛⲉⲙ Ⲅⲁⲗⲗⲓⲛⲓⲕⲟⲥ : ⲛ̇ⲧⲉϥ…	أطلبوا من الرب عنا يا انبا صرابامون الاسقف وابصادى وغلينيكوس ليغفر …
*Pray to the Lord on our behalf, O struggle mantled martyrs, the Forty Saints of Sebasta, that He may...	*Ⲧⲱ̅ : ⲛⲓⲁⲑⲗⲟⲫⲟⲣⲟⲥ ⲙ̇ⲙⲁⲣⲧⲩⲣⲟⲥ : ⲡⲓⲉ̇ⲙⲉ ⲉ̇ⲑⲟⲩⲁⲃ ⲛ̇ⲧⲉ Ⲥⲉⲃⲁⲥⲧⲉ : ⲛ̇ⲧⲉϥ…	*اطلبوا من الرب عنا ايها الشهداء المجاهدون الأربعون قديساً بسبسطية ليغفر …
Pray: Abba Piru and Atom, And John and Simeon, that He may...	Ⲧⲱ̅ : ⲁⲃⲃⲁ Ⲡⲓⲣⲱⲟⲩ ⲛⲉⲙ Ⲇⲟⲱⲙ : ⲛⲉⲙ Ⲓⲱⲁⲛⲛⲏⲥ ⲛⲉⲙ Ⲥⲩⲙⲉⲱⲛ : ⲛ̇ⲧⲉϥ…	أطلبوا من الرب عنا ياأنبا بيروه واتوم ويوحنا وسمعان ليغفر …
*Pray: O struggle mantled martyrs, Abba Pishoi and his friend Peter, that He may...	*Ⲧⲱ̅ : ⲛⲓⲁⲑⲗⲟⲫⲟⲣⲟⲥ ⲙ̇ⲙⲁⲣⲧⲩⲣⲟⲥ : ⲁ̇ⲡⲁ Ⲡϣⲱⲓ ⲛⲉⲙ ⲡⲉϥϣⲫⲏⲣ Ⲡⲉⲧⲣⲟⲥ : ⲛ̇ⲧⲉϥ…	*أطلبا من الرب عنا أيها الشهيدان المجاهدان أبا بشوى وصديقه بطرس ليغفر...

Pray to the Lord on our behalf, Abba Eklog the priest, and Abba Epgol and Abba Kav, that He may...	Ⲧⲱ̄ : ⲁⲡⲁ `Ⲕⲗⲟⲭ ⲡⲓⲡⲣⲉⲥⲃⲩⲧⲉⲣⲟⲥ: ⲛⲉⲙ ⲁ̀-ⲡⲁ Ⲡ̇ⲭⲟⲗ ⲛⲉⲙ ⲁ̀ⲡⲁ Ⲕⲁⲩ:ⲛ̀ⲧⲉϥ...	أطلبوا من الرب عنا ياأبا كلوج القس وابا بجول وأبا كاف ليغفر...
*Pray: Abba John of Heraclia, Master Piphamon and Pistavros, that He may...	*Ⲧⲱ̄ : ⲁⲡⲁ Ⲓⲱⲁⲛⲛⲏⲥ ⲡⲓⲣⲉⲙⲅⲁⲣⲁⲕⲗⲓⲁ̀ : ⲛⲉⲙ ⲕⲩⲣ Ⲡⲓϥⲁⲙⲱⲛ ⲛⲉⲙ Ⲡⲓ̇ⲥⲧⲁⲩⲣⲟⲥ: ⲛ̀ⲧⲉϥ...	*أطلبوا من الرب عنا ياأبا يوحنا الهرقلى والسيد بفام وبسطوروس ليغفر...
Pray: Isidore and Panteleon, Sophia and Euphemia, that He may....	Ⲧⲱ̄ : Ⲏ̇ⲥⲏⲇⲱⲣⲟⲥ ⲛⲉⲙ Ⲡⲁⲛⲧⲉⲗⲉⲟⲛ : Ⲥⲟⲫⲓⲁ̀ ⲛⲉⲙ Ⲉⲩⲫⲟⲙⲓⲁ̀: ⲛ̀ⲧⲉϥ...	أطلبوا من الرب عنا يا ايسيذوروس و بندلاون وصوفيا وإفوميه ليغفر ...
*Pray to the Lord on our behalf, master Abanoub and Ptolomaeus, Apa Ekragon and Sosinius, that He may...	*Ⲧⲱ̄ : ⲕⲩⲣⲓ Ⲇⲡⲁⲛⲟⲩⲃ ⲛⲉⲙ Ⲡ̇ⲑⲟⲗⲟⲙⲉⲟⲥ : ⲛⲉⲙ Ⲇⲡⲁⲕⲣⲁⲅⲟⲛ ⲛⲉⲙ Ⲥⲟⲩⲥⲉⲛⲛⲓⲟⲥ: ⲛ̀ⲧⲉϥ...	*أطلبوا من الرب عنا ياسيدى ابانوب و ابطلماوس ابكراجون و سوسِنِيوس ليغفر...

Pray: O great high priest, Abba Peter seal of the martyrs, that He may…	Ⲧ̅ⲱ̅: ⲱ̀ ⲡⲓⲛⲓϣϯ ⲛ̀ⲁⲣⲭⲏⲉⲣⲉⲧⲥ : ⲁⲃⲃⲁ Ⲡⲉⲧⲣⲟⲥ ⲓⲉⲣⲟⲙⲁⲣⲧⲩⲣⲟⲥ : ⲛ̀ⲧⲉϥ…	أطلب من الرب عنا يارئيس الكهنة العظيم انبا بطرس خاتم الشهداء ليغفر...
*Pray: O new martyrs, Pistavros and Arsenius, that He may...	*Ⲧ̅ⲱ̅ : ⲱ̀ ⲛⲓⲃⲉⲣⲓ ⲙ̀ⲙⲁⲣⲧⲩⲣⲟⲥ : Ⲡⲓⲥⲧⲁⲩⲣⲟⲥ ⲛⲉⲙ Ⲁⲣⲥⲉⲛⲓⲟⲥ : ⲛ̀ⲧⲉϥ…	*أطلبوا من الرب عنا أيها الشهيدان الجديدان بسطوروس وارسانيوس ليغفر ...
Pray to the Lord on our behalf, O Michael the hegumen, and Michael the monk, that He may...	Ⲧ̅ⲱ̅ : ⲱ̀ Ⲙⲓⲭⲁⲏⲗ ⲡⲓϩⲏⲅⲟⲩⲙⲉⲛⲟⲥ : ⲛⲉⲙ Ⲙⲓⲭⲁⲏⲗ ⲡⲓⲙⲟⲛⲁⲭⲟⲥ : ⲛ̀ⲧⲉϥ…	اطلبا من الرب عنا ياميخائيل القمص وميخائيل الراهب ليغفر ...
*Pray: O choirs of the martyrs, who suffered for the sake of Christ, that He may...	*Ⲧ̅ⲱ̅ : ⲛⲓⲭⲟⲣⲟⲥ ⲛ̀ⲧⲉ ⲛⲓⲙⲁⲣⲧⲩⲣⲟⲥ : ⲉ̀ⲧⲁⲩϣⲉⲡⲙ̀ⲕⲁϩ ⲉⲑⲃⲉ Ⲡ̅ⲭ̅ⲥ̅ : ⲛ̀ⲧⲉϥ…	*اطلبوا من الرب عنا ياصفوف الشهداء الذين تألموا من أجل المسيح ليغفر ...

275

Pray: Our masters and fathers who loved their children, Abba Anthony and Abba Paul, that He may...	Ⲧⲱ : ⲛⲁϭⲟⲓⲥ ⲛ̀ⲓⲟϯ ⲙ̀ⲙⲁⲓⲛⲟⲩϣⲏⲣⲓ : ⲁⲃⲃⲁ Ⲁⲛⲧⲱⲛⲓⲟⲥ ⲛⲉⲙ ⲁⲃⲃⲁ Ⲡⲁⲩⲗⲉ:ⲛ̀ⲧⲉϥ...	اطلبا من الرب عنا ياسيدى الابوين محبى أولادهما أنبا انطونيوس وأنبا بولا ليغفر ...
*Pray to the Lord on our behalf, O three saints Abba Macarii, and all their children the cross-bearers, that He may...	*Ⲧⲱ: ⲡⲓϣⲟⲙⲧ ⲉ̀ⲑⲟⲩⲁⲃ ⲁⲃⲃⲁ Ⲙⲁⲕⲁⲣⲓ : ⲛⲉⲙ ⲛⲟⲩϣⲏⲣⲓ ⲛ̀ⲥⲧⲁⲩⲣⲟⲫⲟⲣⲟⲥ:ⲛ̀ⲧⲉϥ...	*اطلبوا من الرب عنا أيها الثلاثة مقارات القديسون وأولادهم لباس الصليب ليغفر...
Pray: Our masters and fathers the archpriests, Abba John and Abba Daniel, that He may...	Ⲧⲱ : ⲛⲁϭⲟⲓⲥ ⲛ̀ⲓⲟϯ ⲛ̀ϩⲏⲧⲟⲩⲙⲉⲛⲟⲥ : ⲁⲃⲃⲁ Ⲓⲱⲁⲛⲛⲏⲥ ⲛⲉⲙ ⲁⲃⲃⲁ Ⲇⲁⲛⲓⲏⲗ:ⲛ̀ⲧⲉϥ...	اطلبا من الرب عنا ياسيدى الابوين القمصين أنبا يوحنا وأنبا دانيال ليغفر ...
*Pray: Our masters and fathers who loved their children, Abba	*Ⲧⲱ:ⲛⲁϭⲟⲓⲥ ⲛ̀ⲓⲟϯ ⲙ̀ⲙⲁⲓⲛⲟⲩϣⲏⲣⲓ : ⲁⲃⲃⲁ Ⲡⲓϣⲱⲓ ⲛⲉⲙ ⲁⲃⲃⲁ	*اطلبا من الرب عنا ياسيدىّ الابوين محبى أولادهما أنبا

276

Pishoi and Abba Paul, that He may...	Ⲡⲁⲩⲗⲉ: ⲛⲧⲉϥ...	بيشوى وأنبا بولا ليغفر ...
Pray to the Lord on our behalf, our saintly Roman fathers, Maximus and Dometius, that He may...	Ⲧⲱ̄: ⲛⲉⲛⲓⲟϯ ⲉⲑⲟⲩⲁⲃ ⲛ̇ⲣⲱⲙⲉⲟⲥ: Ⲙⲁⲝⲓⲙⲟⲥ ⲛⲉⲙ Ⲇⲟⲙⲉⲧⲓⲟⲥ: ⲛ̇ⲧⲉϥ...	أطلبا من الرب عنا ياأبوينا القديسين الروميين مكسيموس و دوماديوس ليغفر ...
*Pray: O forty nine Martyrs, the Elders of Shiheet, that He may...	*Ⲧⲱ̄: ⲡⲓⲉ̅ⲙⲉⲯⲓⲧ ⲙ̇ⲙⲁⲣⲧⲩⲣⲟⲥ: ⲛⲓϧⲉⲗⲗⲟⲓ ⲛ̇ⲧⲉ Ϣⲓϩⲏⲧ: ⲛ̇ⲧⲉϥ...	*اطلبوا من الرب عنا أيها التسعة والاربعون شهيداً شيوخ شيهات ليغفر...
Pray: O strong saint Abba Moses, and John Kame, that He may...	Ⲧⲱ̄: ⲡⲓϫⲱⲣⲓ ⲉⲑⲟⲩⲁⲃ ⲁⲃⲃⲁ Ⲙⲱⲥⲏ: ⲛⲉⲙ Ⲓⲱⲁⲛⲛⲏⲥ ⲡⲓⲭⲁⲙⲏ: ⲛ̇ⲧⲉϥ...	أطلبا من الرب عنا ايها القوى القديس انبا موسي ويحنس كاما ليغفر ...
*Pray to the Lord on our behalf, Abba Pachomious	*Ⲧⲱ̄: ⲁⲃⲃⲁ Ⲡⲁϧⲱⲙ ϧⲁ ϯⲕⲟⲓⲛⲱⲛⲓⲁ: ⲛⲉⲙ	*اطلبا من الرب عنا ياانبا باخوم ابا الشركة و

277

of the Koinonia, and his disciple Theodore, that He may...	Θεοδωρος πεϥμαθη-της: ντεϥ...	تادرس تلميذه ليغفر ...
Pray: Abba Shenouda the Archimandrite, and Abba Wissa his disciple, that He may...	Ϫⲱ : ⲁⲃⲃⲁ Ϣⲉⲛⲟⲩϯ ⲡⲓⲁⲣⲭⲏⲙⲁⲛⲇⲣⲓⲧⲏⲥ : ⲛⲉⲙ ⲁⲃⲃⲁ Ⲃⲓⲥⲁ ⲡⲉϥⲙⲁⲑⲏⲧⲏⲥ: ⲛⲧⲉϥ...	اطلبا من الرب عنا ياانبا شنوده رئيس المتوحدين وانبا ويصا تلميذه ليغفر ...
*Pray: Abba Nopher and Abba Karus, and our father Paphnutius, that He may...	*Ϫⲱ : ⲁⲃⲃⲁ Ⲛⲟⲩϥⲉⲣ ⲛⲉⲙ ⲁⲃⲃⲁ Ⲕⲁⲣⲟⲥ : ⲛⲉⲙ ⲡⲉⲛⲓⲱⲧ Ⲡⲁⲫⲛⲟⲩⲧⲓⲟⲥ :ⲛⲧⲉϥ...	*اطلبوا من الرب عنا ياانبا نفر وانبا كاروس وابانا بفنوتيوس ليغفر ...
Pray to the Lord on our behalf, Abba Samuel the confessor, and Justus and Apollo his disciples, that He may...	Ϫⲱ : ⲁⲃⲃⲁ Ⲥⲁⲙⲟⲩⲏⲗ ⲡⲓⲟⲙⲟⲗⲟⲅⲓⲧⲏⲥ : ⲛⲉⲙ Ⲓⲟⲩⲥⲧⲟⲥ ⲛⲉⲙ Ⲁⲡⲟⲗⲗⲟ ⲛⲉϥⲙⲁⲑⲏⲧⲏⲥ:ⲛⲧⲉϥ...	اطلبوا من الرب عنا ياانبا صموئيل المعترف ويسطس وأبوللو تلميذيه ليغفر...

*Pray: Abba Apollo and Abba Apip, and our father Abba Pigimi, that He may...	*Ⲧⲱ̄ : ⲁⲃⲃⲁ Ⲁⲡⲟⲗⲗⲟ ⲛⲉⲙ ⲁⲃⲃⲁ Ⲁⲡⲓⲡ : ⲛⲉⲙ ⲡⲉⲛⲓⲱⲧ ⲁⲃⲃⲁ Ⲡⲓϫⲓⲙⲓ : ⲛ̀ⲧⲉϥ...	*اطلبوا من الرب عنا ياانبا ابوللو وانبا ابيب وابانا انبا بيجيمى ليغفر ...
Pray: Abba Evkin and Abba Ehron, Abba Hor and Abba Phis, that He may...	Ⲧⲱ̄: ⲁⲃⲃⲁ Ⲉⲩⲕⲓⲛ ⲛⲉⲙ ⲁⲃⲃⲁ Ⲉ̀ⲣⲟⲛ : ⲛⲉⲙ ⲁ̀ⲡⲁ Ⲑⲱⲣ ⲛⲉⲙ ⲁ̀ⲡⲁ Ⲫⲓⲥ : ⲛ̀ⲧⲉϥ...	اطلبوا من الرب عنا ياانبا افكين وانبا إهرون واباهور وابا فيس ليغفر ...
*Pray to the Lord on our behalf, Abba Parsouma and Ephrem, and John and Simeon, that He may...	*Ⲧⲱ̄ : ⲁⲃⲃⲁ Ⲡⲁⲣⲥⲱⲙⲁ ⲛⲉⲙ Ⲉϥⲣⲉⲙ : ⲛⲉⲙ Ⲓⲱⲁⲛⲛⲏⲥ ⲛⲉⲙ Ⲥⲩⲙⲉⲱⲛ : ⲛ̀ⲧⲉϥ...	*اطلبوا من الرب عنا ياانبا برسوما وافريم ويوحنا وسمعان ليغفر ...
Pray: Epiphanius and Ammonius, and Arshillidis and Arsenius, that He may…	Ⲧⲱ̄ : Ⲉ̀ⲡⲓⲫⲁⲛⲓⲟⲥ ⲛⲉⲙ Ⲁ̀ⲙⲙⲱⲛⲓⲟⲥ : ⲛⲉⲙ Ⲁⲣⲭⲏⲗⲓⲧⲏⲥ ⲛⲉⲙ Ⲁ̀ⲣⲥⲉⲛⲓⲟⲥ : ⲛ̀ⲧⲉϥ...	اطلبوا من الرب عنا ياابيفانيوس امونيوس وارشليدس وارسانيوس ليغفر...

*Pray: our masters, the ascetic fathers, Abba Abraam and George, that He may...	*Ⲧⲱ̄ : ⲛⲁϭⲟⲓⲥ ⲛ̇ⲓⲟϯ ⲛ̇ⲁⲥⲕⲏⲧⲏⲥ : ⲁⲃⲃⲁ Ⲁⲃⲣⲁⲁⲙ ⲛⲉⲙ Ⲅⲉⲱⲣⲅⲏ : ⲛ̇ⲧⲉϥ...	*اطلبا من الرب عنا ياسيدى الابوين الناسكين انبا أبرام وجاورجى ليغفر ...
Pray to the Lord on our behalf, Athanasius the Apostolic, Severus and Dioscorus, that He may...	Ⲧⲱ̄ : Ⲁⲑⲁⲛⲁⲥⲓⲟⲥ ⲡⲓⲁ̇ⲡⲟⲥⲧⲟⲗⲓⲕⲟⲥ : Ⲥⲉⲩⲓⲣⲟⲥ ⲛⲉⲙ Ⲇⲓⲟⲥⲕⲟⲩⲣⲟⲥ : ⲛ̇ⲧⲉϥ...	اطلبوا من الرب عنا يا اثاناسيوس الرسولى وساويرس وديسقورس ليغفر ...
*Pray: Basil and Gregory, and our father Abba Cyril, that He may...	*Ⲧⲱ̄ : Ⲃⲁⲥⲓⲗⲓⲟⲥ ⲛⲉⲙ Ⲅⲣⲓⲅⲟⲣⲓⲟⲥ : ⲛⲉⲙ ⲡⲉⲛⲓⲱⲧ Ⲁⲃⲃⲁ Ⲕⲩⲣⲓⲗⲗⲟⲥ : ⲛ̇ⲧⲉϥ...	*اطلبوا من الرب عنا يا باسيليوس و اغريغوريوس . وابانا أنبا كيرلس ليغفر ...
Pray: the three hundred and eighteen gathered, at Nicea for the faith, that He may...	Ⲧⲱ̄ : ⲡⲓϣⲟⲙⲧ ϣⲉⲙⲉⲧ ϣ̇ⲙⲏⲛ ⲉ̇ⲧⲁⲩⲑⲱⲟⲩϯ : ϧⲉⲛ Ⲛⲓⲕⲉⲁ : ⲉⲑⲃⲉ ⲡⲓⲛⲁϩϯ : ⲛ̇ⲧⲉϥ...	اطلبوا من الرب عنا أيها ال٣١٨ الذين اجتمعوا فى نيقيه من اجل الايمان ليغفر ...
*Pray to the Lord	*Ⲧⲱ̄ : ⲱ̇ ⲡⲓϣⲉ ⲧⲉⲃⲓ ⲛ̇ⲧⲉ	*اطلبوا من الرب

280

on our behalf, the one hundred and fifty at Constantinople, and the two hundred at Ephesus, that He may...	Ⲕⲱⲥⲧⲁⲛⲧⲓⲛⲟⲩⲡⲟⲗⲓⲥ ⲛⲉⲙ ⲡⲓ ⲥ̅ⲛⲁⲩ ϣⲉ ⲛ̀ⲧⲉ Ⲉ̀ⲫⲉⲥⲟⲥ⁚ ⲛ̀ⲧⲉϥ...	عنا ايها ال ١٥٠ بمدينة القسطنطينية والمائتين بأفسس ليغفر ...
Pray: Abba Hadid and Abba John, our great father Parsouma and Abba Roweis, that He may...	Ⲧⲱ̅⁚ ⲁⲃⲃⲁ Ⲏ̀ⲁⲇⲓⲇ ⲛⲉⲙ ⲁⲃⲃⲁ Ⲓⲱⲁⲛⲛⲏⲥ⁚ ⲛⲉⲙ ⲡⲉⲛⲓⲱⲧ ⲡⲓⲛⲓϣϯ ⲁⲃⲃⲁ Ⲡⲁⲣⲥⲱⲙⲁ ⲛⲉⲙ ⲁⲃⲃⲁ Ⲧⲉⲭⲓ⁚ ⲛ̀ⲧⲉϥ...	اطلبوا من الرب عنا ياانبا حديد وأنبا يوحنا وأبانا العظيم أنبا برسوما وأنبا رويس ليغفر ...
*Pray: Abba Abraam the hegomen, and our father Abba Mark, that He may...	*Ⲧⲱ̅⁚ ⲁⲃⲃⲁ Ⲁⲃⲣⲁⲁⲙ ⲡⲓ̀ⲏ̀ⲅⲟⲩⲙⲉⲛⲟⲥ⁚ ⲛⲉⲙ ⲡⲉⲛⲓⲱⲧ ⲁⲃⲃⲁ Ⲙⲁⲣⲕⲟⲥ ⁚ ⲛ̀ⲧⲉϥ...	*اطلبا من الرب عنا ياأنبا ابرام القمص وابانا أنبا مرقس ليغفر ...
Pray to the Lord on our behalf, O choirs of the cross-bearers, perfected in the wilderness,	Ⲧⲱ̅⁚ ⲛⲓⲭⲟⲣⲟⲥ ⲛ̀ⲧⲉ ⲛⲓⲥ̀ⲧⲁⲩⲣⲟⲫⲟⲣⲟⲥ⁚ ⲉⲧⲁⲩ ϫⲱⲕ ⲉ̀ⲃⲟⲗ ϩⲓⲛⲓϣⲁϥⲉⲣ⁚ ⲛ̀ⲧⲉϥ...	اطلبوا من الرب عنا يامصاف لبّاس الصليب الذين كملوا فى البرارى ليغفر ...

281

that He may...

*Pray: my master King Constantine, and his mother Queen Helen, that He may...

Pray: O wise virgin ladies, the brides of Christ, that He may...

*Pray: O saints of this day, everyone according to their name, that He may forgive us our sins.

Likewise we glorify You, with David the Psalmist, You are the priest forever, according to the order of Melchizedek.

*Ⲧⲱ̄ : ⲡⲁϭⲟⲓⲥ ⲡ̀ⲟⲩⲣⲟ Ⲕⲱⲥⲧⲁⲛⲧⲓⲛⲟⲥ : ⲛⲉⲙ Ⲏ̀ⲗⲁⲛⲏ ϯⲟⲩⲣⲱ : ⲛ̀ⲧⲉϥ...

Ⲧⲱ̄ : ⲛⲓⲁ̀ⲗⲟⲩ ⲛ̀ⲥⲁⲃⲉ ⲙ̀ⲡⲁⲣⲑⲉⲛⲟⲥ : ⲛⲓϣⲉⲗⲉⲧ ⲛ̀ⲧⲉ Ⲡⲓⲭ̀ⲣⲓⲥⲧⲟⲥ : ⲛ̀ⲧ- ⲉϥ...

*Ⲧⲱ̄ : ⲛⲏⲉ̀ⲑⲟⲩⲁⲃ ⲛ̀ⲧⲉ ⲡⲁⲓ ⲉ̀ϩⲟⲟⲩ : ⲡⲓⲟⲩⲁⲓ ⲡⲓⲟⲩⲁⲓ ⲕⲁⲧⲁ ⲡⲉϥⲣⲁⲛ : ⲛ̀ⲧⲉϥ...

Ⲱ̀ⲥⲁⲩⲧⲱⲥ ⲧⲉⲛϭⲓⲥⲓ ⲙ̀- ⲙⲟⲕ : ⲛⲉⲙ ⲡⲓϩⲩⲙ- ⲛⲟⲇⲟⲥ Ⲇⲁⲩⲓⲇ : ϫⲉ ⲛ̀ⲑⲟⲕ ⲡⲉ ⲡⲓⲟⲩⲏⲃ ϣⲁ ⲉ̀ⲛⲉϩ : ⲕⲁ-

*اطلبا من الرب عنا ياسيدى الملك قسطنطين و هيلانه الملكة ليغفر ...

اطلبن من الرب عنا ايتها الفتيات العذارى الحكيمات عرائس المسيح ليغفر ...

*اطلبوا من الرب عنا ياقديسى هذا اليوم كل واحد باسمه ليغفر ...

كذلك نعظمك مع المرتل داود قائلين انت هو الكاهن إلى الأبد على طقس ملشيصاداق .

*Pray: our saintly father, the pontiff Abba (...), the high priest, that He may forgive us our sins.

ⲧⲁ ⲧⲧⲁⲝⲓⲥ ⲙ̀ⲙⲉⲗⲭⲓⲥⲉⲇⲉⲕ.

*Ⲓ̄ⲱ̄ : ⲡⲉⲛⲓⲱⲧ ⲉⲑⲟⲩⲁⲃ ⲙ̀ⲡⲁⲧⲣⲓⲁⲣⲭⲏⲥ : ⲁ-ⲃⲃⲁ (...) ⲡⲓⲁⲣⲭⲏⲉⲣⲉⲩⲥ : ⲛ̀ⲧⲉϥ...

*اطلب من الرب عنا ياابانا القديس البطريرك انبا (...) رئيس الكهنة ليغفر...

Praises For the Saints مدايح للقديسين:

<u>Praise for St Shenouda</u>   مديحة للأنبا شنوده

<u>*(To the tune of "The Burning Bush...")*</u>

I begin in the name of Almighty God:	أبدى بأسم الله القدير
Ever present without change:	دائم باقى من غير تغيير
And praise this shining star:	وأمدح هذا الكوكب المنير
<u>*(Coptic) Shenouti pi Archimanedritees*</u>	المرد : شينوتي بى أرشى
<u>*(repeat)*</u>	مان إدريتيس.

The saints father lived in a village:	كان والد هذا القديس يقيم
Near the town of Akhmeem:	بقرية من تخوم أخميم
He was given this great star:	فرزق بهذا الكوكب العظيم
<u>*Shenouti ....*</u>	شينوتي.....

Before his birth his father saw:	قبل ميلاده رآه أبوه
A vision and contemplated on it:	فى الرؤيا وتأمل فيه
A great star revealed by God:	كوكب عظيم أشرق عليه
<u>*Shenouti ....*</u>	شينوتي ...

His mother saw a strange vision:	فرأت أمه أمر غريب
The Virgin, mother of the Beloved:	أن العذراء أم الحبيب

284

Appeared to her carrying a cross:
Shenouti ……...

ظهرت لها وبيدها صليب
شينوتي ...

She strengthened her and gave her
-bread:
And told her this good news:
"You will give birth to a chaste son":
Shenouti ……...

قوتها وأعطتها رغيف
وقالت لها قولاً لطيف
ستلدين غلاماً عفيف
شينوتي ...

The Mother of God gave him the
-name:
Shenouda is there a better meaning?:
Its meaning is sweet being "a son of
-God":
Shenouti ……...

دعت أسمه ام الإله
شنودة ما أحلى معناه
تفسيره حلو هو أبن الله
شينوتي ...

He matured in Christianity:
And was devoted to spirituality:
And lived an angelic life:
Shenouti ……...

ينمو فى الإصول المسيحية
ويسير سيرة روحانية
ويعيش عيشة ملائكية
شينوتي ...

When he matured to a youth:
He worked as a shepherd:
And was always fasting:
Shenouti ……...

لما شب ونما هذا الغلام
أهتم برعاية الأغنام
فكان يصوم عن الطعام
شينوتي ...

While he prayed as a young boy:

لما كان يصلى وهو صغير

285

Saying, "Guide my life O Almighty
-God":
His hands would shine bright like
-candles:
Shenouti ……...

يقول دبر حياتى ياقدير
أصابع يديه كالشمع تنير
شينوتى...

When the righteous saint would pray:
He became shining with light:
While sweet incense came from him:
Shenouti ……...

عند صلاة هذا المبرور
كان يحاط كله بالنور
ويفوح منه رائحة بخور
شينوتى...

His father thought and said:
"We must go and receive the blessing
-of Anba Pigol":
They went and when they arrived:
Shenouti ……...

فكر والده وبدأ يقول
نذهب نتبارك من أنبا
بيجول. فقام وذهب وعند
وصول.
شينوتى...

The holy old man Anba Pigol stood:
And held the hand of the young boy:
Placing it respectfully on his own
-head:
Shenouti ……...

قام أنبا بيجول الشيخ الكبير
وأمسك بيد الغلام الصغير
ووضعها على رأسه بكل
تقدير.
شينوتى...

He said, "Bless me O blessed son:
You are worthy of blessings and
-goodness.":
The saint was only nine years old:

قال باركنى يا أبن البركات
يا مستحق الطوبى
والغبطات. وكان يبلغ تسع
سنوات.

Shenouti ……...   ...شـينوتي

His parents were reassured and left: إطمأن والده وتركه وسار
And at the end of that day: وعند مساء هذا النهار
The righteous saint lay down to sleep: ذهب لينام الغلام البار
Shenouti ……...   ... شـينوتي

While he slept Anba Pigol saw: نام بيجول الشيخ ورأى فى
An angel of God guarding the saint: المنام. ملاك الله يحرس
Who said, "Pigol listen to what I say":   الغلام. يقول يابيجول أسمع
                      منى الكلام.
Shenouti ……...   شـينوتي.....

"In the morning you get the 'eskeem':   أنهض فى الصباح تجد
And gird Shenouda the great young boy: اسكيم. بجوار الصبى
The honorable Jesus has ordained   شنودة العظيم. رشمهُ بيده
-him":   يسوع الكريم.
Shenouti ……...   ...شـينوتي

Anba Pigol arose and obeyed: قام أنبا بيجول وألبسه أياه
Ordained him a monk and they lived: ورسمه راهب ومعه أبقاه
-together: فأجهد نفسه بالصوم
They struggled in fasting and prayer: والصلاة.
Shenouti ……...   شـينوتي....

The righteous saint grew older: كبر هذا القديس البار
And began to explain the Bible: ووضع تعاليم فى الأسفار

287

The world has been illuminated by his -teaching:	بتعاليمه العالم استنار
Shenouti ……...	شـينوتي...

He is like a luminous angel:	تشبه بالملائكة النورانية
And lived a saintly life:	وعاش عيشة تقية
Therefore he heard the heavenly -voice:	فسمع من السماء صوت علانية.
Shenouti ……...	شـينوتي...

By the authority of Jesus the -everlasting judge:	أنتصر على قوة الشيطان
He triumphed over the devils' powers:	بقدرة يسوع الرب الديان
And strengthened the other monks:	وكان يقوى الأباء الرهبان
Shenouti ……...	شـينوتي...

He was likened to Elijah the zealous:	تشبه بـإيلـيا الغيور
And attended the council with Saint -Kyrollos:	حضر المجمع مع كيرلس المبرور. دافع عن الإيمان
And defended the faith and -embarrassed Nestor:	وبكت نسطور.
Shenouti ……...	شـينوتي...

He perfected all virtues:	لبس ثوب الفضيلة بكمال
And was carried by a glorious cloud:	فحملته سحابه بإجلال
Which delivered him quickly to his -monastery:	وأوصلته إلى ديره فى الحال.

Shenouti ....شـينـوتـي

With the power of Almighty God: صنع عجائب مع آيات
He performed great signs and   وكان يشفى من به عاهات
-wonders: بقدرة الإله رب القوات
And cured all those with sicknesses: ...شـينـوتـي
Shenouti ....

Before his death he fell sick briefly: عند موته مرض قليل
So the saints surrounded him like a   فاحاط به القديسون مثل
-crown: إكليل. ووجهه ينير بشكل
While his face shone beautifully: .جميل
Shenouti ....شـينـوتـي

The righteous saint was worthy: أستحق هذا القديس البار
Of seeing the highest ranks of the   أن يرى فى رؤيا بيعة
-heavenlies: الأبكار. والمسيح كشف له
And Christ revealed to him the   .الأسرار
-mysteries: ...شـينـوتـي
Shenouti ....

All the heavenly ranks: جميع الطغمات السمائيين
The angels, martyrs and saints: والملائكة والشهداء
Welcomed him chanting and saying: والقديسين. استقبلوه
Shenouti ....   .وهتفوا قائلين
                                                           ...شـينـوتـي

Oh Lord who's nature is perfection:
And whose mercy is plenteous without
-limit:
Accept us through the intercessions of
Anba Shenouda:
Shenouti ....

يارب يامن طبعة الجودة
ومراحمة كثير غير
محدوده. اقبلنا بشفاعة
الأنبا شنودة.
شـينوتـي...

And accept oh Lord all those present:
Who have celebrated this
-remembrance:
Through the intercessions of the
-chosen saint:
Shenouti ....

أقبل يارب جميع الحضار
من إحتفلوا بهذا التذكار
بشفاعة قديسك المختار
شـينوتـي...

The mention of your name in the
mouth of the believers, they all chant
saying, oh God of Anba Shenouda
support us.

تفسير أسمك فى أفواه
كل القديسين الكل يقولون
ياإله انبا شنودة اعنا
أجمعـين.

Praise for St. Bishoy - مديحة للأنبا بيشوي

In the church of the victorious	فى كنيسة الغالبين
The righteous and pure	الأبرار البتوليين
Example to the perfect	مثال للكاملين
Peniot avva Pishoi/Father abba Bishoy	بنيوت أفا بيشوى
In the council of the ascetics	فى مجمع النساك
Your face shines like an angel	يضيء وجهك كملإك
Blessed are you O blessed one	يقولون طوباك طوباك
Peniot avva Pishoi/Father abba Bishoy	بنيوت أفا بيشوى
The "eskeem" and the cross	الآسكيم والصليب
The best in Habib valley	زينة وادى هبيب
From you we smell the aroma	منك يفيح الطيب
Peniot avva Pishoi/Father abba Bishoy	بنيوت أفا بيشوى
Since you were young	إختارك منذ صباك
God chose and called you	الرب و دعاك
And the angel indicated you are the	وأشار عليك الملإك
-one:	بنيوت أفا بيشوى
Peniot avva Pishoi/Father abba Bishoy	
You become an example in Shiheet	صرت لشيهيت مثال
In the way of perfection	فى طريق الكمـال
Throughout all ages	إلى مدى الأجيال

Peniot avva Pishoi/Father abba Bishoy	بنيوت أفا بيشوى
Blessed are you Abba Bishoy	طوباك يا أنبا بيشوى
The beloved of God	يا حبيب ابن الله
He visited you as a friend	زارك مثل صديق
Peniot avva Pishoi/Father abba Bishoy	بنيوت أفا بيشوى
Your hands took water	يدك أخذت مياه
And washed His feet	و غسلت له قدماه
And you lived according to His will	و عشت فى رضاه
Peniot avva Pishoi/Father abba Bishoy	بنيوت أفا بيشوى
Your works enlightened	فاضاءت أعماقك
And your words were blessed	و تباركَت أقوالك
And you became perfect	و صرتَ كملاك
Peniot avva Pishoi/Father abba Bishoy	بنيوت أفا بيشوى
You struggled in prayer	الجهاد فى الصلاِة
With genuine vigil	والسهر فى معناه
We learn from your example	منك تعلمناه
Peniot avva Pishoi/Father abba Bishoy	بنيوت أفا بيشوى
You carried Jesus the righteous	حملت يسوع البار
Upon your shoulders with fear	على منكبيك بوقار
You became a throne for the Chosen	صرت كرسياً للمختار
Peniot avva Pishoi/Father abba Bishoy	بنيوت أفا بيشوى

You carried Him as a poor man	حملته كمسكين
With a joyous and honest heart	بقلب فرح أمين
And He is the worlds Redeemer	و هو فادى العالمين
Peniot avva Pishoi/Father abba Bishoy	بنيوت أفا بيشوى

Then He appeared to you clearly	فتجلى لك بوضح
And the wounds were shining	و أضاءت الجروح
You shouted with spiritual joy	فصرخت بفرح الروح
Peniot avva Pishoi/Father abba Bishoy	بنيوت أفا بيشوى

"You are glorified in Heaven	ياممجد فى سماه
Your humility is wonderful	تواضعك ما احلاه
And I'm the first of all sinners"	انا أول الخطاة
Peniot avva Pishoi/Father abba Bishoy	بنيوت أفا بيشوى

"Heaven is your Throne	السماء هى كرسيك
And the Earth is Your footstool	و الأرض موطى قدميك
And I am the work of Your hand "	و انا صنعة يديك
Peniot avva Pishoi/Father abba Bishoy	بنيوت أفا بيشوى

"I am dust and ashes	أنا تراب ورماد
And you are the God of glories	و أنت رب الأمجاد
To the age of ages"	إلى أبد الأباد
Peniot avva Pishoi/Father abba Bishoy	بنيوت أفا بيشوى

"May the ship of the Cherubim	مركبة الشاروبيم
Which is full of glory	المملوئة تعظيم

Carry You O honoured One"
Peniot avva Pishoi/Father abba Bishoy

تحملك ياكريم
بنيوت أفا بيشوى

"And I the sinner O my Lord
You are my refuge
Forive my sins"
Peniot avva Pishoi/Father abba Bishoy

وانا خاطى ياربى
انت هو حسبى
تغاضى عن ذنبى
بنيوت أفا بيشوى

The Lord of Hosts said
"O Bishoy peace be unto you
Your sins are forgiven"
Peniot avva Pishoi/Father abba Bishoy

فقال الأنام
يا بيشوى لك السلام
مغفورة لك الأثام
بنيوت أفا بيشوى

"I am the Lord of glories
And I commanded that forever
Your body will never decay"
Peniot avva Pishoi/Father abba Bishoy

انا رب الأمجاد
امرت إلى الأباد
لا يرى جسدك فساد
بنيوت أفا بيشوى

He arose happy and joyous
His face illuminated with joy
While he chanted the psalms
Peniot avva Pishoi/Father abba Bishoy

فنهض فرحا مسرور
يضى وجهه بحبور
و يرنم المزمور
بنيوت أفا بيشوى

"I glorify You O my God
For You drew me to You
And You will not let my enemy
-rejoice"

أعظمك يا ربى
لأنك إحتضنتنى
و لم تشمت بى عدوى
بنيوت أفا بيشوى

Peniot avva Pishoi/Father abba Bishoy

"My soul glorifies You   تعظمك نفسى

And my spirit rejoices in You   و تبتهج بك روحى

You are my good Saviour"   يا الله مخلصى

Peniot avva Pishoi/Father abba Bishoy   بنيوت أفا بيشوى

What joy for our church   يا فرحة كنيستنا

For our beloved St Bishoy   بالانبا بيشوى حبيبنا

By your prayers confirm us   بطلباتك ثبتنا

Peniot avva Pishoi/Father abba Bishoy   بنيوت أفا بيشوى

Remember our weaknesses   اذكر نقائصنا

And ask the Father on our behalf   و أطلب من الأب عنا

And by your prayers help us   و بصلاتك أعنا

Peniot avva Pishoi/Father abba Bishoy   بنيوت أفا بيشوى

Your name in "Shiheet" is beloved   أسمك فى شهيت محبوب

O you the light of our hearts   يا ضياء ميزان القلوب

Teach me how to repent   علمنى كيف أتوب

Peniot avva Pishoi/Father abba Bishoy   بنيوت أفا بيشوى

O Lord look after our Patriarch   يارب إحفظ بطركنا

And his partner Anba ....   و شركاؤه أساقفتنا

And our priests and monks   و كهنتنا و رهباننا

Peniot avva Pishoi/Father abba Bishoy   بنيوت أفا بيشوى

And keep O Lord of Lords	و احفظ يارب الأرباب
All your beloved	سائر كل الأحباب
Those present and those absent	الحضار و الغياب
Peniot avva Pishoi/Father abba Bishoy	بنيوت أفا بيشوى

The mention of your name in the mouth of the believers they all chant saying, oh God of Anba Bishoy support us.	تفسير أسمك فى أفواه كل المؤمنين الكل يقولون ياإله الأنبا بيشوى أعنا أجمعين

Praise for St. Anthony the Great — مديحة للأنبا أنطونيوس

In the Church of the virgins	فى كنيسة الأبكار
In the pure assembly	فى مجمع الاطهار
Living in piety	قائم بكل وقار
Peniot Ava Antonios	بنيوت آفا أنطونيوس

You are in a glorious state	قائم بمجد عظيم
In the habit of the eskeem	مع لباس الأسكيم
In the rite of the Seraphim	فى طقس السيرافيم
Peniot Ava Antonios	بين يوت آفا أنطونيوس

With spiritual prayers	بصلاة روحانية
Living a godly life	بحياة إلهية
You consecrated the desert	دشنت البرية
Peniot Ava Antonios	بين يوت آفا انطونيوس

With struggles in prayers	بجهاد فى الصلوات
For many decades	عشرات السنوات
And tears in the metanias	بدموع فى الميطانيات
Peniot Ava Antonios	بين يوت آفا أنطونيوس

In ascetic fasts	بنسك فى الأصوام
For days at a time	على مدى الأيام
With an unfailing spirit	بنفس لاتنام
Peniot Ava Antonios	بين يوت آفا أنطونيوس

With meagerness in pleasures   بزهد فى اللذات

Concerned in Godly matters   بهذيذ فى الإلهيات

And spiritual meditations   وتأمل فى الروحيات

Peniot Ava Antonios   بين يوت آفا أنطونيوس

You were given the spirit of Elijah   أعطيت روح إيليا

And Anna the prophetess   وحنة النبية

And John the son of Zacharias   ويوحنا بن زكريا

Peniot Ava Antonios   بين يوت آفا أنطونيوس

The devils feared you   ارتاع الشياطين

Because of your upright heart   من قلبك الأمين

And your constant prayers   وصلاتك كل حين

Peniot Ava Antonios   بين يوت آفا أنطونيوس

They fought against you daily   حاربوك مدة طويلة

They tried each possible way   بذلوا كل وسيلة

Using many tricks   بكم حيلة وحيلة

Peniot Ava Antonios   بين يوت آفا أنطونيوس

They reminded you of your sister   بأختك ذكروك

In order to worry you   لكيما يقلقوك

So you may return to the world   بهذا ويرجعوك

Peniot Ava Antonios   بين يوت آفا أنطونيوس

They scattered gold and silver   نثروا الذهب والمال

Before you on the mountains	أمامك على الجبال
Glittering in the midst of the sand	يضوى بين الرمال
Peniot Ava Antonios	بين يوت آفا أنطونيوس
They came with chants and songs	أتوك بطرب وغناء
And images of women	وصورة النساء
To make you fall into temptation	لتسقط فى الإغراء
Peniot Ava Antonios	بين يوت آفا أنطونيوس
They came with fierce visions	وأتوك بشكل أسود
Of lions, tigers and leopards	ونمور وفهود
And with sounds of thunder	بصياح كالرعود
Peniot Ava Antonios	بين يوت آفا أنطونيوس
They came with their malice	جاءوك بأذاهم
So you may fear their visions	لتخاف من رؤياهم
Your humility cast them out	تواضعك أخزاهم
Peniot Ava Antonios	بين يوت آفا أنطونيوس
You proclaimed and said to them	صرخت يااقوياء
"O you strong ones	لماذا هذا العناء
I will return to dust and sand"	تراب انا وهباء
Peniot Ava Antonios	بنيوت آفا أنطونيوس
"I am surprised at your gathering	عجبى لتجمهركم
In my weakness and appearance	على ضعفى وتظاهركم
I am the weakest of you all."	أنا أضعف من أصغركم

Peniot Ava Antonios	بين يوت آفا انطونيوس
O strong and high tower	يا برج عالي وحصين
You are an example for us all	يامثال للمنسحقين
In your humility before Satan	تتواضع للشياطين
Peniot Ava Antonios	بين يوت آفا انطونيوس
You are a powerful example	ياقوة ومثال
Throughout the generations	على مدى الأجيال
O dweller of the mountains	ياساكن الجبال
Peniot Ava Antonios	بين يوت آفا أنطونيوس
You are great in struggles	ياعظيم فى جهادك
And wise in counsels	ياحكيم فى إرشادك
Pray on behalf of your children	اشفع فى أولادك
Peniot Ava Antonios	بين يوت آفا انطونيوس
We have not practiced your life	لم نحيا كحياتك
Nor acquired your likeness	لم نسلك فى صفاتك
Remember us in your prayers	فاذكرنا فى صلاتك
Peniot Ava Antonios	بين يوت آفا أنطونيوس
Pray for our iniquities	اشفع فى مذلتنا
And the weakness of our nature	وضعف طبيعتنا
For we are strangers in this world	فى مدة غربتنا
Peniot Ava Antonios	بين يوت آفا أنطونيوس

Praise for Saints Maximos and Domadios

مديحة للقديسين مكسيموس و دوماديوس

In the Name of God	أبدأ باسم الإله
Our Lord Jesus Christ	سيدنا بى اخريستوس
Presenting the life of	واشرح فى شرف معنى
Maximos and Domadios	مكسيموس نيم دوماديوس
They took off their crowns	بدأ بخلع التاجات
And cast them away	وطرحها عن الرؤس
For the love of the Heavenly King	محبة فى ملك السموات
Maximos and Domadios	مكسيموس نيم دوماديوس
Praising with hymns and songs	صاحا بتراتيل وألحان
In the love of the Holy Lord	حباً فى الرب القدوس
Were these two great soldiers	وصارا أجناداً شجعان
Maximos and Domadios	مكسيموس نيم دوماديوس
Our father Abba Macarius	قال عنهم أبوهما
Described the brothers as	أنبا مقاريوس
"The pride of monasticism"	ثوب الرهبنة افتخر بهما
Maximos and Domadios	مكسيموس نيم دوماديوس
They defeated all evils	غلبوا كل الشياطين
By the Name of the Holy Lord	باسم الرب القدوس
And lived with joy in Paradise	واتكئآ فى النعيم فرحين

301

Maximos and Domadios	مكسيموس نيم دوماديوس
They left worldly reign	خلصا من مُلك العالم
Satan was deeply grieved	وخزوا إبليس المنجوس
They were rewarded the everlasting joy	ونالا الفرح الدايم
Maximos and Domadios	مكسيموس نيم دوماديوس
Blessed are you O our fathers	طوباكم ياأبهات
The children of Macarius	ياأولاد مقاريوس
The stars of Shiheet	ياكواكب جبل شيهيت
And the light of Baramous	ومصابيح دير البراموس
Just like Paradise	ياوادى هبيب شبهوك
The Valley of Natroon	الآباء بالفردوس
The king's children dwelt in you	وأولاد الملوك سكنوك
Maximos and Domadios	مكسيموس نيم دوماديوس
A great mountain you are	ياجبل عظيم الشأن
Similar to Paradise	متشبه بالفردوس
The home of our fathers	مسكن الآباء الرهبان
The monastery of Macarius	إسقيط مقاريوس
The righteous dwelt there	سكنه آباء أبرار
Proclaiming and singing Agios	صارخين قائلين قدوس
Watching night and day	سهارىَ ليل ونهار
The children of Macarius	أولاد مقاريوس

302

Home for barbarians you were	يامسكن للأشرار
And shelter for the thieves	ومأوى للصوص
But Macarius converted you	صيرك أبو مقار
To be like Paradise	متشبهاً بالفردوس
Blessed be you Abba Makar	طوباك أيها البار
Blessed be Macarius	طوباك يامقاريوس
The father of Shiheet	أنت لشيهيت فخار
Cleanser of rusting souls	مع الآباء الرؤوس
Hail to the three Macarii	وسلامى للثلاثة مقارات
And all the Abbot fathers	وكل الآباء الرؤوس
Dwelling in Shiheet	السكان بجبل شيهيت
The monastery of Macarius	إسقيط مقاريوس
Hail to Abba Youanis	وسلامى لأنبا يؤنس
The blessed hegomen (protopriest)	بى هيغومينوس
And to Abba Bishoy	والأب أنبا بيشوى
Pi romi ente leeos	بى رومى إنتى ليوس
Hail to Abba Daniel	وسلامى لأنبا دانيال
And to Abba Isidore	والأب أنبا ايسيذورس
And the exceedingly honored	والمكرم بكل الاكرام
Abba Arsanios	الانبا أرسانيوس
Don't forget our Pope	ولاتنسوا بطركنا
When praying to the Holy Lord	عند الرب القدوس

303

Anba (Shenouda) our Patriarch	انبا (شنوده) قدوتنا
And his partners our bishops	نيم نين يوتى إن نى إيبيسكوبوس
Please remember O Lord	لاتنسى ياسيدنا
The ranks of monks	طغمات نى موناخوس
And all the Christians	وكل مراتب ملتنا
Grant them Your mercies	بى أواى إن نى اخريستيانوس
Hail to Saint Mary	وسلامى إلى مريم
The intercessor for all people	الشفيعة فى كل جنوس
The great honored name	صاحبة الاسم الأعظم
Our guide to Paradise	وتوصلنا إلى الفردوس

The Doxologies   الذوكصولوجيات

—

The Doxology for Kiahk - ذكصولوجية كيهك

For if I speak about you, O Cherubimic vessel, my tongue will never quit, blessing you forever.	Ⲕⲉ ⲅⲁⲣ ⲁⲓϣⲁⲛⲥⲁϫⲓ ⲉⲑⲃⲏⲧ: ⲱ ⲡⲓϩⲁⲣⲙⲁ ⲛ̀ⲭⲉⲣⲟⲩⲃⲓⲙⲓⲕⲟⲛ: ⲡⲁⲗⲁⲥ ⲛⲁϭⲓⲥⲓ ⲁⲛ ⲉ̀ⲛⲉϩ: ⲧⲉⲛⲉⲣⲙⲁⲕⲁⲣⲓⲍⲓⲛ ⲙ̀ⲙⲟ.	لأني إذا ما تكلمت من أجلك أيتها المركبة الشاروبيمية فأن لسانى لا يتعب أبداً فى تطويبك.
For I go truly, to the house of David, to be granted a voice, in which I will utter your honor.	Ⲭⲉ ⲟⲛⲧⲱⲥ ⲅⲁⲣ ϯⲛⲁϣⲉⲛⲏⲓ: ϣⲁ ⲛⲓⲁⲩⲗⲏⲟⲩ ⲛ̀ⲧⲉ ⲡ̀ⲏⲓ ⲛ̀Ⲇⲁⲩⲓⲇ: ⲛ̀ⲧⲁϭⲓ ⲛ̀ⲟⲩⲥⲙⲏ ⲉ̀ⲃⲟⲗϩⲓⲧ ⲟⲧϥ: ⲉⲑⲣⲓⲥⲁϫⲓ ⲙ̀ⲡⲉⲧⲁⲓⲟ.	لأننى أمضي حقاً إلى ديار بيت داود لأحظى بصوت به أنطق بكرامتكِ.
For God went, to the border of Judea, and spoke rejoicfully, and was accepted by Judah's tribe.	Ⲭⲉ ⲁ̀ Ⲫϯ ⲟ̀ϩⲓ ⲉ̀ⲣⲁⲧϥ : ϧⲉⲛ ⲛⲓⲑⲱϣ ⲛ̀ⲧⲉ ϯⲓⲟⲩⲇⲉⲁ: ⲁϥϯ ⲛ̀ⲧⲉϥⲥⲙⲏ ϧⲉⲛ ⲟⲩⲑⲉⲗ-	لأن الله وقف فى حدود اليهودية وأعطى صوته بتهليل فقبله سبط يهوذا.

ΗΛ: ἂΤΦΥΛΗ ΝΙΟΥΔΑ
ϣⲟⲡϥ̀ⲉⲣⲟⲥ.

The Virgin is the tribe of Judah, that gave birth to our Saviour, and after His birth, she remained a virgin.	Ϯ̀ΦΥΛΗ ΝΙΟΥΔΑ ΤΕ Ϯⲡⲁⲣⲑⲉⲛⲟⲥ: ⲑⲏⲉ̀ⲧⲁⲥⲙⲓⲥⲓ ⲙ̀Ⲡⲉⲛⲥⲱⲣ: ⲟⲩⲟ̅ⲅ̅ ⲟⲛ ⲙⲉⲛⲉⲛⲥⲁ ⲑ̀ⲣⲉⲥⲙⲁⲥϥ: ⲁⲥⲟ̅ⲅ̅ⲓ ⲉⲥⲟⲓ ⲙ̀ⲡⲁⲣⲑⲉⲛⲟⲥ.	العذراء هى سبط يهوذا التى ولدَت مخلصنا. وبعد ولادته أيضاً بقيت عذراء.
Along with, Archangel Gabriel, we honour you, O Theotokos Mary.	Ⲉ̀ⲃⲟⲗ ⲅⲁⲣ ⲅⲓⲧⲉⲛ Ϯⲫⲱⲛⲏ: ⲛ̀ⲧⲉ Ⲅⲁⲃⲣⲓⲏⲗ ⲡⲓⲁⲅⲅⲉⲗⲟⲥ: ⲧⲉⲛϯ ⲛⲉ ⲙ̀ⲡⲓⲭⲉⲣⲉⲧⲓⲥⲙⲟⲥ: ⲱ̀ Ϯⲑⲉⲟ̀ⲧⲟⲕⲟⲥ Ⲙⲁⲣⲓⲁ̀.	وبصوت الملاك غبريال تُعطيك السلام يا والدة الإله مريم.
Hail to you from God, hail to you from Gabriel, hail to you from us, we magnify you saying "hail to you."	Ⲭⲉⲣⲉ ⲛⲉ ⲉ̀ⲃⲟⲗⲅⲓⲧⲉⲛ Ⲫϯ: ⲭⲉⲣⲉ ⲛⲉ ⲉ̀ⲃⲟⲗ ⲅⲓⲧⲉⲛ Ⲅⲁⲃⲣⲓⲏⲗ: ⲭⲉⲣⲉ ⲛⲉ ⲉ̀ⲃⲟⲗⲅⲓⲧⲟⲧⲉⲛ: ⲭⲉ ⲭⲉⲣⲉ ⲛⲉ ⲧⲉⲛϭⲓⲥⲓ ⲙ̀ⲙⲟ.	السلام لكِ من قِبَل الله. السلام لكِ من قِبَل غبريال. السلام لك من قِبَلنا نعظمك قائلين السلام لكِ.

Gabriel the holy angel, announced to the Virgin, and after granting her peace, he strengthened her saying.	Πιαγγελοc εθⲩ Ⲅⲁⲃⲣⲓⲏⲗ: ⲁ϶ⲓϣⲉⲛⲛⲟⲩϥⲓ ⲛ̀ϯⲡⲁⲣⲑⲉⲛⲟⲥ: ⲙⲉⲛⲉⲛⲥⲁ ⲡⲓⲁⲥⲡⲁⲥⲙⲟⲥ: ⲁ϶ⲧⲁ϶ⲣⲟ ⲙ̀ⲙⲟⲥ ϧⲉⲛ ⲡⲉ϶ⲥⲁⲝⲓ.	غبريال الملاك الطاهر بشر العذراء وبعد ان أهداها السلام قواها بقوله.
"Do not be afraid Mary, for you have found peace unto the Lord, for you shall conceive, and give birth to a Son."	Ⲭⲉ ⲙ̀ⲡⲉⲣⲉⲣ϶ⲟϯ Ⲙⲁⲣⲓⲁⲙ: ⲁⲣⲉⲭⲓⲙⲓ ⲅⲁⲣ ⲛ̀ⲟⲩ϶ⲙⲟⲧ: ϧⲁⲧⲉⲛ Ⲫ̀ⲛⲟⲩϯ ϩⲏⲡⲡⲉ ⲅⲁⲣ ⲧⲉⲣⲁⲉⲣⲃⲟⲕⲓ : ⲟⲩⲟ϶ ⲛ̀ⲧⲉⲙⲓⲥⲓ ⲛ̀ⲟⲩϣⲏⲣⲓ.	لا تخافى يا مريم لأنك قد وجدتِ نعمة عند الله. ها ستحبلين وتلدين إبناً.
"And the Lord God shall give Him, the throne of David His father, and He will reign over the house, of Jacob forever and ever."	Ⲉ϶ⲉϯ ⲛⲁ϶ ⲛ̀ϫⲉ Ⲡⲟⲥ Ⲫϯ: ⲙ̀ⲡⲓⲑⲣⲟⲛⲟⲥ ⲛ̀ⲧⲉ Ⲇⲁⲩⲓⲇ ⲡⲉ϶ⲓⲱⲧ: ϥ̀ⲛⲁⲉⲣⲟⲩⲣⲟ ⲉ̀ϫⲉⲛ ⲡ̀ⲏⲓ ⲛ̀Ⲓⲁⲕⲱⲃ: ϣⲁ ⲉ̀ⲛⲉ϶ ⲛ̀ⲧⲉ ⲡⲓⲉ̀ⲛⲉ϶.	ويعطيه الرب الإله كرسى داود أبيه. ويملك على بيت يعقوب إلى أبد الأبد.

Fo this we glorify you, as the Mother of God, always intercede to God, on our behalf to forgive us our sins.	Ⲉⲑⲃⲉ ⲫⲁⲓ ⲧⲉⲛϯⲱⲟⲩ ⲛⲉ⳿ ⳿ⲱⲥ ⲑⲉⲟⲧⲟⲕⲟⲥ ⳿ⲛⲥⲏⲟⲩ ⲛⲓⲃⲉⲛ⳿ ⲙⲁⲧⲁⲟ ⳿ⲉⲠⲟⲥ ⳿ⲉⲁⲣⲏⲓ ⳿ⲉϫ ⲱⲛ⳿ ⳿ⲛⲧⲉϥ...	من أجل هذا نُمجدك كوالدة الاله كل حين إسألى الرب عنا ليغفر...
Hail to you O Virgin, the very and true Queen, hail to the pride of our race, who gave birth to Emmanuel.	Ⲭⲉⲣⲉ ⲛⲉ ⳿ⲱ ϯⲡⲁⲣⲑⲉⲛⲟⲥ ⳿ ϯⲟⲩⲣⲱ ⳿ⲙⲙⲏⲓ ⳿ⲛⲁⲗⲏⲑⲓⲛⲏ ⳿ ⲭⲉⲣⲉ ⳿ⲡϣⲟⲩϣⲟⲩ ⳿ⲛⲧⲉ ⲡⲉⲛⲅⲉⲛⲟⲥ ⳿ ⲁⲣⲉϫⲫⲟ ⲛⲁⲛ ⳿ⲛⲈⲙⲙⲁⲛⲟⲩⲏⲗ⳿	السلام لك أيتها العذراء الملكة الحقيقية الحقانية. السلام لفخر جنسنا. ولدت لنا عمانوئيل.
We ask you to remember us, O our trusted advocate, before our Lord Jesus Christ, that He may forgive us our sins.	Ⲧⲉⲛϯⲁⲟ ⳿ⲁⲣⲓⲡⲉⲛⲙⲉⲩⲓ⳿ ⳿ⲱ ϯⲡⲣⲟⲥⲧⲁⲧⲏⲥ ⳿ⲉⲧⲉⲛⲁⲟⲧ ⳿ ⲛⲁⲁⲣⲉⲛ Ⲡⲉⲛϭⲟⲓⲥ Ⲓⲏⲥⲟⲩⲥ ⲠⲓⲬⲣⲓⲥⲧⲟⲥ ⳿ ⳿ⲛⲧⲉϥⲭⲁ ⲛⲉⲛⲛⲟⲃⲓ ⲛⲁⲛ ⳿ⲉⲃⲟⲗ⳿	نسألك أن تذكرينا أيتها الشفيعة المؤتمنة أمام ربنا يسوع المسيح ليغفر لنا خطايانا.

St Virgin Mary's Kiahk Doxology
ذكصولوجية العذراء

The adornment of Virgin Mary, the daughter of King David, at the right hand of Jesus Christ, the Beloved Son of God.	Ⲉⲣⲉ ⲡⲥⲟⲗⲥⲉⲗ ⲛ̀ϯⲡⲁⲣⲑⲉⲛⲟⲥ⳱ Ⲙⲁⲣⲓⲁ ϯϣⲉⲣⲓ ⲙ̀ⲡⲟⲩⲣⲟ Ⲇⲁⲩⲓⲇ⳱ ⲥⲁⲟⲩⲓⲛⲁⲙ ⲛ̀Ⲓⲏⲥ Ⲡ̅ⲭ̅ⲥ̅⳱ Ⲡϣⲏⲣⲓ ⲙ̀Ⲫⲛⲟⲩϯ ⲡⲓⲙⲉⲛⲣⲓⲧ.	زينة العذراء مريم يا ابنة الملك داود عن يمين يسوع المسيح. ابن الله الحبيب.
As David the king and psalmist, has said in the psalm, upon the right hand of the throne, did stand the queen.	Ⲕⲁⲧⲁ ⲡ̀ⲥⲁϫⲓ ⲛ̀Ⲇⲁⲩⲓⲇ ⲡ̀ⲟⲩⲣⲟ⳱ ⲡⲓϩⲩⲙⲛⲟⲗⲟⲥ ϧⲉⲛ ⲡⲓⲯⲁⲗⲙⲟⲥ⳱ ϫⲉ ⲁⲥⲟϩⲓ ⲉ̀ⲣⲁⲧⲥ ⲛ̀ϫⲉ ϯⲟⲩⲣⲱ⳱ ⲥⲁⲟⲩⲓⲛⲁⲙ ⲙ̀ⲡⲓⲑⲣⲟⲛⲟⲥ.	كقول داود الملك المرتل فى المزمور قامت الملكة عن يمين العرش.
You are higher than the Cherubim, O Mother of the God of powers, and more honoured than the Seraphim, in	Ⲧⲉϭⲟⲥⲓ ⲉ̀ⲛⲓⲬⲉⲣⲟⲩⲃⲓⲙ⳱ ⲱ̀ ⲑⲙⲁⲩ ⲙ̀Ⲫⲛⲟⲩϯ ⲫⲁ ⲡⲓⲁⲙⲁϩⲓ⳱ⲧⲉⲧⲁⲓⲏⲟⲩⲧ ⲉ̀Ⲛⲓⲥⲉⲣⲁⲫⲓⲙ⳱ ϧⲉⲛ ⲧ̀ⲫⲉ ⲛⲉⲙ ϩⲓϫⲉⲛ ⲡⲓⲕⲁϩⲓ.	أنت ارفع من الشيروبيم يا ام الله ذى العزة. واكرم من السيرافيم فى السماء وعلى الارض.

heaven and on earth.

Blessed are you O Mary, for you have borne the true One, while remaining virgin, and your virginity is ever sealed.

Ⲱⲟⲩⲛⲓⲁϯ ⲛ̀ⲑⲟ Ⲙⲁⲣⲓⲁ: ϫⲉ ⲁⲣⲉϫⲫⲟ ⲙ̀ⲡⲓⲁ̀ⲗⲏⲑⲓⲛⲟⲥ: ⲉⲥⲧⲟⲃ ⲛ̀ϫⲉ ⲧⲉⲡⲁⲣⲑⲉⲛⲓⲁ: ⲁ̀ⲣⲉⲟ̀ϩⲓ ⲉⲣⲉⲟⲓ ⲙ̀ⲡⲁⲣⲑⲉⲛⲟⲥ.

طوباك انت يا مريم لانك ولدت الحقيقى. وبتوليتك مختومة وانت باقية عذراء.

As Isaiah has said, with the voice of rejoicing, "Behold a Virgin shall conceive, and b-ring forth Emm-anuel."

Ⲕⲁⲧⲁ ⲫ̀ⲣⲏϯ ⲉ̀ⲧⲁϥϫⲟⲥ: ⲛ̀ϫⲉ Ⲏⲥⲁⲏⲁⲥ ϧⲉⲛ ⲟⲩⲥⲙⲏ ⲛ̀ⲑⲉⲗⲏⲗ: ϫⲉ ⲓⲥ ⲁⲗⲟⲩ ⲙ̀ⲡⲁⲣⲑⲉⲛⲟⲥ: ⲉⲥⲉ̀-ⲙⲓⲥⲓ ⲛⲁⲛ ⲛ̀Ⲉⲙⲙⲁⲛⲟⲩⲏⲗ.

كما قال اشعياء بصوت التهليل. ها فتاة عذراء ستلد لنا عمانوئيل.

We magnify you every day, saying with Gabriel, Hail to you filled with grace, the Lord is with you.

Ⲧⲉⲛϭ́ⲓⲥⲓ ⲙ̀ⲙⲟ ⲙ̀ⲙⲏⲛⲓ ⲙ̀-ⲙⲏⲛⲓ:ⲉⲛϫⲱ ⲙ̀ⲙⲟⲥ ⲛⲉⲙ Ⲅⲁ-ⲃⲣⲓⲏⲗ: ϫⲉ ⲭⲉⲣⲉ ⲕⲉⲭⲁⲣ-ⲓⲧⲱⲙⲉⲛⲏ: ⲟ̀ Ⲕⲩⲣⲓⲟⲥ ⲙⲉⲧⲁ ⲥⲟⲩ.

نرفعك يوما فيوما قائلين مع غبريال. افرحى يا ممتلئة نعمة. الرب معك.

Hail to you O

Ⲭⲉⲣⲉ ⲛⲉ ⲱ̀ ϯⲡⲁⲣⲑⲉ-

السلام لك ايتها

Virgin, and we call you blessed, with Gabriel the angel, the Lord is with you.

noc：теnершакарızın ѝ-мо：neш Ѕаврінλ піаѕѕ-елос：отоѕ Π̄о̄с̄ ϣоп neше.

العذراء نطوبك مع غبريال الملاك الرب معك.

We ask you remember us, O our faithful advocate, before our Lord Jesus Christ, that He may forgive us our sins.

Ѱenтѕо àрiпеnшері：ѡ ѱпростатнс èтеnѕот：наѕрen Пенбоіс Інсотс ПὶХрістос ：ѝтечха неnnові нан èвоλ.

نسألك اذكرينا ايتها الشفيعة المؤتمنة امام ربنا يسوع المسيح ليغفر لنا خطايانا.

Doxology For Archangel Gabriel for Kiahk
ذكصولوجية الملاك غبريال

You are truly great, O messenger of good tidings, among the choirs of the angels, and the heavenly orders.

Ѝѳок отnіϣ̀ àλнѳос：ѡ піфаіϣennотѵı ѝк-аλѡс：ꬴen nітаꙁіс ѝаѕѕеλікоn ：neш nітаѕша ѝèпотра-nіоn.

انت عظيم حقاً ايها المبشر الحسن فى الطقوس الملائكية والطغمات السمائية.

O Gabriel the evangel, the great among the angels, and the holy orders on high, who carry flaming fiery swords.	Ⲅⲁⲃⲣⲓⲏⲗ ⲡⲓϥⲁⲓϣⲉⲛⲛⲟⲩϥⲓ : ⲡⲓⲛⲓϣϯ ϧⲉⲛ ⲛⲓⲁⲅⲅⲉⲗⲟⲥ: ⲛⲉⲙ ⲛⲓⲧⲁⲅⲙⲁ ⲉⲑⲟⲩⲁⲃ ⲉⲧϭⲟⲥⲓ : ⲉⲧϥⲁⲓ ϧⲁ ⲧⲥⲏϥⲓ ⲛϣⲁϩ ⲛⲭⲣⲱⲙ.	ياغبريال المبشر العظيم في الملائكة و الطغمات المقدسة العلوية حاملي السيف الملتهب ناراً .
Daniel the prophet, has seen your honour, you have revealed unto him, the mystery of the Trinity.	Ⲁϥⲛⲁⲩ ⲅⲁⲣ ⲉⲡⲉⲕⲧⲁⲓⲟ : ⲛ̀ϫⲉ Ⲇⲁⲛⲓⲏⲗ ⲡⲓⲡ̀ⲣⲟⲫⲏⲧⲏⲥ ⲉⲟⲩⲟϩ ⲁⲕⲧⲁⲙⲟϥ ⲉ̀ⲡⲓⲙⲩⲥⲧⲏⲣⲓⲟⲛ : ⲛ̀ϯ̀ⲧⲣⲓⲁⲥ ⲛⲣⲉϥⲧⲁⲛϧⲟ.	قد نظر كرامتك دانيال النبي واعلمته سر الثالوث المحي .
To Zechariah the priest, you have brought the good news, of the birth of the forerunner, John the Baptizer.	Ⲟⲩⲟϩ Ⲍⲁⲭⲁⲣⲓⲁⲥ ⲡⲓⲟⲩⲏⲃ : ⲛ̀ⲑⲟⲕ ⲁⲕϩⲓϣⲉⲛⲛⲟϥⲓ ⲛⲁϥ : ϧⲉⲛ ⲡ̀ϫⲓⲛⲙⲓⲥⲓ ⲙ̀ⲡⲓⲡ̀ⲣⲟⲇⲣⲟⲙⲟⲥ : Ⲓⲱⲁ Ⲡⲓⲣⲉϥ ϯⲱⲙⲥ.	وزكريا الكاهن انت بشرته بميلاد يوحنا المعمداني .
Likewise saying to the Virgin, "Blessed are	Ⲁⲕϩⲓϣⲉⲛⲛⲟϥⲓ ⲟⲛ ⲛ̀ϯⲡⲁⲣⲑⲉⲛⲟⲥ : ϫⲉ ⲭⲉⲣⲉ	وبشرت ايضاً العذراء قائلاً

you, filled with grace, the Lord is with you. You shall bring forth, the Saviour of the whole world."	ⲑⲏⲉⲑⲙⲉϩ ⲛ̀ϩ̀ⲙⲟⲧ : Ⲡⲟ̅ⲥ̅ ⲛⲉⲙⲉ ⲧⲉⲣⲁⲙⲓⲥⲓ : ⲙ̀Ⲡⲥⲱ-ⲑⲏⲣ ⲙ̀ⲡⲓⲕⲟⲥⲙⲟⲥ ⲧⲏⲣϥ.	السلام لك ياممتلئة نعمة. الرب معك. ستلدين مخلص العالم كله.
Intercede on our behalf, O holy Archangel, Gabriel the angel-evangel, that He may forgive us our sins.	Ⲁ̀ⲣⲓⲡ : ⲱ̀ ⲡⲓⲁⲣⲭⲏⲁⲅ-ⲅⲉⲗⲟⲥ : ⲉ̀ⲑⲟⲩⲁⲃ Ⲅⲁⲃⲣⲓⲏⲗ ⲡⲓϥⲁⲓϣ-ⲉⲛⲛⲟⲩϥⲓ : ⲛ̀ⲧⲉϥ ⲭⲁ ⲛⲉⲛⲛⲟⲃⲓ ⲛⲁⲛ ⲉ̀ⲃⲟⲗ.	اشفع فينا امام الرب يارئيس الملائكة المقدس غبريال المبشر ليغفر لنا خطايانا.

Conclusion of the Doxologies ختام الذوكصولوجيات

Be our advocate, in the highest where you are, O Lady of us all the Theotokos, the ever-virgin Mary	Ⲯϣⲱⲡⲓ ⲛ̀ⲑⲟ ⲉⲣⲉ ⲥⲟⲙⲥ ⲉ̀-ⲭⲱⲛ : ϧⲉⲛ ⲛⲓⲙⲁ ⲉⲧϭⲟ-ⲥⲓ ⲉ̀ⲧⲁⲣⲉⲭⲏ ⲛ̀ϧⲏⲧⲟⲩ : ⲱ̀ ⲧⲉⲛϭⲟⲓⲥ ⲛ̀ⲛⲏⲃ ⲧⲏⲣⲉⲛ ϯⲑⲉⲟⲧⲟⲕⲟⲥ : ⲉⲧⲟⲓ ⲙ̀ⲡ-ⲁⲣⲑⲉⲛⲟⲥ ⲛ̀ⲥⲏⲟⲩ ⲛⲓⲃⲉⲛ.	كونى أنت ناظرة علينا فى المواضع العالية التى أنت كائنة فيها. يا سيدتنا كلنا والدة الإله العذراء كل حين.

Ask of Him Whom you have born, our good Saviour, to take away our afflictions, and accord to us His peace.	Ⲙⲁⲧϩⲟ ⲙ̀ⲫⲏⲉⲧⲁⲣⲉⲙⲁⲥϥ : Ⲡⲉⲛⲥⲱⲧⲏⲣ ⲛ̀ⲁⲅⲁⲑⲟⲥ : ⲛ̀ⲧⲉϥⲱⲗⲓ ⲛ̀ⲛⲁⲓϭⲓⲥⲓ ⲉⲃⲟⲗ-ϩⲁⲣⲟⲛ : ⲛ̀ⲧⲉϥⲥⲉⲙⲛⲓ ⲛⲁⲛ ⲛ̀ⲧⲉϥϩⲓⲣⲏⲛⲏ.	إسألى الذى ولدته مخلصنا الصالح أن يرفع عنا هذه الأتعاب ويقرر لنا سلامه.
Hail to you O Virgin, the very and true queen, hail to the pride of our race, who has borne to us Emmanuel.	Ⲭⲉⲣⲉ ⲛⲉ ⲱ̀ ϯⲡⲁⲣⲑⲉⲛⲟⲥ : ϯⲟⲩⲣⲱ ⲙ̀ⲙⲏⲓ ⲛ̀ⲁⲗⲏⲑⲓⲛⲏ : ⲭⲉⲣⲉ ⲡ̀ϣⲟⲩϣⲟⲩ ⲛ̀ⲧⲉ ⲡⲉⲛⲅⲉⲛⲟⲥ: ⲁ̀ⲣⲉⲭ̀ⲫⲟ ⲛⲁⲛ ⲛ̀Ⲉⲙⲙⲁⲛⲟⲩⲏⲗ.	السلام لك أيتها العذراء الملكة الحقيقية الحقانية. السلام لفخر جنسنا. ولدت لنا عمانوئيل.
We ask you to remember us, O our faithful advocate, before our Lord Jesus Christ, that He may forgive us our sins.	Ⲧⲉⲛϯϩⲟ ⲁ̀ⲣⲓⲡⲉⲛⲙⲉⲩⲓ : ⲱ̀ ϯⲡⲣⲟⲥⲧⲁⲧⲏⲥ ⲉⲧⲉⲛϩⲟⲧ : ⲛⲁϩⲣⲉⲛ Ⲡⲉⲛϭⲟⲓⲥ Ⲓⲏⲥⲟⲩⲥ Ⲡⲓⲭ̀ⲣⲓⲥⲧⲟⲥ : ⲛ̀ⲧⲉϥ ⲭⲁ ⲛⲉⲛⲛⲟⲃⲓ ⲛⲁⲛ ⲉ̀ⲃⲟⲗ.	نسألك أن تذكرينا أيتها الشفيعة المؤتمنة أمام ربنا يسوع المسيح ليغفر لنا خطايانا.

Hymn Before Friday Theotokia -
مديح واطس على ثيؤطوكية يوم الجمعة

I begin with the name of the Lord -Jesus:	ابدى باسم الرب يسوع
And ask in awe from His goodness:	وأطلب من فضله بخشوع.
To raise my mind to the heaven:	ان يجعل عقلى مرفوع
To praise the daughter of Zion.	كى امدح فى ابنه صهيون

بدء كلامى ونظامى

I begin my words and praise:
By greeting the Virgin:
Because all my maladies and pain:
Were cured through her.

اهدى البكر سلامى
لان جميع اسقامى
والاوجاع بها يبراؤن

My soul longs for her:
I submit myself to her:
Because I depend on her:
To save me from the evil one.

تاقت نفسى اليها
وانا مطروح بين يديها
لانى توكلت عليها
لكى افوز من الاركون

Come to our help O Mother of Light:
Please Mary save me from all evil:

جيرينا يا ام النور
يامريم من كل شرور

From her came the Well Known: The Creator of all flesh.	يامن جاء منها غير المنظور خالق كل البشريين
All my thoughts became darkened: Because I could not see the light: A Virgin without a spouse: Carried the Hidden Mystery.	صارت كل افكارى كليل اذ لم اجد فيها سبيل عذراء ليس لها بعل قد حملت سرا مكنون
Creator of the seen and the unseen: How could the womb contain Him: All the wise and educated: Tell me how can it be.	خالق ما يرى وما لايرى كيف سعته بطن العذراء يا ذو الالباب والخبرة لم فيها تهتمون
She is called "The mother of Mercy": And also "The full of Grace": The mother of the Logos: Many about her prophesied.	هذه تدعى ام الرحمة هذه المملؤة نعمة هذه والدة الكلمة وكثير عنها قد تنبأوا
Let me praise you and say : Blessed are you pure Virgin: From whom came the Well Known: The Savior of all flesh.	دعنى انا امدح واقول طوباك يابكر بتول يامن جاء منها المنظور ومخلص كل البشريين

The Spirit of Truth the Paraclete:	روح الحق الباراقليط
Came as a mediator with the good -news:	جانا مبشر ووسيط
He is the Spirit of God surrounding -us:	سبحانه رب ومحيط
Knowing of what was and what will be:	يعلم بما كان وما سيكون

He adorned Mary with His Advent: زين مريم بحلول

And fulfilled the prophecies: وأكمل ما قد شهدوا له

The Magi came and worshiped Him: مجوس اتوا وسجدوا له

With precious gifts they were -introduced.   بهداياهم قد دخلوا

Our Lord accepted suffering: سيدنا قبل الالام

Died was buried in the tomb: مات ودفن فى القبر وقام

He arose and Mary was filled with -joyful peace: وابتهجت مريم بسلام

And He also appeared to the Apostles.   وظهر ايضا للحواريين

You were compared to Noah's Ark: شبهتى بسفينة نوح

You healed our wounds: داويتى جرح المجروح

And you made Adam joyful: وصيرتى ادام مشروح

With extraordinary tributes.   بكرامات لا يوصفون

Mary you became a lamp: صرتى يامريم مصباح

And Your Light in the world showed :   ونورك فى العالم قد لاح

The one Whose aroma spread: يامن عنبرها قد فاح

Whom all the righteous smelled.	واشتمه الصديقون

When the sheep lost his way:	ضل الخروف الناطق
The Shepherd sought to redeem him:	والراعى طلب الهابق
When He completed His true promise:	حين وفى وعده الصادق
And appeared to us in the flesh	وظهر أيضا للبشريين

Blessed are you O' full of Grace:	طوباك يامختارة
Who became like a lighthouse:	يامن صرتى كمناره
And you became like a fishing hook:	وتشبهتى بالصناره
To the intellect of mankind.	العليقة للبشريين

You were covered by the Cherubim:	ظللكى الكاروبيم
O' Mary daughter of Joachim:	يامريم يا ابنة يواقيم
Truly it is a great mystery:	حقا انه سر عظيم
Not understood by the scholars.	لم يحوه النظامون

Our Lord Emanuel:	عمانوئيل سيدنا
Meaning God with us:	تفسيرة الله معنا
He came and saved us:	حتى اتى وخلصنا
And we became His children.	وسمينا لله بنين

The Unseen how could we see :	غير المرئى كيف رأوه
The Unlimited how could He be -contained:	الغير محوى كيف حووه
The incomprehensible how could He -be understood:	من لم يدرك كيف نظروه
	اعيننا اللحميون

By any human being.

Jesus opened the doors of Paradise:	فتح يسوع باب الفردوس
And with Him all souls were pleased:	وابتهجت به كل النفوس
He brought back life with His Holy -Name:	واحيانا باسمه القدوس
And Gave to us His body as proof.	و اعطاناجسده عربون

You became a mother to your Lord:	قد صرتى اما لمولاك
O most High and blessed:	يامتعالية طوباك
Your elegance and glory O' Mary:	يامريم بمجدك وبهاك
Cannot be expressed by any poet.	لم يحوك النظامون

All tongues could not speak:	كلت كل الالسن فيك
And I a sinner put my hope in you:	وانا الخاطئ مسترجيك
My mind could not contain you:	ولم يقدر عقلى يحويك
And my thoughts are so weak.	وافكارى فيك قد عجزت

I am still begging you:	لم ازل اطلب منك
To lead me to your Son's way:	تهدينى الي سبل ابنك
We all bless you:	نعطيك الطوبى لانك
Because you became to us Zion.	صرتى يامريم صهيون

I need a wise and rational one:	من كان يوجد عاقل
To help me to be able to say:	ولبيب

Praise and hymns worthy of you:
So I can feel safe in you.

يسعفنى لكى اجيب مدح
يليق بها ويطيب
ولى فيها بر مامون

The Lord saw the lost fallen:
And to David He gave a promise:
"From your seed will be:
The Promise" and He did not relent.

نظر الرب الضال تلف
ولداود اقسم وحلف
وعد الوعد ولم يخلف
ان من ثمرة صلبك
سيكون

The promise He did complete:
In the fullness of time He came:
From the House of David He
-appeared:
And walked on Earth like any human.

ها هوذا تم الموعود
وامتزج الوعد المقصود
وظهر من بيت داود
ومشى كالجسدانيين

I the sinner with all my troubles:
Asking for exceeding joy:
Abu Al-Saad from Abu Teig :
The servant of all who write poetery.

وانا الخاطئ وضجيجى
طالب زايد تفريحى
انا محب التطويب
اصغر جميع النظامين

My mind with guilt made me write:
Because in the Psalms I did read:
"Unless the Lord builds:
They labour in vain who build."

لآمنى عقلى وانشأت
لآنى فى المزمور قرأت
اذ لم يبن الرب البيت
فباطل تعب البنائين

O' Jesus our Savior:	يايسوع مخلصنا
Preserve the life of Anba (.......):	احفظ حياة انبا (.....)
The Patriarch And His companions:	بطركنا
Our Bishops And our gathered	وشركائه اساقفتنا
-brothers.	واخوتنا المجتمعين
And the peace of the Lord be with	وسلام الله يكون معكم
-you:	ياحاضرين باجمعكم
All you gathered together here:	بصوته الفرح يسمعكم
And His pleasant voice shall you:	فى يوم القيامة مجتمعين
Hear On the day of Resurrection.	

Fourth Hoos – Πιϩⲱⲥ ⲙ̅ⲙⲁϩ ⲇ̅ - الهوس الرابع

*Praise the Lord from the heavens Alleluia. Praise Him in the heights.	*Ⲥⲙⲟⲩ ⲉⲠ̅ⲟ̅ⲥ̅ ⲉⲃⲟⲗ ϧⲉⲛ ⲛⲓⲫⲏⲟⲩⲓ Ⲇ̅ⲗ̅ : ⲥⲙⲟⲩ ⲉⲣⲟϥ ϧⲉⲛ ⲛⲏⲉⲧϭⲟⲥⲓ.	*سبحوا الرب من السموات الليلويا. سبحوه فى الأعالى.
Praise Him all His angels Alleluia. Praise Him all His hosts.	Ⲥⲙⲟⲩ ⲉⲣⲟϥ ⲛⲉϥⲁⲅⲅⲉⲗⲟⲥ ⲧⲏⲣⲟⲩ Ⲇ̅ⲗ̅: ⲥⲙⲟⲩ ⲉⲣⲟϥ ⲛⲉϥⲇⲩⲛⲁⲙⲓⲥ ⲧⲏⲣⲟⲩ.	سبحوه ياجميع ملائكته الليلويا. سبحوه يا جميع جنوده.
*Praise Him sun and moon Alleluia. Praise Him all you stars of light.	*Ⲥⲙⲟⲩ ⲉⲣⲟϥ ⲡⲓⲣⲏ ⲛⲉⲙ ⲡⲓⲓⲟϩ Ⲇ̅ⲗ̅ : ⲥⲙⲟⲩ ⲉⲣⲟϥ ⲛⲓⲥⲓⲟⲩ ⲧⲏⲣⲟⲩ ⲛ̀ⲧⲉ ⲡⲓⲟⲩⲱⲓⲛⲓ.	*سبحيه ايتها الشمس والقمر الليلويا. سبحيه ياجميع كواكب النور.
Praise Him you heavens of heavens Alleluia. And you	Ⲥⲙⲟⲩ ⲉⲣⲟϥ ⲛⲓⲫⲏⲟⲩⲓ ⲛ̀ⲧⲉ ⲛⲓⲫⲏⲟⲩⲓ Ⲇ̅ⲗ̅	سبحيه يا سماء السموات الليلويا. ويا ايتها المياه

waters above the heavens.	ⲛⲉⲙ ⲛⲓⲕⲉⲙⲱⲟ ⲉⲧⲥⲁ ⲡ̄-ϣⲱⲓ ⲛ̀ⲛⲓⲫⲏⲟⲩⲓ.	التى فوق السموات.
*Let them praise the Name of the Lord Alleluia. For He commanded and they were created.	*Ⲙⲁⲣⲟⲩⲥ̀ⲙⲟⲩ ⲧⲏⲣ-ⲟⲩ ⲉ̀ⲫⲣⲁⲛ ⲙ̀Ⲡ6ⲟⲓⲥ ⲁ̄ⲗ ⲝ̀ⲭⲉ ⲛ̀ⲑⲟ4 ⲁ4ⲭⲟⲥ ⲟⲩⲟⲅ ⲁⲩϣⲱⲡⲓ.	*لتسبح جميعها لاسم الرب الليلويا. لانه قـال فكانت.
He has ordered and they were created Alleluia. He has established them forever and ever.	`Ⲛ̀ⲑⲟ4 ⲁ4ⲥⲟⲛⲅⲉⲛ ⲟⲩⲟⲅ ⲁⲩⲥⲱⲛⲧ ⲁ̄ⲗ꞉ ⲁ4ⲧⲁ-ⲅⲱⲟⲩ ⲉ̀ⲣⲁⲧⲟⲩ ϣⲁ ⲉ̀ⲛⲉⲅ ⲛⲉⲙ ϣⲁ ⲉ̀ⲛⲉⲅ ⲛ̀ⲧⲉ ⲡⲓⲉ̀ⲛⲉⲅ.	وأمر فخلقت الليلويا. اقامها إلى الأبد والى ابـد الابد.
*He has made a decree and it will be enforced Alleluia. Praise the Lord from the earth.	*Ⲁ4ⲭⲱ ⲛ̀ⲟⲩⲅⲱⲛ ⲟⲩ-ⲟⲅ ⲛ̀ⲛⲉ4ⲥⲓⲛⲓ ⲁ̄ⲗ꞉ ⲥ̀ⲙ-ⲟⲩ ⲉ̀Ⲡ6ⲟⲓⲥ ⲉ̀ⲃⲟⲗⲅⲉⲛ ⲡ̄-ⲭⲁⲅⲓ.	*وضع لها امرا فلن تتجاوزه الليلويا. سبحى الرب من الارض.
All you dragons and all depths Alleluia. Fire and hail, snow	Ⲛⲓⲁ̀ⲣⲁⲕⲱⲛ ⲛⲉⲙ ⲛⲓⲛⲟⲩⲛ ⲧⲏⲣⲟⲩ ⲁ̄ⲗ꞉	ايتها التنانين وجميع الاعماق الليلويا. النار

and vapor and stormy wind fulfilling His word.	ⲟⲩⲭⲣⲱⲙ ⲟⲩⲁⲗ ⲟⲩⲭⲓⲱⲛ ⲟⲩⲭⲣⲩⲥⲧⲁⲗⲗⲟⲥ ⲟⲩ̅ⲡ̅ⲛⲉⲩⲙⲁ ⲛ̀ⲥⲁⲣⲁⲑⲏⲟⲩ ⲛⲏⲉⲧ̀ⲓⲣⲓ ⲙ̀ⲡⲉϥⲥⲁϫⲓ.	والبرد والثلج والجليد والريح العاصفة الصانعة كلمته.
*Mountains and all hills Alleluia. Fruitful trees and all cedars.	*Ⲛⲓⲧⲱⲟⲩ ⲉⲧϭⲟⲥⲓ ⲛⲉⲙ ⲛⲓⲕⲁⲗⲁⲙⲫⲱⲟⲩ ⲧⲏⲣⲟⲩ ⲁ̅ⲗ̅: ⲛⲓϣ̀ϣⲏ ⲙ̀ϧⲁⲓⲟⲩⲧⲁϩ ⲛⲉⲙ ⲛⲓϣⲉⲛⲥⲓϥⲓ ⲧⲏⲣⲟⲩ.	*الجبال العالية وجميع الآكام الليلويا. الاشجار المثمرة وكل الأرز.
Beasts and all cattle Alleluia. Creeping things and flying birds.	Ⲛⲓⲑⲏⲣⲓⲟⲛ ⲛⲉⲙ ⲛⲓⲧⲉⲃⲛⲱⲟⲩⲓ̀ ⲧⲏⲣⲟⲩ ⲁ̅ⲗ̅: ⲛⲓϭⲁⲧϥⲓ ⲛⲉⲙ ⲛⲓϩⲁⲗⲁϯ ⲉⲧⲟⲓ ⲛ̀ⲧⲉⲛϩ.	الوحوش وكل البهائم الليلويا. الهوام وكل الطيور ذات الاجنحة.
*Kings of the earth and all people Alleluia. Princes and all judges of the earth.	*Ⲛⲓⲟⲩⲣⲱⲟⲩ ⲛ̀ⲧⲉ ⲡ̀ⲕⲁϩⲓ ⲛⲉⲙ ⲛⲓⲗⲁⲟⲥ ⲧⲏⲣⲟⲩ ⲁ̅ⲗ̅ : ⲛⲓⲁⲣⲭⲱⲛ ⲛⲉⲙ ⲛⲓⲣⲉϥϯϩⲁⲡ ⲧⲏⲣⲟⲩ ⲛ̀ⲧⲉ ⲡ̀ⲕⲁϩⲓ.	*ملوك الارض وكل الشعوب الليلويا. الرؤساء وكل حكام الارض.

Both young men and maidens Alleluia. Old men and children.	Ⲃⲁⲛⲇⲉⲗϣⲓⲣⲓ ⲛⲉⲙ ⲃⲁⲛ-ⲡⲁⲣⲑⲉⲛⲟⲥ Ⲁ̅ⲗ̅: ⲃⲁⲛⲃ-ⲉⲗⲗⲟⲓ ⲛⲉⲙ ⲃⲁⲛⲁⲗⲱⲟⲩⲓ.	الشبان والعذارى الليلويا. الشيوخ والصبيان.
*Let them praise the Name of the Lord Alleluia. For His Name alone is exalted.	*Ⲙⲁⲣⲟⲩⲥⲙⲟⲩ ⲧⲏⲣ-ⲟⲩ ⲉ̀ⲫⲣⲁⲛ ⲙ̅Ⲡⲟ̅ⲥ̅ Ⲁ̅ⲗ̅ : ⲭⲉ ⲁϥϭⲓⲥⲓ ⲛ̀ⲭⲉ ⲡⲉϥⲣⲁⲛ ⲙ̀ⲙⲁⲩⲁⲧϥ.	*فليسبحوا جميعاً اسم الرب الليلويا. لانه قد تعالى اسمه وحده.
His glory is above the earth and heaven Alleluia. He also exalts the horn of His people.	Ⲡⲉϥⲟⲩⲱⲛⲃ ⲉ̀ⲃⲟⲗ ϣⲟⲡ ⲃⲓⲭⲉⲛ ⲡ̀ⲕⲁⲃⲓ ⲛⲉⲙ ⲛ̀-ⲉ̀ⲣⲏⲓ ϭⲉⲛ ⲧ̀ⲫⲉ Ⲁ̅ⲗ̅ : ϥ̀ⲛⲁϭⲓⲥⲓ ⲙ̀ⲡ̀ⲧⲁⲡ ⲛ̀ⲧⲉ ⲡⲉϥⲗⲁⲟⲥ.	شكره كائن على الارض وفى السماء الليلويا. ويرفع قرن شعبه.
*The praise of all His saints Alleluia. The children of Israel a people near unto Him.	*Ⲟⲩⲥⲙⲟⲩ ⲛ̀ⲧⲉ ⲛⲏⲉ-ⲑⲟⲩⲁⲃ ⲧⲏⲣⲟⲩ ⲛ̀ⲧⲁϥ Ⲁ̅ⲗ̅ : ⲛⲉⲛϣⲏⲣⲓ ⲙ̀Ⲡ-ⲓⲥⲣⲁⲏⲗ ⲡⲓⲗⲁⲟⲥ ⲉⲧ-ϭⲉⲛⲧ ⲉ̀ⲣⲟϥ.	*سبحاً لجميع قديسيه الليلويا. بنى اسرائيل الشعب القريب اليه.

Alleluia, Alleluia, Alleluia.	Ⲁ̅ⲗ̅ Ⲁ̅ⲗ̅ Ⲁ̅ⲗ̅	الليلويا الليلويا الليلويا.
Sing unto the Lord a new song Alleluia. And His praise in the congregation of the saints.	Ⲭⲱ ⲙ̀Ⲡⲟⲥ ⲇⲉⲛ ⲟⲩ-ⲭⲱ ⲙ̀ⲃⲉⲣⲓ Ⲁ̅ⲗ̅ ⲝ ⲝⲉ ⲁⲣⲉ ⲡⲉϥⲥⲙⲟⲩ ⲇⲉⲛ ⲧⲉⲕⲕⲗ-ⲏⲥⲓⲁ̀ ⲛ̀ⲧⲉ ⲛⲏⲉⲑⲟⲩⲁⲃ.	انشدوا للرب نشيداً جديداً الليلويا. لان تسبحته فى بيعة القديسين.
*Let Israel rejoice in Him that made Him Alleluia. Let the children of Zion be joyful in their King.	*Ⲙⲁⲣⲉϥⲟⲩⲛⲟϥ ⲛ̀ⲭⲉ Ⲡⲓⲥⲣⲁⲏⲗ ⲉ̀ⲭⲉⲛ ⲫⲏⲉⲧ-ⲁϥⲑⲁⲙⲓⲟϥ Ⲁ̅ⲗ̅ ⲝ ⲛⲉⲛ-ϣⲏⲣⲓ ⲛ̀Ⲥⲓⲱⲛ ⲙⲁⲣⲟ-ⲩⲑⲉⲗⲏⲗ ⲉ̀ⲭⲉⲛ ⲡⲟⲩⲟ-ⲩⲣⲟ.	*فليفرح اسرئيل بخالقه الليلويا. وبنوا صهيون فليتهللوا بملكهم.
Let them praise His Name in the chorus Alleluia. Let them sing praises unto Him with timbrel and harp.	Ⲙⲁⲣⲟⲩⲥⲙⲟⲩ ⲉ̀ⲡⲉϥⲣⲁⲛ ⲉⲑⲟⲩⲁⲃ ⲇⲉⲛ ⲟⲩⲭⲟⲣⲟⲥ Ⲁ̅ⲗ̅ ⲝ ⲇⲉⲛ ⲟⲩⲕⲉⲙⲕⲉⲙ ⲛⲉⲙ ⲟⲩⲯⲁⲗⲧⲏⲣⲓⲟⲛ ⲙⲁⲣⲟⲩⲉⲣⲯⲁⲗⲓⲛⲉ̀ⲣⲟϥ.	فليسبحوا اسمه القدوس بصف الليلويا. بدف ومزمار فليرتلوا له.
*For the Lord takes	*Ⲭⲉ Ⲡϭⲟⲓⲥ ⲛⲁϯ-	*لان الرب يُسر

pleasure in His people Alleluia. He will raise the meek with salvation.	̅ⲙⲁϯ ⲉ̀ϫⲉⲛ ⲡⲉϥⲗⲁⲟⲥ ⲀⲖ : ϥⲛⲁϭⲓⲥⲓ ⲛ̀ⲛⲓⲣⲉ-ⲙⲣⲁⲩϣ ϧⲉⲛ ⲟⲩⲟⲩϫⲁⲓ.	بشعبه الليلويا. يعلى الودعاء بالخلاص.
Let the saints be joyful in glory Alleluia. Let them sing aloud upon their beds.	Ⲉⲩ̀ϣⲟⲩϣⲟⲩ ⲙ̀ⲙⲱⲟⲩ ⲛ̀ϫⲉ ⲛⲏⲉⲑⲟⲩⲁⲃ ϧⲉⲛ ⲟⲩⲱⲟⲩ ⲀⲖ : ⲉⲩ̀ⲉ-ⲉⲗⲏⲗ ⲙ̀ⲙⲱⲟⲩ ϩⲓϫⲉⲛ ⲛⲟⲩⲙⲁⲛⲉⲛⲕⲟⲧ.	يفتخر القديسون بمجد الليلويا. ويتهللون على مضاجعهم.
*Let the high praises of God be in their mouth Alleluia. And a two edged sword in their hand.	*Ⲛⲓϭⲓⲥⲓ ⲛ̀ⲧⲉ Ⲫϯ ⲉⲧⲭⲏ ϧⲉⲛ ⲧⲟⲩϣⲃⲱⲃⲓ ⲀⲖ : ϩⲁⲛⲥⲏϥⲓ ⲛ̀ⲣⲟ ⲥⲛⲁⲩ ⲉ-ⲧⲭⲏ ϧⲉⲛ ⲛⲟⲩϫⲓϫ.	*تعليات الله فى حناجرهم الليلويا. وسيوف ذات حدين فى أيديهم.
To execute venge-ance upon the hea-then Alleluia. And punishment upon the people.	Ⲉ̀ⲡϫⲓⲛⲓ̀ⲣⲓ ⲛ̀ⲟⲩϭⲓ ⲙ̀ⲡϣ-ⲓϣ ϧⲉⲛ ⲛⲓⲉⲑⲛⲟⲥ ⲀⲖ : ⲛⲉⲙ ϩⲁⲛⲥⲟϩⲓ ϧⲉⲛ ⲛⲓⲗⲁⲟⲥ.	ليصنعوا نقمة فى الامم الليلويا. وتوبيخات فى الشعوب.
*To bind their kings with chains Alleluia.	*Ⲉ̀ⲡϫⲓⲛⲥⲱⲛϩ ⲛ̀ϩⲁⲛ-	*ليوثقوا ملوكهم بقيود الليلويا.

And their nobles with fetters of iron.	oυрωoυ ϧεn ϩαnπε-Δнϲ ⲃⲗⲗⳉ nεⲙ nнε-ттαιнoυт n̄тⲱoυ ϧεn ϩαnπεΔнϲ n̄ϫ-ιϫ m̄Βεnιпι.	واشرافهم باغلال للايدى من حديد.
To execute on them the written judgment Alleluia. This honor have all His saints.	Επϫιnιρι n̄ϧнтoυ n̄-oυϩαπ εϥⲥϧнoυт ⲗⲗ ⁚ παιⲱoυ φαι αϥϣoп ϧεn nнεϑoυαΒ тнρ-oυ n̄тαϥ.	ليصنعوا بهم حكما مكتوباً الليلويا. هذا المجد كائن فى جميع قديسيه.
*Alleluia, Alleluia, Alleluia.	*ⲗⲗ ⲗⲗ ⲗⲗ.	*الليلويا الليلويا الليلويا
*Praise God in all his saints Alleluia.	*Ϲⲙoυ εΦnoυ† ϧεn nнεϑoυαΒ тнρoυ n̄т-αϥ. ⲗⲗ.	*سبحوا الله في جميع قديسيه الليلويا.
*Unto our God is due glory and praise. Praise the Lord our God with a	*Εϥεραnαϥ m̄πεnno-υ† n̄ϫε πιⲱoυ nεⲙ πιⲥⲙoυ. Ϲⲙoυ εΠϭoιⲥ	*يليق لإلهنا المجد والتسبيح. سبحوا الرب الهنا بحسن

joyful psalm.	ⲡⲉⲛⲛⲟⲩϯ ϫⲉ ⲛⲁⲛⲉ ⲟⲩⲯⲁⲗⲙⲟⲥ.	المزمار.
Praise Him in the firmament of His power Alleluia.	Ⲥⲙⲟⲩ ⲉⲣⲟϥ ϧⲉⲛ ⲡⲓⲧⲁϫⲣⲟ ⲛⲧⲉ ⲧⲉϥϫⲟⲙ. Ⲁ̅ⲗ̅.	سبحوه في جلد قوته الليلويا.
Unto our God is due glory and praise. Praise the Lord our God with a joyful psalm.	Ⲉϥⲉⲣⲁⲛⲁϥ ⲙⲡⲉⲛⲛⲟⲩϯ ⲛϫⲉ ⲡⲓⲱⲟⲩ ⲛⲉⲙ ⲡⲓⲥⲙⲟⲩ. Ⲥⲙⲟⲩ ⲉⲠϬⲟⲓⲥ ⲡⲉⲛⲛⲟⲩϯ ϫⲉ ⲛⲁⲛⲉ ⲟⲩⲯⲁⲗⲙⲟⲥ.	يليق لإلهنا المجد والتسبيح. سبحوا الرب الهنا بحسن المزمار.
*Praise Him for His mighty acts Alleluia.	*Ⲥⲙⲟⲩ ⲉⲣⲟϥ ⲉϩⲣⲏⲓ ϩⲓϫⲉⲛ ⲧⲉϥⲙⲉⲧϫⲱⲣⲓ. Ⲁ̅ⲗ̅.	*سبحوه على مقدرته الليلويا.
*Unto our God is due glory and praise. Praise the Lord our God with a joyful psalm.	*Ⲉϥⲉⲣⲁⲛⲁϥ ⲙⲡⲉⲛⲛⲟⲩϯ ⲛϫⲉ ⲡⲓⲱⲟⲩ ⲛⲉⲙ ⲡⲓⲥⲙⲟⲩ. Ⲥⲙⲟⲩ ⲉⲠϬⲟⲓⲥ ⲡⲉⲛⲛⲟⲩϯ ϫⲉ ⲛⲁⲛⲉ	*يليق لإلهنا المجد والتسبيح. سبحوا الرب الهنا بحسن المزمار.

	ⲟⲩⲯⲁⲗⲙⲟⲥ.	
Praise Him according to His excellent greatness Alleluia.	Ⲥⲙⲟⲩ ⲉⲣⲟϥ ⲕⲁⲧⲁ ⲡ̀ⲁ̀ϣⲁⲓ ⲛ̀ⲧⲉ ⲧⲉϥⲙⲉⲧⲛⲓϣϯ. Ⲁ̅ⲗ̅.	سبحوه ككثرة عظمته الليلويا.
Unto our God is due glory and praise. Praise the Lord our God with a joyful psalm.	Ⲉϥⲉ̀ⲣⲁⲛⲁϥ ⲙ̀ⲡⲉⲛⲛⲟⲩϯ ⲛ̀ⲭⲉ ⲡⲓⲱⲟⲩ ⲛⲉⲙ ⲡⲓⲥⲙⲟⲩ. Ⲥⲙⲟⲩ ⲉ̀Ⲡϭⲟⲓⲥ ⲡⲉⲛⲛⲟⲩϯ ⲭⲉ ⲛⲁⲛⲉ ⲟⲩⲯⲁⲗⲙⲟⲥ.	يليق لإلهنا المجد والتسبيح. سبحوا الرب الهنا بحسن المزمار.
*Praise Him with the sound of the trumpet Alleluia.	*Ⲥⲙⲟⲩ ⲉ̀ⲣⲟϥ ϧⲉⲛ ⲟⲩⲥⲙⲏ ⲛ̀ⲥⲁⲗⲡⲓⲅⲅⲟⲥ. Ⲁ̅ⲗ̅.	*سبحوه بصوت البوق الليلويا.
*Unto our God is due glory and praise. Praise the Lord our God with a joyful psalm.	*Ⲉϥⲉ̀ⲣⲁⲛⲁϥ ⲙ̀ⲡⲉⲛⲛⲟⲩϯ ⲛ̀ⲭⲉ ⲡⲓⲱⲟⲩ ⲛⲉⲙ ⲡⲓⲥⲙⲟⲩ. Ⲥⲙⲟⲩ ⲉ̀Ⲡϭⲟⲓⲥ ⲡⲉⲛⲛⲟⲩϯ ⲭⲉ ⲛⲁⲛⲉ ⲟⲩⲯⲁⲗⲙⲟⲥ.	*يليق لإلهنا المجد والتسبيح. سبحوا الرب الهنا بحسن المزمار.
Praise Him with the	Ⲥⲙⲟⲩ ⲉ̀ⲣⲟϥ ϧⲉⲛ	سبحوه بمزمار

psaltery and harp Alleluia.	oⲯⲁⲗⲧⲏⲣⲓⲟⲛ ⲛⲉⲙ oⲩⲕⲑⲟⲁⲣⲁ.‾Ⲁⲗ.	وقيثارة الليلويا.
Unto our God is due glory and praise. Praise the Lord our God with a joyful psalm.	Ⲉϥⲉⲣⲁⲛⲁϥ ⲙ̀ⲡⲉⲛⲛⲟⲩϯ ⲛ̀ⲭⲉ ⲡⲓⲱⲟⲩ ⲛⲉⲙ ⲡⲓ̀ⲥⲙⲟⲩ. Ⲥⲙⲟⲩ ⲉ̀Ⲡ̅ϭⲟⲓⲥ ⲡⲉⲛⲛⲟⲩϯ ⲭⲉ ⲛⲁⲛⲉ ⲟⲩⲯⲁⲗⲙⲟⲥ.	يليق لإلهنا المجد والتسبيح. سبحوا الرب الهنا بحسن المزمار.
*Praise Him with timbrel and chorus Alleluia.	*Ⲥⲙⲟⲩ ⲉ̀ⲣⲟϥ ϧⲉⲛ ⲍⲁⲛⲕⲉⲙⲕⲉⲙ ⲛⲉⲙ ⲍⲁⲛⲭⲟⲣⲟⲥ.‾Ⲁⲗ.	*سبحوه بدفوف وصفوف الليلويا.
*Unto our God is due glory and praise. Praise the Lord our God with a joyful psalm.	*Ⲉϥⲉⲣⲁⲛⲁϥ ⲙ̀ⲡⲉⲛⲛⲟ-ⲩϯ ⲛ̀ⲭⲉ ⲡⲓⲱⲟⲩ ⲛⲉⲙ ⲡⲓ̀ⲥⲙⲟⲩ. Ⲥⲙⲟⲩ ⲉ̀Ⲡ̅ϭⲟⲓⲥ ⲡⲉⲛⲛⲟⲩϯ ⲭⲉ ⲛⲁⲛⲉ ⲟⲩⲯⲁⲗⲙⲟⲥ.	*يليق لإلهنا المجد والتسبيح. سبحوا الرب الهنا بحسن المزمار.
Praise Him with stringed instruments and organs Alleluia.	Ⲥⲙⲟⲩ ⲉ̀ⲣⲟϥ ϧⲉⲛ ⲍⲁⲛⲕⲁⲡ ⲛⲉⲙ	سبحوه بأوتار وأرغن الليلويا.

331

	ⲟⲩⲟⲣⲅⲁⲛⲟⲛ. Ⲁ̅ⲗ̅.	
Unto our God is due glory and praise. Praise the Lord our God with a joyful psalm.	Ⲉϥⲉⲣⲁⲛⲁϥ ⲙ̀ⲡⲉⲛⲛⲟⲩϯ ⲛ̀ϫⲉ ⲡⲓⲱⲟⲩ ⲛⲉⲙ ⲡⲓⲥⲙⲟⲩ. Ⲥⲙⲟⲩ ⲉ̀Ⲡϭⲟⲓⲥ ⲡⲉⲛⲛⲟⲩϯ ϫⲉ ⲛⲁⲛⲉ ⲟⲩⲯⲁⲗⲙⲟⲥ.	يليق لإلهنا المجد والتسبيح. سبحوا الرب الهنا بحسن المزمار.
*Praise Him with loud sounding cymbals Alleluia.	*Ⲥⲙⲟⲩ ⲉ̀ⲣⲟϥ ϧⲉⲛ ϩⲁⲛⲕⲩⲙⲃⲁⲗⲟⲛ ⲉⲛⲉⲥⲉ ⲧⲟⲩⲥⲙⲏ. Ⲁ̅ⲗ̅.	*سبحوه بصنوج حسنة الصوت الليلويا.
*Unto our God is due glory and praise. Praise the Lord our God with a joyful psalm.	*Ⲉϥⲉⲣⲁⲛⲁϥ ⲙ̀ⲡⲉⲛⲛⲟ-ⲩϯ ⲛ̀ϫⲉ ⲡⲓⲱⲟⲩ ⲛⲉⲙ ⲡⲓⲥⲙⲟⲩ. Ⲥⲙⲟⲩ ⲉ̀Ⲡϭⲟⲓⲥ ⲡⲉⲛⲛⲟⲩϯ ϫⲉ ⲛⲁⲛⲉ ⲟⲩⲯⲁⲗⲙⲟⲥ.	*يليق لإلهنا المجد والتسبيح. سبحوا الرب الهنا بحسن المزمار.
Praise Him with cymbals of joy Alleluia.	Ⲥⲙⲟⲩ ⲉ̀ⲣⲟϥ ϧⲉⲛ ϩⲁⲛⲕ-ⲩⲙⲃⲁⲗⲟⲛ ⲛ̀ⲧⲉ ⲟⲩⲉ̀ⲯⲗⲏⲗⲟⲩⲓ. Ⲁ̅ⲗ̅.	سبحوه بصنوج التهليل الليلويا.

Unto our God is due glory and praise. Praise the Lord our God with a joyful psalm.	Ⲉϥ̀ⲉⲣⲁⲛⲁϥ ⲙ̀ⲡⲉⲛⲛⲟⲩϯ ⲛ̀ϫⲉ ⲡⲓⲱⲟⲩ ⲛⲉⲙ ⲡⲓⲥⲙⲟⲩ. Ⲥⲙⲟⲩ ⲉ̀Ⲡϭⲟⲓⲥ ⲡⲉⲛⲛⲟⲩϯ ϫⲉ ⲛⲁⲛⲉ ⲟⲩⲯⲁⲗⲙⲟⲥ.	يليق لإلهنا المجد والتسبيح. سبحوا الرب الهنا بحسن المزمار.
*Let everything that has breath praise the name of the Lord our God Alleluia.	*Ⲛⲓϥⲓ ⲛⲓⲃⲉⲛ ⲙⲁⲣⲟⲩ̀ⲥⲙⲟⲩ ⲧⲏⲣⲟⲩ ⲉ̀ϥ̀ⲣ-ⲁⲛ ⲙ̀Ⲡϭⲟⲓⲥ Ⲡⲉⲛⲛⲟⲩϯ. Ⲁ̅ⲗ̅.	*كل نسمة فلتسبح اسم الرب الهنا الليلويا.
Glory be to the Father, the Son and the Holy Spirit Alleluia.	Ⲇⲟⲝⲁ Ⲡⲁⲧⲣⲓ ⲕⲉ Ⲩⲓⲱ ⲕⲉ Ⲁ̀ⲅⲓⲱ Ⲡⲛⲉⲩⲙⲁⲧⲓ. Ⲁ̅ⲗ̅.	المجد للآب والأبن والروح القدس الليلويا.
*Now and forever and unto the ages of ages Amen Alleluia.	*Ⲕⲉ ⲛⲩⲛ ⲕⲉ ⲁ̀ⲓ ⲕⲉ ⲓⲥⲧⲟⲩⲥ ⲉ̀ⲱⲛⲁⲥ ⲧⲱⲛ ⲉ̀-ⲱⲛⲱⲛ ⲁ̀ⲙⲏⲛ. Ⲁ̅ⲗ̅.	*الآن وكل أوان وإلى دهر الداهرين آمين الليلويا.
Alleluia, Alleluia, Glory be to our God Alleluia.	Ⲁ̅ⲗ̅ Ⲁ̅ⲗ̅ Ⲇⲟⲝⲁ ⲥⲓ ⲟ̀ Ⲑⲉⲟⲥ ⲩⲙⲱⲛ Ⲁ̅ⲗ̅.	الليلويا الليلويا المجد لإلهنا الليلويا.

*Alleluia, Alleluia, Glory be to our God Alleluia.

*Ⲁⲗ Ⲁⲗ Ⲡⲓⲱⲟⲩ ⲫⲁ Ⲡⲉⲛⲛⲟⲩϯ ⲡⲉ Ⲁⲗ.

*المجد لإلهنا الليلويا.

The Sunday Psali –
Ⲯⲓⲕⲱϯ – ابصالية الأحد

I sought after You: from the depths of my heart: My Lord Jesus help me.	Ⲯⲓⲕⲱϯ ⲛ̀ⲥⲱⲕ: ϧⲉⲛ ⲡ̀ϣⲱⲕ ⲙ̀ⲡⲁϩⲏⲧ : Ⲡⲁϭⲟⲓⲥ Ⲓⲏⲥⲟⲩⲥ: ⲁ̀ⲣⲓⲃⲟⲏⲑⲓⲛ ⲉ̀ⲣⲟⲓ.	طلبتك من عمق قلبى. ياربى يسوع أعنى.
Loosen for me: all the bonds of sin: My Lord Jesus Christ help me.	Ⲃⲱⲗ ⲉ̀ⲃⲟⲗ ϩⲁⲣⲟⲓ : ⲛ̀ⲛⲓⲥⲛⲁⲩϩ ⲛ̀ⲧⲉ ⲫ̀ⲛⲟⲃⲓ : Ⲡⲁϭⲟⲓⲥ Ⲓⲏⲥⲟⲩⲥ Ⲡⲓⲭ̀ⲣⲓⲥⲧⲟⲥ: ⲁ̀ⲣⲓⲃⲟⲏⲑⲓⲛ ⲉ̀ⲣⲟⲓ	حلّ عنى رباطات الخطية. ياربى يسوع المسيح أعنى.
*Be a help to me: so that You may save me: My Lord Jesus help me.	*Ϣⲉⲛⲑⲓ ⲙ̀ⲃⲟⲏⲑⲟⲥ : ⲉⲑⲣⲉⲕⲥⲱϯ ⲙ̀ⲙⲟⲓ: Ⲡⲁϭⲟⲓⲥ Ⲓⲏⲥⲟⲩⲥ: ⲁ̀ⲣⲓⲃⲟⲏⲑⲓⲛ ⲉ̀ⲣⲟⲓ.	*كن لى معيناً لكى تخلصني. ياربى يسوع أعنى.
*May Your goodness: come speedily to me: My Lord Jesus Christ help me.	*Ⲇⲉⲕⲙⲉⲧⲁ̀ⲅⲁⲑⲟⲥ: ⲙⲁⲣⲉⲥⲧⲁϩⲟⲓ ⲛ̀ⲭⲱⲗⲉⲙ : Ⲡⲁϭⲟⲓⲥ Ⲓⲏⲥⲟⲩⲥ Ⲡⲓⲭ̀ⲣⲓⲥ-	*صلاحك فليدركنى سريعاً. ياربى يسوع المسيح

	ⲧⲟⲥ: ⲁⲣⲓⲃⲟⲏⲑⲓⲛ ⲉⲣⲟⲓ.	أعنى.
Overshadow me: with the shadow of Your wings: My Lord Jesus help me.	Ⲉⲕⲉⲣϧⲏⲓⲃⲓ ⲉϫⲱⲓ: ϧⲁ ⲧϧⲏⲓⲃⲓ ⲛ̀ⲧⲉ ⲛⲉⲕⲧⲉⲛϩ: Ⲡⲁϭⲟⲓⲥ Ⲓⲏⲥⲟⲩⲥ: ⲁ̀ⲣⲓⲃⲟⲏⲑⲓⲛ ⲉⲣⲟⲓ.	ظلل علّى بظل جناحيك. ياربى يسوع أعنى.
In six days You have made: all the creation: My Lord Jesus Christ help me.	ⲋ̅ ⲅⲁⲣ ⲛ̀ⲉϩⲟⲟⲩ: ⲁⲕⲑⲁⲙⲓⲟ ⲛ̀ⲧⲕ̀ⲧⲏⲥⲓⲥ ⲧⲏⲣⲥ: Ⲡⲁϭⲟⲓⲥ Ⲓⲏⲥⲟⲩⲥ Ⲡⲓⲭ̅ⲣ̅ⲓⲥⲧⲟⲥ: ⲁ̀ⲣⲓⲃⲟⲏⲑⲓⲛ ⲉⲣⲟⲓ.	فى ستة أيام صنعت كل الخليقة. ياربى يسوع المسيح أعنى.
*Seven times eve-ryday: I will praise Your Holy Name: My Lord Jesus help me.	*Ⲯⲁϣϥ ⲛ̀ⲥⲟⲡ ⲙ̀ⲙⲏⲛⲓ: ϯⲛⲁⲥⲙⲟⲩ ⲉⲡⲉⲕⲣⲁⲛ: Ⲡⲁϭⲟⲓⲥ Ⲓⲏⲥⲟⲩⲥ: ⲁ̀ⲣⲓⲃⲟⲏⲑⲓⲛ ⲉⲣⲟⲓ.	*سبع مرات فى اليوم أبارك اسمك. ياربى يسوع أعنى.
*All the creation: glorifies Your Holy Name: My Lord Jesus Christ help me.	*Ⲏⲥ ϯⲕ̀ⲧⲏⲥⲓⲥ ⲧⲏⲣⲥ: ⲥⲉϯⲱⲟⲩ ⲙ̀ⲡⲉⲕⲣⲁⲛ: Ⲡⲁϭⲟⲓⲥ Ⲓⲏⲥⲟⲩⲥ Ⲡⲓⲭ̅ⲣ̅ⲓⲥⲧⲟⲥ: ⲁ̀ⲣⲓⲃⲟⲏⲑⲓⲛ ⲉⲣⲟⲓ.	*ها كل البرية تمجد اسمك: ياربى يسوع المسيح أعنى.

Yours is the Lordship: and the authority: My Lord Jesus help me.	Θωκ τε ϯμετϭοιϲ : νεμ ϯεⲝⲟⲩⲥⲓⲁ : Ⲡⲁϭⲟⲓⲥ Ⲓⲏⲥⲟⲩⲥ : ⲁ̀ⲣⲓⲃⲟⲏ̀ⲑⲓⲛ ⲉ̀ⲣⲟⲓ.	لك الربوبية والسلطان ياربى. يسوع أعنى.
Make haste O my God: so that You may save me: My Lord Jesus Christ help me.	Ⲓⲱⲥ ⲙ̀ⲙⲟⲕ Ⲡⲁⲛⲟⲩϯ : ⲉⲑⲣⲉⲕⲥⲱϯ ⲙ̀ⲙⲟⲓ : Ⲡⲁϭⲟⲓⲥ Ⲓⲏⲥⲟⲩⲥ Ⲡⲓⲭ̀ⲣⲓⲥⲧⲟⲥ : ⲁ̀ⲣⲓⲃⲟⲏ̀ⲑⲓⲛ ⲉ̀ⲣⲟⲓ.	أسرع ياإلهي لتخلصنى. ياربى يسوع المسيح أعنى.
*Every knee: bows down before You: My Lord Jesus help me.	*Ⲕⲉⲗⲓ ⲛⲓⲃⲉⲛ ⲥⲉⲕⲱⲗⲝ : ⲙ̀ⲡⲉⲕⲙⲑⲟ ⲉ̀ⲃⲟⲗ : Ⲡⲁϭⲟⲓⲥ Ⲓⲏⲥⲟⲩⲥ : ⲁ̀ⲣⲓ ⲃⲟⲏ̀ⲑⲓⲛ ⲉ̀ⲣⲟⲓ.	*كل ركبة تجثو أمامك. ياربى يسوع أعنى.
*All the diverse tongues: together bless Your Name: My Lord Jesus Christ help me.	*Ⲗⲁⲥ ⲛⲓⲃⲉⲛ ⲉⲩⲥⲟⲡ : ⲥⲉ̀ⲥⲙⲟⲩ ⲉ̀ⲡⲉⲕⲣⲁⲛ : Ⲡⲁϭⲟⲓⲥ Ⲓⲏⲥⲟⲩⲥ Ⲡⲓⲭ̀ⲣⲓⲥⲧⲟⲥ : ⲁ̀ⲣⲓⲃⲟⲏ̀ⲑⲓⲛ ⲉ̀ⲣⲟⲓ.	*كل الألسنة معاً تبارك اسمك. ياربى يسوع المسيح أعنى.
Turn away Your face: from all of my sins: My Lord Jesus	Ⲙⲁⲧⲁⲥⲑⲟ ⲙ̀ⲡⲉⲕϩⲟ : ⲥⲁⲃⲟⲗ ⲛ̀ⲛⲁⲛⲟⲃⲓ : Ⲡⲁϭⲟⲓⲥ	اصرف وجهك عن خطاياي. ياربى يسوع

help me.	Iⲏⲥⲟⲩⲥ: ⲁ̀ⲣⲓⲃⲟⲏⲑⲓⲛ ⲉ̀ⲣⲟⲓ.	أعنى.
Blot out O God: all my iniquities: My Lord Jesus Christ help me.	Ⲛⲁ̀ⲁⲛⲟⲙⲓⲁ̀ ⲧⲏⲣⲟⲩ: Ⲫ̀ϯ ⲉⲕⲉ̀ⲥⲟⲗϫⲟⲩ: Ⲡⲁϭⲟⲓⲥ Iⲏⲥⲟⲩⲥ Ⲡⲓⲭ̀ⲣⲓⲥⲧⲟⲥ: ⲁ̀ⲣⲓⲃⲟⲏⲑⲓⲛ ⲉ̀ⲣⲟⲓ.	جميع آثامى يا الله امحها. ياربى يسوع المسيح أعنى.
*You know my thoughts: and You search my reins: My Lord Jesus help me.	*Ⲍ̀ⲟⲩⲛ ⲛ̀ⲛⲁⲙⲉⲣⲓ: ⲕ̀ϭⲟⲧϭⲉⲧ ⲛ̀ⲛⲁϭⲗⲱⲧ: Ⲡⲁϭⲟⲓⲥ Iⲏⲥⲟⲩⲥ: ⲁ̀ⲣⲓⲃⲟⲏⲑⲓⲛ ⲉ̀ⲣⲟⲓ.	*أنت تعرف أفكارى وتفحص كليتى. ياربى يسوع أعنى.
*Create in me: a clean heart: My Lord Jesus Christ help me.	*Ⲟⲩⲏⲧ ⲉϥⲟⲩⲁⲃ: ⲉⲕⲉ̀ⲥⲟⲛⲧϥ ⲛ̀ϧⲏⲧ: Ⲡⲁϭⲟⲓⲥ Iⲏⲥⲟⲩⲥ Ⲡⲓⲭ̀ⲣⲓⲥⲧⲟⲥ: ⲁ̀ⲣⲓⲃⲟⲏⲑⲓⲛ ⲉ̀ⲣⲟⲓ.	*قلباً طاهراً أخلقه فيّ. ياربى يسوع المسيح أعنى.
Your Holy Spirit: do not take away from me: My Lord Jesus help me.	Ⲡⲉⲕⲡ̀ⲛⲉⲩⲙⲁ ⲉ̀ⲑⲟⲩⲁⲃ: ⲙ̀ⲡⲉⲣⲟⲗϥ ⲉ̀ⲃⲟⲗϩⲁⲣⲟⲓ: Ⲡⲁϭⲟⲓⲥ Iⲏⲥⲟⲩⲥ: ⲁ̀ⲣⲓⲃⲟⲏⲑⲓⲛ ⲉ̀ⲣⲟⲓ.	روحك القدوس لاتنزعه منى. ياربى يسوع أعنى.

Incline Your ears: make haste and hear me: My Lord Jesus Christ help me.	Ⲣⲉⲕ ⲡⲉⲕⲙⲁϣϫ ⲉⲣⲟⲓ : ⲥⲱⲧⲉⲙ ⲉⲣⲟⲓ ⲛ̀ⲭⲱⲗⲉⲙ : Ⲡⲁϭⲟⲓⲥ Ⲓⲏⲥⲟⲩⲥ Ⲡⲓⲭⲣ-ⲓⲥⲧⲟⲥ: ⲁ̀ⲣⲓⲃⲟⲏ̀ⲑⲓⲛ ⲉ̀ⲣⲟⲓ.	أمل سمعك إلىّ واستجب لى عاجلاً. ياربى يسوع المسيح أعنى.
*Set before me a law: in the way of Your justice: My Lord Jesus help me.	*Ⲥⲉⲙⲛⲉ ⲛⲟⲙⲟⲥ ⲛⲏⲓ : ϩⲓ ϥ̀ⲙⲱⲓⲧ ⲛ̀ⲧⲉ ⲧⲉⲕⲙⲉⲑⲙⲏⲓ : Ⲡⲁϭⲟⲓⲥ Ⲓⲏⲥⲟⲩⲥ : ⲁ̀ⲣⲓⲃⲟⲏ̀ⲑⲓⲛ ⲉ̀-ⲣⲟⲓ.	*قرر لى ناموساً فى طريق عدلك. ياربى يسوع أعنى.
*Your Kingdom O my God: is an eternal kingdom: My Lord Jesus Christ help me.	*Ⲧⲉⲕⲙⲉⲧⲟⲩⲣⲟ Ⲡⲁⲛ-ⲟⲩϯ: ⲟⲩⲙⲉⲧⲟⲩⲣⲟ ⲛ̀ⲉⲛⲉϩ : Ⲡⲁϭⲟⲓⲥ Ⲓⲏⲥⲟⲩⲥ Ⲡⲓⲭⲣⲓⲥⲧⲟⲥ: ⲁ̀ⲣⲓⲃⲟⲏ̀ⲑⲓⲛ ⲉ̀ⲣⲟⲓ.	*ملكوتك ياإلهى ملكوت أبدى. ياربى يسوع المسيح أعنى.
You are the Son of God: I believe in You: My Lord Jesus help me.	Ⲩⲓⲟⲥ Ⲑⲉⲟⲥ ⲛ̀ⲑⲟⲕ ⲁⲓⲛⲁϩϯ ⲉ̀ⲣⲟⲕ : Ⲡⲁϭⲟⲓⲥ Ⲓⲏⲥⲟⲩⲥ : ⲁ̀ⲣⲓⲃⲟⲏ̀ⲑⲓⲛ ⲉ̀ⲣⲟⲓ.	أنت ابن الله آمنت بك. ياربى يسوع أعنى.
You who carries: the	Ⲫⲏⲉⲧⲱ̀ⲗⲓ ⲙ̀ⲫ̀ⲛⲟⲃⲓ: ⲛ̀ⲧⲉ	ياحامل خطية

sins of the world save me: My Lord Jesus Christ help me.	ⲡⲓⲕⲟⲥⲙⲟⲥ ⲛⲁⲓ ⲛⲏⲓ ⳾ Ⲡⲁϭⲟⲓⲥ Ⲓⲏⲥⲟⲩⲥ Ⲡⲓⲭⲣⲓⲥⲧⲟⲥ⳾ⲁ̀ⲣⲓⲃⲟⲏⲑⲓⲛ ⲉ̀ⲣⲟⲓ.	العالم ارحمنى. ياربى يسوع المسيح أعنى.
*Forgive me the multitude: of my transgressions: My Lord Jesus help me.	*Ⲭⲱ ⲛⲏⲓ ⲉ̀ⲃⲟⲗ ⲙ̀ⲡⲁϣⲁⲓ ⳾ ⲛ̀ⲧⲉ ⲛⲁⲁ̀ⲛⲟⲙⲓⲁ̀ ⳾ Ⲡⲁϭⲟⲓⲥ Ⲓⲏⲥⲟⲩⲥ ⳾ⲁ̀ⲣⲓⲃⲟⲏⲑⲓⲛ ⲉ̀ⲣⲟⲓ.	*اغفر لى كثرة آثامى. ياربى يسوع أعنى.
*All of the souls: together bless Your Name: My Lord Jesus Christ help me.	*Ⲯⲩⲭⲏ ⲛⲓⲃⲉⲛ ⲉⲩⲥⲟⲡ ⳾ ⲥⲉⲥⲙⲟⲩ ⲉ̀ⲡⲉⲕⲣⲁⲛ ⳾ Ⲡⲁϭⲟⲓⲥ Ⲓⲏⲥⲟⲩⲥ Ⲡⲓⲭⲣⲓⲥⲧⲟⲥ⳾ⲁ̀ⲣⲓⲃⲟⲏⲑⲓⲛ ⲉ̀ⲣⲟⲓ.	*كل الأنفس معاً تبارك اسمك. ياربى يسوع المسيح أعنى.
Have patience with me: do not hasten to destroy me: My Lord Jesus help me.	Ⲱⲟⲩⲛ̀ϩⲏⲧ ⲛⲉⲙⲏⲓ ⳾ ⲙ̀ⲡⲉⲣⲧⲁⲕⲟⲓ ⲛ̀ⲭⲱⲗⲉⲙ ⳾ Ⲡⲁϭⲟⲓⲥ Ⲓⲏⲥⲟⲩⲥ ⳾ ⲁ̀ⲣⲓⲃⲟⲏⲑⲓⲛ ⲉ̀ⲣⲟⲓ.	تـأن علىّ ولاتهلكنى سريعاً. ياربى يسوع أعنى.
Early in the morning: I will rise and bless Your	Ⲱⲁⲓⲧⲱⲛⲧ ⲙ̀ⲫⲛⲁⲩ ⲛ̀ϣⲱⲣⲡ ⳾ ⲛ̀ⲧⲁⲥⲙⲟⲩ ⲉ̀ⲡ-	أقوم وقت السحر لأبارك اسمك. ياربى

Name: My Lord Jesus Christ help me.	εκραν : Παϭοιс Ιнсотс Πιⲭριстос: ἀριⲃонⲑιн ἐροι.	يسوع المسيح أعنى.
*Your yoke is sweet: and Your burden is light: My Lord Jesus help me.	* Ϥ̀ⲃολⲝ ⲛⲭⲉ ⲡⲉⲕⲛⲁⲁⲃⲉϥ: ⲧⲉⲕⲉⲧⲫⲱ ⲁ̀ⲥ̀ⲓⲱⲟⲩ : Ⲡⲁϭⲟⲓⲥ Ⲓⲏⲥⲟⲩⲥ :ⲁ̀ⲣⲓⲃⲟⲏⲑⲓⲛ ⲉ̀ⲣⲟⲓ.	*حلو هو نيرك وحملك خفيف ياربى. يسوع أعنى.
*In the accepted time: hear me: My Lord Jesus Christ help me.	*Ϧⲉⲛ ⲟⲩⲥⲏⲟⲩ ⲉϥϣⲏⲡ ⲉⲕⲉⲥⲱⲧⲉⲙ ⲉ̀ⲣⲟⲓ : Ⲡⲁϭⲟⲓⲥ Ⲓⲏⲥⲟⲩⲥ Ⲡⲓⲭⲣⲓⲥⲧⲟⲥ: ⲁ̀ⲣⲓⲃⲟⲏⲑⲓⲛ ⲉ̀ⲣⲟⲓ.	*فى زمن مقبول استجب لى. ياربى يسوع المسيح أعنى.
Oh how beloved: is Your Holy Name: My Lord Jesus help me.	Ⲑⲱⲥ ⲟⲩϣⲟⲩⲙⲉⲛⲣⲓⲧϥ : ⲡⲉ ⲡⲉⲕⲁⲣⲁⲛ ⲉ̀ⲑⲟⲩⲁⲃ : Ⲡⲁϭⲟⲓⲥ Ⲓⲏⲥⲟⲩⲥ : ⲁ̀ⲣⲓⲃⲟⲏⲑⲓⲛ ⲉ̀ⲣⲟⲓ.	محبوب هو اسمك القدوس ياربى. يسوع أعنى.
Disperse away from me: all of the devils: My Lord Jesus	Ⲭⲱⲣ ⲉ̀ⲃⲟⲗ ⲅⲁⲣⲟⲓ : ⲛ̀ⲇⲓⲁ̀ⲃⲟⲗⲏ ⲛⲓⲃⲉⲛ :	فرق عنى كل الابالسة. ياربى يسوع المسيح

Christ help me.	Ⲡⲁϭⲟⲓⲥ Ⲓⲏⲥⲟⲩⲥ Ⲡⲓⲭⲣ- ⲓⲥⲧⲟⲥ: ⲁ̀ⲣⲓⲃⲟⲏ̀ⲑⲓⲛ ⲉ̀ⲣⲟⲓ.	أعنى.
*Sow within me: the seed of Your righteousness: My Lord Jesus help me.	*Ϭⲟ ⲛ̀ϧⲣⲏⲓ ⲛ̀ϧⲏⲧ : ⲙ̀ⲡⲟⲩⲧⲁϩ ⲛ̀ⲧⲉ ⲧⲉⲕⲙⲉⲑⲙⲏⲓ : Ⲡⲁϭⲟⲓⲥ Ⲓⲏⲥⲟⲩⲥ : ⲁ̀ⲣⲓⲃⲟⲏ̀ⲑⲓⲛ ⲉ̀ⲣⲟⲓ.	*اغرس فيّ ثمرة برك ياربى. يسوع أعنى.
*Grant us Your true peace: and forgive us our sins: My Lord Jesus Christ help me.	*Ϯⲛⲁⲛ ⲛ̀ⲧⲉⲕϩⲓⲣⲏⲛⲏ ⲙ̀ⲙⲏⲓ : ⲭⲁ ⲛⲉⲛⲛⲟⲃⲓ ⲛⲁⲛ ⲉ̀ⲃⲟⲗ : Ⲡⲁϭⲟⲓⲥ Ⲓⲏⲥⲟⲩⲥ Ⲡⲓⲭⲣⲓⲥⲧⲟⲥ : ⲁ̀ⲣⲓⲃⲟⲏ̀ⲑⲓⲛ ⲉ̀ⲣⲟⲓ.	*أعطنا سلامك الحقيقى وأغفر لنا خطايانا. ياربى يسوع المسيح أعني

I Open my Mouth with Praise - افتح فاىبالتسبيح

I open my mouth with praise	أفتح فاى بالتسبيح
And say with a broken heart	وأقول بقلب جريح
O my Lord Jesus Christ	ياربى يسوع المسيح
Grant me a praising tongue	أعطنى لسان فصيح
That I may praise Your Name	لكى أسبح أسمك
And thank You for Your grace	وأشكر فضل انعامك
O my Lord Jesus Christ	ياربى يسوع المسيح
Teach me Your statutes	علمنى أحكامك
Holy is Your Name and wonderful	قدوس أسمك وعجيب
And glorified in Your saints	وممجد فى قديسيك
O my Lord Jesus Christ	ياربى يسوع المسيح
Have mercy on me	ارحم صنعة يديك
Worthy and right are You	مستحق ومستوجب
To be praised and glorified	التسابيح والتماجيد
O my Lord Jesus Christ	ياربى يسوع المسيح

343

Your praise is sweet and good	تسبيحك حلو ولذيذ
I cried unto You all day	صرخت بطول النهار
I raised my hands to You	مَديت نحوك يداى
O my Lord Jesus Christ	ياربى يسوع المسيح
Your Name is sweet to me	أسمك حلو عندى
I cast my cares on You	جعلت اتكالى عليك
Lord do not neglect me	يارب لا تهملنى
O my Lord Jesus Christ	يارب يسوع المسيح
Do not forsake me	لاتتخلَ عنى
Your Holy Spirit	روحك القدوس
Cast not away from me	لا تنزعه منى
O my Lord Jesus Christ	ياربى يسوع المسيح
With Your might help me	بمعونتك أشملنى
The enemy has injured me	جرحنى العدو بسهام
And has deeply wounded me	وجرحه فى حاق
Give me Your Body as ointment	أعطنى جسدك مرهم
And Your Blood as a bandage	ودمك لى ترياق
Seven times everyday	سبع مرات كل يوم
Everyday I praise Your Name	كل يوم أبارك أسمك

O my Lord Jesus Christ	ياربى يسوع المسيح
Grant me as Your portion	اجعلنى من قسمك
My soul thirsts for You	اشتاقت نفسى اليك
As a barren land	كالأرض العطشانة
O my Lord Jesus Christ	ياربى يسوع المسيح
In Your mercy remember us	برحمتك لاتنسانا
Do not forget our Church	لا تنسى بيعتنا
Fill it with Your goodness	إملأها من خيراتك
O my Lord Jesus Christ	ياربى يسوع المسيح
Establish it in Your laws	ثبتها بشهاداتك
Your laws are sweet on my lips	شهاداتك حلوة فى
As honey is sweet in my mouth	حلقى
O my Lord Jesus Christ	كالشهد داخل فمى
Cleanse me from my sins	ياربى يسوع المسيح
	اغسلنى من أثمى
Let us thank the Beneficent	نشكر صانع الخيرات
And worship the Lord Jesus	نسجد للرب يسوع
Christ the Lord of hosts	المسيح رب القوات
In fear we bow unto Him	فلنركع له بخشوع

345

Confirm us in Your statutes	رتب فينا أحكامك
Establish us in Your oracles	وبقولك ثبتنا
O my Lord Jesus Christ	ياربى يسوع المسيح
Raise the state of the church	ارفع شأن مَلّتنا
Raise the state of the Christians	ارفع شأن المسيحيين
In all the world	فى جميع المسكونة
O my Lord Jesus Christ	ياربى يسوع المسيح
Embrace and support them	اشملهم بمعونة
If we live in poverty	وان كنّا فقراء من
Your Name shall sustain us	المال اسمك هو يكفينا
O my Lord Jesus Christ	ياربى يسوع المسيح
Your goodness shall make us rich	وصلاحك يُغنينا
Unto You is due praise	يجب لك التسبيح
Unto You is due blessing	ينبغى لك البركات
O my Lord Jesus Christ	ياربى يسوع المسيح
The Fountain of goodness	ينبوع كل الخيرات
O Lord save Your people	يارب خلص شعبك
And bless Your inheritance	وبارك ميراثك
Raise their state in Your Name	ارفع شأنهم باسمك
And grant them Your kingdom	وورّثهم ملكوتك

Your Kingdom O my God	ملكوتك يا إلهى
Is an everlasting Kingdom	ملكوت أبدية
And Your Lordship O my King	وسيادتك ياملكى
Is an everlasting Lordship	سيادة أزلية
Everlasting and exalted	أزلية ومرتفعة
And wonderful are Your deeds	وعجيبة هى أفعالك
O my Lord Jesus Christ	ياربى يسوع المسيح
You are the Lord of all kingdoms	سيد كل ممالك
All kingdoms shall perish	ممالك الدنيا تزول
Together with the money of this	والمال كله فانى
-world	ياربى يسوع المسيح
O my Lord Jesus Christ	ٌملكك غير متناهى
Your Kingdom is everlasting	
May the kingdoms perish	تتناهى كل ممالك
With the treasures of this world	تفنى كنوز الأمراء
O my Lord Jesus Christ	ياربى يسوع المسيح
You are the treasure of the poor	أنت كنز الفقراء
The poor make them rich	فقراء شعبك اغنيهم
And the sick please heal them	والمرضى أشفيهم

Comfort all the widows	والايتام ربِّيهم
O Lord make them rich	من فضلك أغنيهم
O please make them rich	أغنيهم من فضلك
And aid those who are in debt	أوفِ عن المديونين
O my Lord Jesus Christ	ياربى يسوع المسح
You're the treasure of the poor	أنت غنى المحتاجين
If we are ever in need	ان كنا محتاجين
We have the Precious Gem	فلنا درة ثمينة
The Rock of great value	لنا الحجر الكريم
Jesus the honored One	يسوع غالى القيمة
More precious and honored	غال القيمة وكريم
Than all things in the world	أغلى من الدنيا تمام
His name is Jesus Christ	إسمه يسوع المسيح
The forgiver of sins	الغافر كل آثام
The forgiver of our debts	غافر كل الذنوب
Who hearkens to him who pleads	سامع لمن يدعوه
All the nations confess Him	تعترف له كل
And all the kings praise Him	الشعوب والملوك
	يسبحوه

Praise Him O you people	سبحوه يا كل الامم
Glorify Him all nations	مجدوه يا كل الشعوب
O my Lord Jesus Christ	ياربى يسوع المسيح
Grant us to do Your will	تُبلغنا المطلوب

We ask for Your Kingdom	مطلوبنا ملكوتك
And Your never-ending mercy	ومراحمك موجوده
O my Lord Jesus Christ	ياربى يسوع المسيح
Whose nature is Almighty	يامن طبعه الجوده

You are powerful and honored	صاحب جوده وكريم
There is no other like You	وليس له قط نظير
O my Lord Jesus Christ	ياربى يسوع المسيح
You are all-observing	أنت على الكل بصير

All-observing who hearkens	بصير ومتطلع
Unto us according to Your plan	علينا بتدابيرك
O my Lord Jesus Christ	يا ربى يسوع المسيح
Cast us not away from You	لا تحوجنا لغيرك

We know no other but You	لا نعرف غيرك اله
In Your Gospel we trust	بإنجيلك صدِقنا
You are the Son of God	أنت هو إبن الله
Confirm us in Your faith	فى ايمانك ثبتنا

Confirm us in the faith	ثبتنا على الأيمان
And raise us up from idleness	وانهضنا من كل ملل
O my Lord Jesus Christ	ياربى يسوع المسيح
Your praise enlightens our soul	باسمك نتهلل
We rejoice with hymns	نتهلل بالالحان
We chant with psalms	ونرتل بالمزمار
O my Lord Jesus Christ	ياربى يسوع المسيح
Your praise is joy and delight	تسبيحك بهجة
	وسرور
Our joy is in Your praise	سرورنا تسابيحك
Our splendor is in Your glory	بهجتنا هى مجدك
O my Lord Jesus Christ	ياربى يسوع المسيح
To You is due all glory	العظمة لك وحدك
I have sinned against You	لك وحدك انا اخطيت
And have transgressed Your law	وصنعت الشر أمامك
You are justified in Your words	لتصدق فى أقوالك
And prevail when You judge	وتغلب فى أحكامك
Your judgments are true and	أحكامك حق وعدل
-righteous	ومراحمك متسعة
And Your mercy is never-ending	ياربى يسوع المسيح

O my Lord Jesus Christ	ارحم نفسى المتضعة
Have mercy on my soul	
I humbled myself before Your glory	اتضعت أمام مجدك
And depended on Your words	وإتكلت على أقوالك
O my Lord Jesus Christ	ياربى يسوع المسيح
Cast me not on Your left	لا تطرحنى على شمالك
On Your left cast me not	على شمالك لا توقفنى
With the evil people	مع القوم الاشرار
I ask You to accept me	اسألك أن تقبلنى
As You accepted the tax collector	كما قبلت العشار
I cry out as the tax collector	أصرخ بصوت العشار
With a broken heart	وأنا بوجه مطاطى
O Lord forgive my sins	اللّهُم أغفر لى الاوزار
For Your servant is a sinner	فإنى عبدك خاطئ
Sin is of my nature	الخطية من طبعى
And Your nature is goodness	وانت طبعك الاحسان
There is no slave without sin	ليس عبد بلا خطية
Nor a Master without forgiveness	ولا سيد بلا غفران
Forgiveness is of You	الغفران من عندك

351

And Your mercy is endless

والرحمة هى من قبلك

O my Lord Jesus Christ

ياربى يسوع المسيح

Guide me to do Your will

اهدينى الى سبلك

I have forgotten Your way

سبلك تاهت عنى

My life is far spent and passed away

والعمر فرغ منى

I ask You to accept me

أسألك تقبلنى

And give me repentance

والتوبة أعطينى

Give me repentance and forgiveness

أعطينى توبة وغفران

And clean me from my sins

ونقينى من كل عيوبى

O my Lord Jesus Christ

ياربى يسوع المسيح

Forgive all my sins

اغفر لى كل ذنوبى

My sins have become

ذنوبى ثقلت فوق

A burden unto me

راسى

O my Lord Jesus Christ

كحمل ثقيل قاسى

Purify all my senses

ياربى يسوع المسيح

اشف كل حواسى

Adam Conclusion   ختام الآدام

Your mercies O my God	مراحمك يا الهى
Are great and plenteous	هى كثيرة جدا
Your mercies O my God	مراحمك يا الهى
Are numerous.	لا يحصى لها عددا

Your mercies O my God   مراحمك يا الهى
Are more than the plants of the   أكثر من نبات الارض
-earth   مراحمك يا الهى
Your mercies O my God   قد فاقت كل عدد
Are beyond measure.

Your mercies O my God   مراحمك يا الهى
Are plentiful   كقطرات الامطار
Your mercies O my God   مراحمك يا الهى
Are more than the sand of the sea .   أكثر من رمل البحار

Your mercies O my God   مراحمك يا الهى
Are as a fountain of water   كينابيع المياه
Your mercies O my God   مراحمك يا الهى
Are like living water.   كالأنهار الجارية

353

O Lord save my soul	يارب ارحم نفسى
O Lord save me	يارب خلصنى
O Lord blot out my sins	يارب امح اثمى
With Your goodness remember me	بصلاحك اذكرنى

Holy, Holy, Holy,	قدوس قدوس قدوس
God the Lord of Sabaoth	الله رب الصاباؤوت
The Creator of the universe	الخالق كل نفوس
And its Provider.	ورازقهم بالقوت

We ask You O Our King	نسألك ياملكنا
Preserve the life of our Patriarch	أدِم رئاسة بطركنا
And the Bishops his companions	وشريكة اسقفنا
Amen Alleluia	اَمين اللـيلويا

And whenever we, gather for prayer, let us bless the Name, of my Lord Jesus.	Ⲗⲟⲓⲡⲟⲛ ⲁⲛϣⲁⲛⲑⲱⲟⲩϯ ⲓ̀ⲉϯ̀ⲡⲣⲟⲥⲉⲩⲭⲏ ⲙⲁⲣⲉⲛⲥⲙⲟⲩ ⲉ̀ⲡⲓⲣⲁⲛ ⲛ̀ⲧⲉ Ⲡⲁϭⲟⲓⲥ Ⲓⲏⲥⲟⲩⲥ.	وايضاً أذا ما اجتمعنا للصلاة فلنبارك اسم ربى يسوع .
* We bless You, O my Lord Jesus, save	* Ⲭⲉ ⲧⲉⲛⲛⲁⲥⲙⲟⲩ ⲉ̀ⲣⲟⲕ ⲱ̀ Ⲡⲁϭⲟⲓⲥ	*لاننا نباركك ياربى يسوع

us through Your name, for we have hope in You.	Ⲓⲏⲥⲟⲩⲥ: ⲛⲁϩⲙⲉⲛ ϧⲉⲛ ⲡⲉⲕⲣⲁⲛ : ϫⲉ ⲁⲛⲉⲣϩⲉⲗⲡⲓⲥ ⲉⲣⲟⲕ	نجنا باسمك لأننا توكلنا عليك .
That we may praise You, with Your Good Father, and the Holy Spirit, for You have come and saved us.	Ⲑⲣⲉⲛϩⲱⲥ ⲉⲣⲟⲕ : ⲛⲉⲙ Ⲡⲉⲕⲓⲱⲧ ⲛ̀ⲁⲅⲁⲑⲟⲥ : ⲛⲉⲙ Ⲡⲓⲡⲛⲉⲩⲙⲁ ⲉ̀ⲑⲟⲩⲁⲃ : ϫⲉ ⲁⲕⲓ ⲁⲕⲥⲱϯ ⲙ̀ⲙⲟⲛ.	لكى نسبحك مع ابيك الصالح والروح القدوس لانك أتيت وخلصتنا.
* Glory be to the Father, the Son and the Holy Spirit, now and forever, and to the ages of all ages Amen.	*Ⲇⲟⲝⲁ Ⲡⲁⲧⲣⲓ ⲕⲉ Ⲩⲓⲱ: ⲕⲉ ⲁⲅⲓⲱ Ⲡⲛⲉⲩⲙⲁⲧⲓ. Ⲕⲉ ⲛⲩⲛ ⲕⲉ ⲁ̀ⲓ ⲕⲉ ⲓⲥⲧⲟⲩⲥ ⲉ̀ⲱⲛⲁⲥ ⲧⲱⲛ ⲉ̀ⲱⲛⲱⲛ ⲁ̀ⲙⲏⲛ	*المجد للآب والابن والروح القدس. الآن وكل اوان والى دهر الداهرين آمين.

The Sunday Theotokia

ثيؤطوكية يوم الأحد

You are called righteous, O blessed one, among women, the Second Tabernacle.	Ⲥⲉⲙⲟⲩϯ ⲉⲣⲟ ⲇⲓⲕⲉⲟⲥ : ⲱ̄ ⲑⲏⲉⲧⲥⲙⲁⲣⲱⲟⲩⲧ : ϧⲉⲛ ⲛⲓϩⲓⲟⲙⲓ : ϫⲉ ϯⲙⲁϩⲥⲛⲟⲩϯ ⲛ̀ⲥⲕⲏⲛⲏ.	مدعوة صدّيقة أيتها المباركة فى النساء القبة الثانية.
*Which is called, the Holy of Holies, wherein are the Tablets, of the Covenant.	*Ⲑⲏⲉⲧⲟⲩⲙⲟⲩϯ ⲉ̀ⲣⲟⲥ : ϫⲉ ⲑⲏⲉⲑⲟⲩⲁⲃ : ⲛ̀ⲧⲉ ⲛⲏⲉⲑ-ⲟⲩⲁⲃ ⲉ̀ⲣⲉ ⲛⲓⲡⲗⲁⲝ ⲛ̀-ϧⲏⲧⲥ.	*التى تدعى قدس الأقداس وفيها لوحا العهد.
Whereupon is, the Ten Commandments, these which are written, by the finger of God.	Ⲛ̀ⲧⲉ ϯⲇⲓⲁ̀ⲑⲏⲕⲏ : ⲛⲉⲙ ⲡⲓⲙⲏⲧ ⲛ̀ⲥⲁϫⲓ : ⲛⲁⲓ ⲉⲧ-ⲁϥⲥϧⲏⲟⲩⲧ : ⲛ̀ϫⲉ ⲡⲓⲧⲏⲃ ⲛ̀ⲧⲉ Ⲫϯ.	والعشر كلمات هذه المكتوبة باصبع الله.
*They have directed us, to the Iota, the	*Ⲥⲉⲉⲣϣⲟⲣⲡ ⲛ̀ⲉⲣⲥⲩ-	*سبقت أن دلتنا على (اليوطة)

Name of Salvation, of Jesus Christ.	ⲙⲙⲉⲛⲓⲛ: ⲛⲁⲛ ⲙ̀ⲡⲓ- ⲓⲱⲧⲁ: ⲡⲓⲣⲁⲛ ⲛ̀ⲟⲩ- ⲭⲁⲓ : ⲛ̀ⲧⲉ Ⲓⲏⲥⲟⲩⲥ Ⲡⲓⲭ̀ⲣⲓⲥⲧⲟⲥ.	اسم الخلاص الذى ليسوع المسيح.
Who was incarnate, of you without change, and became the Mediator, of a New Covenant.	Ⲫⲁⲓ ⲉⲧⲁϥϭⲓⲥⲁⲣⲝ ⲛ̀- ϧⲏⲧ: ϧⲉⲛ ⲟⲩⲙⲉⲧⲁ- ⲧϣⲓⲃϯ: ⲁϥϣⲱⲡⲓ ⲙ̀ⲙⲉⲥⲓⲧⲏⲥ: ⲉⲩⲇⲓⲁ̀- ⲑⲏⲕⲏ ⲙ̀ⲃⲉⲣⲓ.	هذا الذى تجسد منك بغير تغيير . وصار وسيطاً لعهد جديد.
*Through the shed-ding, of His holy blood, He purified the faithful, to be a justified people.	*Ⲉⲃⲟⲗϩⲓⲧⲉⲛ ⲫ̀ⲛⲟⲩⲭⲟ : ⲛ̀ⲧⲉ ⲡⲉϥⲥⲛⲟϥ ⲉ̀ⲑⲟ- ⲩⲁⲃ: ⲁϥⲧⲟⲩⲃⲟ ⲛ̀ⲛⲏ- ⲉⲑⲛⲁϩϯ : ⲉⲩⲗⲁⲟⲥ ⲉⲩⲑ̀ⲙⲁⲓⲟϥ.	*من قبل رشاش دمـه المقدس طهر المؤمنين شعباً مبرراً.
Wherefore every-one, magnifies you, O my lady the Mother of God, the ever holy.	Ⲉⲑⲃⲉ ⲫⲁⲓ ⲟⲩⲟⲛ ⲛⲓⲃⲉⲛ : ⲥⲉϭⲓⲥⲓ ⲙ̀ⲙⲟ : ⲧⲁϭⲟⲓⲥ ϯⲑⲉⲟ̀ⲧⲟⲕⲟⲥ: ⲉⲑⲟⲩ- ⲁⲃ ⲛ̀ⲥⲏⲟⲩ ⲛⲓⲃⲉⲛ.	من أجل هذا كل واحد يعظمك ياسيدتى والدة الاله القديسة كل حين .

*And we too, hope to win mercy, thro-ugh your intercess-ions, with the Lover of mankind.	*Ⲁⲛⲟⲛ ϩⲱⲛ ⲧⲉⲛⲧⲱⲃϩ : ⲉⲑⲣⲉⲛϣⲁϣⲛⲓ ⲉⲩⲛⲁⲓ ϩⲓⲧⲉⲛ ⲛⲉⲡⲣⲉⲥⲃⲓⲁ : ⲛⲧⲟⲧϥ ⲙ̀ⲡⲓⲙⲁⲓⲣⲱⲙⲓ.	*ونحن أيضاً نطلب أن نفوز برحمة بشفاعاتك عند محب البشر.

(1)   **(ⲁ̅)**   **(١)**

Who can speak of, the honor of the Tabernacle, which Moses had made, on Mount Sinai.	Ⲛⲓⲙ ⲡⲉⲑⲛⲁϣ̀ⲥⲁϫⲓ : ⲙ̀ⲡⲧⲁⲓⲟ ⲛ̀ⲧ̀ⲥⲕⲏⲛⲏ : ⲉⲧⲁ Ⲙⲱⲩ̀ⲥⲏⲥ ⲑⲁⲙⲓⲟⲥ : ϩⲓϫⲉⲛ ⲡ̀ⲧⲱⲟⲩ ⲛ̀Ⲥⲓⲛⲁ.	من يقدر أن ينطق بكرامة القبة التى صنعها موسى على جبل سيناء .
*He made it with glory, as comma-nded by the Lord, according to the patterns, shown unto him.	*Ⲁϥⲑⲁⲙⲓⲟⲥ ϧⲉⲛ ⲟⲩⲱⲟⲩ : ⲕⲁⲧⲁ ⲡⲥⲁϫⲓ ⲙ̀Ⲡⲟ̅ⲥ̅ : ⲛⲉⲙ ⲕⲁⲧⲁ ⲛⲓⲧⲩⲡⲟⲥ ⲧⲏⲣⲟⲩ : ⲉⲧⲁⲩⲧⲁⲙⲟϥ ⲉ̀ⲣⲱⲟⲩ.	*صنعها بمجد كقول الرب وكجميع المثالات التى اعلنت له.

Therein Aaron, and his sons served, the example of the highest, in the shadow Of the heavenly ones.	Ѳн ⲉⲣⲉ Ⲁ̀ⲁⲣⲱⲛ: ⲛⲉⲙ ⲛⲉϥϣⲏⲣⲓ ϣⲉⲙϣⲓ ⲛ̀ⲟ̀-ⲏⲧⲥ: ϧⲉⲛ ⲡ̀ⲧⲩⲡⲟⲥ ⲛ̀-ⲧⲉ ⲡ̀ϭⲓⲥⲓ: ⲛⲉⲙ ⲧ̀ϧⲏⲓⲃⲓ ⲛ̀ⲧⲉ ⲛⲁ̀ ⲧ̀ⲫⲉ.	تلك التى كان هرون وبنوه يخدمون فيها بمثال العلاء وظل السمائيات.
*They likened it to you, O Virgin Mary, the true Tabernacle, wherein dwelt God.	*Ⲁⲩⲧⲉⲛⲑⲱⲛⲓ ⲉ̀ⲣⲟⲥ: Ⲙⲁⲣⲓⲁ̀ ϯⲡⲁⲣⲑⲉⲛⲟⲥ ϯⲥⲕⲏⲛⲏ ⲙ̀ⲙⲏⲓ : ⲉ̀ⲣⲉ Ⲫϯ ⲥⲁϧⲟⲩⲛ ⲙ̀ⲙⲟⲥ.	*شبهوك بها يامريم العذراء القبة الحقيقية التى فى داخلها الله.
Wherefore we, mag-nify you befittingly, with prophetic, hymnology.	Ⲉⲑⲃⲉ ⲫⲁⲓ ⲧⲉⲛϭⲓⲥⲓ : ⲙ̀ⲙⲟ ⲁⲍⲓⲱⲥ : ϧⲉⲛ ⲅⲁⲛⲩⲙⲛⲟⲗⲟⲅⲓⲁ̀ : ⲙ̀ⲡ̀ⲣ-ⲟⲫⲏⲧⲓⲕⲟⲛ.	من أجل هذا نعظمك باستحقاق بتماجيد نبوية.
*For they spoke of you, with great honor, O Holy City, of the Great King.	*Ϫⲉ ⲁⲩⲥⲁϫⲓ ⲉⲑⲃ-ⲏϯ : ⲛ̀ϩⲁⲛϩ̀ⲃⲏⲟⲩⲓ̀ ⲉⲩⲧⲁⲓⲏⲟⲩⲧ : ϯⲃⲁ-ⲕⲓ ⲉ̀ⲑⲟⲩⲁⲃ : ⲛ̀ⲧⲉ ⲡⲓⲛⲓϣϯ ⲛ̀ⲟⲩⲣⲟ.	*لانهم تكلموا من أجلك بأعمال كريمة أيتها المدينة المقدسة التى للملك العظيم.

| We entreat and pray, that we may win mercy, through your intercessions, with the Lover of mankind. | Ⲧⲉⲛϯϩⲟ ⲧⲉⲛⲧⲱⲃϩ : ⲉⲑⲣⲉⲛϣⲁϣⲛⲓ ⲉⲩⲛⲁⲓ ϩⲓⲧⲉⲛ ⲛⲉⲡⲣⲉⲥⲃⲓⲁ : ⲛ̀ⲧⲟⲧϥ ⲙ̀ⲡⲓⲙⲁⲓⲣⲱⲙⲓ. | نسأل ونطلب أن نفوز برحمة بشفاعاتك عند محب البشر. |

The First Explanation — التفسير الأول

I start in the Name of God	أبدأ باسم الله
Who dwells in light	الساكن فى النور
Who spoke to Moses	الذى كلم موسى
Upon Mount Tabor	من فوق جبل الطـور

Saying O Moses	قائلاً ياموسى
Arise joyfully	انهض فرحاً مسروراً
So I may show you	لأعلمك بما كان
A place prophesied about	كمــا عنــه تنبــأون

| Arise O Moses | انهض ياموسى |
| And ascend to the highest mount | واصعد إلى اعلى الجبال |

Thereupon it build a dome	وابن هناك قبة
To resemble a tabernacle	تكون لك شبة مظـــــال
And all I say to you	وجميع ما قلته لك
Immediately write down	اكتبه فى الحال
This is a testimony	هذه هى شهادة
For the Israelites	للأسرائيليين
Hasten O Moses	إسرع ياموسى
And observe the place	انظر هذا المكان
Build there a dome	وابن فيه قبة
With granite stone	بالحجر الصوان
Elevate its height	وعلى شوارعها
And for it make four corners	واعمل لها أربعة أركان
And gather what is needed	واجمع مايحتاج
For the builders	إليه البناؤون
Make the outside of the dome	واعمل خارج القبة
And widen its hallway	فسحة كالدهليز
Overlay it O Moses	واطليها ياموسى
With pure gold	بالذهب الإبريز
Within and without	داخل مع خارج

Honour for consecration	كرامة للتكريس
From the top to the base	من أعلى إلى أسفل
With the precious gold	بالذهب الموزون
Make the inside of the dome	واعمل داخل القبة
An altar for the showbread	مذبح للقربان
And around the altar	واعمل حول المذبح
Make four pillars	أربعة عمدان
Make there upon it	يكون من فوقها
Cherubs made out of gold	من الذهب كاروبان
With their wings spread	بأجنحة مفروشة
Upon the cover	إيجين بى إيللاستيريون
And in its place	واجعل فيها تابوت
The overlaid ark of covenant	العهد المطلى
And in it the golden vessel	وفيه القسط الذهب
With the hidden manna	بالمن المخفى
And in it Aaron's censer	وفيه شورية هرون
From pure gold	من الذهب المصفى
And the tablets of the covenant	وفيه لوحا العهد
With Aaron's rod	مع عصاة هارون

And in it the lampstand	وفيه المنارة
With the chosen gold	من الذهب المختار
And the golden vessel	وفيه المايدة ذهب
Burning as the ember	تشعل كجمر النار
Decorate it O Moses	وزينها ياموسى
With various lights	بسائر كل الأنوار
Make also in it	واجعل فيها أيضاً
Seven burning candles	سبعة سرج ينيرون

REFRAIN المرد

Hail to you O Mary	السلام لك يامريم
O you full of grace	يامملوءة نعمة
Who are engulfed in light	يامشتملة بالانوار
O mother of the Merciful	ياام الرحمة
Intercede for us	إشفعى فينا
On judgment day	فى يوم الزحمة
Your Son granted us salvation	بابنك نلنا الخلاص
O daughter of Zion	يابنة صهيون

Holy, Holy, Holy. A reading from	قدوس قدوس قدوس .
the Gospel according to St. Luke	فصل من الانجيل بحسب

[1: 46-50] the Evangelist, may his blessings be with us all. Amen.

"And Mary said: "My soul magnifies the Lord, and my spirit has rejoiced in God my Savior. For He has regarded the lowly state of His maidservant, For behold, from henceforth all generations will call me blessed. For He who is mighty has done great things for me, and Holy is His Name. And His mercy is on those who fear Him from generation to generation." Glory be to God forever. Amen

لوقا(1: 46 – 50)

البشير . بركاته تكون معنا . آمين.

"فقالت مريم تعظم نفسى الرب . وتتهلل روحى بالله مخلصى لأنه نظر إلى تواضع أمته . هوذا منذ الآن تعطينى الطوبى. جميع الأجيال . صنع بى القوى عظائم. قدوس اسمه ورحمته إلى جيل الأجيال لخائفيه" والمجد لله دائماً أبدياً . آمين.

2	Ⲃ̄	٢
*The Ark overlaid, roundabout with gold, that was made, with wood that would not decay.	*Ϯⲕⲓⲃⲱⲧⲟⲥ ⲉⲧⲟⲩϫ ⲛ̀ⲛⲟⲩⲃ ⲛ̀ⲥⲁⲥⲁ ⲛⲓⲃⲉⲛ ⲑⲏⲉⲧⲁⲩⲑⲁⲙⲓⲟⲥ ϧⲉⲛ ⳑⲁⲛϣⲉ ⲛ̀ⲁⲧⲉⲣ-ϧⲟⲗⲓ.	*التابوت المصفح بالذهب من كل ناحية المصنوع من خشب لايسوس.
It foretold the sign, of God the Word, Who became man, without separation.	Ⲁⲥⲉⲣϣⲟⲣⲡ ⲛ̀ⲧⲙⲏⲓⲛⲓ ⲙ̀Ⲫϯ ⲡⲓⲗⲟⲅⲟⲥ ⲫⲏⲉⲧⲁϥϣⲱⲡⲓ ⲛ̀ⲣⲱⲙⲓ ϧⲉⲛ ⲟⲩⲙⲉⲧⲁ ⲧ̀ϥⲱⲣϫ.	سبق أن دلنا على الله الكلمة. الذى صار انساناً بغير افتراق.
*One nature out of two, a Holy divinity, co-Essential with the Father, and incorr-uptible.	*Ⲟⲩⲁⲓ ⲡⲉ ⲉ̀ⲃⲟⲗϧⲉⲛ ⲥ̀-ⲛⲁⲩ ⲟⲩⲙⲉⲑⲛⲟⲩϯ ⲉⲥⲧⲟⲩⲃⲏⲟⲩⲧ ⲉⲥⲟⲓ ⲛ̀-ⲁⲧⲧⲁⲕⲟ ⲛ̀ⲟⲙⲟⲟ-ⲩⲥⲓⲟⲥ ⲛⲉⲙ Ⲫⲓⲱⲧ.	* واحد من اثنين لاهوت قدوس بغير فساد مساو للآب.
A holy humanity, Begotten without seed, coessential with	Ⲛⲉⲙ ⲟⲩⲙⲉⲧⲣⲱⲙⲓ ⲉⲑⲟⲩⲁⲃ ⲭⲱⲣⲓⲥ	وناسوت طاهر بغير مباضعة مساو لنا

365

us, according to the economy.	cⲩⲛⲟⲩⲥⲓⲁ : ⲛ̀ⲟⲙⲟⲟⲩⲥ- ⲓⲟⲥ ⲛⲉⲙⲁⲛ : ⲕⲁⲧⲁ ϯⲟⲓⲕⲟⲛⲟⲙⲓⲁ.	كالتدبير.
*This which He has taken, from you O undefiled, He made one with Him, as a hypostasis.	*Ⲑⲁⲓ ⲉ̀ⲧⲁϥϭⲓⲧⲥ ⲛ̀ⲟ̀ ⲏ ϯ : ⲱ̀ ϯⲁⲧⲑⲱⲗⲉⲃ : ⲉⲁϥϩⲱⲧⲡ ⲉ̀ⲣⲟⲥ : ⲕⲁ- ⲧⲁ ⲟⲩϩⲩⲡⲟⲥⲧⲁⲥⲓⲥ.	*هذا الذى أخذه منك أيتها الغير الدنسة واتحد به كاقنوم.
Wherefore everyone, magnifies you, O my lady the Mother of God, the ever holy.	Ⲉⲑⲃⲉ ⲫⲁⲓ ⲟⲩⲟⲛ ⲛⲓⲃⲉⲛ : ⲥⲉϭⲓⲥⲓ ⲙ̀ⲙⲟ : ⲧⲁϭ̀ⲟⲓⲥ ϯⲑⲉⲟ̀ⲧⲟⲕⲟⲥ : ⲉⲑⲟⲩ- ⲁⲃ ⲛ̀ⲥⲏⲟⲩ ⲛⲓⲃⲉⲛ.	من أجل هذا كل واحد يعظمك ياسيدتى والدة الاله القديسة كل حين .
*And we too, hope to win mercy, through your intercessions, with the Lover of mankind.	*Ⲁⲛⲟⲛ ϩⲱⲛ ⲧⲉⲛⲧ- ⲱⲃϩ : ⲉⲑⲣⲉⲛϣⲁϣⲛⲓ ⲉⲣⲛⲁⲓ : ϩⲓⲧⲉⲛ ⲛⲉⲡ̀ⲣ- ⲉⲥⲃⲓⲁ̀ : ⲛ̀ⲧⲟⲧϥ ⲙ̀ⲡⲓ- ⲙⲁⲓⲣⲱⲙⲓ.	*ونحن أيضاً نطلب أن نفوز برحمة بشفاعاتك عند محب البشر.
All the souls together, of the children Of Israel,	Ⲯⲩⲭⲏ ⲛⲓⲃⲉⲛ ⲉⲩⲥⲟⲡ : ⲛ̀ⲧⲉ ⲛⲉⲛϣⲏⲣⲓ ⲙ̀Ⲡ-	كل الأنفس معاً من بنى إسرائيل قدموا قرابين

brought offerings unto, the Tabernacle of the Lord.	ісранλ : ауіні н̀га-н̀Δωρον : ѐ†скн-нн ̀нте Ⲡ̄бοιс.	إلى قبة الرب.
*Gold and silver, and precious stone, purple and scarlet, and fine linen.	*Ⲡιноуⲃ нем піⲅат : нем піⲱні ̀ммні : нем піϣенс етса† : нем піⲅⲣакунеі-нон.	*الذهب و الفضة والحجر الكريم والحرير المغزول والأرجوان.
And they made an ark, of wood that would not decay, overlaid with gold, within and without.	Δуоаміо ̀ноукіⲃω-тос: бен ⲅанϣе ̀-атерⲅоⲗі : ауλаλ-ωс ̀нноуⲃ : саборн нем саⲃоλ.	صنعوا تابوتاً من خشب لايسوّس. وصفحوه بالذهب داخلاً وخارجاً.
*You too O Mary, are clothed with the glory, of the Divinity, within and without.	*Ⲧехωⲅ ⲅар ⲅωι : Ⲙаріа †парⲑенос ̀м̀п̀ⲱоу ̀нте †ме-ⲑноу† : саборн нем саⲃоλ.	*وأنت أيضاً يامريم العذراء متسربلة بمجد اللاهوت داخلاً وخارجاً.

For you have brought, unto God your Son, many people, through your purity.	Ϫⲉ ⲁⲣⲉⲓⲛⲓ ⲉϧⲟⲩⲛ : ⲛ̀ⲟⲩⲗⲁⲟⲥ ⲉϥⲟϣ : ⲙ̀Ⲫϯ ⲡⲉϣⲏⲣⲓ : ϩⲓⲧⲉⲛ ⲡⲉⲧⲟⲩⲃⲟ.	لانك قدمت شعباً كثيراً لله ابنك من قبل طهارتك.
*Wherefore we, magnify you befittingly, with prophetic, hymnology.	*Ⲉⲑⲃⲉ ⲫⲁⲓ ⲧⲉⲛϭⲓⲥⲓ : ⲙ̀ⲙⲟ ⲁⲍⲓⲱⲥ : ϧⲉⲛ ϩⲁⲛⲩ̀ⲙⲛⲟⲗⲟϯⲁ : ⲙ̀ⲡⲣⲟⲫⲏⲧⲓⲕⲟⲛ.	*من أجل هذا نعظمك باستحقاق بتماجيد نبوية.
For they spoke of you, with great honor, O Holy City, of the Great King.	Ϫⲉ ⲁⲩⲥⲁϫⲓ ⲉⲑⲃⲏϯ : ⲛ̀ϩⲁⲛⲉ̀ⲃⲏⲟⲩⲓ̀ ⲉⲩⲧⲁⲓⲏⲟⲩⲧ : ϯⲃⲁⲕⲓ ⲉ̀ⲑⲟⲩⲁⲃ : ⲛ̀ⲧⲉ ⲡⲓⲛⲓϣϯ ⲛ̀ⲟⲩⲣⲟ.	لانهم تكلموا من أجلك بأعمال كريمة أيتها المدينة المقدسة التى للملك العظيم.
*We entreat and pray, that we may win mercy, through your intercessions, with the Lover of mankind.	*Ⲧⲉⲛϯϩⲟ ⲧⲉⲛⲧⲱⲃϩ : ⲉⲑⲣⲉⲛϣⲁϣⲛⲓ ⲉⲩⲛⲁⲓ ϩⲓⲧⲉⲛ ⲛⲉⲡⲣⲉⲥⲃⲓⲁ̀ : ⲛ̀ⲧⲟⲧϥ ⲙ̀ⲡⲓⲙⲁⲓⲣⲱⲙⲓ.	*نسأل ونطلب أن نفوز برحمة بشفاعاتك عند محب البشر.

The Second Explanation   التفسير الثانى

The Lord said to Moses	قال الرب لموسى
Called him in a loud vioce	بصوت عالى يناديه
Arise and build an ark for Me	قم إصنع لى تابوتاً
And overlay it with gold	وبالذهب إطليه

So therein may dwell My secrets	لأضع سرى فيه
And also My covenant	وأجعل عهدى فيه
From shittim wood	من خشب لايسوس
And overlaid with gold	وبالذهب تطلون

You were likened O Mary	تشبهت يامريم
To the overlaid ark	بتابوت العهد المطلى
And in it the golden vessel	وفيه القسط ذهب
With the rational manna	بالمن العقلى

Your praise on my tongue	مديحك فى فمى
Is sweeter than honey	أحلى من العسل
We offer praise to You	نقرئك كل سلام
O daughter of Zion	ياابنة صهيون

O shining star	يانجمة تضوى

369

As a lit lamp	كمصباح النور
You held the Son of God	حملت إبن الله
The Living who is unseen	الحى غير المنظور
He saved Adam	و أنقذ آدم
After the bondage	بعد أن كان مأسور
And returned him and his sons	وعاد هو وبنوه
Joyfully to Paradise	إلى الفردوس وهم فرحون
You enlightened the world	نورت العالم
After it was in darkness	بعد أن كان ظلمة
And you carried in your womb	وحملت فى أحشاك
The Son the Logos of God	إبن اللة الكلمة
You are the ark	انت هى التابوت
You are wisdom	انت هى الحكمة
You are our strength	انت هى قوتنا
And the joy of the upright	وفرح الصديقون
At the suitable time	لما أراد الله
God desired and chose you	وشاء واختارك
And sent unto you the Logos	وأرسل إليك الكلمة
With the Holy Spirit in you	بروح قدسه زانك

370

You carried in your womb	وحملت فى أحشاك
The Lord your God	الرب إلهك
You nourished Him with your milk	ولدتيه ورضع لبنك
Like all other humans	كسائر البشريين
Ezekiel prophesied	حزقيال تنبأ
In a vision and said	فى رؤياه وقال
"I saw an eastern door	رأيت باباً فى المشرق
Closed from all sides	مقفولا بالأقفال
Therein entered and came forth	دخل فيه وخرج
The most high King	الملك المتعال
And no harm came to it	ولم يمسه ضرر
And it was continuously sealed."	وبحاله مختومون
Many witnessed of you	وكم شهدوا عنك
In prophecies and proverbs	فى نبوات وأمثال
He who shall come forth from you	سوف يظهر منك
Is the exalted Lord	الرب المتعال
He shall save His people	ويخلص شعبه
At the end of days	فى آخر الأجيال
Your Son granted us salvation	بابنك نلنا الغفران

O censer of Aaron	ياشورية هارون

REFRAIN — المرد

Hail to you O Mary — السلام لك يامريم
O you full of grace — يامملوءة نعمة
Who are engulfed in light — يامشتملة بالانوار
O mother of the Merciful — ياام الرحمة

Intercede for us — إشفعى فينا
On judgment day — فى يوم الزحمة
Your Son granted us salvation — بابنك نلنا الخلاص
O daughter of Zion — ياإبنة صهيون

Holy, Holy, Holy. A reading from the Gospel according to our St. Luke [1: 51-55] the Evangelist, may his blessings be with us all. Amen.

قدوس قدوس قدوس . فصل من الانجيل بحسب لوقا (1: 51 - 55) البشير. بركاته تكون معنا . آمين.

"He has shown strength with His arm; He has scattered the proud in the imagination of their hearts. He

"صنع قوة بذراعه. وفرق المستكبرين بفكر قلوبهم. أنزل

372

has put down the mighty from their thrones and exalted the lowly. He has filled the hungry with good things, and the rich He has sent away empty. He has helped His servant Israel, In remembrance of His mercy, As He spoke to our fathers, To Abraham and to his seed forever." Glory be to God forever. Amen

الأقوياء عن الكراسى ورفع المتواضعين أشبع الجياع من الخيرات. وأرسل الأغنياء فارغين. عضد إسرائيل فتاه وذكر رحمة كما قال لآبائنا ابراهيم وزرعه إلى الأبد".والمجد لله دائماً أبدياً آمين.

3	$\overline{\text{Γ}}$	٣
The Mercy Seat, was overshadowed by, the forged Cherubim, from all sides.	Πιλαςτηριον : ετο- τεωβς ̀μμοϥ : ϩιτεν νιⲬερουβιμ : ετοι ̀ν-ϩικων.	الغطاء المظلل عليه بالكروبين المصورين.
*Was a symbol of God the Word, Who was incarnate, of you without change, O undefiled.	*Ⲉτε Ⲫϯ πιλοⲅος : εταϥϭιсαρⲝ ̀νϧηϯ : ̀ω ϯατάϭνι : ϧεν ουμετ-ατϣιβϯ.	*اى الله الكلمة الذى تجسد منك أيتها التى بلا عيب بغير تغير.
He became the purification, of our sins, and the forgiveness, of our iniquities.	Ⲁϥϣωπι ̀ντουⲃο: ̀ντε νεννοβι: νεμ ουρεϥ-ⲭω ̀εⲃολ : ̀ντε νενὰνομιὰ.	وصار تطهيراً لخطايانا وغافراً لآثامنا.
*Wherefore everyone, magnifies you, O my lady the Mother of God, the ever holy.	*Ⲉⲑⲃε ϕαι ουον νιⲃεν : ceⲃιcι ̀μμο : ⲧⲁϭοιc ϯⲑεⲟⲧοκος : εⲑουⲁⲃ ̀νcϩου νιⲃεν.	*من أجل هذا كل واحد يعظمك ياسيدتى والدة الاله القديسة كل حين .
And we too, hope to	Ⲁνον ϩⲱν ⲧεντⲱⲃϩ :	ونحن أيضاً

win mercy, through your intercessions, with the Lover of mankind.	ⲉⲑⲣⲉⲛϣⲁϣⲛⲓ ⲉⲩⲛⲁⲓ : ϩⲓⲧⲉⲛ ⲛⲉⲡⲣⲉⲥⲃⲓⲁ : ⲛⲧⲟⲧϥ ⲙⲡⲓⲙⲁⲓⲣⲱⲙⲓ.	نطلب أن نفوز برحمة بشفاعاتك عند محب البشر.
*The two golden Cherubim, continually cover, with their wings, the Mercy Seat.	*Ⲭⲉⲣⲟⲩⲃⲓⲙ ⲥⲛⲁⲩ ⲛⲛⲟⲩⲃ : ⲉⲧⲟⲓ ⲛϩⲓⲕⲱⲛ : ⲉⲧϩⲱⲃⲥ ⲙⲡⲓⲡⲗⲁⲥⲧⲏⲣⲓⲟⲛ : ϧⲉⲛ ⲛⲟⲩⲧⲉⲛϩ ⲛⲥⲟⲩ ⲛⲓⲃⲉⲛ.	*كروبا ذهب مصوران مظللان على الغطاء باجنحتهما كل حين.
Overshadowing, the place of The Holy, of the Holies, in the Second Tabernacle.	Ⲉⲧⲉⲣϧⲏⲓⲃⲓ ⲉϩⲣⲏⲓ : ϩⲓϫⲉⲛ ⲡⲓⲙⲁ ⲉⲑⲟⲩⲁⲃ : ⲛⲧⲉ ⲛⲏⲉⲑⲟⲩⲁⲃ : ϧⲉⲛ ϯⲥⲕⲏⲛⲏ ⲙⲙⲁϩⲥⲛⲟⲩϯ.	يظللان على موضع قدس الأقداس فى القبة الثانية .
*You too O Mary, thousands of thousands, and myriads of myriads, overshadow you:	* ⲛ̀ⲑⲟ ϩⲱⲓ Ⲙⲁⲣⲓⲁ : ⲛⲓⲁⲛⲁⲛϣⲟ ⲛϣⲟ : ⲛⲉⲙ ⲛⲓⲁⲛⲁⲛⲑⲃⲁ ⲛⲑⲃⲁ : ⲥⲉⲉⲣϧⲏⲓⲃⲓ ⲉϫⲱ.	*وأنت أيضاً يامريم الوف الوف وربوات ربوات يظللون عليك.
Praising their Creator, Who was in your womb, and took	Ⲉⲧϩⲱⲥ ⲉⲡⲟⲩⲣⲉϥⲥⲱⲛⲧ : ⲉϥⲭⲏ ϧⲉⲛ ⲧⲉⲛⲉϫⲓ	مسبحين خالقهم وهو فى بطنك. هذا

our likeness, without sin or alteration.	: ϧⲁⲓ ⲉ̀ⲧⲁϥϭⲓ ⲙⲡⲉⲛⲓⲛⲓ : ⲭⲱⲣⲓⲥ ⲛⲟⲃⲓ ϩⲓ ϣⲓⲃϯ.	الذى أخذ شبهنا ما خلا الخطية والتغيير.
*Wherefore we, magnify you befittingly, with prophetic, hymnology.	*Ⲉⲑⲃⲉ ⲫⲁⲓ ⲧⲉⲛϭⲓⲥⲓ : ⲙ̀ⲙⲟ ⲁⲝⲓⲱⲥ : ϧⲉⲛ ϩⲁⲛⲩⲙⲛⲟⲗⲟⲅⲓⲁ : ⲙ̀ⲡⲣⲟⲫⲏⲧⲓⲕⲟⲛ.	*من أجل هذا نعظمك باستحقاق بتماجيد نبوية.
For they spoke of you, with great honor, O Holy City, of the Great King.	Ⲭⲉ ⲁⲩⲥⲁϫⲓ ⲉⲑⲃⲏⲧ : ⲛ̀ϩⲁⲛϩ̀ⲃⲏⲟⲩⲓ̀ ⲉⲩⲧⲁⲓ̀ⲏⲟⲩⲧ : ϯⲃⲁⲕⲓ ⲉ̀ⲑⲟⲩⲁⲃ : ⲛ̀ⲧⲉ ⲡⲓⲛⲓϣϯ ⲛ̀ⲟⲩⲣⲟ.	لانهم تكلموا من أجلك بأعمال كريمة أيتها المدينة المقدسة التى للملك العظيم.
*We entreat and pray, that we may win mercy, through your intercessions, with the Lover of mankind.	*Ⲧⲉⲛϯϩⲟ ⲧⲉⲛⲧⲱⲃϩ : ⲉⲑⲣⲉⲛϣⲁϣⲛⲓ ⲉⲩⲛⲁⲓ ϩⲓⲧⲉⲛ ⲛⲉⲡⲣⲉⲥⲃⲓⲁ̀ : ⲛ̀ⲧⲟⲧϥ ⲙ̀ⲡⲓⲙⲁⲓⲣⲱⲙⲓ.	*نسأل ونطلب أن نفوز برحمة بشفاعاتك عند محب البشر.

The Third Explanation التفسير الثالث

O Mary, you became	يامريم صرت
An altar for forgiveness	مذبح للغفران
And on it the golden gifts	وعليه المايدة ذهب
And the showbread, which was -the Body	وفيه الجسد قربان

It was the Son of the Living God	هو إبن الله الحى
Who gives forgiveness	المعطى الغفران
To every pure person	لكل نقى طاهر
Who lives in the paradise of Joy	يسكن نعيم الفردوس

You are the high altar	أنت هى المذبح العالى
Who is engulfed in light	المشتملة بالأنوار
And the light shines brightly	ونوره يتلألأ
And fills all the earth	ملأ كل الاقطار

Your light, O Mary	وضوئك يامريم
Exceeds the sun and the moon	فاق كل شموس وأقمار
You're higher than all ranks	فقت كل مراتب
And all the hosts	وسائر كل طقوس

You exceeded the elders	فقت الرؤساء
And the four Living Creatures	والأربعة الحيوانات
And also the Thrones	وأيضاً الكراسى
The Principalities and the Powers	والأرباب والقوات
You held the Son of God	حملت ابن الله
The Creator of all things	خالق كل المخلوقات
The Life Giver	معطى كل حياة
To every body and soul	لكل جسد ونفوس
O flower of incense	يازهرة الأطياب
The aroma of your incense spread	بخورك عنبر فاح
O star that shines	يانجمة تضوى
That shines as a lamp	تضئ كالمصباح
O you full of grace	يامملوءة نعمة
O you who are our joy	يابدء الافراح
Your Son granted us salvation	بابنك نلنا الخلاص
And the Paradise of Joy	ونعيم الفردوس
Daniel prophesied	دانيال تنبأ
In a vision and said	فى رؤياه بثبات
I saw a Throne surrounded by	قال رأيت كرسياً من نور
-light	وعليه رب القوات

And upon it sat the Lord of hosts

Around Him thousands and   وحوله ألوف ألوف
-thousands   ربوات مع طغمات
Myriads and myriads   يسبحون الله
While praising God   الملك القدوس
The Holy King

You were likened O Mary   تشبهت يامريم
To the Throne of God the Creator   بكرسى الله الخالق
You held the Son of God   وحملت ابن الله
The living and unseen   الحى الناطق

The fathers called you   سَمَاك الآباء
The eastern door   باب المشارق
Many spoke of you   وكم وصفوا عنك
O Virgin and bride   يابكرة وعروس

The Lord chose you   الرب إختارك
From the root of Jesse   من أصل يسى
From the pure and sanctified   من نسل نقى طاهر
-seed   بيت النبوة والرؤساء
The house of prophets and rulers

You held Him in your womb	وحملتيه فى أحشاك
O Virgin and bride	يابكر وعروس
You bore Him and fed Him milk	ولدتيه ورضع لبنك
Like any other human.	هوس رومى إنتى ليوس

REFRAIN — المرد

Hail to you O Mary	السلام لك يامريم
O you full of grace	يامملوءة نعمة
Who are engulfed in light	يامشتملة بالانوار
O mother of the Merciful	ياام الرحمة

Intercede for us	إشفعى فينا
On judgment day	فى يوم الزحمة
Your Son granted us salvation	بابنك نلنا الخلاص
O daughter of Zion	ياإبنة صهيون

Holy, Holy, Holy. A reading from the Gospel according to St. Luke [1: 68-72] the Evangelist, may his blessings be with us all. Amen.	قدوس قدوس قدوس . فصل من الانجيل بحسب لوقا 1: 68 – 72) . البشير . بركاته تكون معنا . آمين.

"Blessed is the Lord God of Israel, For He has visited and redeemed His people, and has raised up a horn of salvation for us in the house of His servant David. As He spoke by the mouth of His holy prophets, who have been since the world began, that we should be saved from our enemies and from the hand of all who hate us, to perform the mercy promised to our fathers and to remember His holy covenant,". Glory be to God forever. Amen.

"مبارك الرب إله اسرائيل لأنه افتقد وصنع نجاة لشعبه: وأقام لنا قرن خلاص من بيت داود عبده. ليذكر رحمته كما تكلم من أفواه أنبيائه الأطهار منذ البدء. خلاص من أعدائنا : ومن أيدى كل مبغضينا: ليصنع رحمة مع آبائنا ويذكر عهده القدوس". والمجد لله دائماً أبدياً آمين.

4

You are the pot, made of pure gold, wherein was hidden, the true manna.

*The Bread of Life, which came down for us, from heaven, and gave life unto the world.

Wherefore everyone, magnifies you, O my lady the Mother of God, the ever holy.

*And we too, hope to win mercy, through your intercessions, with the Lover of mankind.

ⲁ̅

Ⲛ̄ⲑⲟ ⲡⲉ ⲡⲓⲥⲧⲁⲙⲛⲟⲥ ⲥ̅ ⲛ̄ⲛⲟⲩⲃ ⲉⲧⲧⲟⲩⲃⲏⲟⲩⲧ ⲥ̅ ⲉ̀ⲣⲉ ⲡⲓⲙⲁⲛⲛⲁ ϩⲏⲡ ⲥ̅ⲛ̄ϧ̀ⲣⲏⲓ ϧⲉⲛ ⲧⲉϥⲙⲏϯ.

*Ⲡⲓⲱⲓⲕ ⲛ̀ⲧⲉ ⲡ̀ⲱⲛϧ ⲥ̅ ⲉⲧⲁϥⲓ̀ ⲉ̀ⲡⲉⲥⲏⲧ ⲥ̅ ⲛⲁⲛ ⲉ̀ⲃⲟⲗϧⲉⲛ ⲧ̀ⲫⲉ ⲥ̅ ⲁϥϯ ⲙ̀ⲡ̀ⲱⲛϧ ⲙ̀ⲡⲓⲕⲟⲥⲙⲟⲥ.

Ⲉⲑⲃⲉ ⲫⲁⲓ ⲟⲩⲟⲛ ⲛⲓⲃⲉⲛ ⲥ̅ ⲥⲉϭⲓⲥⲓ ⲙ̀ⲙⲟ ⲥ̅ ⲧⲁϭⲟⲓⲥ ϯⲑⲉⲟ̀ⲧⲟⲕⲟⲥ ⲥ̅ ⲉⲑⲟⲩⲁⲃ ⲛ̀ⲥⲏⲟⲩ ⲛⲓⲃⲉⲛ.

* Ⲁⲛⲟⲛ ϩⲱⲛ ⲧⲉⲛⲧⲱⲃϩ ⲥ̅ ⲉⲑⲣⲉⲛϣⲁϣⲛⲓ ⲉⲩⲛⲁⲓ ⲥ̅ ϩⲓⲧⲉⲛ ⲛⲉⲡⲣⲉⲥⲃⲓⲁ̀ ⲥ̅ ⲛ̀ⲧⲟⲧϥ ⲙ̀ⲡⲓⲙⲁⲓⲣⲱⲙⲓ.

٤

أنت هى قسط الذهب النقى المخفى المن فى وسطه.

*خبز الحياة الذى نزل لنا من السماء وأعطى الحياة للعالم.

من أجل هذا كل واحد يعظمك ياسيدتى والدة الاله القديسة كل حين.

*ونحن أيضاً نطلب أن نفوز برحمة بشفاعاتك عند محب البشر.

It befits you, to be called, the Golden Pot, where the manna was hidden.	Ϥⲧⲱϣⲓ ⲅⲁⲣ ⲉⲣⲟ ⲉ ⲉⲑⲣⲟⲩⲙⲟⲩϯ ⲉⲡⲉⲣⲁⲛ ⲝ ⲭⲉ ⲡⲓⲥⲧⲁⲙⲛⲟⲥ ⲛ̀ⲛⲟⲩⲃ ⲝ ⲉⲣⲉ ⲡⲓⲙⲁⲛⲛⲁ ⲋⲏⲡ ⲛ̀ϧⲏⲧϥ.	يليق بك أن يدعى اسمك قسط الذهب المخفى فية المن.
*For that was kept, in the Tabernacle, as a testimony, to the children of Israel.	*Ⲫⲏ ⲙⲉⲛ ⲉⲧⲉ ⲙ̀ⲙⲁⲩ ⲝ ϣⲁⲩⲭⲁϥ ϧⲉⲛ ϯⲥⲕⲏⲛⲏ ⲝ ⲛ̀ⲟⲩⲙⲉⲧⲙⲉⲑⲣⲉⲝ ⲛ̀ⲧⲉ ⲛⲉⲛϣⲏⲣⲓ ⲙ̀Ⲡⲓⲥⲣⲁⲏⲗ.	*فذاك وضع فى القبة شهادة لبنى اسرائيل.
Of the good things that the Lord God, did unto them, in the wilderness of Sinai.	Ⲉⲑⲃⲉ ⲛⲓⲡⲉⲑⲛⲁⲛⲉⲩ ⲝ ⲉⲧⲁϥⲁⲓⲧⲟⲩ ⲛⲉⲙⲱⲟⲩ ⲝ ⲛ̀ⲭⲉ Ⲡϭⲟⲓⲥ Ⲫϯ ⲝ ⲋⲓ ⲡ̀ϣⲁϥⲉ ⲛ̀Ⲥⲓⲛⲁ.	من أجل الخيرات التى صنعها معهم الرب الاله فى برية سيناء.
*You too O Mary, have carried in your womb, the rational Manna, that came from the Father.	*`Ⲛⲑⲟ ⲋⲱⲓ Ⲙⲁⲣⲓⲁ ⲝ ⲁⲣⲉϥⲁⲓ ϧⲉⲛ ⲧⲉⲛⲉⲭⲓ ⲙ̀ⲡⲓⲙⲁⲛⲛⲁ ⲛ̀ⲛⲟⲏⲧⲟⲛ ⲝ ⲉⲧⲁϥⲓ ⲉⲃⲟⲗϧⲉⲛ Ⲫⲓⲱⲧ.	*وأنت أيضاً يامريم حملت فى بطنك المن العقلى الذى أتى من الآب.

You bore Him without blemish, He gave unto us, His honored Body and Blood, and we lived forever.	Ⲁⲣⲉⲙⲁⲥϥ ⲁϭⲛⲉ ⲑⲱ-ⲗⲉⲃ : ⲁϥϯ ⲛⲁⲛ ⲙ̀ⲡ-ⲉϥⲥⲱⲙⲁ : ⲛⲉⲙ ⲡⲉϥ-ⲥ̀ⲛⲟϥ ⲉⲧⲧⲁⲓⲏⲟⲩⲧ : ⲁⲛⲱⲛϧ ϣⲁ ⲉ̀ⲛⲉϩ.	وولدته بغير دنس. وأعطانا جسده ودمه الكريمين فحيينا إلى الآبد .
*Wherefore we, magnify you befitt-ingly, with prophe-tic, hymnology.	*Ⲉⲑⲃⲉ ⲫⲁⲓ ⲧⲉⲛϭⲓⲥⲓ : ⲙ̀ⲙⲟ ⲁⲝⲓⲱⲥ : ϧⲉⲛ ϩⲁⲛⲩ̀ⲙⲛⲟⲗⲟⲅⲓⲁ : ⲙ̀ⲡ-ⲣⲟⲫⲏⲧⲓⲕⲟⲛ.	*من أجل هذا نعظمك باستحقاق بتماجيد نبوية.
For they spoke of you, with great honor, O Holy City, of the Great King.	Ⲭⲉ ⲁⲩⲥⲁϫⲓ ⲉⲑⲃⲏϯ : ⲛ̀ϩⲁⲛⲉ̀ⲃⲏⲟⲩⲓ ⲉⲧⲧⲁ-ⲓⲏⲟⲩⲧ : ϯⲃⲁⲕⲓ ⲉⲑⲟⲩⲁⲃ : ⲛ̀ⲧⲉ ⲡⲓⲛⲓϣϯ ⲛ̀ⲟⲩⲣⲟ.	لانهم تكلموا من أجلك بأعمال كريمة أيتها المدينة المقدسة التى للملك العظيم.
*We entreat and pray, that we may win mercy, through your intercessions, with the Lover of mankind.	*Ⲧⲉⲛϯϩⲟ ⲧⲉⲛⲧⲱⲃϩ : ⲉⲑⲣⲉⲛϣⲁϣⲛⲓ ⲉⲩⲛⲁⲓ ϩⲓ-ⲧⲉⲛ ⲛⲉⲡⲣⲉⲥⲃⲓⲁ : ⲛ̀ⲧⲟⲧϥ ⲙ̀ⲡⲓⲙⲁⲓⲣⲱⲙⲓ.	*نسأل ونطلب أن نفوز برحمة بشفاعاتك عند محب البشر.

The Fourth Explanation - التفسير الرابع

O precious golden vessel	ياقسط ذهب غالى
Which concealed the Manna	والمن مخفى فيه
It was a symbol of you	رمزاً وإشارة
O Theotokos	عليك ياوالدة الإله
O the precious gem	ياحجر الجوهر
O ship of our salvation	ياسفينة النجاة
Blessed are you O Mary	طوباك يامريم
The daughter of Zion	ياإبنه صهيون
O ladder of Jacob	ياسلم يعقوب
You held the Judge	حملت الديان
And He dwelt in your womb	وصار فى أحشاك
You gave birth to the Son of Man	المحجوب:
	وولدت ابن الانسان
He healed all the sick,	وشفى كل المرضى
And opened the eyes of the blind	وفتح أعين العميان
And raised the dead	وأقام الميت
After their burial	بعد أن كان مدفون
You are Aaron's rod	ياعصاة هرون

That did blossom	نورت الازهار
O the dome of Moses	ياقبة موسى
That is filled with light	المملوءة أنوار
You are a planted vineyard	وكرمة مغروسة
That bears the Fruit	حاملة الأثمار
Your Son granted us forgiveness	وبابنك نلنا الغفران
O hidden gem	ياجوهر مكنون
David said in the psalm,	داود قال فى المزمور
While playing on his harp	وقال على القيثارات
"The Lord chose Zion	الرب اختار صهيون
And came and dwelt in her."	وسكن فيها بثبات
These are all symbols	هذا كله مثال
Signs that resemble	ورمزاً واشارات
You O Mary	عليك يامريم
O daughter of Zion	ياابنة صهيون
The Lord chose your beauty	الرب اختار حسنك
And God dwelt in your womb	وسكن فيك الإله
You gave birth to Him	ولدتيه ورضع لبن
And He drank your milk	ثدييك بفاه

You are greatly exalted	ارتفعت جداً
You became the highest heaven	وصرت كأعلى سماه
You are above all ranks	فقت كل الرؤساء
The righteous and the saints	والأبرار والصديقين
You're above the Cherubim	فقت الشاروبيم
O the pride of virgins	ياست الأبكار
And higher than the Seraphim	وأيضاً السيرافيم
Which are full of light	المملوءة أنوار
O daughter of Joachim	ياإبنة يواقيم
From the upright seed	من نسل الأبرار
Your Son saved Adam	ابنك خلص آدم
After his bondage	بعد أن كان مسجون
O you full of grace	يامملوءة نعمة
Purer than everyone	ياطهر الأطهار
O mother of the Merciful	يا أم الرحمة
You are brighter than all light	يا نور الأنوار
Your Son illuminated the darkness	بابنك زالت الظلمة
And made us free	وقد صرنا أحرار
We inherited the kingdom	وورثنا الملكوت
Through baptism and Holy Myron	بعمادنا بالميرون

REFRAIN

المرد

Hail to you O Mary

السلام لك يامريم

O you full of grace

يامملوءة نعمة

Who are engulfed in light

يامشتملة بالانوار

O mother of the Merciful

يا ام الرحمة

Intercede for us

إشفعى فينا

On judgment day

فى يوم الزحمة

Your Son granted us salvation

بابنك نلنا الخلاص

O daughter of Zion

يا إبنة صهيون

Holy, Holy, Holy. A reading from the Gospel according to St. Luke [1: 73-77] the Evangelist, may his blessings be with us all. Amen.

قدوس قدوس قدوس . فصل من الانجيل بحسب لوقا (73 – 77 :1) البشير . بركاته تكون معنا . آمين.

"The oath, which He swore to our father Abraham: To grant us that we, being delivered from the hand of our enemies, might serve Him

"القسم الذى حلف لإبراهيم أبينا ليعطينا الخلاص بغير خوف من أيدى أعدائنا :

without fear, in holiness and righteousness before Him all the days of our life. And you, child, will be called the prophet of the Highest; For you will go before the face of the Lord to prepare His ways, to give knowledge of salvation to His people by the remission of their sins,". Glory be to God forever. Amen

لنخدمه بطهارة وبر أمامه كل أيام حياتنا : وأنت أيها الصبى تدعى نبى العلى لأنك تسبق بالمسير أمام الرب لتعد طريقه : وتعطى علم الخلاص لشعبه لمغفرة خطاياهم". والمجد لله دائماً أبدياً آمين.

5	ē	٥
You are the lampstand, made of pure gold, carrying, the ever-burning lamp.	Nθo τε †λγχnιa: ṅnoγβ εττογβηογτ : ετ϶αι ϭα πιλαμπας: εθμοϭ ṅchογ niβen.	أنت المنارة الذهب النقى الحاملة المصباح المتقد كل حين .
*That is the unapproachable, Light of the world, that proceeds from, the unapproachable light.	*Ϭτε ϥογωιni ṁπικοсмос: πιατϣϭωnτ εροϥ : πιεβολ ϭεn πιογωιni : nατϣϭωnτ εροϥ.	*الذى هو نور العالم غير المقترب اليه. الذى من النور غير المُدنى منه.
The True God, out of True God, Who was incarnate, of you without change.	Πιnογ† ṅταϥμηι : εβολϭεn ογnογ† ṅταϥμηι : εταϥϭιсαρϫ ṅϭη† : ϭεn ογμετατϣιβ†.	الاله الحق من الاله الحق .الذى تجسد منك بغير تغيير.
*By His appearance, He gave light to us, we who sit in the	*Ϭιτεn τεϥπαρογсιà : αϥερογωιni ε-	*بظهوره اضاء علينا نحن الجلوس فى

darkness, and in the shadow of death.	ⲣⲟⲛ : ϧⲁ ⲛⲏⲉⲧϩⲉⲙⲥⲓ ϧⲉⲛ ⲡⲭⲁⲕⲓ : ⲛⲉⲙ ⲧϧⲏⲓⲃⲓ ⲙⲫⲙⲟⲩ.	الظلمة وظلال الموت.
And He guided our feet, in the path of peace, through the communion, of His holy sacraments.	ⲁϥⲥⲟⲩⲧⲉⲛ ⲛⲉⲛϭⲁⲗⲁⲩⲝ : ⲉⲫⲙⲱⲓⲧ ⲛⲧⲉ ϯⲉⲓⲣⲏⲛⲏ : ϩⲓⲧⲉⲛ ϯⲕⲟⲓⲛⲱⲛⲓⲁ : ⲛⲧⲉ ⲛⲉϥⲙⲩⲥⲧⲏⲣⲓⲟⲛ ⲉⲟⲟⲩⲁⲃ.	وقوّم أرجلنا إلى طريق السلام بشركة أسراره المقدسة.
*Wherefore everyone, magnifies you, O my lady the Mother of God, the ever holy.	*Ⲉⲑⲃⲉ ⲫⲁⲓ ⲟⲩⲟⲛ ⲛⲓⲃⲉⲛ : ⲥⲉϭⲓⲥⲓ ⲙⲙⲟ : ⲧⲁϭⲟⲓⲥ ϯⲑⲉⲟⲧⲟⲕⲟⲥ : ⲉⲟⲟⲩⲁⲃ ⲛⲥⲏⲟⲩ ⲛⲓⲃⲉⲛ.	*من أجل هذا كل واحد يعظمك ياسيدتى والدة الاله القديسة كل حين.
And we too, hope to win mercy, through your intercessions, with the Lover of mankind.	Ⲁⲛⲟⲛ ϩⲱⲛ ⲧⲉⲛⲧⲱⲃϩ : ⲉⲑⲣⲉⲛϣⲁϣⲛⲓ ⲉⲩⲛⲁⲓ : ϩⲓⲧⲉⲛ ⲛⲉⲡⲣⲉⲥⲃⲓⲁ : ⲛⲧⲟⲧϥ ⲙⲡⲓⲙⲁⲓⲣⲱⲙⲓ.	ونحن أيضاً نطلب أن نفوز برحمة بشفاعاتك عند محب البشر.

391

*All the ranks on high, cannot resemble you, O golden lampstand, that carries the True Light.	*Ⲧⲥⲟⲥ ⲛⲓⲃⲉⲛ ⲉⲧϭ-ⲉⲛ ⲡ̀ϭⲓⲥⲓ : ⲙ̀ⲡⲟⲩϣ̀ⲧ-ⲉⲛⲑⲱⲛⲟⲩ ⲉ̀ⲣⲟ : ⲱ̀ ϯⲗⲩⲭⲛⲓⲁ̀ ⲛ̀ⲛⲟⲩⲃ : ⲉⲧϥⲁⲓ ϧⲁ ⲡⲓⲟⲩⲱ-ⲓⲛⲓ ⲙ̀ⲙⲏⲓ.	*كل الرتب العلوية لم تقدر أن تشبهك أيتها المنارة الذهبية حاملة النور الحقيقي.
That was made of, pure and elect gold, and was placed in, the Tabernacle.	Ⲑⲏ ⲙⲉⲛ ⲉ̀ⲧⲉ ⲙ̀ⲙⲁⲩ : ϣⲁⲩⲑⲁⲙⲓⲟⲥ ϧⲉⲛ ⲟⲩⲛⲟⲩⲃ : ⲉϥⲥⲱⲧⲡ ⲛ̀ⲕⲁⲑⲁⲣⲟⲥ : ϣⲁⲩⲭⲁⲥ ϧⲉⲛ ϯⲥⲕⲏⲛⲏ.	فتلك صُنعت من ذهب مختار نقى ووضعت فى القبة.
*That was made, by the hands of men, who brought oil for its lamps, by day and by night.	*Ⲥⲉⲉⲣⲕⲉⲃⲉⲣⲛⲓⲧⲏⲥ ⲉ̀ⲣ-ⲟⲥ : ϩⲓⲧⲉⲛ ϩⲁⲛϫⲓϫ ⲛ̀ⲣⲱⲙⲓ : ⲉⲩⲧⲛⲉϩ ⲛ̀ⲥⲁ ⲛⲉⲥⲗⲁⲙⲡⲁⲥ : ⲙ̀ⲡⲓⲉ̀ϩ-ⲟⲟⲩ ⲛⲉⲙ ⲡⲓⲉ̀ϫⲱⲣϩ.	*تُدبر بايدى البشر . اذ يُعطىَ زيت لمصابيحها نهاراً وليلاً.
He Who dwells in your womb, O Virgin Mary, gives light to every man, who	Ⲫⲏⲉⲧⲭⲏ ϧⲉⲛ ⲧⲉⲛ-ⲉϫⲓ : Ⲙⲁⲣⲓⲁ̀ ϯⲡⲁⲣ-ⲑⲉⲛⲟⲥ: ⲁϥⲉⲣⲟⲩⲱⲓ-	والذى فى بطنك يا مريم العذراء اضاء لكل انسان آت الى العالم.

comes into the world.	ⲛⲓ ⲉ̀ⲣⲱⲙⲓ ⲛⲓⲃⲉⲛ : ⲉⲑⲛⲏⲟⲩ ⲉ̀ⲡⲓⲕⲟⲥⲙⲟⲥ.	
*For He Whom you have born, is the Sun of Righteousness, and He has healed us, of all our sins.	* Ⲛ̀ⲑⲟϥ ⲅⲁⲣ ⲡⲉ ⲫ̀ⲣⲏ : ⲛ̀ⲧⲉ ϯⲇⲓⲕⲉⲟⲥⲩⲛⲏ : ⲁ̀ⲣⲉⲙⲁⲥϥ ⲁϥⲧⲁⲗϭⲟⲛ: ⲉ̀ⲃⲟⲗ ϧⲉⲛ ⲛⲉⲛⲛⲟⲃⲓ.	*لانه هو شمس البر. ولدته وشفانا من خطايانا.
Wherefore we, magnify you befittingly, with prophetic, hymnology.	Ⲉⲑⲃⲉ ⲫⲁⲓ ⲧⲉⲛϭⲓⲥⲓ : ⲙ̀ⲙⲟ ⲁⲝⲓⲱⲥ : ϧⲉⲛ ϩⲁⲛⲩⲙⲛⲟⲗⲟⲅⲓⲁ : ⲙ̀ⲡⲣⲟⲫⲏⲧⲓⲕⲟⲛ.	من أجل هذا نعظمك باستحقاق بتماجيد نبوية.
*For they spoke of you, with great honor, O Holy City, of the Great King.	*Ϫⲉ ⲁⲩⲥⲁϫⲓ ⲉⲑⲃⲏⲧ : ⲛ̀ϩⲁⲛϩⲃⲏⲟⲩⲓ ⲉⲧⲧⲁⲓⲏⲟⲩⲧ : ϯⲃⲁⲕⲓ ⲉ̀ⲑⲟⲩⲁⲃ : ⲛ̀ⲧⲉ ⲡⲓⲛⲓϣϯ ⲛ̀ⲟⲩⲣⲟ.	*لانهم تكلموا من أجلك بأعمال كريمة أيتها المدينة المقدسة التى للملك العظيم.
We entreat and pray, that we may win mercy, through your	Ⲧⲉⲛϯϩⲟ ⲧⲉⲛⲧⲱⲃϩ : ⲉⲑⲣⲉⲛϣⲁϣⲛⲓ ⲉⲩⲛⲁⲓ	نسأل ونطلب أن نفوز برحمة بشفاعاتك عند

intercessions, with the Lover of mankind.	ϩⲓⲧⲉⲛ ⲛⲉⲡⲣⲉⲥⲃⲓⲁ : ⲛ̀ⲧⲟⲧϥ ⲙ̀ⲡⲓⲙⲁⲓⲣⲱⲙⲓ.	محب البشر.

The Fifth Explanation التفسير الخامس

The Lord spoke to Moses	الله كلم موسى
Upon the mountain saying	فوق جبل الطور أجهار
Arise build a lampstand	قم أصنع منارة
Overlay it with the chosen gold	من الذهب المختار
Place upon it seven candles	وفيها سبعة سراج
To shine by day and night	تنير ليل و نهار
From the inside of the dome	من داخل القبة
And from the ark	نيم تى كيفوتوس
He made it according to the plan	فصنع موسى كما قال
And built the lampstand	وصنع المنارة
Out of precious gold	من الذهب العال
Blessed are you O chosen	طوباك يامختارة
Blessed are you O Mary	طوباك يامريم

You gave meaning to the symbols	فقت كل الامثال
Your light dawned upon us	ونورك اشرق فينا
We the Christians	انون خانى
	إخريستيانوس

You are the lampstand	أنت هى المنارة
That is filled with light	المملوءة انوار
And its light shined	وشعاع نورها أشرق
Upon all the earth	على كل الأقطار

O Mary you are higher	وعليت يامريم
Than all the upright fathers	عن الآباء الأبرار
The Holy Spirit came upon you	حل بروح قدسه
The Holy Lord dwelt in you	فيك الرب القدوس

Moses did see you	رآك موسى
Upon Mount Tabor	فوق جبل الطور
A planted tree	شجرة مغروسة
Engulfed in light	محاطة بالأنوار

Through you O Mary	بك يامريم فزنا
We became victorious	بفرح وبهجة وسرور
No one has received	من نال مانلت
What you have been granted	فى سائر بى كوسموس

There is no one like you	ليس من يشبهك
On Earth or in Heaven	فى الأرض ولا فى
The Lord favored you	السموات
Above all the creations	والرب فَضَّلَكِ
	عن كل المخلوقات

Many spoke of you	وقد شهدوا عنك
In prophesies and proverbs	فى اسفار ونبوات
The fathers called you	سماك الآباء
The fair dove	تى إتشرومبى إثنيسوس

David your father	داود أبوك
Said in the Psalms	فى المزمور قد قال
"The Lord choose your beauty	الرب إختار حسنك
And increased you in splendor."	وزادك نور وجمال

He dwelt in your womb	وحل فى بطنك
Nine full months	تسعة أشهر بكمال
You bore Him and Fed Him milk	ولدتيه ورضع لبنك
According to the angel's decree	كبشارة بى أنجيلوس

He likewise said	وقال ايضاً
O mother of Man	ياأم الإنسان

A Man dwelt in her	وإنسان حل فيها
The Most High King	وهو الملك الديان

He Who overshadowed her	الذى انشأها وأرسل لها
And sent her His Holy Spirit	روح قدسه ببيان
You gave birth to the True God	ووضعت الله الحق
The Creator of souls	الخالق كل نفوس

REFRAIN	المرد

Hail to you O Mary	السلام لك يامريم
O you full of grace	يامملوءة نعمة
Who are engulfed in light	يامشتملة بالانوار
O mother of the Merciful	ياام الرحمة
Intercede for us	إشفعى فينا.
On judgment day	فى يوم الزحمة
Your Son granted us salvation	بابنك نلنا الخلاص
O daughter of Zion	ياابنة صهيون

Holy, Holy, Holy. A reading from the Gospel according to St. Luke [1: 78-79] the Evangelist, may his blessings be with us all. Amen.	قدوس قدوس قدوس . فصل من الانجيل بحسب لوقا [79-78:1] البشير بركاته تكون معنا

. آمين.

"Through the tender mercy of our God, with which the Dayspring from on high has visited us; To give light to those who sit in darkness and the shadow of death, to guide our feet into the way of peace." Glory be to God forever. Amen

"من أجل تحنن رحمة إلهنا بهذه الذى افتقدنا به مشرقاً من العلاء ليضئ للجالسين فى الظلمة وظلال الموت : لتستقيم أرجلنا إلى سبل السلام".
والمجد لله دائماً أبدياً آمين.

6	ⲋ̄	٦
*You are the censer, made of pure gold, carrying the Blessed, and Live Coal.	*Ⲛ̅ⲑⲟ ⲧⲉ ϯϣⲟⲩⲣⲏ : ⲛ̅ⲛⲟⲩⲃ ⲛ̅ⲕⲁⲑⲁⲣⲟⲥ : ⲉⲧϥⲁⲓ ϧⲁ ⲡⲓϫⲉⲃⲥ : ⲛ̅ⲭⲣⲱⲙ ⲉⲧⲥ̅ⲙⲁⲣⲱⲟⲩⲧ.	*أنت هى المجمرة الذهب النقى حاملة جمر النار المباركة.
That is taken, from the altar, to purge the sins, and take away the iniquities.	Ⲫⲏⲉⲧⲟⲩϭⲓ ⲙ̅ⲙⲟϥ : ⲉⲃⲟⲗϧⲉⲛ ⲡⲓⲙⲁⲛⲉⲣϣⲱⲟⲩϣⲓ : ϣⲁϥⲧⲟⲩⲃⲟ ⲛ̅ⲛⲓⲛⲟⲃⲓ : ⲛ̅ⲧⲉ ϥⲱⲗⲓ ⲛ̅ⲛⲓⲁ̀ⲛⲟⲙⲓⲁ̀.	الذى يؤخذ من المذبح يطهر الخطايا ويمحو الآثام.
*Which is God the Word, Who took flesh from you, and offered Himself as incense, to God His Father.	*Ⲉⲧⲉ Ⲫ̄ϯ ⲡⲓⲗⲟⲅⲟⲥ : ⲉⲧⲁϥϭⲓⲥⲁⲣⲝ ⲛ̅ϧⲏϯ : ⲁϥⲟⲗϥ ⲉ̀ⲡϣⲱⲓ ⲛ̅ⲟⲩⲥ̀ⲟⲓⲛⲟⲩϥⲓ : ϣⲁ Ⲫ̄ϯ Ⲡⲉϥⲓⲱⲧ.	*أى الله الكلمة الذى تجسد منك ورفع ذاتة بخوراً إلى الله أبيه.
Wherefore every-one, magnifies you, O my lady the	Ⲉⲑⲃⲉ ⲫⲁⲓ ⲟⲩⲟⲛ ⲛⲓⲃⲉⲛ : ⲥⲉϭⲓⲥⲓ ⲙ̅ⲙⲟ : ⲧⲁϭⲟⲓⲥ	من أجل هذا كل واحد يعظمك ياسيدتى والدة

Mother of God, the ever holy.	ϯⲑⲉⲟⲧⲟⲕⲟⲥ ⲉⲑⲟⲩⲁⲃ ⲛ̀ⲭⲟⲩ ⲛⲓⲃⲉⲛ.	الاله القديسة كل حين .
*And we too, hope to win mercy, through your intercessions, with the Lover of mankind.	*Ⲁⲛⲟⲛ ϩⲱⲛ ⲧⲉⲛⲧⲱⲃϩ ⲉⲑⲣⲉⲛϣⲁϣⲛⲓ ⲉⲩⲛⲁⲓ ϩⲓⲧⲉⲛ ⲛⲉⲡⲣⲉⲥⲃⲓⲁ ⲛ̀ⲧⲟⲧϥ ⲙ̀ⲡⲓⲙⲁⲓⲣⲱⲙⲓ.	*ونحن أيضاً نطلب أن نفوز برحمة بشفاعاتك عند محب البشر.
Wherefore truly, I do not err, whenever I call you, the golden censer:	Ⲧⲟⲧⲉ ⲁ̀ⲗⲏⲑⲱⲥ ⲛ̀ⲧϣⲱϥⲧ ⲁⲛ ⲛ̀ϩⲗⲓ ⲁⲓϣⲁⲛⲙⲟⲩϯ ⲉ̀ⲣⲟ ϫⲉ ϯϣⲟⲩⲣⲏ ⲛ̀ⲛⲟⲩⲃ.	حينئذ بالحقيقة لا أخطيئ فى شئ إذا ما دعوتك المجمرة الذهب.
*For therein, is offered, the choice incense, before the Holies.	*Ⲑⲏ ⲙⲉⲛ ⲉ̀ⲧⲉ ⲙ̀ⲙⲁⲩ ϣⲁⲩⲧⲁⲗⲟ ⲉ̀ⲡϣⲱⲓ ⲛ̀ϧⲏⲧⲥ ⲙ̀ⲡⲓⲥⲑⲟⲓⲛⲟⲩϥⲓ ⲉⲧⲥⲱⲧⲡ ⲙ̀ⲡⲉⲙⲑⲟ ⲛ̀ⲛⲏⲉ̀ⲑⲟⲩⲁⲃ.	*فتلك يَرفع فيها البخور المختار أمام الأقداس.
Wherein God takes away, the sins of the people, through the burnt offerings, and	Ϣⲁⲣⲉ Ⲫϯ ⲱ̀ⲗⲓ ⲙ̀ⲙⲁⲩ ⲛ̀ⲛⲓⲛⲟⲃⲓ ⲛ̀ⲧⲉ ⲡⲓⲗⲁⲟⲥ ⲉ̀ⲃⲟⲗϩⲓⲧⲉⲛ	ويرفع الله هناك خطايا الشعب من قبل المحرقات ورائحةالبخور.

the aroma of incense.	ⲡⲓⲥⲑⲟⲓⲁ : ⲛⲉⲙ ⲡⲓⲥⲑⲟ-ⲟⲓ ⲛ̀ⲧⲉ ⲡⲓⲥⲑⲟⲓⲛⲟⲩϥⲓ.	
*You too O Mary, have carried in your womb, the Invisible, Word Of the Father.	* Ⲛⲑⲟ ϩⲱⲓ Ⲙⲁⲣⲓⲁ : ⲁⲣⲉϥⲁⲓ ϧⲉⲛ ⲧⲉⲛⲉϫⲓ : ⲙ̀ⲡⲓⲁⲧⲱ̀ⲛⲁⲩ ⲉ̀ⲣⲟϥ : ⲛ̀ⲗⲟⲅⲟⲥ ⲛ̀ⲧⲉ Ⲫⲓⲱⲧ.	*وأنت يامريم حملت فى بطنك الغير منظور كلمة الآب.
He who offered Himself, as an acceptable sacrifice, upon the Cross, for the salvation of our race.	Ⲫⲁⲓ ⲉⲧⲁϥⲉⲛϥ ⲉ̀ⲡ̀ϣⲱⲓ : ⲛ̀ⲟⲩⲑⲩⲥⲓⲁ ⲉⲥϣⲏⲡ : ϩⲓ-ϫⲉⲛ ⲡⲓⲥ̀ⲧⲁⲩⲣⲟⲥ : ϧⲁ ⲡ̀ⲟⲩϫⲁⲓ ⲙ̀ⲡⲉⲛⲅⲉⲛⲟⲥ.	هذا الذى أصعد ذاته ذبيحة مقبولة على الصليب عن خلاص جنسنا.
*Wherefore we, magnify you befittingly, with prophetic, hymnology.	*Ⲉⲑⲃⲉ ⲫⲁⲓ ⲧⲉⲛϭⲓⲥⲓ : ⲙ̀ⲙⲟ ⲁⲝⲓⲱⲥ : ϧⲉⲛ ϩⲁⲛⲩ̀ⲙⲛⲟⲗⲟⲅⲓⲁ : ⲙ̀ⲡ̀-ⲣⲟⲫⲏⲧⲓⲕⲟⲛ.	*من أجل هذا نعظمك باستحقاق بتماجيد نبوية.
For they spoke of you, with great honor, O Holy City, of the Great King.	Ⲭⲉ ⲁⲩⲥⲁϫⲓ ⲉⲑⲃⲏ† : ⲛ̀ϩⲁⲛϩ̀ⲃⲏⲟⲩⲓ ⲉⲩⲧⲁ-ⲓⲏⲟⲩⲧ : †ⲃⲁⲕⲓ ⲉ̀ⲑⲟⲩⲁⲃ :	لانهم تكلموا من أجلك بأعمال كريمة أيتها المدينة المقدسة

	ⲚⲦⲈ ⲠⲒⲚⲒϢϮ Ⲛ̀ⲞⲨⲢⲞ.	التى للملك العظيم.
*We entreat and pray, that we may win mercy, through your intercessions, with the Lover of mankind.	*ϮⲈⲚϮϨⲞ ⲦⲈⲚⲦⲰⲂϨ : ⲈⲐⲢⲈⲚϢⲁϢⲚⲒ ⲈⲨⲚⲁⲓ ϨⲒⲦⲈⲚ ⲚⲈⲠⲢⲈⲥⲂⲒⲁ : Ⲛ̀ⲦⲞⲦϤ Ⲙ̀ⲠⲒⲘⲁⲒⲢⲰⲘⲒ.	*نسأل ونطلب أن نفوز برحمة بشفاعاتك عند محب البشر.

The Sixth Explanation التفسير السادس

You are Aaron's censer	ياشورية هرون
Who carries the coal	الحاملة جمر النار
Its' incense and aroma	وبخورها وعنبرها
Filled all the universe	ملأ كل الأقطار
Your presence O Mary	بوجودك يامريم
Saved us from hell's fire	فزنا من حر النار
You fulfilled the promise	وبك تم الموعود
According to the prophesies	كما عنك تنبأون
You are the censer	أنت هى الشورية
In it are the ointment and incense	فيها طيب وبخور
You held the Son of God	حملت إبن الله

Light of Light	إله نور من نور
He dwelt in your womb	وحل فى بطنك
For nine months	تسعة شهور
You bore Him and fed Him milk	ولدتيه ورضع لبنك
Like any other human	كسائر المخلوقين
You are Aaron's censer	ياشورية هارون
In it is the incense amber	فيها بخور من عنبر
O daughter of David	ياإبنة داود
O precious stone	ياحجر الجوهر
You held He Who is worshipped	حملت المعبود
And He appeared from you	وظهر منك أجهار
He freed those in bondage	وفك كل وثاقات
And trampled down Satan	وكسر فخ الاركون
You are the censer	انت هى الشورية
The aroma of your incense spread	بخور طيبك فاح
And filled all the earth	وملأ المسكونة
And through you we received joy	وبك نلنا الأفراح
We offer you praise	نقرئك كل سلام
Evening and morning	فى كل مساء وصباح

403

O pillar of faith	ياعمود دين
For the Orthodox people	الأرثوذكســـــــــيين
Solomon spoke of you	سليمان قال عنك
In the Song of Songs saying	فى نشيد الأنشاد
"My sister and my friend	أختى وصديقتى واليك
The Lord favored her"	الرب اراد
Your sweet aroma spread	روائح طيبك فاح
From the incense and increased	من عنبر وزاد
He gave symbols of you	وقال عنك امثال
In many prophecies	فى النبوات يشهدون
Blessed are you O Mary	طوباك يامريم
O the mother of Jesus Christ	أم ايسوس بى
O pure sanctuary	اخريستوس
And the shelter of the Holy	ياهيكل طاهر
	وحجاب للقدوس
Protect your Son's people	احفظى شعب ابنك
Deacons and presbyters	شمامسة وقسوس
And all the lay people	وجميع من فى البيعة
And those gathered together	الشعب المجتمعون

Hail to you O Mary	السلام لك يامريم
O sanctuary for protection	ياهيكل منصان
Your light dawned upon us	نورك أشرق فينا
And filled all the earth	وملأ كل الأكوان
You held the Creator	وحملت الخالق
The Son of God the Judge	ابن الله الديان
You gave birth to His humanity	وولدتيه انسان
With the united divinity	باللاهوت متحدون

REFRAIN   المرد

Hail to you O Mary	السلام لك يامريم
O you full of grace	يامملوءة نعمة
Who are engulfed in light	يامشتملة بالانوار
O mother of the Merciful	ياام الرحمة
Intercede for us	إشفعى فينا
On judgment day	فى يوم الزحمة
Your Son granted us salvation	بابنك نلنا الخلاص
O daughter of Zion	ياإبنة صهيون

Holy, Holy, Holy. A reading from the Gospel according to St. Luke the Evangelist, may his blessings be with us all. Amen.

قدوس قدوس قدوس فصل من الانجيل بحسب لوقا البشير . بركاته تكون معنا . آمين.

The Gospel According to St. Luke Ch. 2: 29-32)	(Ⲉⲩⲁⲅⲅⲉⲗⲓⲟⲛ ⲕⲁⲧⲁ Ⲗⲟⲩⲕⲁⲛ)(ⲃ̄ · ⲕ̄ⲑ̄-ⲗ̄ⲃ̄)	(الأنجيل من لوقا (٢: ٢٩-٣٢)
"Lord, now You are letting Your servant depart in peace, according to Your word; For my eyes have seen Your salvation which You have prepared before the face of all peoples, a light to bring revelation to the Gentiles, and the glory of Your people Israel." Glory be to God forever. Amen.	Ⲧⲛⲟⲩ ⲡⲁⲛⲏⲃ ⲭⲛⲁⲭⲁ ⲡⲉⲕⲃⲱⲕ ⲉⲃⲟⲗ · ϧⲉⲛ ⲟⲩϩⲓⲣⲏⲛⲏ ⲕⲁⲧⲁ ⲡⲉⲕⲥⲁϫⲓ · ϫⲉ ⲁⲩⲛⲁⲩ ⲛ̀ϫⲉ ⲛⲁⲃⲁⲗ ⲉ̀ⲡⲉ-ⲕⲛⲟϩⲉⲙ · ⲫⲏⲉⲧⲁⲕ-ⲥⲉⲃⲧⲱⲧϥ ⲙ̀ⲡⲉ-ⲙ̀ⲑⲟ ⲛ̀ⲛⲓⲗⲁⲟⲥ ⲧⲏⲣⲟⲩ. Ⲟⲩⲟⲩⲱⲓⲛⲓ ⲁⲩϭⲱⲣⲡ ⲉ̀-ⲃⲟⲗ ⲛ̀ⲧⲉ ϩⲁⲛⲉⲑⲛⲟⲥ · ⲛⲉⲙ ⲟⲩⲱⲟⲩ ⲛ̀ⲧⲉ ⲡⲉⲕⲗⲁⲟⲥ Ⲡⲓⲥⲣⲁⲏⲗ	"الآن ياسيد تطلق عبدك بسلام كقولك. لأن عينيَّ قد ابصرتا خلاصك الذى أعددتة قدام جميع الشعوب. نوراً تجلى للأمم ومجداً لشعبك اسرائيل". والمجد لله دائما.

7	Ⲍ̄	٧
Hail to you Mary, the beautiful dove, who gave birth to, God the Word.	Ⲭⲉⲣⲉ ⲛⲉ Ⲙⲁⲣⲓⲁ : ϯϭ̄-ⲣⲟⲙⲡⲓ ⲉⲑⲛⲉⲥⲱⲥ : ⲑⲏ-ⲉⲧⲁⲥⲙⲓⲥⲓ ⲛⲁⲛ : ⲙ̀Ⲫϯ ⲡⲓⲗⲟⲅⲟⲥ .	السلام لك يامريم الحمامة الحسنة التى ولدت لنا الله الكلمة.
*You are the flower, of incense, that has blossomed, from the root of Jesse.	* Ⲛ̄ⲑⲟ ⲧⲉ ϯϩ̀ⲣⲏⲣⲓ : ⲛ̀ⲧⲉ ⲡⲓⲥⲑⲟⲓⲛⲟⲩϥⲓ : ⲑⲏⲉⲧⲁⲥϥⲓⲣⲓ ⲉ̀ⲃⲟⲗ : ϧⲉⲛ ⲟ̀ⲛⲟⲩⲛⲓ ⲛ̀Ⲓⲉⲥⲥⲉ .	*أنت زهرة البخور التى أينعت من أصل يسىَّ.
The rod of Aaron, which blossomed, without planting or watering, resembles you.	Ⲡⲓϣ̀ⲃⲱⲧ ⲛ̀ⲧⲉ Ⲁⲁⲣⲱⲛ: ⲉ̀ⲧⲁϥϥⲓⲣⲓ ⲉ̀ⲃⲟⲗ : ⲭⲱⲣⲓⲥ ϭⲟ ⲛⲉⲙ ⲧ̀ⲥⲟ : ϥ̀ⲟⲓ ⲛ̀ⲧⲩⲡⲟⲥ ⲛⲉ .	عصا هرون التى أزهرت بغير غرس ولا سقى هى مثال لك.
*O who gave birth to Christ, our true God, without the seed of man, and remained a virgin.	*Ⲱⲑⲏⲉⲧⲁⲥⲙⲉⲥ Ⲡⲓⲭ̀-ⲣⲓⲥⲧⲟⲥ: Ⲡⲉⲛⲛⲟⲩϯ ϧⲉⲛ ⲟⲩⲙⲉⲑⲙⲏⲓ : ⲁϭⲛⲉ ⲥ̀ⲡ-ⲉⲣⲙⲁ ⲛ̀ⲣⲱⲙⲓ: ⲉⲥⲟⲓ ⲙ̀-ⲡⲁⲣⲑⲉⲛⲟⲥ .	*يامن ولدت المسيح إلهنا بالحقيقة وبغير زرع بشر وأنت عذراء.
Wherefore everyo-	Ⲉⲑⲃⲉ ⲫⲁⲓ ⲟⲩⲟⲛ ⲛⲓⲃⲉⲛ :	من أجل هذا كل

ne, magnifies you, O my lady the Mother of God, the ever holy.	сєбісі ѝмо : таϭоіс ⲧⲑⲉⲟⲧⲟⲕⲟⲥ : ⲉⲑⲟⲩⲁⲃ ⲛ̀ⲥⲏⲟⲩ ⲛⲓⲃⲉⲛ.	واحد يعظمك ياسيدتى والدة الاله القديسة كل حين .
*And we too, hope to win mercy, through your inter-cessions, with the Lover of mankind.	*Ⲁⲛⲟⲛ ⳉⲱⲛ ⲧⲉⲛⲧ-ⲱⲃⳉ : ⲉⲑⲣⲉⲛϣⲁϣⲛⲓ ⲉⲩⲛⲁⲓ : ⳉⲓⲧⲉⲛ ⲛⲉⲡ-ⲣⲉⲥⲃⲓⲁ̀ : ⲛ̀ⲧⲟⲧϥ ⲙ̀ⲡⲓ-ⲙⲁⲓⲣⲱⲙⲓ.	*ونحن أيضاً نطلب أن نفوز برحمة بشفاعاتك عند محب البشر.
You are called righteous, O St Mary, the Second Tabernacle, belon-ging to the Holies.	Ⲥⲉⲙⲟⲩϯ ⲉ̀ⲣⲟ ⲁⲓⲕⲉⲟⲥ : ⲱ̀ ⲑⲏⲉⲑⲟⲩⲁⲃ Ⲙⲁⲣⲓⲁ̀ : ϫⲉ ϯⲙⲁⳉⲥⲛⲟⲩϯ ⲛ̀ⲥⲕⲏⲛⲏ : ⲛ̀ⲧⲉ ⲛⲏⲉ̀ⲑⲟⲩⲁⲃ.	مدعوة أنت بالحقيقة أيتها القديسة مريم التى القبة للاقداس.
*Wherein is placed, The rod of Aaron, and the holy flower, of the incense.	*Ⲑⲏⲉⲧⲟⲩⲭⲏ ⲛ̀ⳋⲏⲧⲥ : ⲛ̀ϫⲉ ⲡⲓϣⲃⲱⲧ ⲛ̀ⲧⲉ Ⲁⲁⲣⲱⲛ : ⲛⲉⲙ ϯⲉ̀ⲣ-ⲏⲣⲓ ⲉ̀ⲑⲟⲩⲁⲃ : ⲛ̀ⲧⲉ ⲡⲓⲥⲑⲟⲓⲛⲟⲩϥⲓ.	*تلك الموضوع فيها عصا هرون والزهرة المقدسة التى للبخور.

You are filled with purity, within and without, O pure Tabernacle, the dwelling of the saints.	Ⲧⲉⲭⲟⲗϩ ⲙ̀ⲡⲓⲧⲟⲩⲃⲟ : ⲥⲁϧⲟⲩⲛ ⲛⲉⲙ ⲥⲁⲃⲟⲗ : ⲱ̀ ϯⲥⲕⲏⲛⲏ ⲛ̀ⲕⲁⲑⲁⲣⲟⲥ : ⲫⲙⲁⲛϣⲱⲡⲓ ⲛ̀ⲛⲓⲆⲓⲕⲉⲟⲥ.	أنت مشتملة بالطهارة من داخل ومن خارج أيتها القبة النقية مسكن الصديقين.
*The hosts of the high standings, and the chorus of the just, glorify you, and your blessedness.	*Ⲛⲓⲧⲁⲅⲙⲁ ⲛ̀ⲧⲉ ⲡ̀ϭⲓⲥⲓ : ⲛⲉⲙ ⲡ̀ⲭⲟⲣⲟⲥ ⲛ̀ⲧⲉ ⲛⲓⲑⲙⲏⲓ : ⲥⲉⲉⲣⲉⲩⲆⲟⲝⲁⲍⲓⲛ : ⲛ̀ⲛⲉⲙⲁⲕⲁⲣⲓⲥⲙⲟⲥ.	*طغمات العلاء وصفوف الابرار يمجدون طوباويتك.
Wherefore we, magnify you befittingly, with prophetic, hymnology.	Ⲉⲑⲃⲉ ⲫⲁⲓ ⲧⲉⲛϭⲓⲥⲓ : ⲙ̀ⲙⲟ ⲁⲝⲓⲱⲥ : ϧⲉⲛ ϩⲁⲛϯⲙⲛⲟⲗⲟⲅⲓⲁ : ⲙ̀ⲡⲣⲟⲫⲏⲧⲓⲕⲟⲛ.	من أجل هذا نعظمك باستحقاق بتماجيد نبوية.
*For they spoke of you, with great honor, O Holy City, of the Great King.	*Ⲭⲉ ⲁⲩⲥⲁϫⲓ ⲉⲑⲃⲏϯ ⲓ̀ⲛϩⲁⲛϩⲃⲏⲟⲩⲓ ⲉⲩⲧⲁⲓⲏⲟⲩⲧ : ϯⲃⲁⲕⲓ ⲉ̀ⲑⲟⲩⲁⲃ ⲓ̀ⲛⲧⲉ ⲡⲓⲛⲓϣϯ ⲛ̀ⲟⲩⲣⲟ.	*لانهم تكلموا من أجلك بأعمال كريمة أيتها المدينة المقدسة التى للملك العظيم.

409

| We entreat and pray, that we may win mercy, through your intercessions, with the Lover of mankind. | Ⲧⲉⲛϯϩⲟ ⲧⲉⲛⲧⲱⲃϩ : ⲉⲑⲣⲉⲛϣⲁϣⲛⲓ ⲉⲧⲛⲁⲓ: ϩⲓⲧⲉⲛ ⲛⲉⲡⲣⲉⲥⲃⲓⲁ : ⲛ̀ⲧⲟⲧϥ̀ⲙ̀ⲡⲓⲙⲁⲓⲣⲱⲙⲓ. | نسأل ونطلب أن نفوز برحمة بشفاعاتك عند محب البشر. |

The Seventh Explanation التفسير السابع

O Theotokos You are called | دعيت أم الله
The daughter of Joachim | ياإبنة يواقيم
You became the highest heaven | وصرت كأعلى سماه
You are higher than the Cherubim | وفقت الكاروبيم

The Fountain of Life came from you | ظهر منك ينبوع الحياة
He healed all the sick | وأبرأ كل سقيم
He returned the lost sheep | ورد الخروف الضال
To the Paradise of Joy | وحطم فخ الأركون

You are the dome of Moses | ياقبة موسى
That is filled with Light | يامملوءة انوار
You are the ark of covenant | ياتابوت العهد
Containing the secrets | وفيه كل الاسرار

O the flower of incense | يازهرة الاطياب

Your aroma filled the earth	بخورك ملأ الأقطار
O precious treasure	ياكنز الجوهر
O Aaron's rod	ياعصاة هرون
O golden vessel	ياقسط ذهب غالى
In it the hidden Manna	والمن مخفى فيه
O pure sanctuary	ياهيكل طاهر
Wherein God was delighted and -dwelled	أحبه الله وسكن فيه
He who believes in Him	ومن يؤمن باسمه
Shall live after death	بعد الموت يحييه
O you pure altar	يامذبح طاهر
Carrying the hidden secrets	حامل السر المكنون
Hail to you O Mary	السلام لك يامريم
O favored above all virgins	ياست العذارى
The Fathers called you	سماك الآباء
"The golden lampstand"	كنزاً ومنارة
Many spoke of you	وكم ضربوا عنك
With symbols and proverbs	رمزاً وإشارة
O the aroma of incense	يا بخور العنبر
In Aaron's censer	فى شورية هارون

O sanctuary and protection	ياهيكل وحجاب
A dwelling place for the Trinity	مسكن للثالوث
O Throne of God the Father	ياكرسى الله الآب
The Lord of Hosts	رب الصاباؤوت
Through you we were awarded	بك يا مريم فزنا
The Kingdom of Joy	بنعيم الملكوت
Blessed are you O Mary	طوباك يامريم
The sister of Solomon	إتسونى ان سولومون
Do not forget your servant	لاتنسى عبدك
For I am a poor sinner	لأنى خاطى ومسكين
I plead for your intercessions	وأرجو شفاعتك
On judgment day	فى الموقف يوم الدين
Before Christ your Son	عند يسوع ابنك
Be unto me a helper and provider	كونى لى عوناً ومعين
So He may forgive me	لكى يغفر لى ذنبى
The multitude of my sins	ومن قد سلفون

REFRAIN

المرد

Hail to you O Mary	السلام لك يامريم
O you full of grace	يامملوءة نعمة
Who are engulfed in light	يامشتملة بالانوار
O mother of the Merciful	يا ام الرحمة
Intercede for us	إشفعى فينا
On judgment day	فى يوم الزحمة
Your Son granted us salvation	بابنك نلنا الخلاص
O daughter of Zion	ياإبنة صهيون

Shere ne Maria - Ⲭⲉⲣⲉ ⲛⲉ

Ⲙⲁⲣⲓⲁ – السلام لك يا مريم

Ⲭⲉⲣⲉ ⲛⲉ Ⲙⲁⲣⲓⲁ:	I start my praise	أبدأ فيك بمديح
Ⲭⲉⲣⲉ ⲛⲉ Ⲙⲁⲣⲓⲁ:	Words from my heart	نظم بقلب صحيح
Ⲭⲉⲣⲉ ⲛⲉ Ⲙⲁⲣⲓⲁ:	I cry out and say	وأشرح فيك وأصيح
Ⲭⲉⲣⲉ ⲛⲉ Ⲙⲁⲣⲓⲁ:	A rhythmic song	قول غالي موزون
Ⲭⲉⲣⲉ ⲛⲉ Ⲙⲁⲣⲓⲁ:	Every needy one	بمديحك يرتاح
Ⲭⲉⲣⲉ ⲛⲉ Ⲙⲁⲣⲓⲁ:	Rejoices and feels calm	كل ذليل محتاج
Ⲭⲉⲣⲉ ⲛⲉ Ⲙⲁⲣⲓⲁ:	You brought all joy	يابدء الأفراح
Ⲭⲉⲣⲉ ⲛⲉ Ⲙⲁⲣⲓⲁ:	To every living soul	لك عندي عربون
Ⲭⲉⲣⲉ ⲛⲉ Ⲙⲁⲣⲓⲁ:	O sweet fruit	ثمرة عربونى
Ⲭⲉⲣⲉ ⲛⲉ Ⲙⲁⲣⲓⲁ:	Apple of my eye	هى طب عيونى
Ⲭⲉⲣⲉ ⲛⲉ Ⲙⲁⲣⲓⲁ:	No one can deny	فى مدحك لامونى
Ⲭⲉⲣⲉ ⲛⲉ Ⲙⲁⲣⲓⲁ:	I'm immersed in your love	فى حبك مفتون
Ⲭⲉⲣⲉ ⲛⲉ Ⲙⲁⲣⲓⲁ:	The jealous were lost	تاهوا عزالى
Ⲭⲉⲣⲉ ⲛⲉ Ⲙⲁⲣⲓⲁ:	And did not know my condition	ماعلموا حالى
Ⲭⲉⲣⲉ ⲛⲉ Ⲙⲁⲣⲓⲁ:	Your praise is precious	ومديحك غالى
Ⲭⲉⲣⲉ ⲛⲉ Ⲙⲁⲣⲓⲁ:	Like refined gold	كالذهب الموزون

414

Ϫⲉⲣⲉ ⲛⲉ Ⲙⲁⲣⲓⲁ:	Gabriel came	جاءك غبريال
Ϫⲉⲣⲉ ⲛⲉ Ⲙⲁⲣⲓⲁ:	With tidings and name	ببشائر وأقوال
Ϫⲉⲣⲉ ⲛⲉ Ⲙⲁⲣⲓⲁ:	Emmanuel became	وسكن فيك المتعال
Ϫⲉⲣⲉ ⲛⲉ Ⲙⲁⲣⲓⲁ:	In your womb the same	سر خفي مكنون
Ϫⲉⲣⲉ ⲛⲉ Ⲙⲁⲣⲓⲁ:	The Logos dwelt	حل بكلمته
Ϫⲉⲣⲉ ⲛⲉ Ⲙⲁⲣⲓⲁ:	Shined with power	وأشرق بقدرته
Ϫⲉⲣⲉ ⲛⲉ Ⲙⲁⲣⲓⲁ:	You became heaven	صرت كسمائه
Ϫⲉⲣⲉ ⲛⲉ Ⲙⲁⲣⲓⲁ:	Fruitful and green	ياعوسج بغصون
Ϫⲉⲣⲉ ⲛⲉ Ⲙⲁⲣⲓⲁ:	Savior of the world	مخلص العالم
Ϫⲉⲣⲉ ⲛⲉ Ⲙⲁⲣⲓⲁ:	Became in your womb	صارفيك قائم
Ϫⲉⲣⲉ ⲛⲉ Ⲙⲁⲣⲓⲁ:	Was born of you	واستيقظ النائم
Ϫⲉⲣⲉ ⲛⲉ Ⲙⲁⲣⲓⲁ:	The Holy Spirit in you	ومخمور بفنون
Ϫⲉⲣⲉ ⲛⲉ Ⲙⲁⲣⲓⲁ:	David in the Psalms	داود فى المزمور
Ϫⲉⲣⲉ ⲛⲉ Ⲙⲁⲣⲓⲁ:	Said you are the bride	قال بنات صور
Ϫⲉⲣⲉ ⲛⲉ Ⲙⲁⲣⲓⲁ:	Offerings and gifts	بهدايا ونذور
Ϫⲉⲣⲉ ⲛⲉ Ⲙⲁⲣⲓⲁ:	Were given to the One	قالوا فيك بفنون
Ϫⲉⲣⲉ ⲛⲉ Ⲙⲁⲣⲓⲁ:	In the book of Proverbs	ذكروك فى الامثال
Ϫⲉⲣⲉ ⲛⲉ Ⲙⲁⲣⲓⲁ:	In image and likeness	على شبه ومثال
Ϫⲉⲣⲉ ⲛⲉ Ⲙⲁⲣⲓⲁ:	The fakhory said	والفاخورى قال
Ϫⲉⲣⲉ ⲛⲉ Ⲙⲁⲣⲓⲁ:	Like Aaron's rod	شبه عصاة هارون
Ϫⲉⲣⲉ ⲛⲉ Ⲙⲁⲣⲓⲁ:	Myriads and myriads	ربوات ثم ألوف
Ϫⲉⲣⲉ ⲛⲉ Ⲙⲁⲣⲓⲁ:	Around the throne stands	حول العرش وقوف

Ⲭⲉⲣⲉ ⲛⲉ Ⲙⲁⲣⲓⲁ:	Hosts and ranks	وطغمات وصفوف
Ⲭⲉⲣⲉ ⲛⲉ Ⲙⲁⲣⲓⲁ:	Many martyrs	وشهداء متصلون
Ⲭⲉⲣⲉ ⲛⲉ Ⲙⲁⲣⲓⲁ:	You are beyond any description	زدت في الأوصاف
Ⲭⲉⲣⲉ ⲛⲉ Ⲙⲁⲣⲓⲁ:	High above all explanation	عن كل الأوصاف
Ⲭⲉⲣⲉ ⲛⲉ Ⲙⲁⲣⲓⲁ:	You lived in purity	ومشيتي بعفاف
Ⲭⲉⲣⲉ ⲛⲉ Ⲙⲁⲣⲓⲁ:	And you are called Zion	وسميت صهيون
Ⲭⲉⲣⲉ ⲛⲉ Ⲙⲁⲣⲓⲁ:	Witnessed by Salome	سالومى شهدت
Ⲭⲉⲣⲉ ⲛⲉ Ⲙⲁⲣⲓⲁ:	The Virgin from the womb	بأن العذراء وضعت
Ⲭⲉⲣⲉ ⲛⲉ Ⲙⲁⲣⲓⲁ:	Gave birth to Whom	آمنت وأعتقدت
Ⲭⲉⲣⲉ ⲛⲉ Ⲙⲁⲣⲓⲁ:	While sealed by the One	والخاتم مصون
Ⲭⲉⲣⲉ ⲛⲉ Ⲙⲁⲣⲓⲁ:	Isaiah had said	أشعياء قال عنك
Ⲭⲉⲣⲉ ⲛⲉ Ⲙⲁⲣⲓⲁ:	That your Son Jesus	بأن يسوع ابنك
Ⲭⲉⲣⲉ ⲛⲉ Ⲙⲁⲣⲓⲁ:	Was born of you	وخرج من بطنك
Ⲭⲉⲣⲉ ⲛⲉ Ⲙⲁⲣⲓⲁ:	In the right season	ونظرناه بعيون
Ⲭⲉⲣⲉ ⲛⲉ Ⲙⲁⲣⲓⲁ:	Zephaniah proclaimed	صوفونيوس خبر
Ⲭⲉⲣⲉ ⲛⲉ Ⲙⲁⲣⲓⲁ:	That Jesus appeared	بأن يسوع يظهر
Ⲭⲉⲣⲉ ⲛⲉ Ⲙⲁⲣⲓⲁ:	As rain and dew	شبه ندي ومطر
Ⲭⲉⲣⲉ ⲛⲉ Ⲙⲁⲣⲓⲁ:	Surrounded by nume-rous ranks	حوله صفوف لايحصون
Ⲭⲉⲣⲉ ⲛⲉ Ⲙⲁⲣⲓⲁ:	You are blessed	طوباك ثم طوباك
Ⲭⲉⲣⲉ ⲛⲉ Ⲙⲁⲣⲓⲁ:	You confused them all	حيرت العلماء

416

Ⲭⲉⲣⲉ ⲛⲉ Ⲙⲁⲣⲓⲁ:	By the water and Spirit We conquered Satan	بوجود الروح والماء قهرنا الأركون
Ⲭⲉⲣⲉ ⲛⲉ Ⲙⲁⲣⲓⲁ:		
Ⲭⲉⲣⲉ ⲛⲉ Ⲙⲁⲣⲓⲁ:	Many thought in you	ظنوا فيك أقوام
Ⲭⲉⲣⲉ ⲛⲉ Ⲙⲁⲣⲓⲁ:	That this was illegal	بإن الحبل ده حرام
Ⲭⲉⲣⲉ ⲛⲉ Ⲙⲁⲣⲓⲁ:	Till He raised	حتى حل وأقام
Ⲭⲉⲣⲉ ⲛⲉ Ⲙⲁⲣⲓⲁ:	The dead and healed -the sick	الأموات والمجنون
Ⲭⲉⲣⲉ ⲛⲉ Ⲙⲁⲣⲓⲁ:	The fathers said	شبهك الاباء
Ⲭⲉⲣⲉ ⲛⲉ Ⲙⲁⲣⲓⲁ:	A dome in a cloud	قبة وسحابة
Ⲭⲉⲣⲉ ⲛⲉ Ⲙⲁⲣⲓⲁ:	When they interpreted it	ووضعوا بإجابة
Ⲭⲉⲣⲉ ⲛⲉ Ⲙⲁⲣⲓⲁ:	They were greatly -amazed	وجميعهم فيك محتارون
Ⲭⲉⲣⲉ ⲛⲉ Ⲙⲁⲣⲓⲁ:	Many came before Him	غلب أقوام سبقوه
Ⲭⲉⲣⲉ ⲛⲉ Ⲙⲁⲣⲓⲁ:	But they did not see Him	مدحوا مالحقوه
Ⲭⲉⲣⲉ ⲛⲉ Ⲙⲁⲣⲓⲁ:	Many came after Him	جاءوا بعده وجدوه
Ⲭⲉⲣⲉ ⲛⲉ Ⲙⲁⲣⲓⲁ:	And saw Him the -hidden secret	بسر خفى مكنون
Ⲭⲉⲣⲉ ⲛⲉ Ⲙⲁⲣⲓⲁ:	My heart rejoices	فيك رضا قلبى
Ⲭⲉⲣⲉ ⲛⲉ Ⲙⲁⲣⲓⲁ:	For you are my choice	من شأن طلبى
Ⲭⲉⲣⲉ ⲛⲉ Ⲙⲁⲣⲓⲁ:	O Mary we praise	يامريم حسبي
Ⲭⲉⲣⲉ ⲛⲉ Ⲙⲁⲣⲓⲁ:	We cry with voices	تاجي وأنا دون
Ⲭⲉⲣⲉ ⲛⲉ Ⲙⲁⲣⲓⲁ:	You are Moses dome	قبة موسى كان

Ⲭⲉⲣⲉ ⲛⲉ Ⲙⲁⲣⲓⲁ	Ornamented all	زخرفها بالألوان
Ⲭⲉⲣⲉ ⲛⲉ Ⲙⲁⲣⲓⲁ	In all four corners	وجعل فيها الأركان
Ⲭⲉⲣⲉ ⲛⲉ Ⲙⲁⲣⲓⲁ	With instruments and -arts	بكل آله وفنون

Ⲭⲉⲣⲉ ⲛⲉ Ⲙⲁⲣⲓⲁ	Beautification fulfilled	كفاها تطريز
Ⲭⲉⲣⲉ ⲛⲉ Ⲙⲁⲣⲓⲁ	By gold and alabaster	بالذهب الابريز
Ⲭⲉⲣⲉ ⲛⲉ Ⲙⲁⲣⲓⲁ	Precisely refined	وفعل بالتمييز
Ⲭⲉⲣⲉ ⲛⲉ Ⲙⲁⲣⲓⲁ	Designer of all artwork	الة كل فنون

Ⲭⲉⲣⲉ ⲛⲉ Ⲙⲁⲣⲓⲁ	God has in the dome	لله فى القبة
Ⲭⲉⲣⲉ ⲛⲉ Ⲙⲁⲣⲓⲁ	Many prayers and requests	صلوات وطلبة
Ⲭⲉⲣⲉ ⲛⲉ Ⲙⲁⲣⲓⲁ	The vessel where the manna is stored	والقسط علامة المحبة
Ⲭⲉⲣⲉ ⲛⲉ Ⲙⲁⲣⲓⲁ	Is the sign of love	المن فيه مكنون

Ⲭⲉⲣⲉ ⲛⲉ Ⲙⲁⲣⲓⲁ	A pure censer	مجمرة التصعيد
Ⲭⲉⲣⲉ ⲛⲉ Ⲙⲁⲣⲓⲁ	Holding the aroma	زهرة عطر تقيد
Ⲭⲉⲣⲉ ⲛⲉ Ⲙⲁⲣⲓⲁ	You are the Ark of covenant	ياتابوت عهد جديد
Ⲭⲉⲣⲉ ⲛⲉ Ⲙⲁⲣⲓⲁ	Carrying the True -Word	بصفائح وقرون

Ⲭⲉⲣⲉ ⲛⲉ Ⲙⲁⲣⲓⲁ	You carried the Light	نالوا نور من نور
Ⲭⲉⲣⲉ ⲛⲉ Ⲙⲁⲣⲓⲁ	Like seven minarets lit	سبع سرج ينيرون
Ⲭⲉⲣⲉ ⲛⲉ Ⲙⲁⲣⲓⲁ	You're Aaron's rod	وقضيب كان مذخور
Ⲭⲉⲣⲉ ⲛⲉ Ⲙⲁⲣⲓⲁ	Which alone blossomed	بأسم الأب هرون

Ϫⲉⲣⲉ ⲛⲉ Ⲙⲁⲣⲓⲁ:	You are the altar	هيكل بموائد
Ϫⲉⲣⲉ ⲛⲉ Ⲙⲁⲣⲓⲁ:	With incense offered	وبخور وصعائد
Ϫⲉⲣⲉ ⲛⲉ Ⲙⲁⲣⲓⲁ:	Many prophesied	وآيات وشواهد
Ϫⲉⲣⲉ ⲛⲉ Ⲙⲁⲣⲓⲁ:	And were fulfilled	عنك يتنبأون
Ϫⲉⲣⲉ ⲛⲉ Ⲙⲁⲣⲓⲁ:	All what they said	وجميع ما وضعوه
Ϫⲉⲣⲉ ⲛⲉ Ⲙⲁⲣⲓⲁ:	In the dome they found	في القبة وجدوه
Ϫⲉⲣⲉ ⲛⲉ Ⲙⲁⲣⲓⲁ:	As your purity showed	ولقدسك ذكروه
Ϫⲉⲣⲉ ⲛⲉ Ⲙⲁⲣⲓⲁ:	Her virginity sealed	عذراء بكر مصون
Ϫⲉⲣⲉ ⲛⲉ Ⲙⲁⲣⲓⲁ:	We ask of you	لازم نترجاك
Ϫⲉⲣⲉ ⲛⲉ Ⲙⲁⲣⲓⲁ:	To ask your Son	عند الابن عساك
Ϫⲉⲣⲉ ⲛⲉ Ⲙⲁⲣⲓⲁ:	O blessed Mary	يامريم طوباك
Ϫⲉⲣⲉ ⲛⲉ Ⲙⲁⲣⲓⲁ:	To forgive us	راعينا بعيون
Ϫⲉⲣⲉ ⲛⲉ Ⲙⲁⲣⲓⲁ:	O daughter of Joachim	يا ابنة يواقيم
Ϫⲉⲣⲉ ⲛⲉ Ⲙⲁⲣⲓⲁ:	O paradise of delight	يا فردوس نعيم
Ϫⲉⲣⲉ ⲛⲉ Ⲙⲁⲣⲓⲁ:	Through you we gained glory	فزنا بالتعظيم
Ϫⲉⲣⲉ ⲛⲉ Ⲙⲁⲣⲓⲁ:	And all joy is yours.	ولك الفرح يكون

8	Ⲏ̄	٨
*Seven times every day, I will praise Your Holy name, with all my heart, O God of everyone.	*Ⲍ̄ ⲛ̀ⲥⲟⲡ ⲙ̀ⲙⲏⲛⲓ ⲉ̀ⲃⲟⲗϧⲉⲛ ⲡⲁϩⲏⲧ ⲧⲏⲣϥ: ϯⲛⲁⲥⲙⲟⲩ ⲉ̀ⲡⲉⲕⲣⲁⲛ: Ⲡ̅ϭⲟⲓⲥ ⲙ̀ⲡⲓⲉ̀ⲡ̀ⲧⲏⲣϥ.	*سبع مرات كل يوم من كل قلبى ابارك أسمك يارب الكل.
I remembered Your name, and I was comforted, O King of the ages, and God of all gods.	Ⲁⲓⲉⲣⲫⲙⲉⲩⲓ̀ ⲙ̀ⲡⲉⲕⲣⲁⲛ: ⲟⲩⲟϩ ⲁⲓϫⲉⲙⲛⲟⲙϯ: ⲡ̀ⲟⲩ̀ⲣⲟ ⲛ̀ⲛⲓⲉ̀ⲱⲛ: Ⲫϯ ⲛ̀ⲧⲉ ⲛⲓⲛⲟⲩϯ.	ذكرت اسمك فتعزيت ياملك الدهور وإله الآلهة.
*Jesus Christ our true Lord, who has come, for our salvation, was incarnate.	*Ⲓⲏⲥⲟⲩⲥ Ⲡⲓⲭ̀ⲣⲓⲥⲧⲟⲥ Ⲡⲉⲛⲛⲟⲩϯ: ⲡⲓⲁ̀ⲗⲏⲑⲓⲛⲟⲥ: ⲫⲏⲉⲧⲁϥⲓ̀ ⲉⲑⲃⲉ ⲡⲉⲛⲥⲱϯ: ⲁϥⲉⲣⲥⲱⲙⲁⲧⲓⲕⲟⲥ.	*يسوع المسيح الهنا الحقيقى الذى أتى من اجل خلاصنا متجسداً.
He was incarnate, of the Holy Spirit, and of Mary, the pure bride.	Ⲁϥϭⲓⲥⲁⲣⲝ ⲉ̀ⲃⲟⲗ: ϧⲉⲛ Ⲡⲓⲡ̀ⲛⲉⲩⲙⲁ ⲉ̀ⲑⲟⲩⲁⲃ: ⲛⲉⲙ ⲉ̀ⲃⲟⲗ ϧⲉⲛ Ⲙⲁⲣⲓⲁ̀: ϯϣⲉⲗⲉⲧⲉ̀ⲑⲟⲩⲁⲃ.	وتجسد من الروح القدس ومن مريم العروس الطاهرة.

*And changed our sorrow, and all our troubles, to joy for our hearts, and total rejoicing.	*Ⲁϥⲫⲱⲛϩ ⲙ̀ⲡⲉⲛϩ-ⲏⲃⲓ꞉ ⲛⲉⲙ ⲡⲉⲛϩⲟϫϩⲉϫ ⲧⲏⲣϥ ꞉ ⲉ̀ⲟⲩⲣⲁϣⲓ ⲛ̀ϩⲏ-ⲧ꞉ ⲛⲉⲙ ⲟⲩⲑⲉⲗⲏⲗ ⲉ̀ⲡ-ⲧⲏⲣϥ.	*وقلب حزننا وكل ضيقنا إلى فرح قلب وتهليل كلى.
Let us worship Him, and sing about His mother, the Virgin, Mary, the beautiful dove.	Ⲙⲁⲣⲉⲛⲟⲩⲱϣⲧ ⲙ̀ⲙⲟϥ꞉ ⲟⲩⲟϩ ⲛ̀ⲧⲉⲛⲉⲣϩⲩⲙⲛⲟⲥ ꞉ ⲛ̀ⲧⲉϥⲙⲁⲩ Ⲙⲁⲣⲓⲁ꞉ ϯϭⲣⲟⲙⲡⲓ ⲉⲑⲛⲉⲥⲱⲥ.	فلنسجد له ونرتل لأمه مريم الحمامة الحسنة.
*And let us all proclaim, with the voice of joy, saying Hail to you Mary, the Mother of Emmanuel.	*Ⲟⲩⲟϩ ⲛ̀ⲧⲉⲛⲱϣ ⲉ̀ⲃⲟⲗ ꞉ ϧⲉⲛ ⲟⲩⲥⲙⲏ ⲛ̀ⲑⲉⲗⲏⲗ ꞉ ϫⲉ ⲭⲉⲣⲉ ⲛⲉ Ⲙⲁⲣ-ⲓⲁ꞉ ⲑ̀ⲙⲁⲩ ⲛ̀Ⲉ̀ⲙⲙⲁⲛ-ⲟⲩⲏⲗ.	*ونصرخ بصوت التهليل قائلين السلام لك يامريم أم عمانوئيل.
Hail to you Mary, the salvation of our father Adam, Hail..., the Mother	Ⲭⲉⲣⲉ ⲛⲉ Ⲙⲁⲣⲓⲁ ꞉ ⲡ̀-ⲥⲱϯ ⲛ̀Ⲁⲇⲁⲙ ⲡⲉⲛⲓ-ⲱⲧ꞉ ⲭⲉ ꞉ ⲑ̀ⲙⲁⲩ ⲙ̀ⲡⲓ-	السلام لك يامريم خلاص أبينا آدم. السلام.. أم

421

of the refuge, Hail..., the rejoicing of Eve, Hail..., the joy of all generations.	ⲙⲁⲙ̀ⲫⲱⲧ: ⲭⲉ : ⲡ̀ⲑⲉⲗⲏⲗ ⲛ̀Ⲉⲩⲁ: ⲭⲉ : ⲡ̀ⲟⲩⲛⲟϥ ⲛ̀ⲛⲓⲅⲉⲛⲉⲁ̀.	الملجأ. السلام .. تهليل حواء. السلام.. فرح الأجيال.
*Hail to you Mary, the joy of the righteous Abel, Hail..., the true Virgin, Hail..., the salvation of Noah, Hail..., the chaste and undefiled.	*Ⲭⲉⲣⲉ ⲛⲉ Ⲙⲁⲣⲓⲁ̀ : ⲫ̀ⲣⲁϣⲓ ⲛ̀Ⲁⲃⲉⲗ ⲡⲓⲑ̀ⲙⲏⲓ ⲭⲉ: ϯⲡⲁⲣⲑⲉⲛⲟⲥ ⲛ̀ⲧⲁⲫⲙⲏⲓ ⲭⲉ : ⲫ̀ⲛⲟϩⲉⲙ ⲛ̀Ⲛⲱⲉ: ⲭⲉ : ϯⲁⲧⲑⲱⲗⲉⲃ ⲛⲥⲉⲙⲛⲉ.	*السلام لك يامريم فرح هابيل البار . السلام.. العذراء الحقيقية. السلام.. خلاص نوح. السلام..غير الدنسة الهادئة.
Hail to you Mary, the grace of Abraham, Hail..., the unfading crown, Hail..., the redemption of Saint Isaac, Hail..., the Mother of the Holy.	Ⲭⲉⲣⲉ ⲛⲉ Ⲙⲁⲣⲓⲁ̀ : ⲡⲓϩ̀ⲙⲟⲧ ⲛ̀Ⲁⲃⲣⲁⲁⲙ: ⲭⲉ : ⲡⲓⲭ̀ⲗⲟⲙ ⲛⲁⲑⲗⲱⲙ: ⲭⲉ : ⲡ̀ⲥⲱϯ ⲛ̀Ⲓⲥⲁⲁⲕ ⲡⲉⲑⲟⲩⲁⲃ: ⲭⲉ : ⲑ̀ⲙⲁⲩ ⲙ̀ⲫ̀ⲏⲉⲑⲟⲩⲁⲃ.	السلام لك يامريم نعمة ابراهيم. السلام .. الاكليل غير المضمحل. السلام.. خلاص اسحق القديس. السلام.. أم القدوس.

*Hail to you Mary, the rejoicing of Jacob, Hail..., myriads of myriads, Hail..., the pride of Judah, Hail..., the mother of the Master.	*Ⲭⲉⲣⲉ ⲛⲉ Ⲙⲁⲣⲓⲁ ⲡ̇ⲑⲉⲗⲏⲗ ⲛ̇Ⲓⲁⲕⲱⲃ: ⲭ̅ⲉ̅ ⲅⲁⲛⲑ̇ⲃⲁ ⲛ̇ⲕⲱⲃ: ⲭ̅ⲉ̅ ⲡ̇ϣⲟⲩϣⲟⲩ ⲛ̇Ⲓⲟⲩⲇⲁ: ⲭ̅ⲉ̅ ⲑ̇ⲙⲁⲩ ⲙ̇ⲡⲓⲆⲉⲥⲡⲟⲧⲁ.	*السلام لك يامريم تهليل يعقوب. السلام.. ربوات مضاعفة. السلام.. فخر يهوذا. السلام .. ام السيد.
Hail to you Mary, the preaching of Moses, Hail..., the Mother of the Master, Hail..., the honor of Samuel, Hail..., the pride of Israel.	Ⲭⲉⲣⲉ ⲛⲉ Ⲙⲁⲣⲓⲁ : ⲡ̇ⲉⲓ-ⲱⲓϣ ⲙ̇Ⲙⲱⲧⲥⲏⲥ: ⲭ̅ⲉ̅ ⲑ̇ⲙⲁⲩ ⲙ̇ⲡⲓⲆⲉⲥⲡⲟⲧⲏⲥ: ⲭ̅ⲉ̅ ⲡ̇ⲧⲁⲓⲟ̇ ⲛ̇Ⲥⲁⲙⲟⲩⲏⲗ: ⲭ̅ⲉ̅ ⲡ̇ϣⲟⲩϣⲟⲩ ⲙ̇Ⲡ̇ⲥ̇ⲣⲁⲏⲗ.	السلام لك يامريم كرازة موسى. السلام.. والدة السيد. السلام.. كرامة صموئيل. السلام.. فخر اسرائيل.
*Hail to you Mary, the steadfastness of Job the righteous , Hail..., the precious stone, Hail..., the Mother of the Beloved, Hail..., the daughter of King	*Ⲭⲉⲣⲉ ⲛⲉ Ⲙⲁⲣⲓⲁ ⲡ̇ⲧⲁ-ⲭⲣⲟ ⲛ̇Ⲓⲱⲃ ⲡⲓⲑ̇ⲙⲏⲓ: ⲭ̅ⲉ̅ ⲡⲓⲱ̇ⲛⲓ ⲛ̇ⲁⲛⲁⲙⲏⲓ: ⲭ̅ⲉ̅ ⲑ̇ⲙⲁⲩ ⲙ̇ⲡⲓⲙⲉⲛⲣⲓⲧ : ⲭ̅ⲉ̅ ⲧ̇ϣⲉⲣⲓ ⲙ̇ⲡⲟⲩⲣⲟ Ⲇⲁⲩⲓⲇ.	*السلام لك يامريم ثبات ايوب البار. السلام.. الحجر الكريم. السلام..أم الحبيب. السلام.. ابنة

David.		الملك داود.
Hail to you Mary, the friend of Solomon, Hail..., the exaltation of the just, Hail..., the redemption of Isaiah, Hail..., the healing of Jeremiah.	Ϫⲉⲣⲉ ⲛⲉ Ⲙⲁⲣⲓⲁ: ϯϣⲫⲉⲣⲓ ⲛⲤⲟⲗⲟⲙⲱⲛ: ϫⲉ : ⲡϭⲓⲥⲓ ⲛⲛⲓⲆⲓⲕⲉⲟⲛ: ϫⲉ : ⲡⲟⲩϫⲁⲓ ⲛ̄Ⲏⲥⲁⲏⲁⲥ: ϫⲉ : ⲡⲧⲁⲗϭⲟ ⲛ̄Ⲓⲉⲣⲉⲙⲓⲁⲥ.	السلام لك يامريم صديقة سليمان. السلام.. رفعة الصديقين . السلام.. خلاص أشعياء. السلام.. شفاء أرميا.
*Hail to you Mary, the knowledge of Ezekiel, Hail..., the grace of Daniel, Hail..., the power of Elijah, Hail..., the grace of Elisha.	*Ϫⲉⲣⲉ ⲛⲉ Ⲙⲁⲣⲓⲁ : ⲡⲉⲙⲓ ⲛ̄Ⲓⲉⲍⲉⲕⲓⲏⲗ : ϫⲉ : ⲭⲁⲣⲓⲥ ⲧⲟⲩ Ⲇⲁⲛⲓⲏⲗ: ϫⲉ : ϯϫⲟⲙ ⲛⲎⲗⲓⲁⲥ: ϫⲉ : ⲡⲓϩⲙⲟⲧ ⲛ̄Ⲉⲗⲓⲥⲉⲟⲥ.	*السلام لك يامريم علم حزقيال. السلام.. نعمة دانيال. السلام ..قوة ايليا. السلام.. نعمة اليشع
Hail to you Mary, the Mother of God, Hail..., the Mother of Jesus Christ,	Ϫⲉⲣⲉ ⲛⲉ Ⲙⲁⲣⲓⲁ: ϯⲑⲉⲟⲧⲟⲕⲟⲥ: ϫⲉ : ⲑⲙⲁⲩ ⲛⲒⲏⲥⲟⲩⲥ Ⲡⲓⲭ̅ⲣ̅ⲓⲥⲧⲟⲥ: ϫⲉ	السلام لك يامريم والدة الاله. السلام.. أم يسوع

Hail..., the beautiful dove, Hail..., the Mother of the Son of God.	:ϯϭⲣⲟⲙⲡⲓ ⲉⲑⲛⲉⲥⲱⲥ: ϫⲉ : ⲟ̀ⲙⲁⲩⲛ̀Ⲧⲓⲟⲥ Ⲑⲉⲟⲥ.	المسيح السلام.. الحمامة الحسناء. السلام..أم ابن الله.
*Hail to you Mary, who was witnessed by, all the prophets, and they said,	*Ⲭⲉⲣⲉ ⲛⲉ Ⲙⲁⲣⲓⲁ:ⲉ̀ⲧⲁ- ⲩⲉⲣⲙⲉⲑⲣⲉ ⲛⲁⲥ: ⲛ̀ϫⲉ ⲛⲓ̀ⲡⲣⲟⲫⲏⲧⲏⲥ ⲧⲏⲣⲟⲩ: ⲟⲩⲟⲅⲁⲩϫⲱ ⲙ̀ⲙⲟⲥ.	*السلام لك يامريم التى شهد لها جميع الانبياء وقالوا.
*Behold God the Word, took flesh from you, in an undescribable, unity.	*Ⲟⲏⲡⲡⲉ Ⲫϯ ⲡⲓⲗⲟⲅⲟⲥ :ⲉ̀ⲧⲁϥϭⲓⲥⲁⲣⲝ̀ⲛ̀ϧⲏⲧ: ϧⲉⲛ ⲟⲩⲙⲉⲧⲟⲩⲁⲓ: ⲛ̀ⲁⲧⲥⲁϫⲓ ⲙ̀ⲡⲉⲥⲣⲏϯ.	*هوذا الله الكلمة الذى تجسد منك بوحدانية لاينطق بمثلها.
You are truly exalted, more than the rod, of Aaron, O full of grace.	Ⲧⲉϭⲟⲥⲓ ⲁⲗⲏⲑⲱⲥ: ⲉ̀ⲅ- ⲟⲧⲉ ⲡⲓϣ̀ⲃⲱⲧ: ⲛ̀ⲧⲉ Ⲁ̀- ⲁⲣⲱⲛ: ⲱ̀ ⲑⲏⲉⲑ- ⲙⲉⲅ ⲛ̀ⲅ̀ⲙⲟⲧ.	مرتفعة أنت بالحقيقة أكثر من عصا هرون أيتها الممتلئة نعمة.
What is the rod, but Mary, for it is the	Ⲁϣ ⲡⲉ ⲡⲓϣ̀ⲃⲱⲧ : ⲉ̀ⲃ-	ماهى العصا إلا مريم لانها

symbol, of her virginity.	ⲛⲁ ⲉⲘⲁⲣⲓⲁ ⲝ ϫⲉ ⲛ̅ⲑⲟ ϥ ⲡⲉ ⲡ̅ⲧⲩⲡⲟⲥ ⲝ ⲛ̅ⲧⲉⲥ ⲡⲁⲣ ⲑⲉ ⲛⲓⲁ̅.	مثال بتوليتها.
*She conceived and gave birth, without a man, to the Son of the Highest, the Word Himself.	*Ⲁ ⲥⲉⲣ ⲃ ⲟ ⲕ ⲓ ⲁⲥ ⲙ ⲓⲥ ⲓ ⲝ ⲭⲱⲣ ⲓ ⲥ ⲥⲩ ⲛⲟⲩ ⲥ ⲓⲁ ⲝ ⲙ̅ⲡ̅ ϣ ⲏ ⲣ ⲓ ⲙ̅ⲫ ⲏ ⲉⲧ ϭ ⲟ ⲥ ⲝ ⲡⲓ- ⲗⲟ ⲅⲟ ⲥ ⲛⲁ ⲓ ⲇ ⲓⲁ̅.	*حبلت وولدت بغير مباضعة ابن العلى الكلمة الذاتى.
*Through her prayers, and intercessions, O Lord open unto us, the gates of the Church.	*Ⲉ ⲓⲧ ⲉ ⲛ ⲛⲉ ⲥ ⲉⲩ ⲭ ⲏ ⲝ ⲛ ⲉ ⲙ ⲛⲉ ⲥ ⲡⲣⲉ ⲥ ⲃ ⲓⲁ ⲝ ⲁ ⲟⲩ ⲱ ⲛ ⲛⲁ ⲛ Ⲡ ϭⲟ ⲓ ⲥ ⲝ ⲙ̅ⲫ- ⲣⲟ ⲛ̅ⲧⲉ ϯⲉⲕ ⲕ ⲗ ⲏ ⲥ ⲓ ⲁ̅	*بصلواتها وشفاعاتها أفتح لنا يارب باب الكنيسة.
I entreat You, O Mother of God, keep the gates of the Church, open to the faithful.	Ϯⲧⲃⲟ ⲉⲣⲟ ⲝ ⲱ̅ ϯ ⲑ- ⲉⲟ ⲧⲟ ⲕⲟ ⲥ ⲝ ⲭ ⲁ ⲫ ⲣⲟ ⲛ̅- ⲛ ⲓⲉⲕ ⲕ ⲗ ⲏ ⲥ ⲓⲁ ⲝ ⲉ ⲩ ⲟⲩ ⲏ ⲛ ⲛ̅ⲛ ⲓ ⲡ ⲓ ⲥ ⲧⲟ ⲥ.	اسألك ياوالدة الاله اجعلى ابواب الكنائس مفتوحة للمؤمنين.
Let us ask her, to intercede for us, before her Beloved, that He may forgive us.	Ⲙ ⲁⲣⲉ ⲛ ϯ ⲧ ⲃ ⲟ ⲉⲣ ⲟⲥ ⲝ ⲉ ⲑ ⲣⲉ- ⲥ ⲧⲱ ⲃ ⲏ ⲉ ϫ ⲱ ⲛ ⲝ ⲛⲁ ⲏ ⲣ ⲉ ⲛ ⲡⲉ ⲥ ⲙ ⲉ ⲛ ⲣ ⲓ ⲧ ⲝ ⲉⲑ ⲣⲉ ϥ ⲭ ⲱ ⲛⲁ ⲛ ⲉ ⲃ ⲟ ⲗ.	*فلنسألها أن تطلب عنا عند حبيبها ليغفر لنا.

O Mary - Ya Mem Reh Yeh Mem

يا م ر ى م -

O M A R Y,
Lady of virgins,
you attained greatness,
from the True Light,
you are exalted,
by the Lord Himself,
you bore the Creator,
O what a great marvel!

يا م ر ى م
ياست الأبكار
قد نلت تعظيم
من نور الأنوار
ووهبت تعظيم
من عنده قد صار
وحملت الخالق
من ذا لا يحتار

Wondrous among nations,
wisdom to rulers,
a hidden gem,
and the gospel spoke of you:
they give you blessings,
in all generations,
O daughter of Joachim,
exalted above the Cherubim.

قد صرتِ اعجوبة
للرؤساء مثال
درة محجوبة
وفي الانجيل قد قال
يعطونك الطوبا
في كل الاجيال
يا ابنة يواقيم
قد فقتي الشاروبيم

You attained what no one could,	من نال ما نلتى
O Mother of Mercy,	يا ام الرحمة
and you became,	وانتي قد صرتي
filled with grace,	مملوءة نعمه
to the Divine you became,	وللاهوت صرتي
a veil for the Word,	حجابا للكلمة
and the scholars marveled,	واحتار فيك
greatly about you.	ارباب التفهيم
O tabernacle of the covenant,	يا تابوت العهد
O censer of Aaron,	يا مجمرة هارون
O spirit of glory,	يا روح المجد
O daughter of Zion,	يا ابنة صهيون
O the light of our eyes,	يا نور العيون
with you we rejoice,	بك نسعد
and abide in grace,	ونحظي بالنعيم
O full of grace.	يا مملوءة نعمه
O full of grace,	يا مملوءة نعمه
the fortifying fortress,	انت الحصن الحصين
the jewel of mercy,	انت كنز الرحمة
the aid of the poor,	يا عون المساكين
your son has purged death,	بإبنك زالت النقمة
O the intercessor of saints,	يا شفيعة القديسين

intercede for us,	وشفيعتنا في الزحمة
O Mother of Mercy.	يا ام الرحيم

Hail to you,	نقدم لك التعظيم
O Lady of virgins,	ياست الأبكار
O daughter of Joachim,	يا ابنة يواقيم
the chosen throne,	يا كرسياً مختار
righteous is your Son,	والمولود منك كريم
He purged our shame,	ازال عنا العار
the glorious God,	الاله العظيم
the Creator of ages.	خالق الادهار

The adornment of virgins,	يا زين الأبكار
the holy Mother,	يا قدس الأحبار
the purity of the pure,	يا طهر الأطهار
O light of lights,	يا نور الأنوار
O jewel of grace,	يا كنز النعمة
O Mother of Mercy,	يا ام الرحمة
truly you are the vine,	أنت هي الكرمة
that is filled with fruit.	المملوئة أثمار

O daughter of Joachim,	يا ابنة يواقيم
you attained greatness,	قد نلت التعظيم
you are Jerusalem,	انت هي اورشليم

glorious and honored,	ذات المجد والفخار
you are Zion,	انت هي صهيون
O precious jewel;	يا جوهر مكنون
you released the captive,	فككت المسجون
from the Deceiver's hand.	من يد المكار

Your son saved Adam,	ابنك خلص ادم
the repentant sinner,	الخاطئ النادم
humanity He set free,	وعتق العالم
from all adversaries,	من كل الاضرار
the Lord from your childhood,	ربك من صغرك
witnessed your purity,	لما رأي طهرك
and therefore has blessed you,	قد طيب ذكرك
before all nations.	في كل الاقطار

He sent you Gabriel,	ارسل لك غبريال
the Messenger of His words,	بمحكم الاقوال
and greeted you saying,	وبشرك اذ قال
the Lord has chosen you,	الله لك اختار
His Holy Spirit,	روح قدسه ملاك
filled and dwelt within you,	وسكن في احشاك
blessed are you O Virgin,	يا عذرا طوباك
throughout all ages."	في كل الاجيال

The Unseen and Holy,	ان غير المحسوس
was born from you,	الرب القدوس
and was called Jesus,	منك اتي ودُعي ايسوس
for all eyes to see,	ونظرته الابصار
Moses saw the bush,	موسي رأي العوسج
blazing with fire,	والنار فيه تتأجج
its branches flaming,	وأغصانه تتوهج
yet the bush was not consumed.	ما ضرته النار
The blazing bush,	ان ما رأته العينان
which Moses had seen,	ملتهبا بالنيران
was indeed Mary,	في العوسج والأغصان
the adornment of virgins,	هي مريم زينة الأبكار
the fire is Jesus,	والنار هي إيسوس
the Holy Lord,	الرب القدوس
who gave us the Law,	معطينا الناموس
engraved in stone.	مكتوبا في الاحجار
Isaiah prophesied,	في اشعيا قد قيل
about the birth,	عن هذا التأويل
of Emmanuel,	تلد عمانوئيل
the Almighty King,	الملك الجبار
Ezekiel saw a door,	وحزقيال رأي باب
through which the Lord entered,	دخل فيه رب الارباب

He sealed the door and claimed it,	وختم الباب مهاب
highly exalted.	عالي المقدار
Highly exalted are you,	عال هو قدرك
and your Son Jesus,	لإن يسوع ابنك
when He was born of you,	لما ولد منك
the earth was adorned,	تزينت الاقطار
and also Daniel,	وايضا دانيال
prophesied and said,	تنبأ حيث قال
I saw the high throne,	رأيت الكرسي العال
highly exalted.	عالي المقدار
In the firmaments high I saw,	نظرت فوق الأركان
one like the Son of Man,	شبه ابن الانسان
who has dominion,	وله السلطان
over all the earth,	علي كل الأقطار
He is the Lord of Hosts,	وهو رب القوات
around Him are the ranks,	ومن حوله طغمات
thousands and myriads,	الوف وربوات
glorifying in reverence.	بعظم ووقار
O daughter of Joachim,	ياابنة يواقيم
you are exalted above,	فقت الكاروبيم
the Cherubim and Seraphim,	وايضا السرافيم

and all righteous fathers,	وكل الاباء الابرار
the Lord was born from you,	منك جاء المولود
and David praises you,	الرب المعبود
with his harp he sings,	يمدح فيك داود
playing its ten strings.	بالعشرة أوتار
The sound of the first string,	الوتر الاول
is in honor of your name,	قول مبجل
the Virgin will carry,	والعذراء تحبل
the Almighty King,	بالملك الجبار
and with the second string,	الوتر الثاني
David rejoices,	داود بالتهاني
chanting with hymns,	و يرتل بالالحان
while playing his harp.	مع ضرب القيثار
And the third O daughter,	الثالث يا ابنة
because you were faithful,	أنت مؤتمنة
you were filled with light,	بالنور مشتملة
and the Lord chose you,	والرب لك إختار
the fourth string is sounded,	الوتر الرابع
so that all can hear,	اصغ يا سامع
of her who is praised,	ذا قول شائع
all over the world.	في كل الاقطار

The fifth gave us the news,	الخامس خبر
as a dove she appears,	حمامة هي تظهر
with Ophir gold,	بالذهب الاصفر
upon her shoulders,	علي منكبيها صار
with the sixth he sung,	السادس قال فيه
praises I will not hide,	قولاً ما أخفيه
but I will praise with him,	لكني أرويه
and proclaim to all.	واشهره أجهار

With the seventh string he said,	السابع اذ قال
O mountain of the High God,	يا جبل الله العال
the High took flesh from you,	تجسد منك المتعال
without a doubt,	بلا شك ولا إنكار
and with the eighth he sang,	والثامن رنم
to the Virgin Mary,	للعذ را مريم
the Great chose her,	اختارها المعظم
and crowned her with honor.	وكللها بالفخار

With the ninth string he said,	التاسع قال عنها
from her will surely come,	يظهر حقا منها
God Who is her son,	الإله وهو إبنها
who sealed her virginity,	والبكورية في حفظ ووقار
with the tenth he sang,	الوتر العاشر
the Powerful God,	الله القادر

in Zion He appeared,	في صهيون ظاهر
the dwelling of the righteous.	مسكن الأبرار
There isn't in all ages,	لم يوجد في الدهر
anyone like you O Virgin,	مثلك أيتها البكر
for you released the chains,	لأنك فككت الاسر
and shame of Adam,	عن آدم والعار
O Lady of the creation,	يا سيدة الأكوان
the pride of faith,	يا فخر الإيمان
your servant is in need,	عبدك حيران
drowning because of sins.	غارق في الاوزار
Highly exalted are you,	عالي هو قدرك
do not leave your servant,	لا تتركي عبدك
I hope that your Son,	قصدي من ولدك
accepts me and remits my sins,	توبة و أستغفار
for your intercessions,	و العذراء تشفع
are heard and accepted,	في الحضار اجمع
and defends us from the attacks,	و هي عنا تدفع
of the adversary.	ضربات الاشرار
Arise O poor one,	قم وانهض يا مسكين
and clothe yourself in faith,	والبس ثوب اليقين
and say Amen Amen,	وقل امين امين

for she intercedes for us,	فهي تشفع في الحضار
and the abject composer,	و أنا الخاطي المسكين
who always praises her,	مادحها في كل حين
has no one on the day of Judgment,	مالي يوم الدين
but the Lady of virgins.	سوي سيدة الابكار

9	ō	٩
*You are called, O Virgin Mary, the holy flower, of the incense.	*Ⲁⲩⲙⲟⲩϯ ⲉⲣⲟⲥ Ⲙⲁⲣⲓⲁ ϯⲡⲁⲣⲑⲉⲛⲟⲥ: ϫⲉ ϯϩ-ⲣⲏⲣⲓ ⲉⲑⲟⲩⲁⲃ: ⲛ̀ⲧⲉ ⲡⲓⲥⲑⲟⲓⲛⲟⲩϥⲓ.	*دعيت يامريم العذراء الزهرة المقدسة التى للبخور.
Which came out, and blossomed, from the roots of the patriarchs, and the prophets.	Ⲑⲏⲉⲧⲁⲥϯⲟⲩⲱ ⲉ̀ⲡϣⲱⲓ: ⲁⲥϥⲓⲣⲓ ⲉⲃⲟⲗ: ϧⲉⲛ ⲟ̀ⲛ-ⲟⲩⲛⲓ ⲛ̀ⲛⲓⲡⲁⲧⲣⲓⲁⲣⲭⲏⲥ: ⲛⲉⲙ ⲛⲓⲡ̀ⲣⲟⲫⲏⲧⲏⲥ.	التى طلعت وازهرت من أصل رؤساء الآباء والأنبياء.
*Like the rod, of Aaron the priest, which blossomed, and brought forth fruit.	*Ⲙ̀ⲫⲣⲏϯ ⲙ̀ⲡⲓϣⲃⲱ-ⲧ: ⲛ̀ⲧⲉ Ⲁⲁⲣⲱⲛ ⲡⲓⲟ-ⲩⲏⲃ: ⲉ̀ⲧⲁϥϥⲓⲣⲓ ⲉⲃⲟⲗ: ⲁϥⲟⲡⲧ ⲛ̀ⲕⲁⲣⲡⲟⲥ.	*مثل عصا هرون الكاهن أزهرت وأوسقت ثمراً.

| For you gave birth to the Word, without the seed of man, and your virginity, was not corrupted. | Ϫⲉ ⲁⲣⲉ̀ϫⲫⲟ ⲙ̀ⲡⲓⲗⲟⲅⲟⲥ: ⲁϭⲛⲉ ⲥ̀ⲡⲉⲣⲙⲁ ⲛ̀ⲣⲱⲙⲓ: ⲉⲥⲟⲓ ⲛ̀ⲁⲧⲧⲁⲕⲟ: ⲛ̀ϫⲉ ⲧⲉⲡⲁⲣⲑⲉⲛⲓⲁ. | لأنك ولدت الكلمة بغير زرع بشر وبتوليتك بغير فساد. |
| *Wherefore we glorify you, as the Mother of God, ask your Son, to forgive us. | *Ⲉⲑⲃⲉ ⲫⲁⲓ ⲧⲉⲛϯⲱⲟⲩ ⲛⲉ: ϩⲱⲥ ⲑⲉⲟ̀ⲧⲟⲕⲟⲥ ⲙⲁ̀ϯϩⲟ ⲙ̀ⲡⲉϣⲏⲣⲓ: ⲉ̀ⲑⲣⲉϥ̀ⲭⲱ ⲛⲁⲛ ⲉ̀ⲃⲟⲗ. | *فلهذا نمجدك كوالدة الاله. اسألى ابنك ليغفر لنا. |

I Praise the Virgin -   أمدح فى البتول

REFRAIN: المرد:

Your love embraced me   سباني حُبك

O pride of nations   يافخرَ الرتب

Moses has seen you   موسى رآكِ

A wonder of wonders   عجب من عجب

And the lamps are bright   والقناديل فضة بتضوي

With golden crosses   والصلبان ذهب

O Mary, Moses' dome   ياقبة موسى يامريم

O Aaron's censer   ياشورية هرون

I praise the Virgin   أمدح فى البتول

And explain and say   وأشرح فيها وأقول

O the origin   ياأصل الأصول

And the hidden pearl   ياجوهر مكنون

Through your Son our Lady   بأبنك ياستنا

He saved our race   خلاص جنسنا

We reached the goal   وبلغنا المنى

And you brought us joy	وبك صرنا فرحون
Was truly Incarnate	تجسد بثبات
From a Virgin girl	من فخر البنات
Crucified and died	صلب عنا ومات
For us at Golgotha	عند الاقرانيون
The fruit of my pledge	ثمرة عربونى
O daughter of Zion	يا أبنة صهيون
To love your Son	أحب الهي
And proclaim and say	وأصيح وأقول
REFRAIN:	المرد:
Your love embraced me	سباني حُبك
O pride of nations	يافخرَ الرتب
Moses saw you	موسى رآكِ
A wonder of wonders	عجب من عجب
And the lamps are bright	والقناديل فضة بتضوي
With golden crosses	والصلبان ذهب
O Mary, Moses' dome	ياقبة موسى يامريم
O Aaron's censer	ياشورية هرون

Gabriel came	جاك غبريال
With tidings and sayings	ببشائر وأقوال
You accepted his word	وقبلت ماقال
In calmness and wisdom	بسر خفي مكنون
He dwelt by His Word	حل بكلمته
In strength and power	وشرح قدرته
You became like heaven	صرت كسمائه
O daughter of Zion	ياإبنة صهيون
He saved Adam	خلص آدم
After his sorrow	بعد أن كان نادم
And has freed the world	وعتق العالم
We rejoice in you	ونحن بك فرحون
He is glorified	دائم تمجيده
And promised His Apostles	وعاهد تلاميذه
To save His people	يخلص عبيده
From Satan's bondage	من كيد الأركون
REFRAIN:	المرد:
Your love embraced me	سباني حُبك
O pride of nations	يافخرَ الرتب

Moses saw you	موسى رآكِ
A wonder of wonders	عجب من عجب
And the lamps are bright	والقناديل فضة بتضوي
With golden crosses	والصلبان ذهب
O Mary, Moses' dome	ياقبة موسى يامريم
O Aaron's censer	ياشورية هرون
Concerning you David said	داود قال عنك
"The King rejoiced in you	الملك إشتهى حسنك
And took flesh from you	وتجسد منك
The Lord on His Throne."	رب العرش المكنون
Myriads and thousands	ربوات وألوف
Standing around the Throne	حول العرش وقوف
Ranks and orders	وطغمات وصفوف
Saints and martyrs	وشهداء متصلون
Sorrow was taken away	زالت عنا الأحزان
And we are comforted	وصرنا فى أطمئنان
Through you O Mary	بك يامريم
The pride of the human race	يافخر البشريون
Salome witnessed	سالومي شهدت

That the Virgin gave birth	إن العذراء ولدت
She believed and confirmed	آمنت وأعتقدت
The mystery of mysteries	بالسر المكنون
REFRAIN:	المرد:
Your love embraced me	سباني حُبك
O pride of nations	يافخرَ الرتب
Moses saw you	موسى رآكِ
A wonder of wonders	عجب من عجب
And the lamps are bright	والقناديل فضة بتضوي
With golden crosses	والصلبان ذهب
O Mary, Moses' dome	ياقبة موسى يامريم
O Aaron's censer	ياشورية هرون
Solomon your father	سليمان أباك
Praised in hymns and songs	صار ينشد بفنون
And Jacob saw you	ويعقوب رآك
An upright ladder	سلم مرتفعون
The chiefs had proclaimed	شهد عنك الرؤساء
O fruitful vine	ياكرمة مغروسة
You are a Virgin and a bride	يابكرة وعروسة

As they prophesied	كما عنك تنبأون
Zephaniah proclaimed	صوفونيوس خبر
That Jesus will appear	بأن يسوع يظهر
As rain and dew	شبه ندي ومطر
While her virginity is sealed	والختم حصن مصون
Eve caused Adam to stray,	ضللت حواء آدم
In tears he cried	وصار يبكى نادم
Naked he was exiled	خرج عريان عادم
Without you they would not return	لولاكِ مارجعون
REFRAIN:	المرد:
Your love embraced me	سباني حُبك
O pride of nations	يافخرَ الرتب
Moses saw you	موسى رآكِ
A wonder of wonders	عجب من عجب
And the lamps are bright	والقناديل فضة بتضوي
With golden crosses	والصلبان ذهب
O Mary, Moses' dome	ياقبة موسى يامريم
O Aaron's censer	ياشورية هرون

Your rank is up high	عال هو قدرك
And great is your glory	وعظيم هو مجدك
The Lord honored you	والله شرف ذكرك
O Aaron's censer	يا شورية هرون
Many praised you	غلب فيك المداح
You are the cause of all joy	يابدء الأفراح
You comfort everyone	بمديحك يرتاح
Who is sorrowful and humble	كل ذليل محزون
My heart rejoices in you	فيك رضا قلبى
O Virgin Mary	يامريم طلبى
Ask your Son Jesus	يسوع إبنك حسبى
To protect me by His might	بقوته أكون
Existent before the ages	قديم أزلي دائم
Suffered and was crucified	صلب عنا وتألم
He rose from His sleep	استيقظ كالنائم
And the Disciples preached	والتلاميذ يكرزون
The righteous Apostles	كرزوا في الأقطار
And the four Evangelists	الرسل الأبرار
Preached in all nations	ونادوا باستبشار
The tidings and rejoice	الآباء الإنجيليون

Glory is due to you	لك كل التعظيم
O daughter of Joachim	يا إبنة يواقيم
You bore a great mystery	حملت سر عظيم
And gave birth to the most High	ووضعت المكنون

REFRAIN: المرد:

Your love embraced me سباني حُبك

O pride of nations يا فخرَ الرتب

Moses saw you موسى رآكِ

A wonder of wonders عجب من عجب

And the lamps are bright والقناديل فضة بتضوي

With golden crosses والصلبان ذهب

O Mary, Moses' dome يا قبة موسى يا مريم

O Aaron's censer يا شورية هرون

Moses and Daniel موسى ودانيال

Said many parables ضربوا عنك أمثال

And you fit all that وقبلت ماقال

Mysteriously and more بسر خفي مكنون

You caused the world to shine نورت الأكوان

446

O the pride of faith	يافخر الإيمان
All the creatures were free	لولاك ماكان
Because of you Mary	كل الخلائق يعتقون
Gifts were offered in faith	هدايا بإيمان
To the King of kings	أتوا بهم الأعيان
By the great Magi	مرا وذهباً ولبان
Myrrh, gold and frankincense	بها المجوس حاملون
They worshipped the new born King	وسجدوا للمولود
The Lord of lords	الرب المعبود
And Herod was terrified	وهيرودس صار مرعوب
And his soldiers marveled	وجنده محتارون
Do not forsake me	لاتنسى في ذلك الحين
A poor and humble sinner	عبداً خاطئ مسكين
Intercede on Judgment Day	شفاعتك يوم الدين
And for all the Christians	لشعب إبنك أجمعين
We ask of Him forgiveness	ونسأل من جوده الغفران
Faith and repentance	وتوبة مع إيمان
To be in calmness	لنصبر في أطمئنان
We the believers	نحن المؤمنون

REFRAIN: :المرد

Your love embraced me   سباني حُبك

O pride of nations   يافخرَ الرتب

Moses saw you   موسى رآكِ

A wonder of wonders   عجب من عجب

And the lamps are bright   والقناديل فضة بتضوي

With golden crosses   والصلبان ذهب

O Mary, Moses' dome   ياقبة موسى يامريم

O Aaron's censer   ياشورية هرون

You are More Worthy - Ⲧⲉⲟⲓⲛϩⲓⲕⲁⲛⲟⲥ -

أنت مستحقة

10	ⲓ̄	١٠

10
You are more worthy, than all of the saints, to ask on our behalf, O full of grace.

Ⲧⲉⲟⲓ ⲛϩⲓⲕⲁⲛⲟⲥ: ⲉϩⲟ-ⲧⲉ ⲛⲏⲉⲑⲟⲩⲁⲃ ⲧⲏⲣⲟⲩ : ⲉⲑⲣⲉⲧⲱⲃϩ ⲉϫⲱⲛ : ⲱ̀ ⲑⲏⲉⲑⲙⲉϩ ⲛ̀ϩⲙⲟⲧ.

أنت مستحقة اكثر من جميع القديسين أن تطلبى عنا ايتها الممتلئة نعمة.

*You are exalted, more than the patriarchs, and honored more, than the prophets.

*Ⲧⲉϭⲟⲥⲓ ⲉⲙⲁϣⲱ : ⲉϩ-ⲟⲧⲉ ⲛⲓⲡⲁⲧⲣⲓⲁⲣⲭⲏⲥ : ⲟⲩⲟϩ ⲧⲉⲧⲁⲓⲏⲟⲩⲧ : ⲉϩ-ⲟⲧⲉ ⲛⲓⲡⲣⲟⲫⲏⲧⲏⲥ.

*أنت مرتفعة جداً أكثر من رؤساء الآباء. ومكرمة أفضل من الانبياء.

And you have a seeking, more special, than the Cherubim, and the Seraphim.

Ⲟⲩⲟⲛ ⲧⲉ ϫⲓⲛⲙⲟϣⲓ : ϧⲉⲛ ⲟⲩⲡⲁⲣⲣⲏⲥⲓⲁ: ⲉ̀-ϩⲟⲧⲉ ⲛⲓⲬⲉⲣⲟⲩⲃⲓⲙ : ⲛⲉⲙ ⲛⲓⲤⲉⲣⲁⲫⲓⲙ.

ولك سعي بدالة أكثر من الشاروبيم والسارافيم.

*For you are truly, the pride of our

*Ⲛⲑⲟ ⲅⲁⲣ ⲁⲗⲏⲑⲱⲥ :

*لانك أنت بالحقيقة فخر

449

race, and the intercessor, of our souls.	ⲡⲉ ⲡ̇ϣⲟⲩϣⲟⲩ ⲙⲡⲉⲛⲅⲉⲛⲟⲥ : ⲟⲩⲟϩ ϯⲡ̇ⲣⲟⲥⲧⲁⲧⲏⲥ : ⲛ̇ⲧⲉ ⲛⲉⲛ̇ⲯⲩⲭⲏ.	جنسنا وشفيعة نفوسنا .
Intercede for us, before our Savior, that He may keep us firm, in the upright faith.	Ⲁⲣⲓⲡ̇ⲣⲉⲥⲃⲉⲩⲓⲛ ⲉ̇ϫⲱⲛ : ⲛⲁϩⲣⲉⲛ Ⲡⲉⲛⲥⲱⲧⲏⲣ : ϩⲟⲡⲱⲥ ⲛ̇ⲧⲉϥⲧⲁϫⲣⲟⲛ : ϧⲉⲛ ⲡⲓⲛⲁϩϯ ⲉⲧⲥⲟⲩⲧⲱⲛ.	اشفعى فينا أمام مخلصنا لكى يثبتنا فى الإيمان المستقيم .
*That He may grant us, the forgiveness of our sins, in order to win mercy, through your intercessions.	*Ⲛ̇ⲧⲉϥⲉⲣϩ̇ⲙⲟⲧ ⲛⲁⲛ : ⲙ̇ⲡⲓⲭⲱ ⲉ̇ⲃⲟⲗ ⲛ̇ⲧⲉ ⲛⲉⲛⲛⲟⲃⲓ : ⲛ̇ⲧⲉⲛϣⲁϣⲛⲓ ⲉⲩⲛⲁⲓ : ϩⲓⲧⲉⲛ ⲛⲉⲡ̇ⲣⲉⲥⲃⲓⲁ̀.	*وينعم لنا بمغفرة خطايانا . لنفوز برحمة بشفاعاتك.
11 All the high names, of the incorporeal, thousands of angels, and archangels.	ⲓ̅ⲁ̅ Ⲣⲁⲛ ⲛⲓⲃⲉⲛ ⲉⲧϭⲟⲥⲓ : ⲛ̇ⲧⲉ ⲛⲓⲁ̀ⲥⲱⲙⲁⲧⲟⲥ : ⲛⲓⲁ̀ⲛⲁⲛϣⲟ ⲛ̇ⲁⲅⲅⲉⲗⲟⲥ : ⲛⲉⲙ ⲁⲣⲭⲏⲁⲅⲅⲉⲗⲟⲥ.	١١ كل الاسماء العالية التى لغير المتجسدين الوف الملائكة ورؤساء الملائكة.

*They did not attain, your high blessedness, O who is clothed in, the glory of the Lord of Hosts.	*Ⲙⲡⲟⲩϣⲫⲟϩ ⲉ̀ⲡϭⲓⲥⲓ : ⲛ̀ⲧⲉ ⲛⲉⲙⲁⲕⲁⲣⲓⲥⲙⲟⲥ : ⲱ̀ ⲑⲏⲉⲧϫⲟⲗϩ ⲙ̀ⲡⲓⲱⲟⲩ : ⲛ̀ⲧⲉ Ⲡϭⲟⲓⲥ ⲥⲁⲃⲁⲱⲑ.	*لم يبلغوا عظمة طوباوياتك أيتها المشتملة بمجد رب الجنود.
You are brighter, than the sun, and more sparkling, than the Cherubim.	Ⲧⲉϯⲁⲕⲧⲓⲛ ⲉ̀ⲃⲟⲗ : ⲉ̀ϩⲟⲧⲉ ⲫ̀ⲣⲏ: ⲧⲉⲟⲓ ⲛ̀ⲗⲁⲙⲡⲣⲟⲥ : ⲉ̀ϩⲟⲧⲉ ⲛⲓⲬⲉⲣⲟⲩⲃⲓⲙ.	أنت مضيئة أكثر من الشمس ولامعة أكثر من الشاروبيم.
*And the Seraphim, with the six wings, which are joyfully, hovering over you.	*Ⲛⲉⲙ ⲛⲓⲤⲉⲣⲁⲫⲓⲙ : ⲛⲁ ⲡⲓⲥⲟⲟⲩ ⲛ̀ⲧⲉⲛϩ: ⲥⲉⲉⲣⲣⲓⲣⲓⲣⲓⲛ ϧⲁϫⲱ : ϧⲉⲛ ⲟⲩⲉ̀ϣⲗⲏⲗⲟⲩⲓ̀.	*والسيرافيم ذوى الستة الأجنحة يرفرفون عليك بتهليل.
12 Your glory O Mary, is higher than heaven, you are more honored than the earth, and its inhabitants.	ⲓⲃ̄ Ⲡⲉ̀ⲱⲟⲩ Ⲙⲁⲣⲓⲁ : ϭⲟⲥⲓ ⲉ̀ϩⲟⲧⲉ ⲧ̀ⲫⲉ : ⲧⲉⲧⲁⲓⲏⲟⲩⲧ ⲉ̀ⲡⲕⲁϩⲓ : ⲛⲉⲙ ⲛⲏⲉⲧϣⲟⲡ ⲛ̀ϧⲏⲧϥ.	١٢ مجدك يامريم أرفع من السماء وأنت أكرم من الأرض وسكانها.

*For you are truly, the real path, leading up, to the heavens.

*Ⲛⲑⲟ ⲅⲁⲣ ⲁ̀ⲗⲏⲑⲱⲥ : ⲧⲉ ϯⲥⲧⲣⲁⲧⲁ ⲙ̀ⲙⲏⲓ : ⲉⲧⲟⲓ ⲙ̀ⲙⲁ̀ⲙⲙⲟϣⲓ : ⲉ̀ⲡϣⲱⲓ ⲉ̀ⲛⲓⲫⲏⲟⲩⲓ.

*لأنك أنت بالحقيقة الطريق الحقيقى المؤدى إلى السموات.

You are clothed, with joy and gladness, and gird-led with power, O daughter of Zion.

Ⲁⲣⲉϯ ϯⲓⲱⲧ : ⲛ̀ⲫⲁϣⲓ ⲛⲉⲙ ⲡ̀ⲑⲉⲗⲏⲗ : ⲁ̀ⲣⲉⲙⲟⲣⲧ ⲛ̀ⲟⲩϫⲟⲙ : ⲱ̀ⲧϣⲏⲣⲓ ⲛ̀Ⲥⲓⲱⲛ.

لبست الفرح والتهليل وتمنطقت بالقوة يا ابنة صهيون.

*O who was clothed, with the garments of the heavenly, so that you covered Adam, with the garments of grace.

*Ⲱ̀ⲑⲏ ⲉ̀ⲧⲁⲥϯϩⲓⲱⲧⲥ : ⲛ̀ⲧϩⲉⲃⲥⲱ ⲛ̀ⲛⲁ ⲛⲓⲫⲏⲟⲩⲓ : ϣⲁ ⲛ̀ⲧⲉⲥϩⲱⲃⲥ ⲛ̀-Ⲁⲇⲁⲙ : ⲛ̀ⲧϩⲉⲃⲥⲱ ⲙ̀-ⲡⲓϩⲙⲟⲧ.

*يامن لبست لباس السمائيين حتى سترت آدم بلباس النعمة.

And restored him again, to the Paradise, the rejoic-ing place, and dwelling of the

Ⲁ̀ⲣⲉⲧⲁⲥⲑⲟϥ ⲛ̀ⲕⲉⲥⲟⲡ : ⲉ̀ⲡⲓⲡⲁⲣⲁⲇⲓⲥⲟⲥ : ⲡ̀ⲧⲟ-ⲡⲟⲥ ⲙ̀ⲡⲟⲩⲛⲟϥ : ⲫⲙ-ⲁ̀ⲛϣⲱⲡⲓ ⲛ̀ⲛⲓⲇⲓⲕⲉⲟⲥ.

وردته مرة أخرى إلى الفردوس موضع الفرح ومسكن

righteous.		الصديقين.

13

*A true tabernacle, is Mary the Virgin, placed in its midst, the true testimonies.

ⲓⲅ̄

*Ⲟⲩⲥⲕⲏⲛⲏ ⲙ̀ⲙⲏⲓ : ⲧⲉ Ⲙⲁⲣⲓⲁ ϯⲡⲁⲣⲑⲉⲛⲟⲥ : ⲉⲩⲭⲏ ϧⲉⲛ ⲧⲉⲥⲙⲏϯ : ⲛ̀ϫⲉ ⲛⲓⲙⲉⲧⲙⲉⲑⲣⲉ ⲉ̀ⲧⲉⲛϩⲟⲧ.

١٣

*قبة حقيقية هى مريم العذراء موضوع فى وسطها الشهادات الصادقة.

The undefiled Ark, overlaid roundabout with gold, and the Mercy Seat, of the Cherubim.

Ⲧ̄ⲕⲓⲃⲱⲧⲟⲥ ⲛ̀ⲁⲧⲑⲱⲗⲉⲃ : ⲉⲧⲟⲩϫ ⲛ̀ⲛⲟⲩⲃ ⲛⲥⲁⲥⲁ ⲛⲓⲃⲉⲛ : ⲛⲉⲙ ⲡⲓ̀ⲗⲁⲥⲧⲏⲣⲓⲟⲛ ⲛ̀Ⲭⲉⲣⲟⲩⲃⲓⲙⲓⲕⲟⲛ.

التابوت الغير الدنس المصفّح بالذهب من كل ناحية. والغطاء الكاروبى .

*The golden vessel, where the manna was hidden, behold the Word of the Father, came and took flesh from you.

*Ⲡⲓⲥⲧⲁⲙⲛⲟⲥ ⲛ̀ⲛⲟⲩⲃ : ⲉ̀ⲣⲉ ⲡⲓⲙⲁⲛⲛⲁ ϩⲏⲡ ⲛ̀ϧⲏⲧϥ : ⲓⲥ ⲡⲓⲗⲟⲅⲟⲥ ⲛ̀ⲧⲉ Ⲫ̀ⲓⲱⲧ : ⲓ̀ ⲁϥϭⲓⲥⲁⲣⲝ ⲛ̀ϧⲏϯ.

*القسط الذهبى المخفى فيه المن هوذا كلمة الآب أتى وتجسد منك.

The golden lampstand, carrying the True Light, who is the unapproachable, Light of the world.	Ϯⲗⲩⲭⲛⲓⲁ ⲛ̀ⲛⲟⲩⲃ : ⲉⲧϥⲁⲓ ϧⲁ ⲡⲓⲟⲩⲱⲓⲛⲓ ⲙ̀ⲙⲏⲓ : ⲉ̀ⲧⲉ ⲫ̀ⲟⲩⲱⲓⲛⲓ ⲙ̀ⲡⲓⲕⲟⲥⲙⲟⲥ : ⲡⲓⲁⲧⲱ̀ϣⲱⲛⲧ ⲉ̀ⲣⲟϥ.	المنارة الذهبية الحاملة النور الحقيقى الذى هو نور العالم الذى لا يُدنى منه.
*The golden censer, carrying the live coal, and the chosen incense, with a rich aroma.	*Ϯϣⲟⲩⲣⲏ ⲛ̀ⲛⲟⲩⲃ : ⲉⲧϥⲁⲓ ϧⲁ ⲡⲓⲭⲉⲃⲥ ⲛ̀ⲭ̀ⲣⲱⲙ : ⲛⲉⲙ ⲡⲓⲥ̀ⲑⲟⲓⲛⲟⲩϥⲓ ⲉⲧⲥⲱⲧⲡ : ⲛ̀ⲁ̀ⲣⲱⲙⲁⲧⲁ.	*المجمرة الذهبية الحاملة جمر النار والبخور المختار العنبرى .
The rod of Aaron, that blossomed, and the holy flower, of incense.	Ⲡⲓϣ̀ⲃⲱⲧ ⲛ̀ⲧⲉ Ⲁ̀ⲁⲣⲱⲛ : ⲉⲧⲁϥ̀ϥⲓⲣⲓ ⲉ̀ⲃⲟⲗ : ⲛⲉⲙ ϯⲉ̀ⲣⲏⲣⲓ ⲉ̀ⲑⲟⲩⲁⲃ : ⲛ̀ⲧⲉ ⲡⲓⲥ̀ⲑⲟⲓⲛⲟⲩϥⲓ.	عصا هارون التى أزهرت والزهرة المقدسة التى للبخور.
*All these together, direct us to, the miraculous birth, O Virgin Mary.	*Ⲛⲁⲓ ⲧⲏⲣⲟⲩ ⲉⲩⲥⲟⲡ : ⲥⲉⲉⲣⲥⲩⲙⲙⲉⲛⲓⲛ ⲛⲁⲛ : ⲙ̀ⲡⲉⲭⲓⲛⲙⲓⲥⲓ ⲛ̀ϣ̀ⲫⲏⲣⲓ : ⲱ̀Ⲙⲁⲣⲓⲁ ϯⲡⲁⲣⲑⲉⲛⲟⲥ.	*هذه جميعها معاً تدُلنا على ولادتك العجيبة يامريم العذراء.

14

You decorated our souls, O Moses the prophet, by the honor of the Tabernacle, which you have adorned.

*The first Tabernacle, which Moses had made, was the place of the forgiveness, for the children of Israel.

He made it with glory, as commanded by the Lord, and according to the patterns, shown unto him.

*There was an Ark, in the Tabernacle, overlaid with gold,

ⲓ̅ⲇ̅

Ⲁⲕⲥⲟⲗⲥⲉⲗ ⲛ̀ⲛⲉⲛⲯ-
ⲩⲭⲏ· ⲱ̀Ⲙⲱ̀ⲩⲥⲏⲥ ⲡⲓ̀ⲡⲣ-
ⲟⲫⲏⲧⲏⲥ · ϧⲉⲛ ⲡ̀ⲧⲁⲓⲟ
ⲛ̀ϯⲥⲕⲏⲛⲏ · ⲉ̀ⲧⲁⲕ-
ⲥⲉⲗⲥⲱⲗⲥ ⲉ̀ⲃⲟⲗ.

*Ϯ̀ⲥⲕⲏⲛⲏ ⲛ̀ϩⲟⲩⲓ̀ⲧ ·
ⲉⲧⲁ Ⲙⲱ̀ⲩⲥⲏⲥ ⲑⲁⲙⲓⲟⲥ ·
ⲛ̀ⲟⲩⲙⲁⲛ̀ⲭⲁⲛⲟⲃⲓ ⲉ̀ⲃⲟⲗ ·
ⲛ̀ⲧⲉ ⲛⲉⲛϣⲏⲣⲓ ⲙ̀Ⲡⲓⲥ-
ⲣⲁⲏⲗ.

Ⲁϥⲑⲁⲙⲓⲟⲥ ϧⲉⲛ ⲟⲩⲱ̀ⲟⲩ
· ⲕⲁⲧⲁ ⲡ̀ⲥⲁϫⲓ ⲙ̀Ⲡϭⲟⲓⲥ
· ⲛⲉⲙ ⲕⲁⲧⲁ ⲛⲓⲧⲩⲡⲟⲥ
ⲧⲏⲣⲟⲩ · ⲉⲧⲁⲩⲧⲁⲙⲟϥ
ⲉ̀ⲣⲱⲟⲩ.

*Ⲟⲩⲟⲛ ⲟⲩⲕⲓⲃⲱⲧⲟⲥ ·
ⲭⲏ ϧⲉⲛ ϯⲥⲕⲏⲛⲏ

زينت نفوسنا
ياموسى النبى
بكرامة القبة
التى زينتها.

*القبة الأولى
التى صنعها
موسى موضع
مغفرة خطايا
بنى اسرائيل.

صنعها بمجد
كقول الرب
وكجميع المُثل
التى أعلمه بها.

*كان فى القبة
تابوت مصفّح
بالذهب من داخل

within and without.	ⲉⲥⲗⲁⲗⲏⲟⲩⲧ ⲛ̇ⲛⲟⲩⲃ : ⲥⲁϧⲟⲩⲛ ⲛⲉⲙ ⲥⲁⲃⲟⲗ.	ومن خارج.
There was a Mercy Seat, in the Tabernacle, and the golden Cherubim, overshadowed it.	Ⲟⲩⲟⲛ ⲟⲩⲓⲗⲁⲥⲧⲏⲣⲓⲟⲛ : ⲭⲏ ϧⲉⲛ Ϯⲥⲕⲏⲛⲏ : ϩⲁⲛⲭⲉⲣⲟⲩⲃⲓⲙ ⲛ̇ⲛⲟⲩⲃ : ⲥⲉⲉⲣϧⲏⲓⲃⲓ ⲉ̇ⲝⲱϥ.	كان فى القبة غطاء وكاروبا ذهب يظللان عليه.
*There was a golden pot, in the Tabernacle, and a measure of the manna, was hidden in it.	*Ⲟⲩⲟⲛ ⲟⲩⲥⲧⲁⲙⲛⲟⲥ ⲛ̇ⲛⲟⲩⲃ : ⲭⲏ ϧⲉⲛ Ϯⲥⲕⲏⲛⲏ : ⲉ̇ⲣⲉ ⲟⲩϣⲓ ⲙ̇ⲙⲁⲛⲛⲁ ϩⲏⲡ : ⲛ̇ⲟ̇ⲣⲏⲓ ⲛ̇ϧⲏⲧϥ.	*كان فى القبة قسط ذهبى وكيل مّن مخفى فيه .
There was a golden lampstand, in the Tabernacle, and the seven lamps, shone upon it.	Ⲟⲩⲟⲛ ⲟⲩⲗⲩⲭⲛⲓⲁ ⲛ̇ⲛⲟⲩⲃ : ⲭⲏ ϧⲉⲛ Ϯⲥⲕⲏⲛⲏ : ⲉ̇ⲣⲉ ⲡⲓϣⲁϣϥ ⲛ̇ϧⲏⲃⲥ : ⲉⲣⲟⲩⲱⲓⲛⲓ ⲉ̇ⲝⲱⲥ.	كان فى القبة منارة من ذهب وسبعة سرج تضئ عليها.
*There was a golden censer, in the Tabernacle, and the	*Ⲟⲩⲟⲛ ⲟⲩϣⲟⲩⲣⲏ ⲛ̇ⲛⲟⲩⲃ : ⲭⲏ ϧⲉⲛ Ϯⲥⲕⲏⲛⲏ	*كان فى القبة مجمرة من ذهب والعود المختار

chosen aloe, was in its midst.	: ⲉⲣⲉ ⲡⲓⲕⲧⲛⲁⲙⲱⲛⲟⲛ : ⲉⲧⲥⲱⲧⲡ ϧⲉⲛ ⲧⲉⲥⲙⲏϯ.	فى وسطها.
There was a flower of incense, in the Tabernacle, inhaled by all, the house of Israel.	Ⲟⲩⲟⲛ ⲟⲩϩⲣⲏⲣⲓ ⲛ̀ⲥ- ⲑⲟⲓⲛⲟⲩϥⲓ : ⲭⲏ ϧⲉⲛ ϯⲥⲕⲏⲛⲏ : ⲉⲩϣⲱⲗ- ⲉⲙ ⲉ̀ⲣⲟⲥ ⲧⲏⲣⲟⲩ : ⲛ̀ⲭⲉ ⲛⲁ ⲡ̀ⲏⲓ ⲙ̀Ⲡⲓⲥⲣⲁⲏⲗ.	كان فى القبة زهرة بخور يستنشق رائحتها جميع آل بيت اسرائيل.
*There was the rod of Aaron, in the Tabernacle, this which has bloss- omed, without plan- ting or watering.	*Ⲟⲩⲟⲛ ⲟⲩϣⲃⲱⲧ ⲛ̀ⲧ- ⲉ Ⲁ̀ⲁⲣⲱⲛ : ⲭⲏ ϧⲉⲛ ϯⲥⲕⲏⲛⲏ : ⲫⲁⲓ ⲉ̀ⲧⲁϥ- ⲫⲓⲣⲓ ⲉ̀ⲃⲟⲗ : ⲭⲱⲣⲓⲥ ϭⲟ ⲛⲉⲙ ⲧⲥⲟ.	*كان فى القبة عصا هرون هذه التى أزهرت بغير غرس ولاسقى.
There was a golden table, in the Tabernacle, and the oblation bread, was placed upon it.	Ⲟⲩⲟⲛ ⲟⲩⲧⲣⲁⲡⲉⲍⲁ ⲛ̀- ⲛⲟⲩⲃ : ⲭⲏ ϧⲉⲛ ϯⲥⲕⲏⲛⲏ : ⲡ̀ⲱⲓⲕ ⲛ̀ϯⲡⲣⲟⲑⲉⲥⲓⲥ : ⲭⲏ ⲉ̀ϩⲣⲏⲓ ⲉ̀ϫⲱⲥ.	كان فى القبة مائده ذهبية وخبز التقدمة موضوعا عليها.
*There was a high priest, in the Tabe-	*Ⲟⲩⲟⲛ ⲟⲩⲁⲣⲭⲏⲉ̀ⲣⲉⲩⲥ :	*كان فى القبة رئيس كهنة

rnacle, offering sacrifices, on account of the peoples' sins.	ⲭⲏ ϧⲉⲛ ⲧ̀ⲥⲕⲏⲛⲏ ⲉ ⲉϥⲉⲛ ϣⲟⲩϣⲟⲩϣⲓ ⲉ̀ⲡϣⲱⲓ ⲉ̀ ⲉⲝⲉⲛ ⲛⲓⲛⲟⲃⲓ ⲛ̀ⲧⲉ ⲡⲓⲗⲁⲟⲥ.	يُصعد الذبائح عن خطايا الشعب.
When the Pantocrator, smelled the aroma, He lifted up the sins, of the people.	Ⲁϥϣⲁⲛϣⲱⲗⲉⲙ ⲉ̀ⲣⲟϥ ⲛ̀ϫⲉ ⲡⲓⲡⲁⲛⲧⲟⲕⲣⲁⲧⲱⲣ ⲉ ϣⲁϥⲱⲗⲓ ⲙ̀ⲙⲁⲩ ⲉ ⲛ̀ⲛⲓⲛⲟⲃⲓ ⲛ̀ⲧⲉ ⲡⲓⲗⲁⲟⲥ.	إذا اشتم رائحتها ضابط الكل يرفع هنالك خطايا الشعب.
*Through Mary, the daughter of Joachim, we learned of the true sacrifice, for the forgiveness of sin.	*Ⲉⲃⲟⲗϩⲓⲧⲉⲛ Ⲙⲁⲣⲓⲁ ⲉ ⲧ̀ϣⲉⲣⲓ ⲛ̀Ⲓⲱⲁⲕⲓⲙ ⲉ ⲁⲛⲥⲟⲩⲉⲛ ⲡⲓϣⲟⲩϣⲟⲩϣⲓ ⲙ̀ⲙⲏⲓ ⲉ ⲛ̀ⲭⲁⲛⲟⲃⲓⲉ̀ⲃⲟⲗ.	*من قبل مريم ابنة يواقيم عرفنا الذبيحة الحقيقية لمغفرة الخطايا.
15 Who can speak of, the honor of the Tabernacle, which was decorated, by the prophet.	ⲓⲉ Ⲛⲓⲙ ⲡⲉⲑⲛⲁϣⲥⲁϫⲓ ⲉ ⲙ̀ⲡⲧⲁⲓⲟ ⲛ̀ⲧ̀ⲥⲕⲏⲛⲏ ⲉ ⲉⲧⲁϥⲥⲉⲗⲥⲱⲗⲥ ⲉ̀ⲃⲟⲗ ⲉ ⲛ̀ϫⲉ ⲡⲓⲡⲣⲟⲫⲏⲧⲏⲥ.	١٥ من يقدر أن يصف كرامة القبة التى زينها النبى .

*When the chosen scholars, of the Holy Books, saw it, they were greatly amaz-ed.	*Ⲉⲧⲁⲩⲛⲁⲩ ⲉⲣⲟⲥ ⲷ ⲛⲝⲉ ⲛⲓⲥⲱⲧⲡ ⲛⲥⲁϧ ⲷ ⲛⲧⲉ ⲛⲓⲅⲣⲁⲫⲏ ⲉⲑⲟⲩⲁⲃ ⲷ ⲁⲩϭⲓϣⲫⲏⲣⲓ ⲉⲙⲁϣⲱ.	*لما رآها المعلمون المختارون للكتب المقدسة تعجبوا جداً.
They thought, with their sublime minds, and explained it, through the Holy Books.	Ⲁⲩⲙⲟⲕⲙⲉⲕ ⲉⲃⲟⲗ ⲷ ϧⲉⲛ ⲡⲟⲩⲕⲁϯ ⲉⲧϭ̄ⲟⲥⲓ ⲷ ⲁⲩⲉⲣⲙⲏⲛⲉⲩⲓⲛ ⲙ̄ⲙⲟⲥ ⲷ ϧⲉⲛ ⲛⲓⲅⲣⲁⲫⲏ ⲉⲑⲟⲩⲁⲃ.	وفكروا بفهمهم السامى. وفسروها من الكتب المقدسة.
*They called Mary, the daughter of Joachim, the True Tabernacle, of the Lord of Hosts.	*Ⲁⲩⲙⲟⲩϯ ⲉⲘⲁⲣⲓⲁ ⲷ ⲧϣⲉⲣⲓ ⲛ̄Ⲓⲱⲁⲕⲓⲙ ⲷ ⲭⲉ ϯⲥⲕⲏⲛⲏ ⲙ̄ⲙⲏⲓ ⲷ ⲛⲧⲉ Ⲡϭⲟⲓⲥ ⲥⲁⲃⲁⲱⲑ.	*ودعوا مريم ابنة يواقيم القبة الحقيقية التى لرب الجنود.
They likened the Ark, to the Virgin, and its chosen gold, to her purity.	Ⲁⲩⲉⲛ ϯⲕⲓⲃⲱⲧⲟⲥ ⲷ ⲉⲓⲭⲉⲛ ϯⲡⲁⲣⲑⲉⲛⲟⲥ ⲷ ⲡⲉⲥⲕⲉⲛⲟⲩⲃ ⲉⲧⲥⲱⲧⲡ ⲷ ⲉⲓⲭⲉⲛ ⲡⲉⲥⲧⲟⲩⲃⲟ.	شبهوا التابوت بالعذراء وذهبه المختار بطهارتها.
*They likened the	*Ⲁⲩⲉⲛ ⲡⲓ̈ⲗⲁⲥⲧⲏⲣⲓ-	*شبهوا الغطاء

Mercy Seat, to the Virgin, and the Cherubim of glory, overshadowing her.	ⲟⲛ : ⲉⲓϫⲉⲛ ϯⲡⲁ-ⲣⲑⲉⲛⲟⲥ : ⲓⲥ ⲛⲓⲬⲉⲣⲟ-ⲩⲃⲓⲙ ⲛ̀ⲧⲉ ⲡ̀ⲱⲟⲩ : ⲥⲉⲉⲣϭⲏⲓⲃⲓ ⲉ̀ϫⲱⲥ.	بالعذراء. وكاروبا المجد يظللان عليها.
They likened the golden pot, to the Virgin, and the measure of the manna, to our Saviour.	Ⲁⲩⲉⲛ ⲡⲓⲥⲧⲁⲙⲛⲟⲥ ⲛ̀-ⲛⲟⲩⲃ: ⲉⲓϫⲉⲛ ϯⲡⲁ-ⲣⲑⲉⲛⲟⲥ : ⲡⲉϥⲕⲉϣⲓ ⲙ̀ⲙ-ⲁⲛⲛⲁ : ⲉⲓϫⲉⲛ Ⲡⲉⲛ-ⲥⲱⲧⲏⲣ.	شبهوا القسط الذهبى بالعذراء وكيلة المن بمخلصنا.
*They likened the golden Candlestand, to the church, and the seven lamps, to its seven orders.	*Ⲁⲩⲉⲛ ϯⲗⲩⲭⲛⲓⲁ̀ ⲛ̀-ⲛⲟⲩⲃ : ⲉⲓϫⲉⲛ ϯⲉⲕⲕ-ⲗⲏⲥⲓⲁ̀ : ⲡⲉⲥⲕⲉ ϣⲁϣϥ ⲛ̀ϭⲏⲃⲥ : ⲉⲓϫⲉⲛ ⲡⲓ ϣⲁ-ϣϥ ⲛ̀ⲧⲁⲅⲙⲁ.	*شبهوا المنارة الذهبية بالكنيسة وسُرجُها السبعة بالسبع طغمات.
They likened the golden Censer, to the Virgin, and its aloes, to Emmanuel.	Ⲁⲩⲉⲛ ϯϣⲟⲩⲣⲏ ⲛ̀ⲛⲟⲩⲃ: ⲉⲓϫⲉⲛ ϯⲡⲁⲣⲑⲉⲛⲟⲥ : ⲡⲉⲥⲕⲩⲛⲁⲙⲱⲛⲟⲛ : ⲉⲓϫ-ⲉⲛ Ⲉⲙⲙⲁⲛⲟⲩⲏⲗ.	شبهوا المجمرة الذهبية بالعذراء وعنبرها . بعمانوئيل .

*They likened the flower of incense, to Mary the Queen, and the chosen incense, to her virginity.	*Ⲁⲩⲉⲛ ϯⲉ̀ⲣⲏⲣⲓ ⲛ̀ⲥⲟⲟⲓⲛⲟⲩϥⲓ: ⲋⲓⲭⲉⲛ Ⲙⲁⲣⲓⲁ̀ ϯⲟⲩⲣⲱ: ⲡⲉⲥⲕⲉⲥ̀ⲑⲟⲓⲛⲟⲩϥⲓ ⲉⲧⲥⲱⲧⲡ: ⲋⲓⲭⲉⲛ ⲧⲉⲥⲡⲁⲣⲑⲉⲛⲓⲁ̀.	*شبهوا زهرة البخور بمريم الملكة. وبخورها المختار ببتوليتها.
They likened the rod of Aaron, to the wood of the cross, which my Lord was crucified upon, in order to save us.	Ⲁⲩⲉⲛ ⲡ̀ϣⲃⲱⲧ ⲛ̀ⲧⲉ Ⲁⲁⲣⲱⲛ: ⲋⲓⲭⲉⲛ ⲡ̀ϣⲉ ⲛ̀ⲧⲉ ⲡⲓⲥⲧⲁⲩⲣⲟⲥ: ⲉ̀ⲧⲁⲩⲉϣ Ⲡⲁϭⲟⲓⲥ ⲉ̀ⲣⲟϥ: ϣⲁ̀ⲛⲧⲉϥⲥⲱϯ ⲙ̀ⲙⲟⲛ.	شبهوا عصا هرون بخشبة الصليب التى صُلب ربى عليها حتى خلصنا.
*They likened the golden table, to the altar, and the oblation bread, to the Body of the Lord.	*Ⲁⲩⲉⲛ ϯ̀ⲧⲣⲁⲡⲉⲍⲁ ⲛ̀ⲛⲟⲩⲃ: ⲋⲓⲭⲉⲛ ⲡⲓⲙⲁⲛⲉⲣϣⲱⲟⲩϣⲓ: ⲡ̀ⲱⲓⲕ ⲛ̀ϯⲡ̀ⲣⲟⲑⲉⲥⲓⲥ: ⲋⲓⲭⲉⲛ ⲡⲥⲱⲙⲁ ⲙ̀Ⲡϭⲟⲓⲥ.	*شبهوا المائدة الذهبية بالمذبح وخبز التقدمة بجسد الرب.
They likened the high priest, to our Saviour, the true sacrifice, for the	Ⲁⲩⲉⲛ ⲡⲓⲁⲣⲭ̀ⲏⲉⲣⲉⲩⲥ: ⲋⲓⲭⲉⲛ Ⲡⲉⲛⲥⲱⲧⲏⲣ: ⲡⲓϣⲟⲩϣⲱⲟⲩϣⲓ ⲙ̀ⲙⲏⲓ	شبهوا رئيس الكهنة بمخلصنا الذبيحة الحقيقية لمغفرة الخطايا.

forgiveness of sins.	ⲤⲚ̀ⲬⲀⲚⲞⲂⲒ ⲈⲂⲞⲖ.	
*He who offered Himself, as an acceptable sacrifice, upon the Cross, for the salvation of our race.	*Ⲫⲁⲓ ⲉⲧⲁϥⲉⲛϥ ⲉ̀ⲡ̀-ϣⲱⲓ : Ⲛ̀ⲟⲩⲑⲩⲥⲓⲀ ⲉⲥϣ-ⲏⲡ : ⲊⲒⲬⲈⲚ ⲡⲓⲤⲧⲀⲩ-ⲣⲞⲤ : ϧⲀ Ⲡ̀ⲞⲩⲬⲀⲒ ⲙ̀-ⲡⲈⲚⲄⲈⲚⲞⲤ.	*هذا الذى أصعد ذاته ذبيحة مقبولة على الصليب عن خلاص جنسنا.
His Good Father, smelled Him, in the evening, on Golgo-tha.	Ⲁϥϣⲱⲗⲉⲙ ⲉ̀ⲣⲞϥ: Ⲛ̀-ⲬⲈ ⲠⲈϥⲒⲰⲦ Ⲛ̀ⲀⲄⲀⲐⲞⲤ : ⲙ̀ⲪⲚⲀⲨ ⲚⲦⲈ ⲊⲀⲚⲀ̀-ⲣⲞⲨⲊⲒ : ⲊⲒⲬⲈⲚ Ⲧ̀ⲄⲨ-ⲞⲖⲄⲞⲐⲀ.	فاشتمه أبوه الصالح وقت المساء على الجلجلة.
*He opened the gate, of Paradise, and restored Adam again, to his authority.	*ⲀϥⲞⲨⲰⲚ ⲙ̀ⲪⲣⲞ : ⲙ̀-ⲠⲒⲠⲀⲣⲀⲆⲒⲤⲞⲤ : ⲀϥⲦⲀ-ⲤⲐⲞ Ⲛ̀ ⲀⲇⲀⲙ : ⲈⲦⲈ-ϥⲀⲣⲬⲎ Ⲛ̀ⲔⲈⲤⲞⲠ.	*فتح باب الفردوس وردّ آدم إلى رئاسته مرة اخرى.
Through Mary, the daughter of Joach-im, we learned of	ⲈⲂⲞⲖⲊⲒⲦⲈⲚ ⲘⲁⲣⲓⲀ̀ : Ⲧ̀ϣⲈⲣⲒ Ⲛ̀ⲒⲰⲀⲔⲒⲙ :	من قبل مريم ابنة يواقيم عرفنا الذبيحة

the true sacrifice, for the forgiveness of sins.	ⲁⲛⲥⲟⲧⲉⲛ ⲡⲓϣⲟⲩϣⲟⲩϣⲓ ⲙ̀ⲙⲏⲓ : ⲛ̀ⲭⲁⲛⲟⲃⲓ ⲉ̀ⲃⲟⲗ.	الحقيقية لمغفرة الخطايا.
*And we too, hope to win mercy, through your intercessions, with the Lover of mankind.	*Ⲁⲛⲟⲛ ϩⲱⲛ ⲧⲉⲛⲧⲱⲃϩ : ⲉⲑⲣⲉⲛϣⲁϣⲛⲓ ⲉⲩⲛⲁⲓ : ϩⲓⲧⲉⲛ ⲛⲉⲡⲣⲉⲥⲃⲓⲁ̀ : ⲛ̀ⲧⲟⲧϥ ⲙ̀ⲡⲓⲙⲁⲓⲣⲱⲙⲓ.	*ونحن أيضاً نطلب أن نفوز برحمة بشفاعاتك عند محب البشر.

463

Conclusion of Adam Theotokias –
Ⲛⲉⲕⲛⲁⲓ ⲱ̀ Ⲡⲁⲛⲟⲩϯ   ختام الثيؤطوكيات الآدام

Your mercies O my God, are countless, and exceedingly plenteous, is Your compassion.	Ⲛⲉⲕⲛⲁⲓ ⲱ̀ Ⲡⲁⲛⲟⲩϯ ⲥⲁ-ⲛⲁⲧϭⲓⲏⲡⲓ ⲙ̀ⲙⲱⲟⲩ : ⲥⲉⲟϣ ⲉ̀ⲙⲁϣⲱ : ⲛ̀ϫⲉ ⲛⲉⲕⲙⲉⲧϣⲉⲛϩⲏⲧ.	مراحمك ياإلهى غير محصاة. وكثيرة جداً هى رأفاتك.
*All the rain drops, are counted by You, and the sand of the Sea, are before Your eyes.	*Ⲛⲓⲧⲉⲗⲧⲓⲗⲏ ⲙ̀ⲙⲟⲩⲛ-ϩⲱⲟⲩ : ⲥⲉⲏⲡ ⲛ̀ⲧⲟⲧⲕ ⲧⲏⲣⲟⲩ : ⲡⲓⲕⲉϣⲱ ⲛ̀ⲧⲉ ⲫ̀ⲓⲟⲙ : ⲥⲉⲭⲏ ⲛⲁϩⲣⲉⲛ ⲛⲉⲕⲃⲁⲗ.	*قطرات المطر محصاة عندك جميعها ورمل البحر كائن أمام عينيك.
How much more are, the sins of my soul, manifest before You , O my God.	Ⲓⲉ ⲁⲩⲏⲣ ⲙⲁⲗⲗⲟⲛ : ⲛⲓⲛⲟⲃⲓ ⲛ̀ⲧⲉ ⲧⲁⲯⲩⲭⲏ : ⲛⲁⲓ ⲉⲑⲟⲩⲱⲛϩ ⲉ̀ⲃⲟⲗ : ⲙ̀ⲡⲉⲕⲙ̀ⲑⲟ Ⲡⲁϭ̅ⲟ̅ⲓ̅ⲥ̅.	فكم بالحرى خطايا نفسى هذه الظاهرة أمامك ياربى.
*The sins that I have committed, do	*Ⲛⲓⲛⲟⲃⲓ ⲉ̀ⲧⲁⲓⲁⲓⲧⲟⲩ:	*الخطايا التى صنعتها ياربى

not remember my Lord, and do not count, my iniquities.	Ⲡⲁϭⲟⲓⲥ ⲛ̀ⲛⲉⲕⲉⲣⲡⲟⲩⲙⲉ-ⲣⲓ̀ⲥⲟⲩⲇⲉ ⲙ̀ⲡⲉⲣϯϭ̀ⲑ-ⲏⲕ: ⲉ̀ⲛⲁⲁ̀ⲛⲟⲙⲓⲁ̀.	لاتذكرها ولا تحسب اثامى.
For You have chosen the Publican, and the adulteress You have saved, And the right hand thief, my Lord You have remembered.	Ϫⲉ ⲡⲓⲧⲉⲗⲱⲛⲏⲥ ⲁⲕⲥⲟⲧⲡϥ: ϯⲡⲟⲣⲛⲏ ⲁⲕⲥⲱϯ ⲙ̀ⲙⲟⲥ: ⲡⲓⲥⲟⲛⲓ ⲉⲧⲥⲁⲟⲩ̀ⲛⲁⲙ: Ⲡⲁϭⲟⲓⲥ ⲁⲕⲉⲣⲡⲉϥⲙⲉⲩⲓ.	فان العشار اخترته والزانية خلصتها. واللص اليمين ياسيدى ذكرته.
*And me too, the sinner, teach me O my Master , to offer repentance.	*Ⲁⲛⲟⲕ ϩⲱ Ⲡⲁϭⲟⲓⲥ: ϧⲁ ⲡⲓⲣⲉϥⲉⲣⲛⲟⲃⲓ: ⲙⲁⲧ̀ⲥⲁⲃⲟⲓ ⲛ̀ⲧⲁⲓⲣⲓ: ⲛ̀ⲟⲩⲙⲉⲧⲁ̀ⲛⲟⲓⲁ̀.	*وأنا أيضاً الخاطئ ياسيدى علمنى أن اصنع توبة.
For You do not desire, the death of a sinner, but rather that he returns, and that his soul may live.	Ϫⲉ ⲭⲟⲩⲱϣ ⲙ̀ⲫⲙⲟⲩ ⲁⲛ: ⲙ̀ⲡⲓⲣⲉϥⲉⲣⲛⲟⲃⲓ: ⲙ̀ⲫⲣⲏϯ ⲛ̀ⲧⲉϥⲧⲁⲥⲑⲟϥ: ⲛ̀ⲧⲉⲥⲱⲛϧ ⲛ̀ϫⲉ ⲧⲉϥⲯⲩⲭⲏ.	لانك لا تشاء موت الخاطئ مثل أن يرجع وتحيا نفسه.

*Restore us O God, To Your salvation, and deal with us, according to Your goodness.	*Ⲙⲁⲧⲁⲥⲑⲟⲛ Ⲫϯ : ⲉϧⲟⲩⲛ ⲉⲡⲉⲕⲟⲩⲭⲁⲓ : ⲁⲣⲓⲟⲩⲓ ⲛⲉⲙⲁⲛ : ⲕⲁⲧⲁ ⲧⲉⲕⲙⲉⲧⲁ̀ⲅⲁⲑⲟⲥ.	*ردنا ياالله إلى خلاصك وعاملنا كصلاحك.
For You are good, and merciful, let Your compassion, come speedily to us.	Ⲭⲉ ⲛ̀ⲑⲟⲕ ⲟⲩⲁ̀ⲅⲁⲑⲟⲥ : ⲟⲩⲟϩ ⲛ̀ⲛⲁⲏⲧ : ⲙⲁⲣⲟⲩⲧⲁϩⲟⲛ ⲛ̀ⲭⲱⲗⲉⲙ : ⲛ̀ϫⲉ ⲛⲉⲕⲙⲉⲧϣⲉⲛϩⲏⲧ.	لانك أنت صالح ورحوم. فلتدركنا رأفاتك سريعاً.
*Have compassion upon us all, O Lord God our Savior, and have mercy upon us, according to Your great mercy.	*Ϣⲉⲛϩⲏⲧ ϧⲁⲣⲟⲛ ⲧⲏⲣⲉⲛ : Ⲡϭⲟⲓⲥ Ⲫϯ Ⲡⲉⲛⲥⲱⲧⲏⲣ : ⲟⲩⲟϩ ⲛⲁⲓ ⲛⲁⲛ : ⲕⲁⲧⲁ ⲡⲉⲕⲛⲓϣϯ ⲛ̀ⲛⲁⲓ.	*تراف علينا كلنا أيها الرب الاله مخلصنا وارحمنا كعظيم رحمتك.
Remember those, O Christ our Master, be among us, and proclaim and say.	Ⲛⲁⲓ ⲁ̀ⲣⲓⲡ ⲙ̀ⲡⲟⲩⲙⲉⲩⲓ : ⲱ̀ ⲡⲉⲛⲛⲏⲃ Ⲡⲓⲭ̅ⲣⲓⲥⲧⲟⲥ: ⲉⲕⲉ̀ϣⲱⲡⲓ ϧⲉⲛ ⲧⲉⲛⲙⲏϯ : ⲉⲕⲱϣ ⲉ̀ⲃⲟⲗ ⲉⲕϫⲱ ⲙ̀ⲙⲟⲥ.	هؤلاء أذكرهم ياسيدنا المسيح كن فى وسطنا صارخاً قائلاً:

*My peace, I give to You, the peace of my Father, I leave with you.	*Ϫⲉ ⲧⲁϩⲓⲣⲏⲛⲏ ⲁⲛⲟⲕ : ϯϯ ⲙⲙⲟⲥ ⲛⲱⲧⲉⲛ : ⲧ̅ϩⲓⲣⲏⲛⲏ ⲙⲠⲁⲓⲱⲧ : ϯⲭⲱ ⲙⲙⲟⲥ ⲛⲉⲙⲱⲧⲉⲛ.	*سلامى أنا اعطيكم سلام أبى أتركه معكم.
O King of peace, grant us Your peace, render unto us Your peace, and forgive us our sins.	ˋⲠⲟⲩⲣⲟ ⲛ̅ⲧⲉ ϯϩⲓⲣⲏⲛⲏ: ⲙⲟⲓ ⲛⲁⲛ ⲛ̅ⲧⲉⲕϩⲓⲣⲏⲛⲏ: ⲥⲉⲙⲛⲓ ⲛⲁⲛ ⲛ̅ⲧⲉⲕϩⲓⲣ- ⲏⲛⲏ: ⲭⲁ ⲛⲉⲛⲛⲟⲃⲓ ⲛⲁⲛ ⲉ̀ⲃⲟⲗ.	ياملك السلام أعطنا سلامك قرر لنا سلامك واغفر لنا خطايانا.
*Disperse the ene-mies, of the church, and fortify her, that she may not be shaken forever.	*Ϫⲱⲣ ⲉ̀ⲃⲟⲗ ⲛ̅ⲛⲓϫⲁ- ϫⲓ: ⲛ̅ⲧⲉ ϯⲉⲕⲕⲗⲏⲥⲓⲁ : ⲁ̀ⲣⲓⲥⲟⲃⲧ ⲉ̀ⲣⲟⲥ: ⲛ̅ⲛⲉⲥⲕⲓⲙ ϣⲁ ⲉ̀ⲛⲉϩ.	*فرق أعداء الكنيسة وحصنها فلا تتزعزع إلى الابد.
Emmanuel our God, is now in our midst, with the glory of His Father, and the Holy Spirit.	Ⲉⲙⲙⲁⲛⲟⲩⲏⲗ Ⲡⲉⲛⲛⲟⲩϯ : ϧⲉⲛ ⲧⲉⲛⲙⲏϯ ϯⲛⲟⲩ : ϧⲉⲛ ⲡ̀ⲱⲟⲩ ⲛ̅ⲧⲉ Ⲡⲉϥⲓⲱⲧ: ⲛⲉⲙ Ⲡⲓⲡ̀ⲛⲉⲩⲙⲁ ⲉ̀ⲑⲟⲩⲁⲃ.	عمانوئيل إلهنا فى وسطنا الآن بمجد أبيه والروح القدس .
*May He bless us	* Ⲛ̅ⲧⲉϥⲥⲙⲟⲩ ⲉ̀ⲣⲟⲛ	*ليباركنا كلنا

all, and purify our hearts, and heal the sicknesses of our soul and bodies.	ⲦⲎⲢⲈⲚ: ⲚⲦⲈϥⲦⲞⲩⲂⲟ ⲚⲚⲈⲚϨⲎⲦ : ⲚⲦⲈϥⲧ- ⲁⲗϭⲟ ⲚⲚⲓϢⲱⲚⲓ: ⲚⲦⲈ ⲚⲈⲚⲮⲩⲬⲎ ⲚⲈⲙ ⲚⲈⲚ- ⲥⲱⲙⲁ.	ويطهر قلوبنا ويشفى أمراض نفوسنا وأجسادنا.
We worship You O Christ, with Your Good Father, and the Holy Spirit, for You have come and saved us.	ⲦⲉⲛⲟⲩⲱϢⲦ ⲙⲙⲟⲕ ⲱ- ⲠⲓⲬⲣⲓⲥⲦⲟⲥ: ⲛⲉⲙ Ⲡⲉ- ⲕⲓⲱⲦ Ⲛⲁⲅⲁⲑⲟⲥ: ⲛⲉⲙ Ⲡⲓⲡⲛⲉⲩⲙⲁ ⲉⲑⲟⲩⲁⲃ : ϫⲉⲁⲕⲓ ⲁⲕⲥⲱϯ ⲙⲙⲟⲛ.	نسجد لك ايها المسيح مع ابيك الصالح والروح القدس لانك أتيت وخلصتنا.

Your Mercies O my God -
مراحمك يا إلهى

Your mercies O my God	مراحمك ياإلهى
Are countless	كثيرة جداً
Your mercies O my God	مراحمك ياإلهى
Have no boundaries	لايحصى لها عددا
All the drops of rain	قطرات الأمطار
Are counted in Your hands	معدودة بين يديك
Also the sand of the sea	وأيضاً رمل البحار
Is present before Your eyes	كائن قدام عينيك
How much more are my sins	كم بالأكثر خطاياى
My trespasses are before You	وآثامى قدامك
And all that I have done	وما صنعته يداى
Are present before You	ظاهر كله امامك
The sins of my youth	خطايا صباى وجهلى
Do not remember O Lord	يارب لاتذكرها
Do not contemplate	ولا تتأمل آثامى

On my sins O God	ياإلهى بل اتركها
For You do not desire	فإنك لاتشاء موت
The death of sinners	الخاطىء
But You are ever pleased	بل تحب رجوعه إليك
That they return to You	ياإلهى اقبل طلباتى
	رجعت وتبت إليك
The tax-collector was chosen	فإن العشار اخترته
The adulteress You forgave	والزانية غفرت لها
The thief You remembered	واللص يارب ذكرته
Your mercy is boundless	رحمتك لانهاية لها
I am a sinner too	وأنا خاطىء ايضاً
O Lord teach me	يارب علمنى
To offer repentance	لكى اصنع توبة
Accept me like the adulteress	مثل الزانية اقبلنى
Return us O God unto Your -salvation	ردنا يارب الى خلاصك
For You are good and gracious	فإنك صالح ورحيم
Grant us Your salvation	إصنع معنا كصلاحك
For you are our Savior	لأنك قادر وكريم

If You judge us in Your uprightness

وإن حاكمتنا بعدلك

We shall have no excuse

فلا نجد حجة

We await Your compassion

لكن ننتظر فضلك

And plead for Your mercy

ومراحمك نترجى

Your mercies O my God

مراحمك ياإلهى

Are beyond all measure

تعلو كل الابعاد

Your mercies O my God

مراحمك ياإلهى

Are as countless as the sand

كالرمل بغير عدد

Your mercies O my God

مراحمك ياإلهى

Are more than the stars in heaven

أكثر من عدد النجوم

And the plants of the earth

وأكثر من نبات الأرض

The mountains and little hills

والجبال وكل النجوم

O King of peace

ياملك السلام

Grant us Your peace

سلامك أعطنا

Render unto us Your peace

قرر لنا سلامك

And forgive us our sins

وحل بروحك فينا

Disperse the enemies

فرق أعداء البيعة

Of the Church

وحصنها بالإيمان

Fortify her stronghold

بحصون عالية منيعة

That she may never be shaken

فلا تتزعزع لزمان

Emmanuel our God	عمانوئيل نفسه
Is now in our midst	فى وسطنا الآن
With the Glory of His Father	بمجد أبيه وروح قدسه
And the Holy Spirit	الآن وكل أوان
May He bless us all	فليباركنا كلنا
And purify our hearts	ويطهر قلوبنا
And heal the sickness	ويشفى أمراضنا
Of our souls and bodies	ويخلص نفوسنا
We worship the Father the Son	نسجد للآب والأبن
And the Holy Spirit	والروح القدس
Both now and forever	الآن وكل أوان
And to the end of ages Amen.	والى الأبد آمين

The Conclusion - الختام

The Introduction to the Creed and The Creed. Conclude with the following, each verse is preceded by Kϒⲣⲓⲉ̀ⲉ̀ⲗⲉⲏⲥⲟⲛ.

(هنا تقال نعظمك يا أم النور و بالحقيقة نؤمن. ثم يقال الختام على Kϒⲣⲓⲉ̀ⲉ̀ⲗⲉⲏⲥⲟⲛ)

Lord Have Mercy (3)	Kϒⲣⲓⲉ̀ⲉ̀ⲗⲉⲏⲥⲟⲛ (3)	يارب إرحم(3)
O God have mercy on us	Ⲫϯ ⲛⲁⲓ ⲛⲁⲛ.	ياالله ارحمنا.
O God hear us	Ⲫϯ ⲥⲱⲧⲉⲙ ⲉ̀ⲣⲟⲛ.	ياالله اسمعنا.
O God look to us	Ⲫϯ ⲥⲟⲙⲥ ⲉ̀ⲣⲟⲛ.	ياالله انظر الينا.
O God behold us	Ⲫϯ ⲭⲟⲩϣⲧ ⲉ̀ⲣⲟⲛ.	ياالله اطلع علينا.
O God have compassion on us	Ⲫϯ ϣⲉⲛϩⲏⲧ ϧⲁⲣⲟⲛ.	يا الله تراءف علينا.
We are Your people	Ⲁⲛⲟⲛ ϧⲁ ⲡⲉⲕⲗⲁⲟⲥ.	نحن شعبك.
We are Your creation	Ⲁⲛⲟⲛ ϧⲁ ⲡⲉⲕⲡ̀ⲗⲁⲥⲙⲁ.	نحن جبلتك.
Deliver us from our enemies	Ⲛⲁϩⲙⲉⲛ ⲉ̀ⲃⲟⲗϧⲉⲛ ⲛⲉⲛⲭⲁϫⲓ	نجنا من أعدائنا.
Deliver us from inflation	Ⲛⲁϩⲙⲉⲛ ⲉ̀ⲃⲟⲗϩⲁ ⲟⲩϩ̀ⲃⲱⲛ	نجنا من الغلاء.
We are Your servants	Ⲁⲛⲟⲛ ϧⲁ ⲛⲉⲕⲉ̀ⲃⲓⲁⲓⲕ	نحن عبيدك .
You are the Son of God	Ⲩⲓⲟⲥ Ⲑⲉⲟⲥ ⲛ̀ⲑⲟⲕ.	أنت ابن الله.

473

We believe in You	Ⲁⲛⲛⲁϩϯⲉⲣⲟⲕ.	آمنا بك.
For You Have come and saved us	Ϫⲉ ⲁⲕⲓ ⲁⲕⲥⲱϯ ⲙ̇ⲙⲟⲛ	لأنك أتيت وخلصتنا.
Visit us with Your salvation	Ϫⲉⲙⲡⲉⲛϣⲓⲛⲓ ϧⲉⲛ ⲡⲉⲕⲟⲩϫⲁⲓ	تعهدنا بخلاصك.
And forgive us our sins.	Ⲟⲩⲟϩ ⲭⲁ ⲛⲉⲛⲛⲟⲃⲓ ⲛⲁⲛ ⲉ̇ⲃⲟⲗ.	واغفر لنا خطايانا.

This is concluded by "Holy Holy Holy, Lord of Hosts". The priest reads the Absolution of the Midnight Psalmody. The First Hour psalms and Morning Doxology is then prayed.

هنا تقال قدوس قدوس قدوس رب الصاباؤوت.ثم يقول الكاهن تحليل نصف الليل و تقرأ مزامير باكر وذكصولوجية باكر.